FIEKE HOOGVELT

The Garden

 **REBO** PRODUCTIONS

© 1997 Rebo Productions, Lisse
© 1997 Published by Rebo Productions Ltd
Cover design: Ton Wienbelt, The Netherlands
Illustrations: Rik Slinger, The Netherlands
Production and layout: TextCase, The Netherlands
Translation: Mary Boorman for First Edition Translations
Ltd, Cambridge, Great Britain
Typesetting: Hof&Land Typografie, The Netherlands

ISBN 1 901094 154

Contents

Foreword

Before you begin laying out your garden, making radical alterations to it, or altering parts of it you will need to collect the necessary background information. You must then adapt this information to fit in with your own circumstances and what you want. This book contains a large amount of the information you will need: facts about the green mantle that covers our gardens as well as about the static ele-

Left: *Every garden needs a corner just in or out of the sun in which to relax.*

You will also find a lot of information in this book about ponds.

ments that can be used in all kinds of gardens. These are the two elements, of course, that are of prime importance. But planning your garden doesn't just end there.

It is a great advantage if you can put your own ideas down on paper in the form of a plan. You can then make clear to yourself and others what you do and do not want, and by using one or two tricks you can check whether your ideas are practicable and will produce the results you want. With the help of the first part of this book, 'The design,' you can try this out. There are a number of handy tips here for you to use. It is a good idea to do this in winter so that you have plenty of time to mull over your ideas and

to test them on paper and perhaps modify them. Then gradually the time will come for the garden to be laid out. Many jobs, for example measuring up the garden, making a shadow plan, measuring the height of trees, casting a garden ornament, planting trees and conifers, making an arbour and suchlike, are explained in the text and illustrations.

In The Garden a great deal of space is devoted to maintenance because in these days of "so much to do and so little time to do it," people are naturally concerned with carrying out the maintenance of their gardens as efficiently as possible. Not all the jobs that have to be done in the garden are equally attractive but there are certain things that have to be done at regular intervals, whether they are pleasant or not. This book includes tips to limit the work you

The owner of a small garden can always create a splendid display on a balcony or in a tiny space by filling all kinds of containers with flowering annuals or perennials.

don't enjoy to the minimum. Nice things, such as various methods of propagation and topiary, are of course covered comprehensively, sometimes in great detail.

The vegetable garden has also regained its place in western gardens. Many amateur gardeners like to know exactly what is being dished up in the vegetables they eat, and they certainly do not appreciate the use of pesticides. If you grow your own vegetables you can decide what is done about the control of pests. It is not usually necessary to use toxic substances in ornamental or vegetable gardens because specific laws of nature are obeyed as far as is possible. In the vegetable garden, too, respect for everything that grows is a basic assumption of good husbandry.

It is sometimes said that, in theory, it is easy to give out advice and directions but that, in practice, things turn out differently — certainly for gardeners who are not yet very experienced. In the last part, 'Practical examples,' the theory is tested against its practical application.

Nor have the owners of small gardens been neglected in The Garden. Such gardeners will benefit from the examples of solutions to problems in "difficult" gardens.

In this book, the theory and practice of gardening go hand in hand. Some background knowledge is indispensable, but the pleasures of having your own garden, its layout, working out solutions for difficult plots, growing your own vegetables or raising herbs, and designing a lovely border, are paramount. A garden is a restful place and must be a space the gardener is able to enjoy, whether sitting on the terrace with a cup of coffee or working among the plants at the busy times. This book has been written with that enjoyment in mind.

Fieke Hoogvelt

Part 1

Garden design

1 Background information

You buy or rent a house for all sorts of reasons. What applies to the house does not usually also apply to the garden, because the garden that goes with it is hardly ever the deciding factor.

Making the best of what you have

Because of his work, Mr X has to live in town. He is lucky, because the house has a garden; it is just a pity that the walled garden is rather small and dark. Mrs X has just found the house of her dreams, but unfortunately it has one drawback - the garden is tiny. After a lot of thought she decides to pursue her passion for gardening on an allotment. You will appreciate the position of a couple who have bought a fantastic building plot on a new development in the country. The area intended for the garden is ideal, the only problem is that the new owners have to come to an agreement with four neighbours about the fencing!

The possible situations are endless. A detached

The more sunlight there is in the garden, the greater the possibilities for planting. There will also be fewer problems with moss, which makes the surface slippery.

A herbaceous border demands a great deal of maintenance.

house may have a row of apartments back onto giving opportunity for being overlooked. An existing house may have a woodland garden whereas the new owner wants to plant herbaceous perennials that need plenty of sun; the inhabitants of the whole street plus the local government officers could turn up if he decides to start felling. These are just two examples: an existing garden is hardly ever completely to the liking of the new owner. It is also clear that when choosing where to live you have to make the house your main priority. It rarely happens that a house is bought, for instance, because of the old walnut tree in the garden.

Take your time

The important tasks of moving house, settling in, and modifying the building and furnishings all take time. A brand new house is generally handed over complete with a narrow path to the front door and a small paved area. This may take the form of large concrete slabs. The path is no luxury, because furniture has to be moved into the house without taking in all the mud as well.

If there is no path to the front door or garage, then lay a temporary one. Often they are whether keen gardeners or not, people decide to put down a permanent path, and they do it without any thought for the rest of the garden. Later on the design of the garden has to be made to fit in with the existing path and the new drive. This is a great pity!

Frequently bricks are left behind by the builders. So you decide to build raised flower beds round the edge of the patio that has yet to be laid. It seems like a good idea: the bricks do not cost anything and you can tidy the place up at the same time.

Moving house does not always happen at the most suitable time of year for making a garden. If you move in May you will probably want to have an attractive garden for sitting out in summer. Unfortunately, many garden centres have very little choice by then so make the most of this opportunity to get to know the existing garden. What is there that you can use? Do you want a low maintenance garden, often very expensive to create, or do you want to do a lot of the work yourself? What shape do you want the garden to have? Do you want to give it a clear, recognizable style?

The next chapter gives a summary of various styles of gardening. Only after that is the matter of design considered in detail. You can put to very good use the six months before you begin. Get your bearings, and try to adapt the style or

Plant herbs near the kitchen. They are then within easy reach, even in wet or cold weather.

An enclosed back garden. Strips have been left in the paving for plants. This means they will need less water than if all the plants were in pots.

But you can guarantee that you will regret it. Whatever the garden is like – already laid out, new or old, pretty or ugly – it is certainly advisable to wait at least six months before you "put a spade in the ground", so to speak.

In the mean time, you will be getting used to the house and the neighbourhood. After six months you will know which rooms you use most.

You discover that sitting in the kitchen is not so pleasant, because it is relatively dark in there. The view from the sitting room window will be more important if you spend most of your time there. However, you may find that the garden by the kitchen gets a lot of sun. Remember that when you are looking for somewhere to plant flowers for cutting and arranging in the house. It is helpful to bear in mind certain features of the house when you come to design the garden.

Tip

If you are itching to get into the garden in your first summer, grow some vegetables and flowers for cutting. You can buy various kinds of vegetable plants on the market or at a garden centre.
You can sow many annual flower seeds in May where they are to flower: sow them in rows to make weeding easier.

features that you want to recreate to what your garden has to offer.

The major garden styles

Some gardens present a clear layout composed of straight lines and symmetrical elements. By contrast, in some gardens the paths wind through the shrubbery and the whole design is unpredictable. Again, in other gardens, the area is divided into smaller sections, so-called rooms or garden rooms, which are not all visible at once, but reveal themselves gradually as you move through the garden.
Presentday gardens are very much influenced in their style and shape by the gardens of the past.

The Persian garden

The layout of the Persian gardenparticularly has had a strong influence on the development of later styles of garden. In Persia and other sub-tropical areas water was, and still is,more important than in tem-perate regions. There was always a reservoir in the garden and either a well, or water led along channels from outside. The well was situated in the centre of the garden and the surrounding area was paved. Four paths radiated out from it, thus dividing the garden into four segments. These four squarebeds represented the four parts of the universe. Useful plants, including herbs, were raised in the beds. Many trees were planted round the edge of the garden, especially cypresses, which were a symbol of eternity.

The water channels were often widened in the middle to form a pool. Later the beds and the watersystem became more elaborate. Flowers for ornamental use and ornamental fountains became popular, and mosaic tiles were laid as paths along the edge of the water. Flowers for purely decorative effect were already being used in Persian gardens. The present-day arbour also dates from that time. Grapes were often grown in Persian gardens, and arbours supported the heavy vines. As well as providing fruit, they gave protection from the sun and very soon these arbours were being made more elaborate.

The sharp divisions, the well, the channels, and the arbour, of the Persian garden, reappear in later designs.

The medieval garden

The Middle Ages was a time of upheaval throughout Europe. Many wars were being fought and there was little time for gardening -

The Persians were the first to decorate pools with ceramic tiles.

A modern alternative to the turf bank: a box bench, which is just as comfortable. Chamomile is growing in front of it.

people were more intent on saving their skins. Dwelling places were fortified to become towers and castles surrounded by a double ring of walls and moats. Inside the castle walls there was always a kitchen garden where enough fruit and vegetables could be grown for the lean times, because the supplies had to sustain the inhabitants during a siege. The kitchen garden was therefore well tended. The remainder of the garden was a sandy area which became a mud bath in wet weather and a dust bowl during dry spells. That continued until carts became used much more. These naturally followed the same path and these cart tracks were eventually paved so that a tree-lined drive evolved. The sandy area inside the walls was put down to grass to reduce the dust and prevent the growth of weeds.

The well in the castle was always flanked by a lime tree to give protection during thunderstorms. It was also a favourite spot for courting couples. The central grass area, the tree-lined-drive, well and lime tree are still important elements in gardens today. Characteristics of monastic and town gardens of the Middle Ages also recur in present day gardens. The cloister garden had two paths at right angles dividing it into four beds edged with box (*Buxus sempervirens*) and filled with flowers and herbs.

Wealthy townspeople had gardens planted with ornamentals, fruittrees, vegetables and herbs. Roses, apples, pears and figs were the most popular flowers and fruit of the time. The turf bank became a common feature; it was a comfortable place to while away the hours and of course the turf contained not only grass but all kinds of wild flowers.

These small towngardens were enclosed by walls. If there were no walls, a solution was found in fences and trellises which were allowed to become heavily overgrown.

One part, "room", of the garden of Barnsley House. The classical temple, the round pool and the ornamental wrought ironwork are typical of the Renaissance style.

The Renaissance garden

The early Renaissance garden was almost always made up of various terraces. This is still the case in Italy. No account was taken of the surroundings or the shape of the terrace. The garden was divided into a number of squares, each of which had its own theme, and there was always a decoration in the centre. The squares, which were surrounded by hedges, were divided from each other by identical paths, and no connection was made between the house and the garden.

Popular elements included statues, fountains, a sundial, mazes, pergolas, overgrown arbours, trellis with espalier fruit trees, low-growing fruit trees and low ornamental planting such as the flower meadow with thyme, pinks, and chamomile. Formal topiary also reached a high point in these gardens. The division into different rooms, topiary, and statues have stood the test of time and which are often found in modern gardens.

The baroque garden

It was the French who refined the concept of enclosure, bringing formality and order to a highpoint in garden design.
The main characteristic of the baroque garden

> **Tip**
> Is your garden laid out in an informal style with a fussy, multi-coloured border? You can make that part of the garden more restful by introducing a few shapes that are repeated in a pattern, such as box balls or yew pillars.

This beautiful perspective has a fountain as the focal point.

Page 18 above: *The combination of blocks, paths and hedges looks very like a modern interpretation of a Renaissance maze.*

Page 18 below: *The gaze is led along the central axis, the green carpet, to the arbour.*

was the monumental layout in which the strongly emphasized central axis linked up with the main room in the house. House and garden formed a unity.

The enclosed squares of the Renaissance garden gave way to open rectangles with side based on a ratio of 3:5. There was no longer any ornament in the centre of the rectangles, only at the intersection of the axes. The view was created by placing fewer large garden rooms on the long axis. The beds were enclosed by low hedges of box in symmetrical designs with elaborate curves.

Framing these beds were long strips planted with flowers. In the French garden the plants stood in closely, absolutely straight rows.

In the Dutch baroque garden the box bushes were planted a little apart. This was so that each plant could be seen to full advantage. There is a theory that because various plants, including bulbs such as the tulip – at that time just being imported – were so expensive, the thrifty Dutch wanted to make the best use of them. You can still find some baroque features in present-day gardens one of the most important is undoubtedly the unity of house and garden.

The rococo garden

The baroque merges into the rococo. During this period the main features of the garden remained unchanged except that the main axis became divided into three or more equal axes. Ornament became very important, and the curving box hedges became more and more complicated. Meandering paths were laid out in the woods around the garden.

The romantic garden

By the end of the eighteenth century, following the French Revolution, the people had begun to revolt. The citizens were demanding "liberty, equality, fraternity". Very elaborate gardens met with disapproval – they symbolized the might and wealth of the well to do, who until then had been the ruling classes. The straight lines and rigidity of the baroque garden were being done away with. People were also coming into contact with a completely different style of gardening through their trade with China and Japan. The Chinese landscape style had a centuries-old tradition.

In 1753 Linnaeus wrote his *Species Plantarum* in which made a systematic cataloque of all the plants available to him. Up until then there had been quite a small choice of plants on offer for gardens. Now the so-called "plant hunters" were

A curving woodland path needs a large area of land.

bringing back many plants from other countries. There were more large towns and the townsfolk who had less contact with the countryside began to glamorize life in the country. All these developments found expression in a new style of gardening. The romantic garden became a symbol of the purity and goodness of nature, of the countryside. Hermitages, or just their front walls, were built in the gardens, preferably with an ornamental hermit on a not-too-sturdy chair in front. Meandering through dark woods, overhanging trees, and weeping willows drooping over an urn, all these were designed to evoke the romantic images of mourning, peace, and the picturesque. The virtues of life in the countryside were extolled in rustic cottages that had to resemble a farmhouse with a milking goat beside the door.

In the gardens of today, anything from the past is acceptable. You can find rustic summerhouses with an old plough and harrow, a wash tub, and the cart wheels in some gardens. They all have a special significance for people.

It is just not possible to create a completely new garden style.

The informal garden

The informal style has its roots in China and Japan. The Chinese appreciated the landscape, and originally the garden was just a separate, natural area. There were absolutely no straight lines or geometric shapes. Because the Chinese had always revered mountains, there was always a "mountain" created in the vicinity of the house. Water, rocks, and trees were the most important ingredients for a garden.

Almost all the elements in the Chinese garden had a symbolic meaning. The round moon gate, a circular opening in a wall or fence, symbolized eternal life. The chrysanthemum represented long life, the plum hope and courage, the pine tree venerable old age.

In Japan, too, nature was imitated precisely. If a tree did not look natural enough, it was pruned to a "natural" shape. Topiary was very important in Japanese garden design.

The great art was to disguise the artificial and to make the garden look like a complete, harmonious, and natural world. Stones and the way they were placed, had a significance based on religious conviction.

The West has learnt from the Japanese the art of making a so-called "dry garden." Stones, sand, and gravel are used to represent waterfalls, river beds, the sea, lakes and islands. Here too, the materials must be placed in a special way because of their symbolic meaning.

The landscape style

A new, informal style of garden took root in the Romantic period. In England the great exponent was Sir Lancelot Brown. The new style was called the landscape style.

Sir Lancelot was nicknamed "Capability" Brown because he could see capability for change in any garden that he looked at. The English landscape, particularly along the River Thames, served as his ideal.

"Informal" did not mean that the landscape garden had no set criteria to fulfil. The garden had to and did look like a landscape. The shape of a real lake was taken from that of a broad sweep of the river. Running water always had to look like a stream so the outlet had to be concealed. Another condition was that the house should be at a higher level than the garden.

It can be done like this too. Here is a modern interpretation of the Japanese concept.

The lawn, which came right up to the house, had to be lower in the middle, and the clumps of trees had to be placed on mounds.

The most important paths led through a belt of woodland that enclosed the garden on all sides. Conifers were definitely out because they were not considered natural enough in these gardens, while deciduous trees were in vogue.

Classical buildings were not allowed. A bridge over the water or a solitary temple were permitted, at least they made the garden appear larger. In Capability Brown's time nature was very carefully designed.

Brown's successors replaced the terraces, balustrades, and fountains by the house once again and gave a lot of space to flowers and flowering shrubs.

Even the walled garden came back. The pure landscape style was watered down.

The urban garden

The urban garden was already in existence by the nineteenth century. More and more people now belonged to the middle classes. They lived in detached or terraced houses and were keen to discover how to lay out and maintain a garden. In 1826 the publisher John Claudius Loudon brought out the first edition of *The Gardener's Magazine*. Loudon emphasized the collection of new plants and described the work of planting the vegetable garden, the nursery, the greenhouse, and cold frames. He tried to put together the best features of all the existing styles of gardening. According to Loudon, the garden should look different from the surrounding landscape. Horticultural societies were springing up like mushrooms. There were just so many new ideas. Opinion on the natural garden

William Robinson would have intended a support like this, the rose, for the clematis.

This lovely composition is typical of Gertrude Jekyll's-garden designs.

Walls that are almost completely overgrown belong in the cottage garden.

changed markedly. Irish horticultural writer William Robinson thought that the garden should fit into the landscape and not the other way round. Flowers should be allowed to grow in the grass and why should a climbing plant grows over an arbour when it could just as well grow in a natural way up a tree? Robinson also spread the idea of winter-hardy plants. Flowers in narrow strips along the edge of the lawn and Victorian flower beds could not withstand the blast of his criticism, although Robinson had nothing against exotic plants provided they were hardy. Right up to the present day there is more of the informal than the formal in garden design.

The cottage style

 Besides the natural style, there was also the cottage style. In the middle of the nine-

teenth century a group of architects wanted to break with the building style of the past. They were searching for a new style, suited to contemporary circumstances. The old craft work was given an important place, and simple materials were used. The English cottage served as the model. The arrangement of the cottage garden was inspired by the small holding where each section had its own special use – the vegetable plot, a working space, the orchard, a section for silage and so on. Translated into the cottage garden that became, for instance, the peaceful green space by the study, the flower garden beside the living room and the vegetable and herb garden by the kitchen. The separate sections were enclosed by hedges and connected along a series of axes, recalling the formal garden. At the junction of the paths statues, birdbaths, fountains, and sun dials appeared once

Water is in fashion in the garden. A statue does not have to be placed in the centre. Here the round shapes of the ceramic elements are repeated in the shape of the water lily leaves.

more. Gertrude Jekyll, the famous garden designer, made a totally new contribution with the border in which flowering plants were grouped according to colour, height, and flower.

Present-day gardens

Compared with the past, there is less space for gardens nowadays, while the choice of plants is very much wider. There is a lot of interest in, and knowledge of plants among garden owners. Perhaps the biggest difference is, however, that people usually have to look after the garden themselves, and indeed are very happy to do so. The garden has become an extension of the house. For many, gardening has become a pleasant, healthy, and relaxing hobby. Modern gar-

dens do not conform to any particular style. Elements from the past are included: the fashion for containers, box topiary, and – if screening is needed in a hurry – ivy growing up netting. Gardens still tend to be divided into rooms. The whole garden is not visible at once, so an element of surprise is created. There is a marked tendency to go back to a more natural ecosystem, which needs little modification and is low-maintenance. It is not so much a new style of gardening, more a way of working with nature, using for instance ground-cover plants. Woodland and wild gardens, with the planting adapted to the local soil and climate, are also becoming increasingly popular. On the other hand, there has been a resurgence of the formal garden. Box edging in geometric designs, beds filled with *Rosa* 'Iceberg' or perennials, these are all part of current layout. The plants of the

Page 25 above: *A practical shady roof has been made from simple materials and* Rosa 'New Dawn.'

Page 25 below: *This way of using ornamental plants blends perfectly with the farmhouse.*

There is plenty of room for reflections in this open pool. It has been designed with oriental ideas in mind.

> **Tip**
>
> If you are starting a garden from scratch, bear in mind that, giving the western European climate ,you will often be looking at the garden from the house. Allow for this at the design stage.

cottage garden are included in the design of a formal kitchen garden from the Middle Ages. Nostalgia is running high. People nowadays give the impression of wanting to withdraw into their own private Utopia – the secure back garden of the late twentieth and early twenty-first centuries.

The pre-design stage

 The earlier sections have given some idea of the way gardens were laid out in the past. The great and the good naturally had enough staff to look after their gardens. There was plenty of money, too, for the design and construction. Nowadays most people find themselves in a rather different situation and have to do all the gardening themselves.

When the move into your new house is complete and the interior work is finished, it is time to turn your attention to the garden. Before you think about the actual design, it is useful to know something about plants and their possibilities.

Plant names

They can be an awful problem for gardeners – those difficult plant names! Most plants have a common name in English, such as beech or bay, forget-me-not or loosestrife. Why make things more difficult?

Here two paths intersect to form four enclosed beds. In the centre of each is a standard Rosa *'Iceberg.'*

A good example is *Tradescantia* x *andersoniana*, which is known variously as boat lily (it is not actually a lily) and Moses-in-the-cradle. Other closely related plants are known as spider plant or Wandering Jew. Common names of plants are often very local, and a plant can have several in one country.

The English plant foxglove has the Latin name *Digitalis purpurea*. The Dutch common name translates as "thimble herb". The French, more sensibly, use *digitale* which is close to the Latin. You can see, however, that it is better to stick to the Latin names since these are internationally understood. If there were not internationally agreed names for plants, there would be enormous confusion both within and between countries. Plant research and horticultural trade would be impossible.

Linnaeus laid the foundations for plant names. In his time, the mid-eighteenth century, Latin was the language of science. In his *Species Plantarum* each plant was given a two part name - one for the family and one for the species. This was still a very rough division: later on, other scientists, among them Charles Darwin, refined the system.

Here is an example of Latin names to show how the system works and how useful it is. If you want to have a large bed of violet-blue bellflowers in front of the house, because they will flower throughout the summer, you can go to the nursery and ask for bellflowers. When the plants begin to grow and flower you may find that the effect is totally different from what you saw in your friends' garden. Instead of a low border, you have plants 1m (3′3″) high. It is not the fault of the nurseryman; he gave you what you asked for. If you had asked for *Campanula portenschlagiana* you would have produced violet-blue flowers on plants about 20cm (8″) high. What you actually bought was *Campanula latifolia* var. *macrantha*.

The same thing can happen with colour. If you give the nurseryman the full Latin name, then you will be certain to get what you want. If you

There are many species in the onion genus, Allium. *This is the ornamental* Allium spaerocephalon, *which flowers in July. It is good for cutting and is also suitable as a dried flower.*

only use the common name there may be a choice of ten or more different plants.

The common name for *Crataegus laevigata* 'Paul's Scarlet' is hawthorn. All hawthorns – *Crataegus* – belong to the family *Rosaceae*. *Crataegus* is the name of the genus, and *laevigata* the name of the species. Latin names are always written in italics. The last name, 'Paul's Scarlet', denotes a cultural variety. A cultural variety, usually shortened to cultivar, differs from the species. This difference has arisen through crossing, sowing, and selection of the forms found in the wild. A cultivar is always written in Roman type with capital letters and enclosed in single quotation marks. There is also the question of a variety. In this case the plant also has three names but the last name is preceded by the abbreviation "var." This last name is written in italics with a lower case first letter and has no quotation marks; for example *Geranium sanguineum* var. *striatum*. A variety may arise through natural selection under different conditions of climate, soil or altitude. The plant differs from the species. If the seed of these varieties is sown the plants that germinate will be identical to those of the parent, that is of the variety. This may not be the case if seeds of a cultivar are sown.

Finally, you will often come across hybrids. A hybrid results from the crossing of two species and is denoted by "x" before the name. *Forsythia* x *intermedia* is a cross between *Forsythia suspensa* and *Forsythia viridissima*.

Ranunculus aconitifolius *has foliage, folius, that looks like that of monkshood,* Aconitum.

Cultivars differ widely

Cultivars can vary widely within a species. The cherry laurel, *Prunus* (genus) *laurocerasus* (species) 'Rotundifolia' (cultivar), is a laurel that is used for hedging in sheltered places where it can grow 3 to 4m (9'10" to 13'). *Prunus laurocerasus* 'Mount Vernon' in contrast, has very much smaller leaves and a different growth form. It makes a round bush no higher than 1m (3'3").

Remembering names

You can sometimes deduce the origin, behaviour or appearance of a plant from its Latin name. The ending of the name may vary.

alba = white
nigra = black

Judging by the name, Eupatorium purpureum, *Joe Pye weed, must be purple.*

glauca	=	blue
purpurea	=	purple
rubra	=	red
sanguinea	=	blood-red
aurea	=	yellow, golden-yellow
argentea	=	silvery-white
variegata	=	variegated
laciniata	=	deeply cut
stolonifera	=	with stolons - creeping underground stems
folia	=	leaf
alternifolia	=	with alternate leaves
salicifolia	=	with leaves like the willow, *Salix*
heli	=	sun, so sun-loving e.g. *Helianthus, Heliopsis*
erecta	=	upright
mollis	=	soft

fastigiata	=	upright, pillar-shaped
pendula	=	hanging
tristis	=	sad, sombre-coloured
japonica	=	Japanese
sinensis, and		
chinensis	=	Chinese

Looking at gardens and photographs

In the pre-design phase, do visit gardens and nurseries, because you can get a lot of ideas from looking at other gardens. The owner will tell you about his or her successes and failures, and you can profit from other people's mistakes. Before you know it, you will have a list of ideas on design and maintenance. Look at a number of gardens. You may well find that the

The weeping pear tree by the pool has the Latin name Pyrus *(pear)* salicifolia *(with leaves like* Salix *- willow)* 'Pendula *(hanging).*

Do you recognize the lady's mantle, Alchemilla mollis*? Mollis refers to the soft, hairy leaf.*

various situations are directly to your own garden.

The usual time to visit gardens is in the spring and summer. Ask about any gardens that are open in the winter. You can then see whether you like the main lines and the several theme of the garden. Is there still something to appreciate in winter? If you visit a garden at different times of the year, you will get to know and recognize the plants better. You will always discover something new in a garden. It is a fact that the plants that are in flower are always the first to catch the eye. However you must be careful when you are looking round gardens that are regularly open to the public. These gardens are open just because they are lovely and almost perfect. In most cases the owners, whether individuals or organizations, can afford to have staff to help with the upkeep. If you have only limited time to spend in the garden, it could be a mistake to base your design or choice of plants on a garden like that.

Useful advice can be gained by looking carefully at the gardens in your neighbourhood. Do they have some attractive features? Try to work out why you think the garden at number 3 looks so awful while the one at number 18 is so pretty. Is it the design or the combination of plants? What is missing or what has been overdone?

Another important point is to find out what plants grow well in the soil in your area and under the local climatic conditions. Which plants find it difficult to survive? It is better not to include those in your garden.

Photographs in books always show the border or the tree at the best time of the year or day. Besides, the photograph is just part of the scene. How will that border look in a fortnight's time?

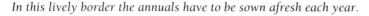

In this lively border the annuals have to be sown afresh each year.

Perhaps you prefer a more restful border in a single colour. The foliage provides variety.

Perhaps the photograph was taken in another country where the climate and soil are not the same as yours. It is actually a good idea to visit a well stocked nursery or garden centre at set times of the year to get to know more flowering and foliage plants. Incidentally the latter also flower - take a look at the *Hosta* species. Trees and shrubs must be looked at carefully, too. Are they still attractive before and after the flowering season?

Look at fencing and wind breaks. What will those concrete slabs look like in a few years time? Many slabs and tiles fade and soon lose their original colours. In short, it is time to draw up lists, look round, and make notes.

Topiary is very popular again today.

2 The design phase

 In this chapter, before getting down to the actual design, various aspects of the garden will be considered in more detail. You have no doubt already collected a lot of information and the catalogues of seeds and plants are to hand. Winter is a very good time for making plans and outline sketches.

The aim of your garden

 Before you decide for certain what sort of garden you are going to lay out, it is a good idea to make a list of what exactly you expect from your garden and what you are going to use it for. Do you want a neat and tidy garden with lawns and borders in which perennials are combined with annuals that flower profusely? You must realize that this will entail a time-consuming programme of mowing, hoeing, weeding, tying up, pruning, dead-heading, and trimming! Moreover, plants "spread" and also self-seed. Annuals have to be sown each year, then pricked out and hardened off. It will certainly become a beautiful garden, but you will have to expend a great deal of time and effort on it.

Looking after this border with so many annuals takes a lot of time.

This wild garden needs careful management to prevent other plants from encroaching on and eventually smothering the clump of white-flowering Rodgersia.

You may think that people interfere with nature quite enough and that the garden, once planted, should be allowed to go its own way. Of course this is one option, but do remember that then it will no longer be a question of what you like or dislike. You will not be able to predict how the plants will evolve or how the garden will look.

Always remember that you are dealing with living material, so that whether the design is formal or informal, each garden is a dynamic entity. Plants go on spreading, or even worse, escape under hedges or grow towards the edge of the bed: you never have absolute control.

The ground has a natural tendency to become covered with plants which protect it against cold, damp, sun and drying out.

If you do not cover the ground with plants that fit in with the particular environment of the garden, nature will provide them in the form of weeds. Hoeing bare ground means you are fighting a losing battle and wasting time and energy.

Tip

Grass has a tendency to mingle with plants in the border. Setting bricks on their sides along the edge of the lawn will keep the grass in its place.

Tip

There are various organic materials available in the shops, for example cocoa shells, which cover and protect the surface of the soil. They rot down gradually and need to be topped up each year. A layer 3-4cm (1-2") thick discourages weeds, and saves a lot of work.

Bark chippings also serve as ground cover. A layer 4cm (1 ½″) deep will discourage weeds.

In general you can expect a garden with borders, lawn, hedges, and topiary shapes to demands a great deal of attention. This increases if the borders are filled with annual and biennial plants, and if a lot of pots and containers of plants are added. But the fact is that many garden owners like a rich, colourful planting that is repeated each year and will do anything for the sake of a

---

Tip

Do not attach tendrils and branches of climbing and espalier plants directly to the fence, but fix them to a removable frame of mesh or trellis. Hang the frame from two large hooks on the fence. If the fence has to be timber treated the frame can be lifted down complete with the plant and laid on the ground.

---

lovely, colourful garden. Low hedges, essential for the straight lines of the design, have to be clipped regularly. Wooden railings, trellises, and fences have to be maintained, unless they are made of tropical hardwood. This work can take even longer if there are climbing plants growing against them, because the plants have to be taken down regularly when painting or treating the timber.

Borders with hedges need less maintenance. The combination of hedge and perennial plant border needs less work than a border with perennials only. A beautiful lawn kept within fixed lines demands a great deal of energy.

Hedges and trees require comparatively little maintenance. A garden in which there is a great deal of stone or concrete needs, relatively speaking, the least effort. But not under estimate the work involved with pots and containers, because planting, feeding and especially watering take a lot of time.

Know your soil

It is very important indeed to get to know the structure and condition of the soil in your garden. As a rule you can work out for yourself whether it is clay, sandy or peaty soil. Some plants simply will not grow in clay soils, while others will die in sandy and/or peaty soils. Clay soils usually have a high pH (a measure of the soil's ability to release hydrogen ions, which determines the acidity of the soil). This means that clay soils tend to have a high lime content, and may be described as alkaline. Peat-based soils usually have a low pH, which means that they are acid and contain little lime. This kind of soil is particularly suitable for growing heathers and rhododendrons. You can look up in many plant books and catalogues which plants

Page 35: *This is a labour-saving garden: a double border with a flagged path. Effort is saved because there is no grass path and no annuals or biennials.*

Various DIY pH test kits are available at garden centres. They are used as follows:

1   With the point of a knife take some soil from the top layer (5-15cm).

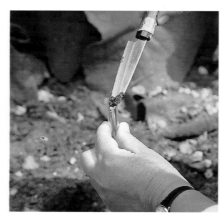

2   Fill the test tube with soil to the level indicated.

3   Add the necessary volume of distilled water.

4   Add a tablet and close the tube with the lid supplied.

5   Shake the tube for a minute until the tablet has dissolved completely.

6   Set the tube upright so that the soil settles. The solution will have cleared after two or three minutes.

7   Compare the colour with the colour chart. Each colour on the chart corresponds to a particular pH.

feel at home in either lime-rich or acid soils. Sandy soils can be divided up according to whether they are acid or alkaline.

The range for optimal plant growth lies between pH 7 and pH 5.5. For clays the pH should be ± 7; for sandy soil ± 5 – 6; for loam, ± 6.5, and for peat, approximately 5 – 5.5. You need to know the pH of the soil in your garden before you begin the layout and planting. DIY soil test kits are available at most garden centres; some centres may even test a soil sample for you on the spot.

The Royal Horticultural Society offers a soil analysis service for gardeners in conjunction

You see lavish growth and flowering of rhododendrons in soils with a low pH.

with a private analytical laboratory at a relatively modest cost. In general garden soil should be well-aerated, moisture-retaining, rich in plant nutrients, and free-draining (for more detailed information see Chapter 7, p. 262. If your garden fulfils these requirements you can count on being rewarded by a wealth of plants.

Climate and microclimate

The difference in climate between, say, the West of England and the central areas may not appear very great but for some plants it makes a difference whether they grow inland, in the east or south, or along the west coast where the winters are generally mild, and where the wind off the sea has a clear influence on plant

> **Tip**
> If you want to grow acid-loving plants, such as skimmia and rhododendron, on lime-rich soil the pH will have to be reduced. Peat can be mixed with the upper layer of soil. Add extra in the hole in which you set the plant.
> The pH of acid soil can be raised by spreading lime on the surface.

growth. Very few plants can stand the salt-laden, chill wind off the sea, which blows the buds off many shrubs so that they become misshapen. The same goes for flower buds. Along the coast the right choice of plants, with hedges that filter and protect from the wind, is absolutely essential.

There are great variations, too, in the amount of precipitation in different regions, in terms of the seasonal pattern as well as the overall total. Many plants die during the winter from too much moisture rather than from cold: they simply rot away. Take note in the catalogues of any comments such as "frost-sensitive", or "needs protection in winter" in the description of plants. Windbreaks and shelter belts can reduce the wind sufficiently to render the garden suitable for plants that prefer a sheltered environment.

When these ornamental onions emerged from the ground they were nipped by a late frost. The results are visible throughout the season.

Tip	
Hedging shrubs that resist the sea wind are:	
Canadian poplar	*Populus x canadensis*
white poplar	*Populus alba*
aspen	*Populus tremula*
white willow	*Salix alba*
alder	*Alnus glutinosa*
field maple	*Acer campestre*
hawthorn	*Crataegus*
elder	*Sambucus nigra*
privet	*Ligustrum vulgare*
Austrian pine	*Pinus nigra* ssp. *nigra*
Leyland cypress	x *Cupressocyparis leylandii*

Sometimes a plant, for example houseleek (*Sempervivum tectorum*), will grow in one garden and not in a neighbouring garden, although the climate is exactly the same. You will probably find that in the first garden the houseleek has a posi-

The hawthorn hedge is impenetrable.

tion which faces south, while in the other garden it faces north east, and has to make do with a damp situation and little sun. You can influence the microclimate in your garden by introducing, for example, differences in height. You can lay slopes in any direction. The temperature will vary on the slope between the top, middle, and bottom, as well as the moisture content of the soil and the degree of shelter. There is a difference in microclimate beside walls, by stones, under trees, and alongside hedges.

Drainage

 An excess of soil water can pose a problem when laying out a new garden. There may be a number of causes – an exceptionally high water table, a hard layer or pan in the soil, or slow drainage of rainwater. The hard-pan can be broken through, and drainage of rainwater to ditches can be speeded up. If the water-table is permanently at a high level drainage will not be an option and the planting will have to be suited to the conditions – it would be as well to consider laying out a bog garden.

Obviously drainage must be put in before you begin to lay out the garden. The method is described in the section: *Maintenance, the hard work.*

Cables and excavation

There are still a number of things to consider that have top priority in the garden layout.

Even different parts of a wall can have their own microclimate. On top of the wall it is nice and sunny, warm and dry. This side of the wall, by the Corydalis, is in shade. Warmth does reach the stones, but it is rather damper there.

Do you want lighting in the garden, and if so where? Of course you can only decide on that when you know how the garden is going to be divided up. At the very least any "hazards" such as a pond or steps, should be lit. It is not essential, but pleasant, to add lighting to the second terrace, along the path to the front door, and behind the little hedge that leads the eye to the second garden room during the day. The power supply for the lighting and for any water pump must not use the same cable, and must have separate switches.

The cables, even if armoured, must be 60cm (2') down in the ground. The water supply will also have to be extended. Electrical fittings for outdoor use must be waterproof. In any case go and consult your local electrical dealer and show him your wiring diagram.

> ### Tip
> Make a scale drawing of the network of mains services in the garden. Do not forget to show which is water and which electricity. Thinking "Oh well, I'll remember which is which" has caused no end of damage to pipes and cables. With the help of a clear drawing you will be able to trace the supply later, perhaps if there is a problem.

Paths

Paths are usually laid out before planting starts. You will find more about the different kinds of stone and the various possibilities for using them in Chapter 4, p. 175.

One important point is: do not make paths that are too narrow. You must have enough room to

You can no longer tell that this path, covered in stone chippings, was too wide when it was laid. The plants spread over the path and cover up the hard edges.

be able to wheel a bicycle or a sturdy wheelbarrow. Another criterion is that two people should be able to walk abreast on the path. Remember there are always plants along the edge or even growing over the path. No doubt you have discovered how annoying it is to have to walk along a path that is too narrow, between tall, over-hanging plants, immediately after a shower. You can shelter from the rain but the plants cannot avoid getting wet. A path that seems to be too wide in a garden before it is planted will be perfect once the plants are fully established.

Because flagstones are set into sand, the ground must first be dug out to a depth of at least 10cm (4″). This bed is filled with a layer of sand on which the flagstones are then laid. The path is later compacted. It will be higher than the immediate surroundings, so the soil that has been dug out is then spread along the sides of the path.

In small gardens the ground can end up 4–5cm (1½–2″) higher after the paths and terraces have been laid. This can cause problems if you want to dig out a relatively large pond. The solution lies in either taking the soil away or in using it elsewhere in the garden to create differences in height.

Differences in height

If a garden slopes down towards the back it appears to be larger. This impression can be further emphasized through the planting. The opposite is also true – if it slopes upwards it seems to be coming towards you, and so appears smaller. You should really not be bothering with differences in height in gardens that are less than 100m² (106yd²) in area because they will make the garden look smaller. If height differences are to be incorporated in the design they must be appropriate. If the garden is situated on a sloping site in hilly surroundings then it will not be difficult to fit them in. On level ground such differences will appear exaggerated and artificial. Small

A large garden that slopes up at the back always seems to be coming towards you and therefore appears shorter.

differences such as hollows for sitting areas, sunken paths, flights of steps, and raised beds are of course easier to design. The relief must be established before the garden is planted. Differences can also be achieved through the planting scheme itself. You must make a place for everything that will need ground excavating for it, including the rotary clothes drier or washing line, the sunken posts for the pergola or fencing, and the sandpit.

Harmony between house, garden and surroundings

It is satisfying when house and garden fit well together. Now you can look at that phrase "fit well together" in a narrow sense, meaning the use in the garden of authentic mate-

The flagpole can be seen clearly from the second terrace.

rials, with regard to form, texture and colour, and dating from the right period. Often, however, the right material is not available or is very expensive. "Fitting well together" can also be understood in a wider context. To emphasize the point with an extreme example: an austere modern house clad with concrete does not unite comfortably with a garden that has curved, bark-covered paths, a terrace paved with old bricks, and rustic planks for fencing: concrete slabs and lacquered steel would have been better in this context. Harmony between house and garden is often achieved by careful planning. For instance, it is advisable to site the sandpit where you can see it from the room in which you spend most of the day and not outside a child's bedroom win-

Most people site the terrace close to the house. It is then within earshot of the doorbell, and it also makes eating out of doors simpler because the dishes do not have to be carried right across the garden.

The style and shape of the house are mirrored exactly in the garden; even the colours of the two harmonize.

dow. Small children prefer to play close to their parents. Put the sandpit near the terrace (the place where you often happen to be) and not 5m (16') further away. Later on, when the children are older, the sandpit can be turned into a pond, extra barbecue space, or a flower box.

Choose a site for the terrace in the same way. This paved area is usually laid near the living room or the kitchen. This makes answering the doorbell or even just fetching something much easier. If the garden is big enough then think about a second terrace. People like to look at the garden from another angle or give the part of the garden beside the second terrace a different theme. The choice of boundary should match the style of the house and of the garden. A rustic fence goes well with a farmhouse on the edge of the woods, but it would be totally out of place beside a glass office block in the heart of the city. You can also apply the standard measurements that are used in the walls of the house, in the garden. This will tie the two in together. The same goes for colour - the colour of the window frames can be reflected, for example, in the garden furniture or fencing, not forgetting the planting.

The same really applies to all the materials that have been used for the house. Does the house

Laze around on the lower terrace and no-one can find you.

have a thatched roof? If so, the shed must have one too - a corrugated iron roof would be totally out of character.

Line of sight or perspective

It is important to emphasize certain main features in the garden, such as a statue or a view. It is then a case of constructing the garden in such a way that the eye is drawn, in that direction. A grass path between a double border can fulfil this role, but so can a hedge, a pergola, an unusual pattern of paving, and so on. It is obvious that a perspective like this should be visible from where you spend the most time, such as the sitting room or the terrace.

In larger gardens where there are more possibilities for terraces and resting places, you can also construct more perspectives. These views which draw your attention to particular features create an atmosphere of tranquillity in the garden as the eye does not need to roam around restlessly.

At this stage you do not need to know whether the perspective will be achieved by means of a border, a small stream or something else, but only that there will be a perspective in that place. The same goes for another kind of view— people looking in from outside. This is not usually appreciated by the garden owner. It is mainly people living in a built-up area who have this problem and they have to find a solution to it themselves. Going to the garden centre with a list of plants that grow tall and quickly is not the answer and is in fact the worst thing to do. At this stage do no think about planting, but decide in which room and which part of the garden you want to avoid being overlooked. There will have to be some obstacle in the garden whether or not it is green. It need not always be a hedge on

When you walk along here your attention is drawn to the mysterious dark gap. What are you going to find there?

Here you can see the boundary between garden and landscape.

the boundary. It can be nice, for example, if a tall hedge stands to one side of the terrace, to form a windbreak and prevent people looking in. Because you cannot see exactly what is behind it, a feeling of excitement and interest is created.

Wide open or enclosed

Whether to leave your garden open to the surrounding landscape or neighbourhood, or to enclose it, is one of the most important choices that you have to make. Do you want to leave the garden open so that it merges into the surrounding landscape? Naturally that can only happen if the materials used and the planting scheme of the garden fit into the landscape. The garden will appear larger because it merges imperceptibly with the countryside. You can also

consider a border of hedges with an opening here and there, to allow a glimpse of the surroundings. This usually gives a surprising and exciting effect. It is better not to plant straight hedges round an over-cultivated garden, because as well as making the garden appear smaller, the contrast between the garden and its setting will be too great.

In a hilly situation a rather looser line using natural materials would fit well in sloping landscapes with wooded banks. In the polder landscape of Holland it is more difficult to create a transition between the individual small gardens and the landscape. I can imagine that more straight lines would be considered when designing a garden there, so that it fitted better into the immediate surroundings.

In urban areas it is much more difficult. There, most gardens are enclosed and more focused on the interior rooms – the garden is regarded more as an extension of the house. A small, enclosed town garden has completely different possibilities, and also needs a totally different planting scheme compared with other, more open gardens. If you want to separate the garden from its surroundings, remember that the height of the boundary must be appropriate for the human scale as well as for the height of the house and the size of the garden. Also bear in mind that a young hedge needs several years to reach its full height.

Proportions

When dividing up the garden, do take account of the balance between planted areas, lawns, pools, and terraces, and provide a logical connection between the various parts. It goes

> **Tip**
>
> Anyone wanting to prevent the neighbours looking in thinks immediately of an impenetrable evergreen hedge or a fence. Ready-made fencing is not usually higher than 1.80m (5′6″) and for hedging the most common solution is the very tall and broad cherry laurel (*Prunus laurocerasus*).
> If you want to avoid being overlooked from the first floor a stilt hedge is a good, narrow alternative.

without saying that the structure of each part should be in proportion to the rest of the garden. A woodland pool of 50m² (58yd²) with an adjacent copse a tenth the area is totally out of proportion. If the pool and the copse are together situated in an open space 2500m² (2934yd²) near

This hornbeam (Carpinus betulus) *stilt hedge will quickly prevent the garden from being overlooked.*

a large country house, the part and the whole are again out of proportion. The interplay between the various features –trees, shrubs, flower beds, buildings, and spaces, everything level and flat, not the lawn, paths, terraces, and pools – must produce a balanced effect.

Interplay of lines

In general it can be said that the horizontal and vertical lines must alternate in order to create a sense of equilibrium in the garden, although in practice more horizontal than vertical lines will be used.

If most of the vegetation consists of plants with vertical lines such as golden rod, delphiniums, purple loosestrife, standard roses, mullein, salvias, and columnar trees, set against a background of vertical trellis, the garden will look as if it is about to take off. There is scarcely a line that does not force the gaze upwards to the clouds. Try to keep to the lines that you have chosen for your design. If the garden is oblong, and you have used straight lines – a rectangular lawn, a long border, a square shrub bed, and a rectangular terrace - a curved path does not belong. Sometimes, a roque element may creep in, probably because at the last minute the gardener has doubts. Don't worry if it all looks too severe. You will be able to soften the geometric shapes by using groups of plants to provide enough "organic" curved forms in the garden.

Different elements

The garden does not need to be a single unit. It usually divides naturally into a number of main and secondary elements. Many important

A garden with many horizontal lines clearly stands with "both feet on the ground".

Here vertical lines contrast with the massive building; they serve to draw the building upwards. Notice the vertical lines in the various lower-growing plants.

elements are sited close to the house, such as the terrace, herb bed and sandpit. The vegetable garden, the beds for cut flowers, the play area, and a second garden seat are less obtrusive. Those sections can be partly or completely enclosed. If the elements are adjacent to or behind each other the divisions make the garden appear larger. A garden that cannot be seen immediately – because the dimensions are not apparent.

Use of colour

Nowadays colour plays an important part in the garden. People from the urban environment seem to be somewhat alienated from the natural world – they no longer have to rely on it, they are no longer dependent on it. For that reason there is not so much feeling for nature. Perhaps that is why primary colours, large and double forms of flowers, bizarre and variegated

cultivars appeal to them. Besides, everyone is in a hurry. No one is prepared to wait.

The "instant garden" mentality is not conducive to the planting of slow-growing plants that promise rewards for the future.

Remember that even the most vigorously flowering plant will only bloom for three months of the year at the most and that you will be looking at the shape of the plant and the form of the leaves for the other nine months.

If you are making a colour scheme for your garden you need to be aware that colours change with the intensity of the daylight and the angle of the sun. The cool colour blue can be very striking in the mid-day sun but towards dusk blue flowers will fade into the background while white flowers will stand out. Pastel shades look good in a damp atmosphere with indirect sunlight but appear bleached in bright sunlight. Red and yellow are warm colours, blue and white are

cool. Warm colours appear come towards us –
so the garden seems smaller– and cool colours
appear to recede. Grey-green and grey are neutral colours that can have a unifying effect.
Fortunately in the cacophony of colours green
comes over as very restful, although within
green itself there are many variations– just think
of blue-green, grey-green, and yellowish-green.
Yellowish-green and light green light up in the
shade, while in the same situation dark green
makes a dark gap.

There are many rules about colour that you can
use for filling in the planting, but you will often
have some idea already of the colour combinations that you would like to see in the garden.
Do not be put off by the rule book, because
colour is very much a question of taste.

Furthermore, each person has his or her own
range of colours, that is their own personal
interpretation of colour combinations. What is
or is not allowed according to the book does not
really come into it. You are the one who is going
to lay out the garden and look at it, so you must
decide what you think is attractive or unattractive, whatever the book may say about it. In
general you do not need any particular knowledge of plants in order to divide up the garden
space, because at this stage which colours are
going to be used in the garden is not important.
You only need to indicate where there is going
to be a group of flowering plants and how much
space they will take up. In the mean time you
can always indulge in a few day-dreams about
colours and moods, perhaps with the help of
some attractive and practical gardening books.

*You are led along the beautiful border towards the patch
of light. That is the place for the second terrace, the play
area or vegetable garden.*

White peps up the garden but beware of overdoing it.

> ### Tip
> To help you put together a colour scheme you can use a colour wheel. The colours opposite each other provide maximum contrast, while adjacent colours harmonize. Remember that in the garden colours will never be separate, but always combined with other colours, with green as a dominant undertone.

Think about the neighbours

Not all gardeners have the same ideas about gardens and naturally that can cause problems. There can be friction and in some cases legal implications if, for instance, a tall hedge blocks out the light.

Tree planting is monitored by local authorities because trees must be set back from the road.

Felling a tree generally requires permission from the local council, which is often conditional on replacing it. In any case you should take specialist advice before planting a tree since the roots could eventually upset the water balance of the soil and cause subsidence in adjacent buildings. Owners of corner plots have a duty to ensure that there is good visibility for traffic.

There can be problems with water draining off your land if you are changing the contours of the garden, and your neighbour will soon complain if his land is flooded as a result of your actions.

It would be wise to consult the relevant authority, either the local council or the river authority, before making any major changes to your garden.

A garden can also be made up entirely of green and greenish-yellow shades.

Your wish list

If you want to lay out a garden in which everyone will feel comfortable and at home, then you must find out what everyone in your household expects of the garden. A big mistake, alas often made, is mentally to divide up the garden jobs among all the members of the family, when you are the only one who actually enjoys gardening. What is the point of a beautiful lawn if every week you have to move heaven and earth to get your student son behind the mower? And it is just as much a problem if your teenage daughter is always sun-bathing round at her friend's house – and so is never at home – because you categorically insist on having a natural woodland garden.

You can avoid a lot of aggravation by making a list of all possible requirements for the garden. Look at how much time you think will be needed for work in the garden. Finally, remember that you will probably only lay out the garden once, whereas the maintenance will continue week in week out, year in year out.

So now you have your wish list. Another consideration is the existing planting or a background that is already there. The previous owners will not always have gardened to your liking and there are some things that will have to be changed or removed. Removing grass and perennials and perhaps re-siting plants does not present a problem, nor does taking out shrubs, but trees are another matter. A tree has taken a long time to grow to its present size. A fully grown tree has a character of its own and gives instant structure to the garden, so you can probably include it in your design. If the tree really does not fit in the garden it will have to be felled and for that you need expert advice and a permit.

You can work out the height of a tree, to find out the area of shade, with home-made equipment. You will need:
- a wooden lath 65 x 2 x 4cm (26 x 1 x 1 1/2″),
- a length of dowel 65cm long and 1.2cm diameter (26″ long and 1/2″ diameter),

> **Tip**
> When you are making a list of all the jobs that have to be done in the garden, make a note of how often they have to be done and at what time of year. This will provide a model which will show when you can expect to have the most work to do in the garden. You can then adjust your design.

- a length of string 75cm (30″) long,
- a woodscrew 1.5mm (1/16″) diameter and 15mm (5/8″) long, no.4,
- a nut.

Drill a 1.2cm (1/2″) hole 5cm (2″) from the end of the lath. Then mark 20 equal divisions of 3cm (1-1/4″), beginning with the hole which is the zero point.

Tie the string 5cm (2″) from the end of the dowel. The nut is tied on the end of the string. Make a scale division on the dowel identical to the one on the lath beginning where the string is fixed, which is the zero point. Push the dowel through the hole in the lath. The screw serves to lock the dowel in the position required. It is put

The height meter is simple to make and is just the job.

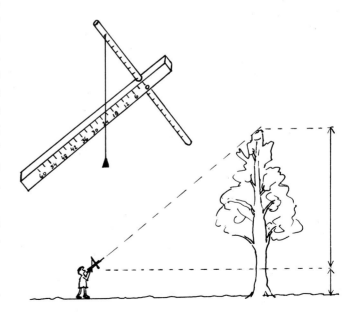

into the side of the lath with the help of a pre-drilled 1.2mm hole. The height meter is now ready for use.

Go into the garden and stand where you can see the top of the tree. Measure the distance to the tree and set the distance scale on the dowel. If you are 12m (40′) from the tree you move the distance scale so that the 12 coincides with the zero of the height scale on the lath.

Point the height scale at the top of the tree. The eye, the height scale, and the top of the tree are now in a direct line. The string, with the weight on the end, will give the height of the tree on the height scale from eye level. You will have to add the height of your eye above the ground - your height minus 12cm (4 1/2″) - to work out the height of the tree.

The sketch

For many people it is a problem that only the length and breadth of the various parts of the garden are given on garden designs. Because the heights are not given on the plan it is difficult to visualize the garden. There may be shadows in the drawings but that is as far as it goes in most of them. Garden designers often make perspective drawings or work with a computer program that can change the two-dimensional plan into a perspective drawing almost instantly.

For the amateur there is another solution: a sketch based on a photograph. Take black and white photographs from various points in the garden looking towards your house, and similarly take photographs of the garden from the most important viewpoints in the house. Have

With the aid of a photograph of your house and some transparent paper, you can sketch out various designs. This makes it easier to decide whether or not to have a tree or path in a particular place.

large prints made on which you can sketch your ideas with a felt-tipped pen. You do not have to draw directly on to the photographs: you can lay tracing paper or transparent film over them and draw on that instead. If you can build up a clear picture of the garden for yourself, and make definite decisions, then it will be easier to transfer the final idea on to a plan of the garden. If you have Lego bricks, trees, and boards in the house you could even build a scale model of your garden.

Drawing a plan

Before you can draw out your design you will need drawing and tracing paper. Graph paper, ruled in millimetres, is even easier to use. You can buy it in pads. Useful sizes are European A4 (21 x 29cm) and A3 (29 x 42cm). Graph paper ruled in inches and tenths is also available in A4 and A3.

You will also need a tape measure to measure the distances on the ground and an HB pencil and a rule. A pair of compasses can be useful for drawing circles, but are also templates, available

with circles in various sizes. There are templates, too, with all kinds of garden details on them. Finally you will need a pen, preferably a fineliner, or a technical drawing pen with Indian ink. To remove an ink line you can use an ink rubber, a scraper or a razor blade.

On rough paper you can now make a sketch of the garden and put in all the walls, sheds, and other buildings. The wall of the house must be included, together with doors and windows. The dimensions of all these, including doors and windows, must be noted on the drawing. After that everything is transferred to transparent paper or graph paper.

Making a scale drawing

It is impossible to draw the garden at its actual size, so it has to be drawn proportionately smaller, that is to scale.

For a drawing of the whole garden a scale of 1:100 or 1:50 is generally used, and for details - border, bed or pool - a scale of 1:20 or 1:25. A scale of 1:50 means that 1 centimetre on paper represents 50cm on the ground. A house wall 6m wide would be represented on paper at a scale of 1:50 by a line 12cm long. A piece of ground is very rarely perfectly square. To find out whether it is you need to measure a diagonal as well as the sides.

For example, supposing you measure the four sides of the garden: side A to B is 4.4m, the side B to C is 5.6m, from C to D 3.4m, and from A to D is 5.8m. A diagonal line now has to be measured - from B to D is 6.9m. When you want to put these measurements on paper you work as follows:

- You draw the line AB = 4.4cm (4.4m, scale 1:100) on paper.
- From point B you draw with the compasses an arc of radius 5.6cm, that is distance BC.
- Then the distance BD = 6.9cm is drawn on paper with the compasses.
- From point A you draw the distance AD = 5.8cm with the compasses. Now point D is fixed on paper.

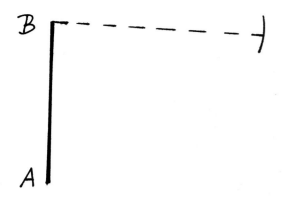

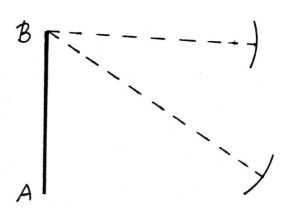

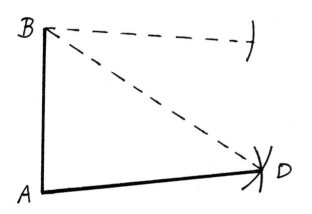

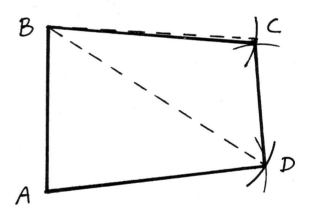

This is how you can work out the dimensions of your garden.

- From point D draw an arc of radius DC = 3.4cm. Point C is now also fixed.

When working in feet and inches use a scale of 1:60 in which two tenths of an inch equals one foot. The method is the same as above. When all the points have been joined up by lines you have the exact dimensions of the garden on paper. It is useful to transfer the shape directly onto sheets of transparent paper to give yourself clean copies to work on.

When the boundary line and the outline of the house have been drawn on paper, you fill in the buildings, hollows, the trees that are to be kept, and so on. You must also put an arrow on the drawing to indicate which direction is north. You can find the north point by putting a ver-

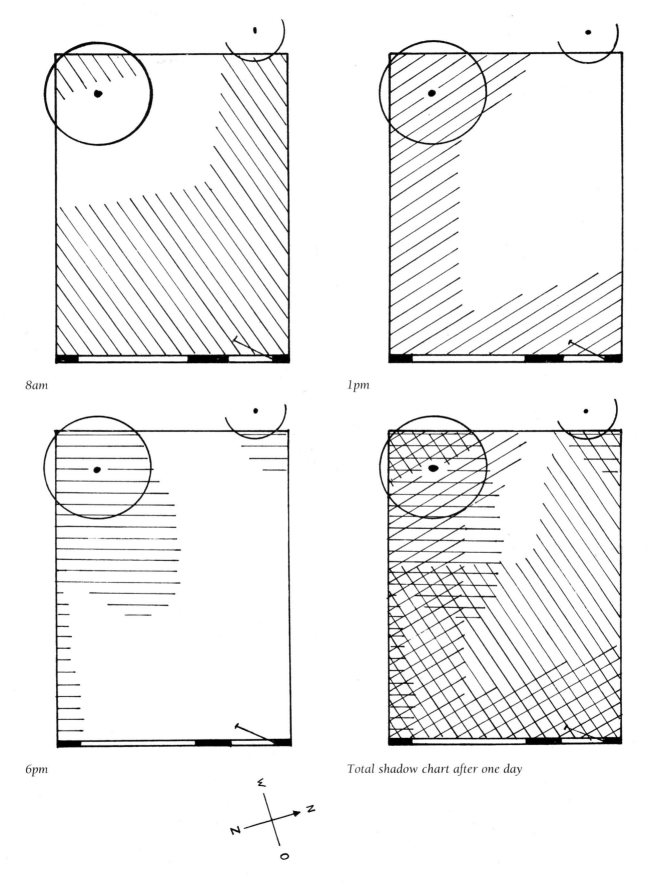

8am

1pm

6pm

Total shadow chart after one day

Symbols

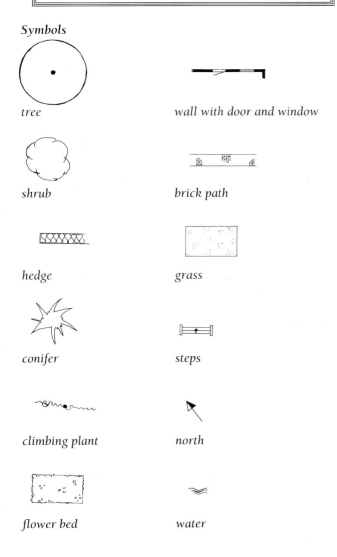

tree	*wall with door and window*
shrub	*brick path*
hedge	*grass*
conifer	*steps*
climbing plant	*north*
flower bed	*water*

Using these symbols in your design will make it easier to read the drawing.

tical stick in the ground on a sunny day. At 12 noon, when the sun is at its highest point, the shadow will point due north.

Various kinds of garden

Gardens can be classified according to their style, their most important features, or the level of maintenance. There is a further division, into front or back garden.

In the foregoing discussion about how the garden will be divided, what the owner wants to achieve and what is possible, the focus has inevitably been on the private garden at the back or side of the house. The garden facing the street is another story.

The front garden

Most people have no idea how to make something attractive out of the front garden where no one lives, works or plays. That garden merely has to be looked after, and yet it does form part of the property. Front gardens can liven up a street very effectively and can "dress up" the houses. These gardens also function as a buffer zone to absorb dust, noise, and smells.

In the front garden there should really be more emphasis on the communal element. After all it is often one street with one pavement and one kind of tree – planted by the council. But most people want to mark out their property very obviously. So between two different drives you have the inevitable conifer hedges, which start off nice and small, but after a year or two have grown too big for the narrow space available for them. You will often see barberry hedges that are so prickly it is nearly impossible to prune them. People trend to vary as much as possible the boundaries between the houses - 6m (20′) of rustic fencing here, 6m (20′) of screen walling there, 6m (20′) of conifers or paling and so on. There is of course no question of unity, on the contrary, most of the materials used do not suit each other at all.

People often have a small patch of lawn 2 x 3m (6 x 10′) surrounded by a border of bedding plants. The crowning glory is the silver fir or blue cedar right in the centre of the lawn, directly in front of the window. This too, was once quite small, but has now grown to such a height that it takes all the light, even from the first floor window. Many owners of small gardens like this would appreciate something different, but do not know how to create an attractive front garden. It is worth talking to the neighbours about having a joint garden. Often what they would like to do with their front garden can be combined with your ideas.

The shared drive
The shared drive can lead to two adjacent gara-

ges and leave just enough space for that one tree that cannot be planted elsewhere. The division on the pavement side need not go along the whole length of the pavement; gaps can be left here and there. If you make a boundary with sleepers, or palings, then this material can be seen from the street as a raised feature, while the ground can be raised on the garden side. In that case though you must ensure that water does not drain onto the garden or even into the living room.

Page 59 above: The front garden and house harmonize. The boundary hedge is continued in the line of topiary shapes in the front garden.

page 59 below: There is not much space in this front garden, yet plants, colours, and materials blend perfectly with each other.

A similar fragmentation of the green area is common in all kinds of streets. Each house owner has chosen a different style of planting, paving and boundary.

The interplay of light and dark is only made possible by the formal lines of the ivy.

Fences can also be omitted completely. The pavement can merge into ground-cover plants with taller plants here and there.

You could plant a single, not too vigorous, tree at the pavement end between the houses. Ask the local authority about regulations on distance from the public highway. If the houses are linked up by greenery they form a whole, and you will gain a pleasant impression of space without all those hedges and fences.

Decorating the front

Often people make an effort to draw attention to the frontage of their house. They do everything to make their house and front door welcoming and adorn the front wall with a bor-

Looking down on it from an even higher roof garden you can see that this is a true urban garden, but nevertheless for those who relax here it is a green oasis in the midst of the built up area.

der of flowers. This does not look right from the street because the flowers are out of proportion with their immediate surroundings: the high wall.

A single climbing plant to decorate the wall can be much more attractive, but beware of smothering the whole wall with foliage.

A well-placed, well-trained climbing plant offers various advantages. It provides extra insulation against the winter cold and summer sunshine and it is also pretty. Ugly house walls will be less obvious with a certain amount of camouflage. In gardens that only have ground cover the vertical climbing plant can break up the horizontal line. This is true of other situations apart from the front wall, such as supports for climbers or roses, and especially the posts of pergolas.

There are plenty of solutions to the problem of the front garden and again it makes a considerable difference if you can look at it with your neighbours. If you do have to do it by yourself then avoid dividing up the tiny front garden. It is often so small that it is better to confine yourself to one theme, for example *Prunus* x *subhirtella* 'Autumnalis' with an evergreen underplanting and some spring bulbs. Other possibilities are a rose garden and a garden with ground-cover plants only, and a single vertical accent.

The urban garden

Is there something special about an urban garden? Not for the inveterate town dwellers, but people who come to live in the town from outside notice the difference compared with a garden in the country. They are amazed to find that in the more enclosed urban gardens plants are less sensitive to frost.

On the other hand they are unlucky, the gardens are more shaded and there is nothing they can do about that, because it is a consequence of neighbouring fences and trees. It is much warmer in an urban garden. The walls of the surrounding house, naturally give out heat, and in general the gardens are so sheltered that it is

Tip

"Plants for full sun" means that the plants need at least seven hours sunlight per day. Plants suitable for half shade need three to five hours full sun, and shade plants are satisfied with less than three hours of sun per day in summer.

sometimes possible to sit out even in February. This makes it sound as if there are only advantages attached to the urban garden, but of course that is not the case.

For example you have no control over the outlook, which might be a beautiful old church tower, but could equally well be your neighbour's extension. The old fencing may be attractive, but it does throw a lot of shadow, while sometimes in the midday sun the garden becomes so warm that you are forced to retreat indoors.

Playing with shadow

Different parts of the garden will be in shadow at different times of the day. It is a good idea to make a shadow chart for a garden like this (see p. 56). In the areas where the deepest shadow falls you put shade plants. Did you know that most shade plants have white flowers? White shows up in the shade so this cannot just be coincidence. You can then see on the shadow chart where the half-shade plants should go, and there are many suitable ones.

Many half-shade plants can survive in the sun and are strictly speaking shade-tolerant, which means that they originally grew in sunny places but were driven into the shade by competition from other plants retreating to the woods. With the grubbing up of many hawthorn hedges in Europe, especially in England, a great deal of hop, *Humulus lupus*, has disappeared. The hop had retreated under the hawthorn where the thorns protected the plant. These shade plants can survive in the sun if there is sufficient water. A plant such as barrenwort, *Epimedium*, does

well in the sun, provided that the soil does not dry out completely.

In the urban garden there are some places left where the sun can blaze down, for instance, beside walls and fences that are in the sun the whole day. It is a good idea to plant a tree there which will give some shade. The solution is a tree in a pot, which must have a capacity of at least 12 litres (2 ½ gallons). A concrete container would be even better. There are various small trees and large shrubs suitable for the purpose. You can prune the crown of the tree into a parasol shade and move it around if need be. A tree gives cooler shade than could ever be thrown by a wall or fence. It is only a small step from the small, enclosed urban garden to the patio garden which is often totally paved. It is not for nothing that people used to have a well or pool in the

Barrenwort is a shade plant that can tolerate full sun providing the soil does not dry out.

centre. In such paved areas the temperature rises and it can become very warm but the water and the plants in tubs and pots provide some cooling. Here too you can sit out of doors in comfort under your container tree.

Try to make your urban or patio garden into an outdoor room to give a smooth transition between house and garden.

The country garden

The opposite of the urban garden is the country garden. In gardening circles the country garden is not mentioned so often nowadays because gardens are usually classified by their main feature, such as the water garden, rock garden or patio garden, and not according to where they are situated.

A country garden is more likely to be referred to as a cottage garden in England. The country garden was originally adapted to the way of life of the farmer or farm labourer who was involved with plants and animals the whole day and preferred to do something different in his spare time.

He did not usually want to spend a long time in his garden, particularly in the summer when farm work was at its peak. The original country garden was first and foremost a simple garden.

Gravel and box

You will not come across a lawn in that kind of garden, and the range of plants is limited to vigorous species. To keep maintenance to a minimum these plants were put in small round or oval beds, surrounded by narrow gravel paths to discourage the weeds, thus saving a

A modern interpretation of the cottage garden. The beds, which are edged with box, are filled with old-fashioned perennials. The paths are surfaced with bark chippings, rather than gravel.

great deal of time. Often there was a border of the slow-growing box, Buxus sempervirens, which only has to be clipped once a year. The original country garden was very exposed to the wind and for that reason a hedge was indispensable.

Meanwhile, thanks to modernization and automation the life of the farmer and farm worker has changed radically. Farmhouses are now surrounded by walled gardens with flower borders edging wide lawns which look as if they need very little upkeep although nothing could be farther from the truth.

Next to the ornamental garden you will find the kitchen garden, a feature that has become much more common in town gardens over the last twenty years. There is a separate section devoted to the vegetable garden (see p. 218).

Cottage garden plants

Very vigorous plants that you can use in a cottage garden include Michaelmas daisy, yarrow, poppy, lupin, bearded iris, bleeding heart, peony, phlox, delphinium, columbine, monkshood, and sunflowers. These sturdy plants do not demand much attention.

What does take more time, among the plants in a traditional cottage garden, are the annual and biennial plants, together with some bulbs and tubers. Annuals include, for example, African marigold, marigold, nasturtium, cornflower, toadflax, balsam and asters. The most popular of the biennials are Canterbury bells, honesty, wallflower, sweet William, and hollyhock. Among the tubers the dahlia, tuberous-rooted begonia, fleur-de-lis, and gladiolus deserve a mention. Making a completely new garden can be a very expensive exercise, with the costs of the non-living material such as stone, planking, cables, brickwork, and such like costing large sums. The cost of the plants themselves is insignificant in comparison, however strange that may sound to the owner of a new garden. Fortunately, it is possible to spread out the construction, and therefore the cost, over several years.

Excavations and ground works in connection with cables and water supply to the pool will have to take priority, together with the work for the main terrace and one usable path.

Much of the planting can wait for a year, or two years if need be. If necessary you can sow some annuals and grow some vegetables. Soil that has yet to be planted can be put down to grass or a green manure to prevent soil erosion. The single tree that needs plenty of time to grow and will determine the perspective of the design can also be put in during the first year. If shrubs are going to form the skeleton and boundaries of your garden then planting them should also have high priority. After a year or two features such as pergolas, ornaments, and perennials can be added.

Nowadays dahlias are available in a wide range of colours, heights, and sizes. A group of different cultivars in one colour need not look too stiff or formal.

Part 2

The layout of your ornamental garden

3 The green mantle

What is the most important thing to consider in an ornamental garden? Do you begin by putting in fencing, terraces, and paths or by planting trees and shrubs? Everyone with a garden is likely to plant something in it, but paths, fences, and pergolas may not be included in the design.

The emphasis in the first chapter, therefore, will be on the different kinds of plants available. Why are particular plants used, and the effect can be created with them? The structures and hard surfaces will be dealt with in Chapter four, p. 174.

Trees, the roof of the garden

Don't imagine that you can skip this chapter, because you think your garden is too small to have space for a tree. Some trees are suitable for small gardens. Once you are aware of how much oxygen is produced by trees, and moreover, that they give a much cooler shade than an awning or parasol, you will have to admit that every garden, however small, needs a tree.

A tree gives a feeling of protection. It forms the roof of the garden.

The green lungs of the world

The tree is a living entity. Its leaves take carbon dioxide from the atmosphere with the help of sunlight, while the roots take up water, nutrients, and carbon from the soil. From these the tree makes the carbohydrates that it needs for growth and for the formation of leaves and buds. The tree can do this thanks to chloroplasts, which give the green colour to the leaves. They enable them to absorb sunlight, transforming it for the process of assimilating carbon. In this process, known as photosynthesis, oxygen, which is essential for humans and animals, is released. Greenery is the only producer of oxygen on earth and that is a vital reason for treating it with respect. If you are wondering whether to have a certain tree in the garden cut down to make way for shrubs

Large trees are important oxygen producers.

and perennials, remember that one old tree produces much more oxygen and traps more dust than hundreds of newly planted saplings. So a hundred-year-old beech, *Fagus sylvatica*, with a leaf surface area of 1500m² (1800yd²) (the space it takes up is only 150m² (180yd²)) can satisfy the annual oxygen requirements of ten people. Moreover, the foliage of a tree that size absorbs 2.83m³ (3.68yd³) dust and can remove that amount of dust after each shower of rain. So you can see that there are plenty of good reasons for planting trees.

Trees set the mood

The tree forms the roof of the garden and gives a feeling of shelter and protection, even in winter when the leaves have fallen. It is precisely during the winter, when so many plants have died back and the garden looks bare, that trees maintain their silhouette and liven up the garden, for example, by giving shelter to the birds. With birds nesting in the branches in spring and shade to sit under in summer, the tree provides enjoyment in every season. Partial shade cast by a tree onto a terrace enables a group of people to sit together with the choice of sun or shade without the frustrations of a wobbly parasol! Don't forget that a tree can shade the sandpit during the heat of the day and provides much cooler shade than a parasol, house wall or verandah.

A tree strategically placed in the foreground lends depth to the garden and makes it look bigger. A tree gives a sense of security, it creates a pleasant atmosphere in the garden, and it offers protection, since it keeps the wind out, or rather, it filters the wind and humidifies the air. If you plant trees with a distinctive shape at regular intervals in the garden it will emphasize the structure. In the past people used to plant a screen of pleached lime trees in front of the farmhouse to keep cool the rooms where food was kept, and nowadays such a screen can still be used to keep out the sun.

The tree takes all the nutrients

✻ If you believe that other plants cannot grow in the shade of a tree, remember that it is essentially lack of food and moisture that prevents the plants from growing there. Many plants and shrubs can grow in the shade providing they are given generous amounts of compost every so often. The tree, which is much more deeply rooted, can be pampered by giving it a mixture of leaf mould and well-rotted cow manure. Make holes in the ground round the tree with a soil augur and fill them with the mixture.

A few drawbacks

When you are choosing a tree for your garden you must consider the shape of its crown.

Geranium macrorrhizum *does not suffer much competition from tree roots.*

If you intend to create a vertical line in a particular area, then you could plant a tall, narrow columnar tree such as the oak, *Quercus robur* 'Fastigiata', though it will not provide much shade. On the other hand trees with a broad crown will cast a large shadow. Not all trees have the same density of leaf cover and they do not all create the same amount of work clearing up the fallen leaves. One of the southern beeches, *Nothofagus antarctica*, has leaves 1.5cm (1/2in) long at most and the branches are sparse, so a lot of light penetrates the crown. Compare the amount of shadow that it gives with, for example, a bean tree, *Catalpa bignonioides*, or a chestnut, both of which cast much denser and deeper shadows. Tree roots may well start to lift the garden paving. Leave plenty of space between the tree and any paving or give it room by leaving a large area of bare soil round the trunk. If you want to sit under your trees, you must make sure that they will not drip sticky honeydew like the lime, for example, or drop fruit, like the black mulberry, *Morus nigra*. The latter drops its fruit throughout the summer, leaving large stains on both your clothes and the paving. Take account of these characteristics in your design.

Planting a tree

✻ When you have chosen which tree you want you need to order it as early as possible. It is often said that "A tree planted in the autumn (after leaf fall) *will* take, one planted in

Choose a tree that you can sit under without the danger of fruit falling on you.

the spring *might*". Nurseries and garden centres order their stocks in summer for the following autumn, winter, and spring. The later you order, the greater the chance that the tree will be sold out and no longer available. Those in the horticultural trade need to think ahead. The concealed roots are at least as important as the crown and the trunk of the tree. Prepare the ground carefully before planting. It is important not to mix up the soil that is dug out: keep the top soil separate from the deeper layers. Dig a hole larger than the diameter of the root ball. Mix compost with each layer of soil dug out and pour some of the mixture into the hole to form a small mound on the soil that you have already loosened at the bottom. Put the root ball on the mound and gradually fill in the hole with the remaining soil. Use a stout stick to work the earth in round the roots. If the soil is dry, water

it well at this stage. Carry on filling the hole with the mixture, firm it well down and cover the surface with a layer of compost. With a young tree placed in a windy situation you will need to put in a stake on the windward side. It seems like a lot of work for one small tree but remember that it has got to thrive in that position for many years.

> **Tip**
> If the tree is in an exposed position, put in a short stake next to it. Secure the tree to the stake with a tree tie, no higher than 60cm (24in) above the ground. If the tie is higher there will be too much movement in the root ball, which will delay the firm establishment and growth of the tree.

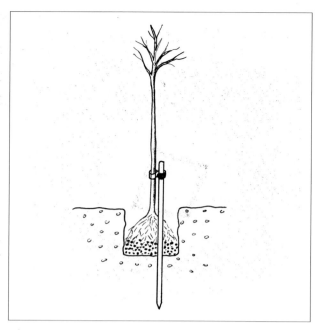

Planting a tree with a stake. The soil is loosened in the bottom of the hole and covered with a layer of the soil that was dug out, mixed with compost. If the tree is in an exposed situation, put in a short stake before you fill the hole completely.

Whether this is a grassed or paved area, a circle of bare ground is always left around the tree. This 60 x 60cm (24 x 24″) space for a trunk 20cm (8″) in circumference at 1m (3′3″) above the ground is necessary to prevent grass competing with the trunk and stem of the young tree and to allow as much light and moisture as possible to reach the ground.

This area may, however, be covered with a layer of organic material.

Tip

Do not add any fertilizer when you are planting. The tree needs only to become established during its first year, and it cannot make use of extra nutrients during that time. If you do want to give it something extra, plant it in compost. In the second year the tree will start to grow and you can then apply fertilizer.

Dos and don'ts

In your design take account of the fact that the roots of a tree must be able to breathe and therefore must grow in aerated soil. That means you should never plant a tree within closed paving; always keep an open space around the trunk. Another possibility is to use pavers with sufficient holes in them. In icy weather never put salt on a path that runs past the tree. No plant can cope with that kind of treatment and the tree will react by developing discoloured and shrivelled leaves.

In a new garden design be careful about where you plant trees in relation to gas mains. Leaking gas will kill the tree, while aggressive tree roots can damage gas pipes. Before digging up an established tree you need to know exactly where the pipes run underground, in order to avoid fracturing the mains removing the tree.

Small trees

There are very few amateur gardeners who know much about trees. For some reason, they always seem to know more about greenery at eye level and below: the shrubs and perennials. Colours are easier to remember and more appealing. At school everyone learns to recognize a beech, birch, oak, or chestnut tree. Because they are familiar, people tend to plant them in their gardens.

But there is nothing worse than planting a beautiful young tree and then being forced to cut it down after fifteen years. You would never have

---

Tip

Ivy, *Hedera*, can grow in trees for several years. Remember, however, that the foliage of the ivy can trap water and snow, the extra weight will increase the chance of branches breaking off the tree in wet or snowy weather.

The ivy has almost completely covered this prunus.

Immediate action required! Ivy growing up the trunk does little harm, but keep the climber well away from branches and foliage.

expected that bean tree, *Catalpa bignonioides*, to develop such a broad crown. You may think that you can keep a tree small by pruning it, but unfortunately that is not usually possible.

A number of trees count as small trees: that is they do not reach more than 8m (26″) and are therefore suitable for small gardens. In addition there are borderline cases that become taller if allowed to grow freely but which can be kept within bounds by pruning. The following are particularly recommended: if you are looking for a couple of attractive trees in the maple genus then consider *Acer negundo* 'Variegatum' and *Acer griseum*.

The former has beautiful silver variegated foliage, which is pinkish at first. It has a broad, round crown and thrives on light soils. The maple, *Acer griseum*, has attractive cinnamon-brown bark, which peels off the trunk and thick branches.

In the autumn the leaves turn scarlet. The globe maple, *Acer platanoides* 'Globosum', is a well known ball form. Don't wait years be-

The Norway maple can grow very large and take over a small garden completely. You need to cut it back regularly.

fore pruning because the old wood is rock hard. If you like attractive bark *Acer pensylvanicum* with its green and white stripes is a good choice. *Acer davidii* has similar bark and remains somewhat smaller. It also has pretty purple twigs in both summer and winter. Maples like the sun and grow in almost all soils providing they are not too wet. The snowy mespil *Amelanchier lamarckii* 'Robin Hill' has a narrower, pyramidal crown. It has pink blossom in the spring and can tolerate as little as three hours sunshine per day. It looks good planted along the borders of narrow driveways.

The upright golden alder, *Alnus incana* 'Aurea', has yellow leaves. The trunk and branches are brownish-yellow and go beautifully with the orange-yellow catkins.

All the birches are really too big for small gardens but I would not want to omit one of them, large or not: *Betula nigra*. In young trees the bark is silvery-white to grey, peeling off in curling, paper-thin strips, to reveal a hint of the reddish-brown trunk. It is suitable for damp, well-drained sandy soil.

The peeling bark of Betula nigra *produces splendid contours.*

You can buy the paper mulberry, *Broussonetia papyrifera*, as a multi-stemmed shrub or a standard tree. It has a rounded crown and the twigs have brownish-grey hairs. The grey-green, hairy leaves vary widely in shape, from a pointed oval to irregular and deeply lobed. The tree produces orange-red, spherical fruits 2cm (1″) in diameter. This lovely tree needs to be planted in a sunny, sheltered position witha fertile, lime-rich soil.

The bean tree, *Catalpa*, is well worth considering, although *C. bignonioides* grows too big for the small garden. Its yellow relative, *C. bignonioides* 'Aurea', remains smaller. The bean tree has foliage that starts off golden yellow, becoming yellowish-green in summer. *C. speciosa* is rather narrower than the very broad *C. bignonioides* but is nevertheless a tall tree. The globe-shaped *C. bignonioides* 'Nana' is an elegant standard tree which does not flower. It is not uniform in growth so in each case you have to wait and see if the specimen you have planted grows into the desired shape.

The katsura tree, *Cercidiphyllum japonicum*, is perfect in every respect. The broad oval crown provides plenty of shade for your terrace and the brownish-red branches produce small round leaves that are bronze initially. The leaves, which have a blue-green underside in summer, develop magnificent autumn colours. This tree does not like clay soil but you can improve the soil in the hole in which you plant it.

The Judas tree, *Cercis siliquastrum*, has an irregular shape and is strongly branched. It is really a large shrub, but is also available as a tree with a short trunk. It has quite large, heart-shaped leaves which are blue-green underneath. It produces pink to mauve flowers on the bare, old wood at the end of April. Later in the year it

It is lovely to sit in the shade of a silver birch.

The weeping ash in full splendour.

develops brown pods. Late night frosts make flowering uncertain, so it is better to plant it in a sunny, sheltered place.

Among the dogwoods there are many fine examples that can be grown as trees. The following species are notable for their flowers and foliage: *Cornus mas* has yellow flowers in winter while *Cornus controversa* has horizontal branches that form distinct layers. It has white, relatively large flowers in June, and is suitable for any fertile soil.

It is very pleasant to laze under the weeping ash, *Fraxinus exelsior* 'Pendula', which can stand a lot of wind so long as it does not come off the sea. A tree for better and damper soils, it can be pruned and thus kept within bounds.

The pride of India, *Koelreuteria paniculata*, forms a loose, broad crown. It has compound or double compound leaves which are reddish when young, turning yellow in the autumn. The yellow flowers clustered in upright sprays develop into bladder-shaped fruit. It prefers a fer-

tile, lime-rich soil. It can be somewhat frost-sensitive when young, but the damage is limited to the branches being frosted. Over the years, as the tree becomes used to the conditions in your garden, it will become much more resistant.

The common laburnum, *Laburnum anagyroides*, is possibly not so common as an ornamental tree these days. *Laburnum* x *watereri* 'Vossii', a small tree about 5m (16') high, with trailing flower racemes up to 50cm (20") long, is certainly worth growing. It is, however, only suitable for fertile soils.

There are many ornamental apples and they are all attractive, but *Malus* 'Liset' deserves a special mention. It reaches 6m (20'6") at the most and has very healthy foliage. When the leaves are emerging they are clearly purple in colour, very attractive alongside the lavender-pink flowers. It is the best pink-flowered cultivar. Of course it also bears fruit, which are a shiny purplish red and remain hanging on the tree for a long time.

The medlar, *Mespilus germanica*, is perhaps

rather old-fashioned, but very decorative thanks to its beautiful, big leaves and large flowers. It is really a multi-stemmed shrub but with a little care and attention it can be grown and pruned into a tree. How about planting it in the vegetable garden? *Mespilus germanica* 'Westerveld' is a heavy cropper and frost-hardy. The soil does need to be damp.

The Antarctic beech, *Nothofagus antarctica*, is a small tree or shrub with a broad, loose crown. The herring-bone pattern of the branches and the lovely bark combine to make a pretty picture even in winter. The tiny leaves turn yellow in the autumn. It is a 'see-through' tree suitable for half shade, which can even be grown by the pond because its small leaves will cause little pollution. Do not plant it in very heavy soil.

If you need a perfect rounded shape, buy a *Prunus fruticosa* as standard or half standard. It has thin, reddish branches and twigs, and very small, dark green leaves. The flowers, which are white and tiny, later form 1cm (½″) red fruit. This slow-growing tree has a naturally rounded shape, and is suitable for narrow lanes.

The hop tree, *Ptelea trifoliata*, is a half standard (or standard) tree with a broad, open crown and strongly aromatic twigs which branch sparsely. Each leaf consists of three leaflets which have a leathery feel. The large bunches of yellow flowers, which are beautifully scented, emerge in the spring, to be followed by winged fruits. With a little imagination these seem to resemble bundles of hops. It has the same yellow autumn colour as the Antarctic beech. Even if the garden is tiny there will always be room for a *Ptelea trifoliata*. There is also a yellow form, *Ptelea trifoliata* 'Aurea'.

The pear *Pyrus calleryana* 'Chanticleer' has a

Prunus fruticosa has a perfect, rounded shape. The tree is available in various heights.

Everything about Malus 'Liset' *is beautiful: the shape of the tree, the colour of the new foliage, and the flowers. It is a small, neat tree, ideally suited to small gardens.*

small, spherical crown with healthy, shiny green foliage that turns orange, yellow, and red in autumn. The leaves fall very late which is a problem for tree nurseries. In March you can enjoy abundant white pear blossom.

Pyrus salicifolia 'Pendula' is best bought as a standard. The branches droop down somewhat, as the word *pendula* suggests. It forms a broad crown and has willow-like, felted grey leaves. The creamy-white pear blossom emerges at the same time as the leaves.

The clammy locust, *Robinia viscosa*, is a less well known *Robinia* with a broad, rounded crown, and spreading twigs; the young twigs and leaf-stalks are dark red and sticky. In contrast to other false acacias, this one has very few thorns. The leaves are long and compound, with a lot of leaflets. It has slightly overhanging, pale lavender-pink flowers in May and June, and a second crop in August. Have you got somewhere suitable for an ornamental corkscrew tree? The *Robinia pseudoacacia* 'Tortuosa' is a shrubby upright tree on a short stem, with fantastically twisted and contorted branches and short, twisted twigs. It still looks very attractive in winter. This corkscrew false acacia looks much more attractive than the corkscrew hazel. Another attractive specimen tree is the willow *Salix matsudana* 'Tortuosa'. In general most of the ornamental apples (*Malus*), ornamental cherries (*Prunus*), hawthorns (*Crataegus*), and rowans and whitebeams (*Sorbus*) remain small. Most of these species belong to the small tree category.

Trees that can be pruned

As well as those in the previous section there are a few species in the genera of the

For centuries lime trees have been used to create pleached avenues.

well known large trees that will tolerate pruning and can be kept more or less under control, or if you so wish, can remain small. The lime, *Tilia*, can be pleached. Generally the large-leaved lime, *Tilia platyphyllos*, and the cultivars *Tilia* x *europaea* 'Pallida' and *Tilia* x *europaea* 'Zwarte Linde' are used for this purpose.

The hornbeam, *Carpinus betulus*, and many of its cultivars also have tremendous powers of regeneration: they tolerate pruning extremely well. That is why they are used for hedges and stilt hedges.

The London plane, *Platanus* x *hispanica*, with its flaking bark rather like a jigsaw puzzle, can be grown as a green "roof", which is appropriate in both formal and informal gardens.

The black mulberry, *Morus nigra*, can just be included among the small trees up to 8m (26'). In the past it was often seen in gardens in northern Europe. It produces small, edible fruits. Unfortunately these fall readily and stain any paving under the tree. The white mulberry,

Morus alba, which in fact grows rather bigger and forms a broader crown, would not be out of place in the garden. The young branches can be vulnerable frost. Fortunately to both mulberries stand up well to pruning. You can make a good sun screen with mulberries beside the terrace, but choose the white one which does not stain.

Conifers

Conifer means "cone bearer". The yew, *Taxus baccata*, also belongs to the conifers although it has a false berry, not a cone. In both old and new garden designs you will come across conifers.

Where do they belong?

Most conifer genera and species have a well defined shape, such as a column or a pyramid. They therefore stand out against shrubs and deciduous trees which generally have a looser growth form. They really fit in best with shrubs such as birch (*Betula*), broom (*Cytisus*), and buckthorn (*Hippophae*), which like the conifers are even at home on sandy soil. The Corsican pine (*Pinus nigra* ssp. *laricio*) and Scots pine (*Pinus sylvestris*), which are naturalized on areas with sandy soils and do very well in the gardens there, are rarely seen in arable landscapes on clay soils. Juniper, *Juniperus communis*, fits in extremely well in a heathland setting or a heather garden, but is not appropriate in a river valley or flat arable landscape. Conifers really do best among other conifers. A hedge is a good example of this. There are cultivars and sub-varieties of the various conifers available, but it is better to be fairly restrained and not plant too many striking yellow straggling forms, green columnar, or blue globe-shapes together. A single striking example a-

mong neutral neighbours is seen to the best advantage.

Give them plenty of space!

Always give conifers plenty of space. The reason is that almost all conifers are wider at the bottom, as well as frequently being sold as "dwarf" varieties. The cedar, *Cedrus libanus* ssp. *atlantica* 'Glauca', which has been popular for a long time, should be planted about 5m (about 16′) from its nearest neighbour because within ten years or so it can reach a diameter of 3.5 to 4m (11′4″ to 13′). And meanwhile, of course, the neighbouring trees will keep growing too. You may know from experience what happens when conifers grow towards each other and eventually touch. This causes the scales or leaves to go brown where they meet and, worse,

Do not use too many different shapes and colours together in a small space.

This cedar has grown too big for its surroundings.

Although the trees are far enough apart the effect is rather overwhelming.

after pruning or taking a conifer out of the group the branches do not produce any new green growth.

To avoid this, you could plant the conifers at what seems to be an excessive distance from

---

Tip

From the middle of the 1980's the ball-shaped tree, shrub, perennial and conifer have been on the up and up.

Sometimes an old conifer that has outgrown its strength and gone brown in places has to be cut back. But rather half bald and lop-sidedthan leave it as a eyesore , you cab trim it into a ball or cone shape. Cut out the lower branches that have gone brown up to the level of the healthy green foliage. Cut out the top of the tree and try to clip the green part into a ball, cone or oval shape.

---

each other. However, the wind will blow through a young conifer bed and it will look ugly for the first few years. So it is better to plant rather closer together, placing between the slow-growing specimens a number of fast-growing, often cheaper conifers. You could use fast-growing shrubs for this, too. As soon as the conifers are touching each other the fast-growing ones can be removed. The same method applies to low-growing species such as juniper, *Juniperus media* 'Pfitzeriana Aurea'. In this case "low-growing" can still mean up to 1.5m (5'). This small, rounded conifer, planted by the front door, will grow so fast that within five years you will no longer be able to get in or out through the door! In general conifers like light, quite-fertile to humus-rich, dry soil. They need plenty of light and space but they hate wind, especially wind off the sea.

The conifer is put in the planting hole with the root ball and sacking.

Once the root ball is in place the knife is brought out.

The knot of the sacking is cut through.

During sunny spells the newly planted conifer is protected with shade netting.

Newly bought conifers should preferably be planted any time from August to mid-September: the soil has warmed up by then and in western Europe those months can be quite wet. These are optimum conditions for the conifers to settle in and start to grow before the winter. Another good time to plant is in late spring. Always plant conifers in a deep hole. The top of the root ball needs to be 5 to 10cm (2 to 4″) below the surface of the ground when you have finished planting. Put some of the soil that has been dug out, perhaps mixed with some compost (if the ground is calcareous), round the root ball. Remove the hessian or netting from the root ball and water the tree. Fill the hole with soil and lightly firm the soil round the roots (do not pack it too tightly because the roots need to be able to breathe). Then give the tree some more water. In normal circumstances you should not need to water the roots any more but the crown must be sprayed daily. Spraying will keep the foliage damp and minimize evaporation, while moisture can be taken up by the foliage and trunk. Shade netting will protect a newly planted conifer from evaporation and scorching.

Transplanting larger conifers

If you had not reckoned that your conifer would grow so fast, you will be able to transplant it, but with a certain amount of effort. Most conifers are evergreen. Their roots are continually taking up water for the needles and scales, which lose water the whole year round. It is therefore essential to cause as little damage as possible to the roots during transplanting, so that they can begin taking up water again immediately afterwards.

In the spring mark a circle about 40cm (16″) from the trunk and stick in a spade all round to about the same depth, severing the roots round the side in the process. The roots *under* the root ball should not be cut through. Dig a trench at that depth and fill it with leaf mould (not compost, because that contains lime), without packing it down too hard.

You may need to anchor the tree. During the summer fine hair roots, necessary for taking up water and nutrients, will grown into the leaf mould. In August the root ball is dig out very carefully.

The roots underneath are severed and the conifer is immediately placed in the newly dug hole in the new position. The hole is now filled with leaf mould. You need to give the tree plenty of water during transplanting. If need be, the conifer can be anchored again.

August is chosen for this operation because it is generally quite a wet month in northern Europe, which means that the tree will receive plenty of water over the top of it. Newly planted and transplanted conifers can suffer in the winter. When there is a prolonged hard frost the roots will be set in ice and unable to absorb water. Protect your conifers from sun and wind in frosty weather with horticultural fleece, shade netting, old curtains or panes of glass.

Tip

If you are buying a perennial, conifer, or tree, do not ask questions along the lines of: "It will grow in the sun, won't it?" or: "It is suitable for pruning, isn't it?" The chances are that the person selling it will want to please you and reply with a wholehearted "yes." It is better simply to ask "Is the plant suitable for shade or for sun?" and "Does it need to be pruned?"

Tip

Whereas snow serves as a welcome blanket against the cold for many plants, it can spell danger for conifers with horizontal branches. The branches can collect so much snow that they break off under the weight. Avoid damage by shaking snow off the branches after a heavy fall.

List of conifers

You have already come across large conifers and have grubbed them all up. Yet they do have the advantage of being evergreen and they can have attractive shapes. The following conifers can be kept in the garden for a number of years.

Name	Colour	Shape	Height	Comments
Firs:				
Abies balsamea 'Nana'	dark green	wide ball	1m (3'3")	dwarf, prefers lime
Abies lasiocarpa 'Compacta'	silvery-grey-green	conical	1.5m (5')	
Abies procera 'Blauwe Hexe'	grey-green	ball	0.6m (24")	
Columnar cypresses:				
Calocedrus decurrens 'Intricata'	green	ball	1m (3'3")	
Calocedrus decurrens 'Compacta'	light green	ball	2m (6'7")	columnar cypress, difficult to obtain
Cedars:				
Cedrus deodara 'Pendula'	green	broad	3m (9'10")	weeping form, difficult to obtain
Cedrus deodar 'Pygmy'	grey	ball	0.5m (20")	
Cedrus deodara 'Verticillata Glauca'	blue-green	narrow upright	4m (13')	slow growing
Cedrus libani 'Sargentii'	blue-green	dwarf	1.5m (5')	fertile soil
Cephalotaxus harringtonia	dark green	broad	3m (9'10")	needs shelter, shiny leaf, likes lime
Dwarf cypresses:				
Chamaecyparis lawsoniana 'Chilworth Silver'	grey	broad upright	3m (9'10")	
Chamaecyparis lawsoniana 'Filiformis compacta'	green	round	0.5 (20")	
Chamaecyparis lawsoniana 'Forsteckensis'	blue-green	round	1m (3'3")	
Chamaecyparis lawsoniana 'Green Globe'	green	ball	1m (3'3")	
Chamaecyparis lawsoniana 'Lutea Nana'	yellow	conical	0.5m (20")	
Chamaecyparis lawsoniana 'Minima Glauca'	blue-green	oval	1m (3'3")	
Chamaecyparis obtusa 'Contorta'	green	dwarf	1m (3'3")	
Chamaecyparis obtusa 'Nana Gracilis'	light green	irregular cone	1m (3'3")	
Chamaecyparis obtusa 'Pygmaea'	brownish-green	ball	1.5m (5')	
Chamaecyparis pisifera 'Filifera Aurea'	golden yellow	overhanging and round	2m (6'7")	
Chamaecyparis pisifera 'Filifera Nana'	dark green	dwarf	1m (3'3")	
Chamaecyparis pisifera 'Plumosa Compressa'	yellow	pyramidal	1m (3'3")	
Japanese cedars:				
Cryptomeria japonica 'Bandai-sugi'	green	irregular ball	1m (3'3")	
Cryptomeria japonica 'Globosa'	blue-green	ball	1.5m (5')	
Cryptomeria japonica 'Jindai-sugi'	light green	conical	2m (6'7")	
Junipers:				
Juniperus chinensis 'Blaauw'	grey-blue	vase-shaped	1.5m (5')	
Juniperus communis	grey-green	natural	2m (6'7")	
Juniperus communis 'Hibernica'	blue-green	column	3m (9'10")	
Juniperus communis 'Hornibrookii'	green	broad	0.5m (20")	ground cover, very broad
Juniperus communis 'Repanda'	green	broad	0.3m (12")	spreading
Juniperus horizontalis 'Wiltonii'	blue	broad	0.3m (12")	forms very thick mats
Juniperus media 'Pfitzeriana'	green	loose	2m (6'7")	
Juniperus media 'Pfitzeriana Aurea'	greenish-yellow	broad overh.	2.5m (8'2")	becomes very broad
Juniperus media 'Sargentii'	blue-green	broad	1m (3'3")	

Name	Colour	Shape	Height	Comments
Sabine junipers:				
Juniperus sabina	green	irregular	2m (6'7")	
Juniperus virginiana 'Grey Owl'	blue-grey	broad	0.5m (20")	ground cover
Microbiota decussata	green	broad	0.5m (20")	prunes well, greenish-brown in winter
Spruces:				
Picea abies 'Clanbrasseliana'	green	ball	1m (3'3")	
Picea abies 'Gregoryana'	green	cushion	0.6m (2')	
Picea glauca 'Conica'	light green	conical	1m (3'3")	in dry periods suffers from red spider mite, goes brown
Picea omorika 'Nana'	grey-green	irregular	1m (3'3")	
Picea pungens 'Glauca Globosa'	silver-blue	compact ball	1m (3'3")	fertile soil, full sun
Pines:				
Pinus mugo 'Gnom'	green	broad, stocky	1.5m (5')	
Pinus mugo var. *pumilo*	green	broad dwarf	1m (3'3")	
Podocarpus lawrencii alpinus	green	irregular	2m (6'7")	tolerates lime and shade
Podocarpus nivalis	bright green	broad	2m (6'7")	tolerates lime and shade
Douglas fir:				
Pseudotsuga menziesii 'Fletcheri'	silver-grey	irregular	2m (6'7")	
Yews:				
Taxus baccata 'Adpressa'	dark green	broad shrub	2.5m (8'2")	yews prune well, tolerate shade
Taxus baccata 'Procumbens'	green	spreading	0.5m (20")	
Taxus baccata 'Repandens'	blue-green	horizontal	0.5m (20")	
Taxus baccata 'Standishii'	yellow	broad upright	2m (6'7")	
Taxus baccata 'Summergold'	yellow	broad	1m (3'3")	
Taxus cuspidata 'Nana'	green	very broad	1m(3'3")	lime, fertile soil
Taxus media 'Hicksii'	green	broad shrub	1m (3'3")	
Red cedars				
Thuja occidentalis 'Alba'	white tips	pyramidal	2.5m (8'2")	
Thuja occidentalis 'Globosa'	greenish-yellow	ball	1m (3'3")	
Thuja occidentalis 'Rheingold'	golden yellow	irregular ball	1.5m (5')	
Thuja occidentalis 'Umbraculifera'	green	flattened ball	1m (3'3")	
Thujopsis dolabrata 'Nana'	green	flattened ball	0.5m (20")	
Western hemlocks:				
Tsuga canadensis 'Jeddeloh'	light green	ball	1m (3'3")	
Tsuga canadensis 'Pendula'	dark green	weeping	2m (6'7")	dwarf form

Shrubs, the framework of the garden

Shrubs form a category somewhere between trees and herbaceous plants. Most of the characteristics of trees apply to shrubs except that shrubs tend to be lower-growing. It is sometimes difficult to tell whether a particular woody plant is a tree or a shrub, but in general a tree has a single trunk and then develops branches, while a shrub branches immediately above the soil.

Most shrubs have numerous branches so they occupy a larger area of ground than a tree, something that tends to be forgotten in planning a layout. Once shrubs have been planted, the garden immediately acquires depth. Shrubs are at eye level and make the greatest contribution to the framework of a garden, particularly where trees cannot be planted.

Planting distance depends on growth

Supposing you plant a mock orange, *Philadelphus*, which has three branches about 70cm (27″) long when you buy it. After a couple of years it may have to be removed because it has grown 2m (6′7″) high and the same in width. One problem is that you cannot see, when you are buying a shrub, whether it is going to grow big or remain small: the size when you buy it is no guide.

Buxus sempervirens 'Rotundifolia' is a cultivar that can reach a height of 2m (6′7″) in western Europe. It can cause problems if you don't realize that when you buy a young plant only 20cm (8″) high.

The *Hypericum* 'Hidcote', on the other hand, is sometimes supplied 50cm (20″) high. Surely that is going to grow into a tall shrub! But it won't: it only reaches 70cm (27″). To avoid such unpleasant surprises you need to look up what height a shrub can be expected to reach and find out whether or not it will tolerate regular pruning. Then it is advisable to keep to the following planting distances:

Buxus sempervirens 'Rotundifolia' *is a cultivar that can reach a height of 2m (6′7″).*

Final height	Distance apart
up to 6m (up to 20′)	3m (10′)
3 to 6m (10 to 20′)	1.5 to 3m (5 to 10′)
1 to 2m (3 to 6′)	1.5m (5′)
0.5 to 1m (20 to 36″)	0.75m (30″)
less than 0.5m (less than 20″)	0.5m (20″)

Different flowering seasons

Generally the most popular shrubs in gardens these days are those with striking, colourful blossom. There is a group that flowers before the leaves emerge, which includes the witch hazel, *Hamamelis mollis*; the cornelian cherry, *Cornus mas*; *Viburnum* x *bodnantense*; *Viburnum fragrans*; and *Prunus* x *subhirtella* 'Autumnalis'. The largest group, which flowers in the spring, comprises the Guelder rose, *Viburnum opulus*; mock orange, *Philadelphus coronarius* and the Jew's mallow *Kerria japonica*. Naturally a large number flower in the summer, including the butterfly bush *Buddleja davidii*; *Potentilla fruticosa*, and the *Hydrangea*.

Many shrubs give added pleasure with their lovely autumn colours and fruit which in some cases is edible, such as that of the flowering quince, *Chaenomeles japonica*.

Evergreen or deciduous

Among the shrubs there are both evergreen and deciduous species. The evergreen ones in particular are appreciated because they liven up the garden during the winter, with their show of greenery. However, many of the evergreens are dark green and look the same all the year round. Try to strike a balance, therefore, between the ones that do not respond to the seasons and the livelier shrubs that flower and will have rich colours from late summer.

In winter it looksunnatural for a strip to be planted with a regular pattern of evergreen shrubs among the deciduous shrubs and perennials. The effect is less artificial if the evergreens are grouped together in a particular part of the garden.

Set apart

Deciduous shrubs include a number of specimen shrubs that are best planted on their own on account of their blossom, shape, or colour. The Japanese maple, *Acer palmatum*, and a cultivar of the smoke tree *Cotinus coggygria* 'Royal Purple' are examples of such shrubs. The corkscrew hazel, *Corylus avellana* 'Contorta' perhaps ought to be set apart, too. It is splendid in winter but looks very odd in summer, when it has large crumpled leaves that look diseased.

The smooth sumach, *Rhus glabra*, is a beauty and it can be a real pleasure to sit in the shade of its broad crown. The one disadvantage is that it produces suckers, but this is more than compensated by the beautiful flowers and for bril-

> **Tip**
> Evergreen shrubs often suffer during the winter. Although the bush appears to be resting, the leaves go on losing moisture and can become dehydrated. Winter sunshine can make matters worse. A screen of fine shade netting can protect the shrub from the sun and from drying out.

liant scarlet colour in the autumn. If several different specimen shrubs are planted amongst others they can give a rather restless impression, as if they are competing with each other. Do not make too much use of such "prima donnas", especially in small gardens. Choose one, or at the most two, and plant them where they will be noticed, for instance by the terrace or the pond, where they are not in competition with other plants.

Other possibilities

Shrubs make first class wind breaks and they are used a great deal for hedging. If you have the space, a living hedge is preferable to a wall or solid wooden fence can actually create wind turbulence in the lee of the barrier. A hedge filters the wind, avoiding eddies. Some shrubs have tangled, even thorny, branches and provide edible fruits for the birds. Just think of the quinces on *Chaenomeles japonica* and the fruits of the blackthorn, *Prunus spinosa*. Grouped together in an undisturbed corner of the garden these shrubs provide nesting sites and feeding places for the birds.

In small gardens the plants are seen at close quarters. Remember that some shrubs such as mock orange and cherry laurel, *Prunus laurocerasus*, have rather coarse leaves which are not so noticeable from a distance, as infilling, but can be an eyesore close to.

In a small area it would perhaps be more sensible to plant a shrub with finer leaves such as *Spiraea*, or *Indigofera heterantha*.

The flowers of the smooth sumach are very prominent and remain on the tree throughout the winter.

Lavender is a sub-shrub that has to be pruned each spring.

Sub-shrubs are the odd ones out

Sub-shrubs present us with a problem: at first sight you would classify them with the perennials (they often appear under perennials in the catalogues), but on closer inspection they do look very like shrubs. In winter they keep their woody branches, often complete with leaves, while a perennial usually dies back to ground level. There are a number of sub-shrubs: lavender cotton, *Santolina chamaecyparissus*;

> **Tip**
>
> It is better to select a shrub because of its silhouette, and the shape and colour of its leaves, than because of its flowers. The flowers only last about three weeks, while you can enjoy the foliage for about eight months of the year.

> **Tip**
>
> Most sub-shrubs actually prefer conditions in the Mediterranean region. In colder areas, such as northern Europe, they are always pruned just after winter, in such a way that some green shoots are always left on the plant underneath the points where clipping has been done.

lavender, *Lavandula angustifolia*; thyme, *Thymus vulgaris*; rock rose, *Helianthemum*; sage, *Salvia officinalis*; hyssop, *Hyssopus officinalis*; winter savory, *Satureja montana*; rue, *Ruta graveolens*; *Hebe* species; rosemary, *Rosmarinus officinalis*; bell heather, *Erica* spp. and heather, *Calluna vulgaris*; *Alyssum montanum*; *Iberis sempervirens*; germander, *Teucrium* x *lucidrys*. Many of these plants are classified as herbs, others as flowering plants. In medieval and Elizabethan times the herbs were used as a clipped edging round the

Heaths are sub-shrubs.

beds in both the herb garden and the ornamental garden.

Top shrubs

 Everyone has his or her favourite shrubs, and the following are mine.

Nandina domestica, heavenly bamboo, is a narrow, upright shrub, that reaches a maximum height of 2m (6'7").

It has bamboo-like branches and evergreen, bipinnate leaves about 30cm (12") long. In spring and autumn these have a reddish tinge. In the middle of the summer *Nandina* has large panicles of white flowers. Plant it in reasonably fertile soil and a sunny, sheltered position.

The creeping blue blossom, *Ceanothus* genus, contains both deciduous and evergreen species. You can see *Ceanothus thyrsiflorus* var. *repens* with its 1cm (1/2") leaves in the photographs on page 87, before and after frost damage. It flowers in May and June with beautiful blue flower heads and spreads in (up to 1.5m (5') each direction) to make perfect ground cover. Although it grows no taller than 50cm (20"), it looks taller on the photograph because it has been attached to a frame and forced to grow higher. During the flowering season the *Ceanothus* becomes alive with buzzing bees. It needs some shelter or protection during hard frosts.

A relative of the bramble, *Rubus thibetanus* 'Silver Fern' is terribly prickly. Although it can only be handled with stout gardening gloves, it is exceptionally pretty with large grey-green, fern-like leaves on purplish red stems with white "frosting". This bramble is an open and upright shrub, with the ends of the branches slightly drooping. Even when the leaves have fallen, the branches of this lovely shrub, which reaches a height of 1.8m (5'11"), still look very

A wall-shrub Ceanothus thyrsiflorus *var.* repens *in full bloom in 1995.*

Above right: *the same ceanothus after the 1995-1996 winter. The plant has suffered severe damage.*

Below right: *the ceanothus at the beginning of June 1996. It is flowering but it will be several years before it looks as good as it did in the first photo.*

decorative in the garden, especially in a large border. You need to remove the old branches in early spring. Although it would make an impenetrable hedge it is not used as such; perhaps such a mass of grey-green would be too much of a good thing. It is best suited to sun and half shade. This also applies to *Rubus tricolor* 'Dart's Evergreen', a flat-growing cultivar, which makes perfect ground cover especially for large areas. It is not so prickly as *R. thibetanus* and are spreading its long branches covered in dark green leaves which stay on the plant all winter. This bramble grows about 30cm (12″) high and is ideal as a boundary – you can keep the front garden unfenced as no one will walk, run, or cycle through it.

Salix exigua is a 4m (13′) high willow that is also grown as a tree. The willow has many slender, upright branches and long narrow silver-grey willow leaves. It has something of the bamboo about it and is pretty all through the year. Give it a place in the sun or light shade.

Viburnum x *burkwoodii* is a snowball tree which flowers in April. Although it tolerates frost very well and is said to be evergreen, it does lose some leaves in winter. A position in half shade is fine, where it will come through the winter, despite severe frosts, undamaged. The blossom is white and sweetly scented, while the leaves are matt and elegantly shaped. Almost all the viburnums are well worth growing. *Viburnum* x *bodnantense* 'Dawn' is a rather narrow, upright,

Viburnum x burkwoodii *likes half shade.*

winter-flowering cultivar that can reach a height of 2.5m (8′2″). The scented flowers, smaller than those of *Viburnum x brukwoodii*, appear after the leaves have fallen. The shrub goes on flowering until the leaves begin to appear again. The edges of the new foliage and the young stems are tinged with red. The plant is also attractive in summer, and it tolerates sun and half shade.

The evergreen *Viburnum tinus* 'Eve Price' is in flower from November to April with white blossom that has a hint of pink. In bud the flowers are crimson. Everything about this shrub is lovely but there seems to be a misconception that it does not grow very tall – in fact it can reach 1.75m (5′9″). It needs a sheltered position and must be protected during hard frosts. *Viburnum tinus* 'Gwenllian' is rather more compact.

Hydrangeas are a familiar sight. Here are a couple of less well known and very lovely ones. *Hydrangea arborescens* 'Annabelle', which produces its heavy, creamy-white balls of flowers in August and September, only reaches 1m (3′3″) in height. It likes lime. *Hydrangea macrophylla* 'Ayesha' (see page 65) has large, shiny leaves, and bowl-shaped, waxy, lavender-pink flowers from July to September. Most hydrangeas prefer a fertile, humus-rich soil which retains moisture.

Generally speaking the blue varieties of the *macrophylla* cultivars become pink or mauve on calcareous soil, while the pink varieties turn blue on neutral and acid soil.

Abelia grandiflora grows to 1.25m (4′), is semi-evergreen and produces clusters of small, bell-shaped, white flowers with a pink tinge from August through to November. The small, slightly shiny leaves grow on overhanging branches. It is suitable for a sheltered, sunny place because winter cold can damage the leaves.

The black chokeberry, *Aronia melanocarpa*, deserves to be planted more widely. It is a small, pretty shrub with a natural look and an open, upright growth habit giving white flowers in

Tip

If you want your pink hydrangeas to have blue flowers, you must dose them once in August and once in September with alum, either dry or dissolved in water. A dessert spoonful per plant is sufficient. A proprietary hydrangea colourant is on sale at garden centres.

later in the season. It is not a tall shrub, 1.5m (5′) high at most, and is suitable for sun and half shade. *Enkianthus campanulatus* grows slowly but can reach 3m (9′10″). It is a narrow shrub which sprouts reddish-purple twigs at the top. The hand-shaped compound leaves turn bright red in autumn. In May and June it produces clusters of pink, bell-shaped flowers which are striped with white. It does best in light shade on acid soils. Buy *Caryopteris* x *clandonensis* 'Heavenly Blue' if you need a small blue shrub that flowers in August and September. It has small, grey-green leaves on greyish twigs. The blue flowers fade to turquoise. The cultivars are rather deeper in colour and *Caryopteris incana* has grey felt-like leaves. These 1.5m (5′) high shrubs like a very sunny, sheltered position. They are frost hardy although the twigs can be damaged, but fortunately they flower on the young shoots.

April and May, followed by black berries. Add to that the lovely brownish-red autumn foliage and your friends will wonder why this 2m (6′7″) high shrub they have not come across this. The shrub tolerates both sun and shade. The yellow flowers of the *Diervilla* x *splendens*, which appear in July and August, resemble those of the weigela. *Diervilla* is a rather bushy plant with arching branches. The new leaves are bronze, turning green

Caryopteris x clandonensis *flowers in late summer.*

Choisya ternata would seem to be the ideal shrub: it is evergreen, can grow in sun or shade, has compound leaves, a bushy round shape, and does not grow more than 1.5m (5') high. However, it is only hardy down to -10°C (14°F) and has to be covered during hard frosts. The fragrant, white, star-shaped flowers that appear in June will really impress you.

Some dogwoods have very pretty flowers and some have colourful twigs, but almost all of them have attractive foliage. *Cornus mas* has pale yellow flowers on bare branches in February and March. This bushy, branching shrub can be pruned into a hedge or arbour. *Cornus kousa* and *C. kousa* var. *chinensis* have large creamy-white bracts during flowering and then develop vibrant autumn colours. The latter variety prefers acid soil. The dogwoods mentioned so far are sturdy shrubs that can reach 5m (16'3") in height. *Cornus alba* and its various cultivars are planted for the colour of their twigs. In *C. alba* 'Sibirica' they are bright red, in the case of *C. alba* 'Kesselringii' blackish red. *Cornus stolonifera* 'Flaviramea' has greenish-yellow twigs. It grows into a shrub 3 to 4m (9'10" to 13') high and is worth growing for the colour of the bare stems.

Corylopsis spicata and *Corylopsis pauciflora* both merit consideration. They have bunches of pale yellow flowers in April and May but they do

The flower of Cornus kousa *var.* chinensis.

grow very slowly. *C. pauciflora* reaches 1.25m (4'), while *C. spicata* is more upright and has more open growth: it can reach 1.5m (5') or even a little more. Both tolerate sun and half shade.

The hazel, *Corylus avellana*, thrives in sun and half shade. It is a suitable shrub for the larger garden because it can easily grow to 3 or 4m (9'10" or 13'). You can harvest hazelnuts after a few years. There is also *Corylus maxima* 'Purpurea' which has brownish-red leaves.

An early flowering shrub is *Fothergilla major*. It has creamy-white catkins in April and May and grows very slowly, reaching no more than 1.5m (5') in height. It has fabulous autumn colouration in orange and yellow. It prefers light shade and does not like clay soil.

Hydrangea quercifolia is grown for its foliage rather than its flowers and is attractive throughout the year. It has an upright growth form with thick branches on which the large, oak-like leaves grow. In the autumn these turn red and purple. The white flowers eventually fade to lilac-pink. This 2.5m (8') high shrub thrives in both sun and shade but develops the best autumn colours if grown in a sunny position.

Indigofera heterantha is a pretty shrub for the herbaceous border. In severe winters it can be damaged by frost but it does survive. It needs to be pruned back hard each spring because it flowers on the young shoots. It then reaches a good metre (3'3") high, with an upright, open growth form, and beautifully divided grey-green leaves. This shrub will grow in the sun, and tolerate any type of soil, providing it is well drained.

Another beauty is the Himalayan honeysuckle, *Leycesteria formosa*. This grows upright with oval leaves and has long bunches of white flowers with purple bracts from July to September followed by purple berries. This shrub can be damaged by frost but sprouts again and flowers on the young shoots. It needs sun or half shade and will reach 1.75m (5'9") in height.

More use should be made of honeysuckles, preferably the winter-flowering species. The shrub honeysuckle *Lonicera fragrantissima* sometimes produces yellow-white flowers before winter. It certainly flowers in February and March and smells delicious. Plant it where you will walk past it so that you can enjoy the fragrance. As a rule it grows to about 2m (6′7″) high. It tolerates either sun or half shade.

Magnolia liliiflora 'Nigra' can be recommended for western Europe because it flowers for a long time in that climate. Very few magnolias are completely hardy there. They will eventually reach about 5m (16′3″), except for *Magnolia stellata*, and produce a dense cover of leaves under which nothing will grow. They flower in April, if the buds have not been damaged by frost, and if there are strong winds the blossom is soon over. The flowers are nevertheless magnificent. *Magnolia liliiflora* has dark red flowers

and goes on producing buds so that you can still enjoy the flowers in August. Magnolias need acid, peaty soil and a sunny position.

Myrica pensylvanica is a relative of the sweet gale. *M. pensylvanica* can grow in drier places. This bushy plant is evergreen, with upright branches and attractive leaves. In April and May it produces reddish-brown catkins followed later by blue-grey berries. This is also a shrub for acid soil and prefers sun or light shade. It will not grow taller than 1.5m (5′) high.

Osmanthus x *burkwoodii* is an evergreen shrub suitable for sun and light shade. It grows very slowly with an upright habit, and a regular pattern of branches with small, leathery leaves. The jasmine-like flowers, which are very fragrant, appear in May. This slow growing shrub will not reach more than 2m (6′7″).

Another shrub for the herbaceous border is

Magnolia liliiflora 'Nigra' is a shrub that goes on flowering more or less continuously through spring and summer.

Perovskia atriplicifolia 'Blue Spire' which at first sight can be mistaken for a large lavender. It is a plant with a strong vertical line, grey twigs, and lavender-blue flowers.

Photinia x *fraseri* 'Red Robin' is planted on account of its lovely, evergreen leaves. In western Europe it reaches 2.5m (8'3") and is useful in a sheltered site in the half shade.

Sarcococca hookeriana var. *humilis* is really an evergreen dwarf shrub, since it does not reach more than 60cm (24"). It has shiny green leaves and flowers early, from January to March. The female flowers are insignificant, in contrast to the male flowers which are sweetly scented.

You do not need both male and female plants of *Skimmia japonica* ssp. *revesiana* to produce berries since it is self-pollinating. The plants form attractive mounds. They produce white flowers in May, and the red berries that follow remain on the twigs throughout the winter. This shrub, which barely reaches 1m (3'3"), likes acid soil and a position in the shade.

Make sure you buy a specimen of *Spiraea veitchii*, which is a beautiful, tall shrub that can reach 2.5 to 3m (8'2" to 9'10"). The long, attractive arching branches carry bunches of white flowers in June and July, which are still decorative even after they have withered.

The lilac, *Syringa microphylla* 'Superba', is rather shorter than the more usual cultivars. The leaves and flowers, too, are rather smaller. It produces loose bunches of pink flowers from May to September and reaches about 2m (6'7") in height.

The young shoots of Photinia x fraseri *'Red Robin' are a magnificent red.*

The Siberian pea shrub Caragana arborescens *'Pendula' is a weeping form which has its place even in the smaller garden.*

Shrubs for different purposes

My choice of favourite shrubs has not answered the question of which shrubs to use for specific conditions of soil or climate. The following lists will give you more to choose from for your own garden.

Shrubs for exposed sites

These shrubs can tolerate wind, so they will survive in an exposed situation. They will, however, grow equally well, if not better, in a sheltered spot.

Shrub	Comments
Amelanchier canadensis	
Berberis vulgaris	
Caragana arborescens	
Colutea arborescens	
Cornus albus	
Cornus mas	
Cornus sanguinea	
Corylus avellana	
Cotoneaster	only the low-growing species on account of fireblight
Crataegus monogyna	also coastal sites
Crataegus laevigata	previously C. oxycantha
Eleagnus	all species
Eleagnus x ebbingii	also coastal sites
Euonymus europaeus	also coastal sites
Hippophae rhamnoides	also coastal sites
Lavatera olbia	
Ligustrum vulgare	also coastal sites
Lonicera tartarica	
Physocarpus opulifolius	
Prunus serotina	
Prunus spinosa	
Rhamnus frangula	
Ribes alpinum	
Rosa canina	
Rosa eglanteria	
Rosa rugosa	also coastal sites

Salix caprea	
Salix repens	
Sambucus nigra	also coastal sites
Tamarix ramosissima	also coastal sites
Viburnum lantana	
Viburnum opulus	

Shrubs for deep shade

Shrub	Comments
Acer campestre	
Alnus glutinosa	
Alnus incana	
Amelanchier	all species
Aucuba japonica	
Buxus sempervirens	
Clethrea alnifolia	
Cornus alba	
Cornus sanguinea	
Euonymus europaeus	
Hedera helix 'Arborescens'	
Lonicera pileata	
Lonicera tartarica	
Ribes alpinum	
Sambucus nigra	
Sambucus racemosa	
Sorbaria sorbifolia	
Symphoricarpus	all species

Shrubs for calcareous soil

Shrub	Comments
Aralia elata	
Berberis	all species and varieties
Buddleja	all species and varieties
Buxus sempervirens	
Caragana	all species and varieties
Ceanothus	some species and varieties
Chaenomeles	some species and varieties
Colutea arborescens	
Cornus mas	

Cornus sanguinea	
Corylus	all species
Cotinus coggygria	and varieties
Cotoneaster	low-growing species
Cytisus x praecox	
Cytisus purpureus	
Daphne cneorum	frost-sensitive
Daphne mezereum	
Ilex aquifolium	
Koelreuteria paniculata	
Laburnum x watereri 'Vossii'	
Ligustrum vulgare	
Ligustrum ovalifolium	
Ligustrum obtusifolium var. *regelianum*	
Lonicera	some species
Philadelphus	some species and varieties
Rhus typhina	
Rosa	some species, not too much lime
Symphoricarpus	
Syringa vulgaris	
Viburnum opulus	

Shrubs with aromatic leaves

Can you picture the scene, or rather, imagine the fragrance, relaxing on the terrace with a cup of coffee, enveloped in the scent of these shrubs?

Leycesteria formosa smells of caramel. The bracts remain on the plant for a long time.

Shrub	Comments
Artemisia abrotanum	sub-shrub, grey leaves, lemon scent
Caryopteris	both species, *C. incana* with grey leaves
Eleagnus angustifolia	plant towards the back
Escallonia	towards the back, grows taller
Gaultheria	
Lavandula	in all shades, grey, grey-blue grey-green
Leycestria formosa	smells of caramel
Magnolia liliiflora 'Nigra'	tall, background, flowers smell of oranges
Myrica	all species
Perovskia atriplicifolia	grey underside to leaves
Ptelea trifoliata	large shrub or small tree
Ribes sanguineum	pretty leaf, grows taller
Rosmarinus officinalis	frost-sensitive
Santolina	some species, frost damages leaves
Sarcococca hookeriana var. *humilis*	
Skimmia	can be clipped into a ball

Sometimes a shrub has scented flowers, with others you need to touch the leaves or crush them in your fingers to enjoy the scent.

Shrubs for bees

With the exception of *Buddleja*, shrubs are not visited much by butterflies, but more by bees. Do not site your terrace along their flight path.

Shrub	Comments
Aesculus parviflora	
Amelanchier ovalis	
Berberis	all species
Buddleja globosa	
Buxus	all species
Calluna vulgaris	
Ceanothus	all species
Chaenomeles	

Shrub	Comments
Colutea	all species
Cornus sanguinea	
Cotoneaster	
Cytisus	all species
Daphne mezereum	
Eleagnus	all species
Escallonia	all species
Hypericum androsaemum	
Ilex	all species
Prunus laurocerasus	
Pyracantha	all species
Rhamnus frangula	
Rhus	all species
Ribes sanguineum	
Salix	all species
Skimmia	all species
Spiraea	all species
Staphylea	all species
Stephanandra	all species
Symphoricarpus	all species
Syringa	all species
Ulex europaeus	
Viburnum opulus	
Viburnum tinus	
Weigela	all species

Shrubs for autumn colour

Some shrubs may not have very striking flowers but, for them, the summer ends in a blaze of autumn glory.

Shrub	Comments
Acer	many species
Aronia	all species
Berberis	many deciduous species
Buddleja	all species
Callicarpa	all species
Cercidiphyllum japonicum	
Clethra	all species
Cornus	all species
Corylopsis	all species
Cotinus coggygria 'Rubrifolius'	

Shrub	Comments
Cotoneaster	many deciduous species
Enkianthus	all species
Euonymus	many deciduous species
Fothergilla	all species
Hamamelis	all species
Hydrangea quercifolia	best colours in full sun
Parrotia persica	
Potentilla	all species
Rhamnus cathartica	
Rhus	all species
Ribes	all species
Rosa glauca	
Rosa rugosa	
Sambucus	all species
Stephanandra	all species
Vitis	many species

Flowering shrubs all year round

It is natural to think of flowering shrubs first and foremost in spring and summer but you can find them for every month of the year.

In summer the foliage of Rosa glauca *is very attractive. In autumn it turns orange-yellow and the shrub bears rosehips.*

The witch hazel sometimes flowers as early as January.

Shrub	Colour	Height	Comments
January:			
Garrya elliptica	yellowish-green	2m (6'7")	to -5°C (23°F)
Hamamelis japonica	yellow	4m (13')	autumn colour
Hamamelis mollis	yellow	4m (13')	autumn colour
Jasminum nudiflorum	yellow	2.5m (8'2")	free-growing
Lonicera standishii	creamy-white	2m (6'7")	evergreen
Prunus x subhirtella 'Autumnalis'	white	4m (13')	flowers in frost-free weather
Viburnum bodnantense	pink	3m (9'10")	
Viburnum farreri	pink	3m (9'10")	
Viburnum tinus	white	3m (9'10")	evergreen, blue fruits
February:			
Cornus mas	yellow	5m (16'3")	
Daphne mezereum	mauve	1.2m (4')	poisonous
Hamamelis japonica	yellow	4m (13')	autumn colour
Hamamelis mollis	yellow	4m (13')	autumn colour
Mahonia japonica	yellow	2m (6'7")	evergreen
Jasminum nudiflorum	yellow	2.5m (8'2")	free-growing
March:			
Chaenomeles	various	1–2.5m (3'3"–8'2")	

Shrub	Colour	Height	Comments
Corylopsis	yellow	up to 2m (6'7")	
Forsythia	yellow	2.5m (8'2")	
Magnolia stellata	white	3m (9'9")	
Osmanthus	white	2m (6'7")	evergreen, to -5°C (23°F)
Pieris japonica	white	2.5m (8'2")	evergreen
Skimmia	white to pink	1m (3'3")	evergreen
April:			
Amelanchier	white or pink	4m (13') plus	
Berberis	yellow,orange,red	to 2.5m (8'2")	evergreen and deciduous
Chaenomeles	various	1–1.5m (3'3"–4'11")	
Corylopsis	yellow	up to 2m (6'7")	
Kerria	yellow	2.5m (8'2")	tips often frosted
Magnolia x soulangeana	pink to white	5m (16'3")	
Mahonia aquifolium	yellow	1.5m (5')	evergreen
Pieris floribunda	white	1.5m (5')	evergreen
Ribes	white, pink, red	2m (6'7")	
Spiraea x arguta	white	2.5m (8'2")	

Corylopsis pauciflora *grows about 1m (3'3") high. The taller* Corylopsis spicata *has larger flower heads.*

Shrub	Colour	Height	Comments
May:			
Callicarpa	mauve	2.5m (8'2")	tiny flowers, striking purple fruits
Caragana arborescens	yellow	6m (19'6")	
Cytisus x praecox	yellow	1m (3'3")	
Cytisus scoparius	yellow	2m (6'7")	
Cotoneaster	white	various heights	deciduous and evergreen
Deutzia gracilis	white	1.2 m (4')	
Enkianthus	pink	3m (9'10")	autumn colour
Kalmia	pink, white, red	up to 2m (6'7")	evergreen
Kolkwitzia	pink	3m (9'10")	
Magnolia liliiflora		4m (13')	dark purple with light pink and white
Paeonia	various	2m (6'7")	
Potentilla	various	1m (3'3")	
Syringa	white, pink, purple	1–4m (3'3"–13')	
Viburnum	various	1–4m (3'3"–13')	
June:			
Buddleja alternifolia	lilac	3.5m (11'4")	willow leaf
Buddleja globosa	yellow	4m (13')	to -5°C (23°F)
Colutea arborescens	yellow	3m (9'10")	bladder-shaped seed pods
Cornus kousa	white	4m (13')	
Eleagnus angustifolia	greenish-white	5m (16'3")	scented blossom
Gaultheria	pink, white	1.5m (5')	need male and female shrubs for berries, evergreen
Genista	yellow	up to 1m (3'3")	
Hypericum	yellow	up to 1.25m (4.1')	
Philadelphus	white	1–3.5m (3'3"–11'4")	
Potentilla	various	1m (3'3")	
Rhododendron	various	0.5–4m (1'8"–12'3")	
Sambucus	white, cream	2–5m (6'7"–16'3")	
Spiraea	white, pink	0.5–2.5m (1'8"–8'2")	
Ulex europaeus	yellow	1m (3'3")	almost leafless
Weigela	various	1–3m (3'3"–9'10")	
July:			
Buddleja davidii	various	up to 4m (13')	
Ceanothus x delilianus 'Gloire de Versailles'	blue	1.5m (5')	to -5°C (23°F)
Ceonothus x pallidus	pink	1.5m (5')	to -5°C (23°F)
Colutea arborescens	yellow	3m (9'10")	
Fuchsia magellanica	various reds	1m (3'3")	can be frosted
Gaultheria procumbens	white–pink	15cm (6")	red berries, evergreen
Hydrangea	various	1–2m (3'3"–6'7")	taller species flower later
Indigofera	mauve-pink	1.5m (5')	to -5°C (23°F)
Lavandula	white, pink, blue	1m (3'3")	to -5°C (23°F) or hardy, evergreen
Potentilla	various	1m (3'3")	

The shrub Potentilla fruticosa *has many cultivars, none of which grow taller than 1m (3'3").*

Shrub	Colour	Height	Comments
August and September:			
Buddleja davidii	various	4m (13')	
Caryopteris	blue	1.2m (4')	to -5°C (23°F)
Ceanothus	blue, pink	1.5m (5')	to -5°C (23°F)
Colutea	yellow	3m (9'10")	
Fuchsia magellanica	various reds	1m (3'3")	can be frosted
Hebe	white, blue, pink	1m (3'3")	evergreen, to -5°C (23°F)
Hedera helix	greenish-yellow	2m (6'7")	shrub ivy, bee plant, evergreen
Hibiscus syriacus	pink, white, blue, red	2.5m (8'2")	
Hydrangea	various	2m (6'7")	
Leycesteria formosa	purplish red with white	2m (6'7")	to -5°C (23°F)
Perovskia	blue	1m (3'3")	like a large lavender
Potentilla	various	1m (3'3")	
Tamarix ramosissima	pink	4m (13')	
October:			
Caryopteris	blue	1.2m (4')	to -5°C (23°F)
Colutea	yellow	3m (9'10")	
Fuchsia magellanica	red	1m (3'3")	can be frosted

Shrub	Colour	Height	Comments
Hamamelis virginiana	yellow	3.5m (11'4")	
Hedera helix	greenish-yellow	2m (6'7")	bee plant, evergreen
Potentilla	various	1m (3'3")	
November:			
Jasminum nudiflorum	yellow	2.5m (8'2")	also as wall shrub
Hamamelis virginiana	yellow	3.5m (11'4")	
Prunus x subhirtella 'Autumnalis'	pink, white	4m (13')	also as a tree
Viburnum x bodnantense	pink	3m (9'10")	
Viburnum farreri	pink	3m (9'10")	
December:			
Hamamelis mollis	yellow	4m (13')	
Jasminum nudiflorum	yellow	2.5m (8'2")	can also be trained
Viburnum	pink, white	3m (9'10")	flowers in frost-free weather

When to plant trees and shrubs

Bare-root deciduous trees and shrubs can be planted or moved from the time the leaves fall until the new leaves appear, unless there is frost in the ground. The trees and shrubs recover well at that time because they have a limited surface area for transpiration, and in autumn the soil is still warm. With evergreen shrubs it is rather different, as you have already seen with the conifers. In both winter and summer evergreen plants are covered in leaves so that transpiration continues normally throughout the winter. Transplanting these shrubs just before a frost can be fatal because the roots that have been damaged during the move are not able to take up enough water to make up for losses due to transpiration. These shrubs are therefore best planted from mid-August to mid-October to give them the chance to develop new roots before the winter. This group of shrubs can also be planted from mid-April until the end of May. They will then continue growing both above and below ground.

On dry sandy and clay (mostly light clay) soils autumn planting is preferable, while in wet soils it is better to plant in the spring.

Trees with fleshy roots, such as tree of heaven (*Ailanthus*), bean tree (*Catalpa*), foxglove tree (*Paulownia*), tulip tree (*Liriodendron*), and wing nut (*Pterocarya*) are transplanted in the spring. It is also preferable to transplant in the spring woody species that have a symbiotic relationship with fungi and bacteria in the soil (beech, birch, and alder). Always dig a large planting hole and loosen the soil round the sides of it.

Container plants

A great deal of plant material is grown in containers in order to extend the season for nurseries and garden centres. The roots of the plant are not damaged when moved from the container to the ground and the plants can go on growing undisturbed. This makes it possible to transplant them throughout the summer.

Tip
Trees, conifers, and shrubs that are planted in spring must be given a lot of water during planting. Unless the soil is very dry watering can be omitted after the summer. Plants put into warm earth in autumn suffer stress if they are doused in cold water. They will then find it difficult to become properly established before winter.

Hedges to shelter and protect

When you are laying out a new garden, creating boundans to the area is the most important consideration. It is often the first work that people tackle in the garden, seeking protection from trespassers, prying eyes, and the wind. Sitting out in the open is not always pleasant and can give a feeling of exposure. The best way to overcome this is to plant shrubs that are long lasting.

From box edging to green room

From ancient Egyptian gardens to the current cottage-garden style, hedges have always been a feature of garden design.
People seek to mark off and protect their property. In times of war and knights on horseback, castles and domains were surrounded by walls but within them the space was divided up with lower hedges. Parts of the ornamental garden were enclosed by low hedges. Hedges were even planted to form mazes. When the garden at Hidcote Manor (England) was laid out in 1907 it was the start of a new garden style whereby the garden is divided into various "rooms", each of which is a separate entity with its own character.

A hedge as divider

An old Chinese saying maintains that a garden without a hedge is like a jacket without a collar. When a hedge is mentioned nowadays it is thought of first and foremost as the boundary of the garden, which, because it is not solid, can break or filter the wind.

The space within one garden room can be further divided by low hedges.

A hedge can also screen the play area or the vegetable garden. Dividing up the garden into different "rooms", means that it cannot be seen all at once. The garden thus appears larger and more exciting because through each gap there is yet another surprise.

Gertrude Jekyll, the English garden designer, discovered a new function for the hedge at the end of the nineteenth century with her designs for the present-day border: the hedge formed the background to the border. All plants look beautiful against restful greenery and in fact you can kill several birds with one stone: the hedge provides the boundary for the garden, the background for the border, and a windbreak all at the same time.

> **Tip**
> A rather taller hedge round your rose or herb garden will not only protect it from the wind but will trap the scents in that area.

A colourful hedge

The advantage of a living boundary, as opposed to a fence, is that it can provide interest throughout the year. It does so, because seasonal variations occur among the deciduous components of the hedge. Space permitting, a rose hedge of, for example, *Rosa rugosa* 'Alba' with its white flowers, is a lovely solution. If you prefer a hedge with autumnal interest, you should consider the barberries, *Berberis* species: most of them (not just the best known which is

The yew hedges trap the fragrances within the herb garden.

Tip

The hedge between two properties, providing both parties agree, can be planted on the line of the boundary. If this is not the case then the hedge must be planted inside your boundary. Ask the local planning department for the exact rules and regulations.

red the whole year) have beautiful autumn colours as well as bearing colourful berries. They are all very prickly. Firethorn (*Pyracantha*), hornbeam (*Carpinus betulus*), species roses, and *Cotoneaster* are a few of the shrubs that, if planted as a loose hedge, provide nesting sites for birds. You can also make a choice from various flowering shrubs for a more open hedge. These do take up very much more space, but because they need to be planted further apart from each other, there is a financial advantage. Low hedges of box or lavender fit in very well with the scale of herb beds and kitchen gardens or round rose beds.

Leave a gap

A hedge is ususally intended to grow in the same place for years. The choice of the hedge must therefore be determined mainly by the type of soil, since you want to keep your hedge free of gaps and above all healthy. The chance of this is greatest if the shrubs feel at home and are well pruned and fed.

When a border is to be planted in front of a hedge keep a strip clear, 30–50cm (12–20″) wide, between hedge and border. That path is useful to walk along when you have to prune the hedge or weed the border.

There is plenty of choice of hedging shrubs.

> **Tip**
>
> If the roots of the hedge tend to spread, chop them through with a spade along the outside edge. Dig a trench and then partly fill it with manure. Fill in the trench completely with the soil that was dug out.

Conifer hedges

If you look around in northern Europe you will see that conifer hedging is rather popular. Conifers actually only grow well on reasonable sandy, peaty, or loamy soils.

The red-cedar, *Thuja occidentalis*, is a fast growing conifer that can tolerate wind, though not wind off the sea, and does reasonably well in shade. The fact that it turns brown in the winter is, however, seen as a drawback by many people. *Thuja* tolerates pruning. The cultivar *Thuja occidentalis* 'Pyramidalis Compacta', which is blue-green, and *Thuja occidentalis* 'Holmstrup', which is a deep green, are both suitable for hedges. The latter does not grow as fast and needs to have plenty of room, so plant it at intervals of 2m (6'7"). If *Thuja* is not free-standing the lower part becomes brown.

The dwarf cypress, *Chamaecyparis lawsoniana*, and various cultivars such as *C. lawsoniana* 'Triumf van Boskoop' and *C. lawsoniana* 'Green Hedger' also grow reasonably well and are suitable for hedges. They do not tolerate shade and dislike wind. The dwarf cypress can be lightly pruned.

If you have a large garden and want to ensure

A yew hedge offers more or less unlimited possibilities. It is, however, slow growing.

your privacy quickly you can use x *Cupresso-cyparis leylandii*. This indestructible grower remains thick even low down and reacts extremely well to pruning. It is suitable for coastal sites. It eventually grows too tall for many gardens.

The much undervalued yew, *Taxus baccata*, is the last in this list of conifers. The yew is not fussy about soil and will grow on heavy, alkaline soil and even in the shade. Yews, including those grown as standards, tolerate hard pruning, and are popular for topiary. It is a pity that they grow very slowly and that they are expensive. The foliage and the berries are poisonous to both humans and animals.

Evergreen hedges

Shrubs suitable for tall hedges which can be pruned include holly, *Ilex aquifolium*; privet, *Ligustrum ovalifolium* (deciduous in hard frosts); cherry laurel, *Prunus laurocerasus* 'Caucasica', and *P. laurocerasus* 'Rotundifolia'. The cherry laurels are better trimmed rather than clipped hard.

For medium height deciduous hedges you can choose from privet, *Ligustrum ovalifolium*; the slightly spiny holly *Ilex aquifolium* 'J.C. van Tol' and *I. aquifolium* 'Laurifolia'; and firethorn *Pyracantha* 'Golden Glow'. The holly, *Ilex meservae* 'Blue Prince' with its soft, non-spiny leaves, comes through the winter very well, but is unsuitable for poor soils and an exposed situation.

For low-growing, deciduous hedges from the evergreen shrub honeysuckle *Lonicera nitida*;

Tip
Distance apart for planting conifer hedges: *Thuja occidentalis* 3 per metre (3'3") length, *Chamaecyparis lawsoniana* 2 per 1.5m (5') length, x *Cupressocyparis leylandii* 1 per metre (3'3") length, *Taxus baccata* 3 per 2m (6'7") length.

Tip
Compared with shrubs and trees conifers have a rather small and compact root system. They are therefore more affected by strong winds and storms. They blow over, or down, more easily than shrubs.

Ilex crenata 'Convexa' or box, *Buxus sempervirens*, *B. sempervirens* 'Suffruticosa', and *B. sempervirens* 'Hansworthiensis'. The last has rather larger leaves and is also suitable for slightly taller hedges. The sub-shrub, *Lavendula officinalis*, which is lime-loving, and its various varieties, some *Hebe* species such as *Hebe armstrongii*, and the lavender cotton, *Santolina*, can be used for small hedges. These sub-shrubs grow best in a sheltered position.

Deciduous hedges

The beech, *Fagus sylvaticus*, is suitable for tall hedges that need to be pruned hard and can form one of the most beautiful hedges. Unfortunately it is rather slow growing. It is familiar as a hedging shrub used in the gardens of country houses, particularly round the kitchen garden. The soil there was always well dug and manured. The beech grows well on light soil, but it is sensitive to changes in the groundwater table and does not do well in coastal sites. The hornbeam, *Carpinus betulus*, is less fussy about soil, is not sensitive to wet ground, and also makes a nice hedge. It grows well on a limed clay soil. The field maple, *Acer campestre*, can put up with virtually anything but does sometimes suffer from mildew. Its cultivar *A.*

Tip
Evergreen hedges, either tall or low-growing, can be made from the common ivy, *Hedera helix*. Fix strong wire netting to a frame and let the ivy climb over it. Two plants per metre (3'3") are sufficient.

It is true that privet has to be pruned more often, but it makes a good dense hedge and is not fussy about its situation.

campestre 'Elsrijk', with its smaller leaves, is resistant to this fungal disease. The privet, *Ligustrum vulgare*, 'Atrovirens', grows fast on any soil. The leaf is longer and narrower than that of *Ligustrum ovalifolium*, but it has a nice, pure green colour. The leaves are shed late in the autumn.

The hawthorn, *Crataegus monogyna*, is unfortunately sensitive to atmospheric pollution but is otherwise very tough. Cornelian cherry, (*Cornus mas*) hawthorn, and currant (*Ribes alpinum*) form outstanding hedges of middle height that can be pruned.

Finally, lower hedges can be formed with snowberry, *Symphoricarpus chenaultii*; the currant *Ribes alpinum*, and *Ligustrum vulgare* 'Lodense'.

Open evergreen hedges

If more space is available, open, evergreen hedges can form suitable, less dense barriers. The great advantage of this type of hedge is that it does not demand much maintenance. For the open, evergreen hedge there is a choice of shrubs including the barberries, *Berberis darwinii*, *B. gagnepainii*, *B. julianae*, and *B. stenophylla*; *Cotoneaster franchetii*; the spindle *Euonymus fortunei* var. *vegetus*; holly, *Ilex aquifolium*; the firethorn, *Pyracantha coccinea*, and *Osmanthus heterophyllus*.

Open deciduous hedges

There is quite a wide choice of shrubs in this category, including the crab apple, *Malus toringo*; barberry, *Berberis aggregata*; *Cotoneaster divaricatus*, *C. dielsianus*, and *C. simonsii*; *Eleagnus multiflora*; *Forsythia* x *intermedia*; *Hypericum hookerianum*; mock orange, *Philadelphus coronarius*; *Potentilla fruticosa*; *Rhamnus frangula*; elderberry, *Sambucus nigra*; and *Spiraea* x *arguta*, *S.* x *bumalda*, and *S. salicifolia*.

Species roses do not look out of place as a hedge. The dog rose, *Rosa canina*, can tolerate some shade; it has pink flowers followed by scarlet hips. The leaves of *Rosa rubiginosa*, with pink flowers and orange hips, give off a lovely apple scent. *Rosa glauca* (formerly *Rosa rubrifolia*) will steal the show with its red-veined, mauve-grey leaves, and splendid autumn colours. In addition there are small pink flowers and red hips to admire. The medium hedge can be planted with *Rosa rugosa* which is a healthy species that does well even on poor soils. The red flowers are followed by scarlet hips which can be used to make rose-hip syrup or jelly. *Rosa nitida*, with its dark red hips and lovely autumn colours makes a low hedge that can even tolerate some shade. *Rosa virginiana* 'Harvest Song', with pink flowers and orange hips, has breathtaking, mainly yellow, autumn colours.

> ### Tip
>
> A willow screen, or diamond weave screen, could make an attractive partition. It grows tall and yet is reasonably narrow. You plant the roughly 3.5m (11'4") long osiers at an angle of 45°, 20cm (8") apart. You plant a second row in front of this, the same distance apart but sloping at 45° in the opposite direction. The whole hedge is tied to and supported by posts and wire. You must cut it regularly at least four times a year. In two years you will have a closed screen.

Planting distance

You can take the planting distances for shrubs used as a hedge from those mentioned in the section "Shrubs: the framework of

Two weeks after planting the osiers are already sprouting.

The osiers a year later, at the same time of year.

the garden" (see p. 83). Because the shrubs are being planted as a loose hedge, they need to be set closer together. It is a different matter when you are dealing with shrubs that will form a closed screen, a hedge that will be clipped.

Shrub	Number per metre (39″) length
beech	
Fagus sylvatica	4 to 5
hornbeam	
Carpinus betulus	4
field maple	
Acer campestris	4
hawthorn	
Crataegus monogyna	3 to 4
privet	
Ligustrum	4
cornelian cherry	
Cornus mas	3
flowering currant	
Ribes alpinum	3
holly	
Ilex aquifolium	3 to 4
cherry laurel	
Prunus laurocerasus	2 to 3
firethorn	
Pyracantha coccinea	3
shrub honeysuckle	
Lonicera nitida	3 to 4
box	
Buxus sempervirens	5
lavender	
Lavandula angustifolia	4
hebe	
Hebe	4
lavender cotton	
Santolina chamaecyparissus	4

Tip

When you are planting trees, conifers, and hedges it is better not to add any fertilizer to the soil. The plants cannot make use of it in the first year while they are becoming established. You can give them plenty of fertilizer from the second year onwards, so keep a broad strip of soil clear of vegetation alongside the hedge to make this easier.

Page 108 above: *The weeds under the beech hedge must not be hoed (root damage) but do need to be removed.*

Page 108 below: *Weeds must be removed by hand to avoid damaging the surface-growing roots of the beech as far as possible.*

Above: *Now just wait until the next round.*

Shrubs for hedges are planted in the same way as in other situations except that you first dig a wide trench in which to position them. String stretched between two pegs in the ground provides a guide to planting in a straight line.

Grass, the green surface

Grass provides a permanent, green "floor-covering" for the garden. This surface is restful to look at and provides a base line for the garden. It is a neutral background against which the various elements of the garden stand out, while at the same time it provides a link between them. The big advantage of grass is that it can be walked on and there are very few substitutes that can tolerate that. In a garden where children are allowed to play a patch of grass is indispensable.

The biggest problem is that so many demands are made on the grass. From the point of view of the garden layout it is really only the neutral effect of the green surface that is important.

Grass makes twice the work

Some people think that if you want a garden with not too much work involved you should just have a large lawn. Nothing could be further from the truth. A lawn takes a lot of time, energy, nutrients, tools, and the determination to keep it looking nice. Much depends on what you understand by a nice lawn. A surface like a bowling green, made up of fine grass species, that will have to be mown twice a week? Then you had better not let the children play on it and not walk on it too often yourself. The choice of seed mixture will depend on the intended use, the type of soil, the moisture content of the ground, and whether the site is in full sun or shade. With these details you can then consult your local supplier of grass seed. For a close turf you will need 2–3kg seed per 100m² (¾ to ⅞oz per sq.yd).

Tip
Since the beginning of 1996 the slow-motion or minimum-mow lawn has been available in the Netherlands. This particular grass mixture grows so slowly that it does not require frequent mowing, while the lawn remains nice and green. The most important constituent of this lawn is crested hair-grass, *Koeleria macrantha*; it grows very slowly and scarcely needs any maintenance. The advertisements claim a 40% reduction in mowing.

The foundation of the lawn

✳ Before the lawn is laid out the soil should be thoroughly prepared. In a new garden you generally have to dig down to a depth of two spits, removing any rubble. Then the future lawn must be manured. If you are using organic manure you will need to allow one to one-and-a-half barrow loads per 10m² (12yd²). Trials suggest that grass roots very well in soil into which peat has been incorporated. Use 20 to 30 litres (4 to 6 gallons) of peat per 10m² (12yd²): the more alkaline the soil, the more peat is needed. Heavy, moisture-retaining soil can be made lighter by mixing the top soil with sharp sand. The recommended time for sowing grass seed is between mid-April and September. Earlier spring sowing is possible but less successful, partly because it is often dry at that time of year. Germination is delayed and then the birds help themselves to the seed and disturb the surface

Bare patches are best sown in August and September.

Tip

In the country, ground is often prepared for a lawn by digging and manuring it in winter or spring and then planting early potatoes in late March or early April. The ground is weeded during the summer, the potatoes are lifted in July and immediately afterwards the ground is prepared for sowing the grass seed.

---

by taking a dust bath. The result is obvious: bare patches. It is better therefore to sow in August and September. The soil is warm and often damp, which gives the grass a better start. Besides, this grass can be walked on straightaway the following spring, which is not the case with spring-sown grass.

Establishing a lawn step by step

✳ To make a lawn, work through the following steps one by one:
– After digging and fertilizing break up the clods.

– Then, if possible, leave it for at least a month, during which time you should dig up any weeds that appear. (If time is short roll the soil with a heavy roller).

– Rake the soil.

– Sow the seed. The sowing surface must be divided into small equal portions. For each piece of ground take two pots of seed in order to sow in both directions. The seed is mixed with sand to make it easier to distribute. Sow the edges first and then the central areas.

– Rake the surface lightly after sowing. Seed that is deeper than 1.5cm (1/2″) will not germinate!

– Light soils only must now be rolled with a heavy roller.

– You can mow the grass for the first time when it is 6cm (2 ½″) high with the mower blades set as high as possible. Mow when the turf is dry but the soil is still damp.

– For the first six months only walk on the lawn with care.

A ready-made lawn

Perhaps you would prefer to have an "instant" lawn, which you can achieve by laying turf instead of sowing seed. This method is quicker but considerably more expensive. The best time to lay turf is during April and May. If it cannot be laid immediately after it has been delivered you will need to unroll the turf to prevent it going yellow and overheating. You should stagger the joins so that the seams do not run right across the lawn. A mixture of compost and peat spread in the seams will ensure a lawn without gaps. Water the turf regularly until the grass is growing vigorously. Do not be tempted by so-called cheap offers at the door; don't buy any old bit of pasture and do check the quality!

It is better to use a coarse grass mixture, for example sports turf with perennial ryegrass, for grass paths that get a lot of wear.

Tip

Make sure that the turf you order is of the same soil type as that in your garden. Trying to grow turf from a clay soil on sandy soil will not work!

A flower-rich alternative

We have seen already that a nice lawn can make the garden look more spacious and neater, but also that a good, weed-free lawn is demands a lot of time and effort.

If you want to devote less time to the lawn, find the use of weedkillers unacceptable, do not want to apply fertilizer too often, and yet still want to have a lawn that can stand hard wear, then youwill have to adjust your expectations of the lawn. Dandelions, clover, daisies, speedwell, and other "weeds" are going to grow in it. At the same time these weeds have the advantage that they survive better than the lawn grasses during dry spells. Nor do they pose any threat to the grass, although you will still have

Why should daisies be removed from the lawn? They look cheerful and in dry spells they survive better than the lawn grasses.

to mow it regularly. If you really do not need to walk on the grass you can make a wild-flower meadow. Paths can be mown across it and round it, for instance, as a boundary along the flower border.

Making a wild-flower meadow

Suppose you have moved into your new house, and you have made plans for the garden. The flower and shrub borders and the vegetable patch can be dug and manured but whatever you do don't put even a pinch of fertilizer on the future wild-flower meadow. The most beautiful meadows develop on the poorest soil, so you may decide that the soil is going to be too rich in plant nutrients to grow a wild-flower meadow and that you will have to think again. However, although the top layer of soil may contain more plant food, the layers underneath it are always less rich. You can therefore reverse the soil profile by burying the top spit of soil beneath the second spit you dig out. When the area you have prepared for the meadow is big enough, you can then bury the topsoil at various depths beneath the lower layer. That will soon encourage a more species-rich meadow. You can also build up small mounds, in which case the richer soil should be buried under the mounds.

Variations in both soil and relief will determine the richness in species and abundance of flowers. A combination of sowing and planting will give you a meadow more quickly, but it is not absolutely necessary. Wild plants from the surrounding land will soon begin to establish themselves. If these are absent or you do not want to have to wait, you can sow your wild-flower meadow. Choose a seed mixture for grassland or grass verges that is appropriate for your soil; it will contain the seeds of perennial grasses, herbs, and perennial plants. At the same time you could use an annual meadow or arable weed mixture which will give the garden more colour in the first year.

This flower border looks like a flower meadow. It contains a wide range of perennials including phlox, golden rod, yarrow, spurge, and Geranium.

Bulbs and tubers can also find a home in a permanent meadow.

You can make paths in your meadow; regular mowing will prevent plants from flowering, so you will have genuine grass paths.

Other ideas for lawns

Another possibility is to cover an area with evergreen ground-cover plants, and you could consider this if you have to renew a lawn.

For small areas, two very low-growing perennial species make runners very easily and can be walked on. The first is the evergreen pearlwort, *Sagina subulata*, which looks like a small mossy cushion. In summer the "moss" produces tiny white flowers which do not mind being crushed underfoot. This 5cm (2″) high plant never needs mowing. Another good substitute for grass is *Leptinella squalida* which has fern-like leaves and greenish-yellow flowers in June. This "grass" does not need to be mown, but you will need to spend some time removing the weeds that come up among the plants.

Two plants that are often mentioned for lawns are not, in fact, sturdy enough to stand much in the way of trampling. The camomile, *Chamaemelum nobile* 'Treneague' and the Corsican mint, *Mentha requienii* are not satisfactory substitutes for grass.

The juniper *Juniperus horizontalis* var. *saxatilis* 'Wiltonii' and *Hedera helix* 'Walthamensis' are sometimes used in place of a lawn. These plants form very dense mats. If a conifer carpet is not really suitable for your garden, then you can still use the ivy, *Hedera helix* 'Baltica'. This cultivar has noticeably smaller leaves than *Hedera*

Hedera helix 'Walthamensis' provides close ground cover for shade.

hibernica and makes outstanding ground cover. It will provide a lovely green foreground for your colourful border and is, moreover, evergreen.

Ornamental grasses and bamboos

Because lawns are mown regularly you miss out on seeing how attractive some grass species can be in their full glory. They have lovely forms and their flowers are also worth waiting for. The flower is referred to as a spike, and it can have many different forms.

Most ornamental grasses occur naturally in the wild and have only been introduced into gardens with the increasing popularity of the natural look. They cannot be planted at random, because they need to be seen against a suitable background. As with all other green elements in the garden, you need to take account of the growing conditions required by the various grass species, which come from all over the world. In contrast to the species that are used for lawn grasses, the ornamental grasses each have their own individual character. It is better to plant too few than too many of them. In many types of garden there is a place for ornamental grasses, for example in the rock garden, between the lawn and the terrace, and sometimes in the shade garden. Ornamental grasses also perform extremely well beside water, creating attractive vertical and oblique reflections.

> ### Tip
> Pampas grass is a naturalized clump-forming grass. You can bleach the flower heads by hanging them out of doors in the early morning mist.

In this part of a grass garden we can see centre back: Sesleria nitida, *right: the herbaceous perennial* Liriope muscari, *and centre left: the ornamental grass* Hakonechloa macra *'Aureola.'*

For lily enthusiasts there is a very natural combination that originates on the steppes of Asia: the ground is covered with ornamental grasses interspersed with groups of lilies. The grasses keep the roots of the lilies cool.

Most ornamental grasses that are planted in the garden are perennial, that is, they sprout from the same root stock every spring; but there are also annual grasses, which have to be sown each year. The latter are often used in dried-flower arrangements.

Interesting grasses for the ornamental garden

Name	Height in cm (in)	Flowering season	Situation	Comments
mosquito grass				
Bouteloua gracilis	30 (12)	7–9	sun and dry	dried bouquet
quaking grass				
Briza media	40 (16)	5–7	sun, some moisture	evergreen, dried bouquet
small reed				
Calamagrostis x *acutiflora* 'Karl Foerster'	150 (59)	7–8	sun	
tufted sedge				
Carex elata 'Aurea'	75 (29)	4–5	sun, half shade, near water	
mace sedge				
Carex grayi	60 (24)	6–10	damp	evergreen, dried bouquet
Carex murrowii 'Variegata'	30 (12)	3–5	sun, half shade	evergreen
Carex muskingumensis	75 (29)	7–8	half shade, damp	leaf like papyrus
Chasmanthium latifolium	80 (31)	9–10	sun, light shade	dried bouquet
pampas grass				
Cortaderia selloana	200–300 (67–118)	8–10	sun	frost-sensitive

Name	Height in cm (in)	Flowering season	Situation	Comments
tufted hair grass				
Deschampsia cespitosa 'Goldschleier'	50 (19)	6–7	sun, dry to damp	evergreen, dried bouquet
couch grass				
Elymus magellanicus (syn. *Agropyron pubiflorum*)	60 (24)	6–7	sun	not invasive, blue green leaf
blue fescue				
Festuca glauca	25 (10)	5–6	sun, dry	grey-blue clumps, evergreen
Festuca gautieri	10 (4)	6	half shade, dry	needs space
Hakonechloa macra 'Aureola'	40 (16)	7–8	sun, dry	yellow-bronze striped leaf
blue oat grass				
Helictotrichon sempervirens	50 (19)	5–7	sun, dry	blue-green, evergreen
Imperata cylindrica 'Rubra'	35 (14)	-	sun, half shade slightly damp	leaf blood red
crested hair grass				
Koeleria glauca	20 (8)	5–8	sun, dry, lime	blue-grey, good evergreen
wood-rush				
Luzula nivea	30 (12)	6–8	damp	dried bouquet
melic				
Melica ciliata	40 (16)	5–7	sun, calcareous soil	dried bouquet
wood millet				
Milium effusum 'Aureum'	60 (24)	4–6	half shade, shade	for dark corners
Miscanthus sinensis 'Graziella'	180 (71)	9–11	sun	dried bouquet
purple moor grass				
Molinia caerulea				
ssp. *caerulea* 'Moorflamme'	30 (12)	8–10	sun, half shade	dried bouquet
Panicum virgatum 'Rehbraun'	100 (39)	8–10	sun	leaf turns red-brown dried bouquet
fountain grass				
Pennisetum orientale	80 (31)	8–10	sun, damp	ornamental species dried bouquet
blue moor grass				
Sesleria nitida	30 (12)	7–8	sun, calcareous	grey-blue leaf
Sorghastrum avenaceum	130 (51)	8–10	sun, calcareous	
pheasant grass				
Stipa brachytrica	100 (39)	8–10	sun	dried bouquet
Stipa capillata	100 (39)	7–8	sun, calcareous	grey green dried bouquet
Stipa pulcherrima	140 (55)	7–8	sun, calcareous	silvery flower spike, dried bouquet

Page 117, above left: Imperata cylindrica 'Rubra' has blood-red leaves which emerge in spring and last until autumn.

Page 117, above right: There are many cultivars of Miscanthus sinensis. *This is* Miscanthus sinensis *'Morning Light'.*

Page 117, below left: The evergreen Carex murrowii *'Variegata'.*

Page 117, below right: Hakonechloa macra *'Aureola' forms a mop head. It needs fertile, well-drained soil.*

Bamboos for an exotic setting

The evergreen bamboo is an easy plant to grow. It likes any type of soil, providing the roots are not under water. Bamboos are divided into those that spread, sometimes even becoming invasive and penetrating pond linings, and those that form clumps. Loosen the soil where you are going to plant bamboos, and give them plenty of water especially in the first season. Species that may be invasive can be contained within the beds by sinking plastic containers about 60cm (24in) high, open top and bottom, into the soil. Bamboos do not root deeper than 45 to 55cm (18 to 22in).

Division of bamboo species into the main groups

Name changes in the bamboos seem to occur be an annual leading to great confusion. The names used here follow current usage.

Ornamental or clump-forming bamboos:

Name	Height	Use]
Sinarundinaria (Fargesia) nitida	3m (9'10")	hedges
Sinarundinaria (Fargesia) nitida 'Nymphenburg' (syn. jaunsarensis or anceps)	2.5m (8'2")	specimen and hedges

Name	Height	Use
Fargesia murielae dana 'Simba'	1.5m (5')	slower growing than well-known Fargesia murielae

Dwarf bamboos:

Name	Height	Use
Pleioblastus humilis	1.2m (4')	ground cover
Pleioblastus auricomus (syn. P. viridistriatus)	1m (3'3")	ground cover
Pleioblastus chino	2m (6'7")	ground cover
Pleioblastus pygmeus var. distichus	80cm (31in)	ground cover
Pleioblastus linearis	2.5m (8'2")	ground cover
Sasaella masamuneana f. albostriata	50cm (20in)	ground cover

The dwarf bamboos are hardy but are usually cut down to ground level by frost. *Sasaella masamuneana* f. *albostriata* has survived through severe winters successfully and remains green.

Broad-leaved bamboos:

Name	Height	Use
Sasa palmata	3m (9'10")	by natural water
Sasa tessellata	2m (6'7")	by natural water
Sasa veitchii	1.5m (5')	ground cover specimen, hedges
Sasa tsuboiana	2m (6'7")	all purposes
Pseudosasa japonica	4m (13')	hedges and specimen

Taller bamboos:

Name	Height	Use
Phyllostachys aurea	5m (16'3")	specimen/group
Phyllostachys aureosulcata	4m (13')	specimen/group
Phyllostachys bissettii	4m (13')	hedges, specimen and in group
Phyllostachys decora	4m (13')	specimen/group
Phyllostachys glauca	4m (13')	hedges, specimen and in group
Phyllostachys humilis	3.5m (11'4")	hedges, specimen and in group
Phyllostachys nigra var. henonis	5m (16'4")	specimen/group
Phyllostachys viridiglaucescens	4.5m (14'7")	specimen/group

Planting distance for bamboos:		
Height of bamboo	Distance apart in garden	Distance apart for hedge
up to 100cm (39″)	50cm (20″)	30cm (12″)
100–250cm (3–9′)	80cm (31″)	50cm (20″)
250–500cm (9–16′)	150cm (59″)	100cm (39″)

Little is known about the flowering of bamboos. Some species flower after 40 years, others after 120 years, and there are two types of flowering, occasional and continuous.

With occasional flowering you can trim off the branch or stem that has flowered. With continuous flowering that occurs suddenly the plant sometimes has had no leaves for years and the stems and branches are bent over under the weight of the seeds. In the end occasional flowering becomes continuous flowering. It is not at all certain whether the plants do die off completely after flowering. If it is well cared for, a flowering plant will probably not die but it will not be a pretty sight for ten to twelve years afterwards and will therefore not be of much value.

The *Fargesia* 'Simba' is a representative of the new generation of bamboos. It is a seedling of *Fargesia murielae dana* and it will probably be some time before it begins to flower. It reaches 1.5m (5′) in height and is seen to best advantage in shade and half shade.

So far *Phyllostachys flexuosa*, *Fargesia murielae*, *Phyllostachys propinqua*, and *Phyllostachys aurea* 'Albovariegata' have been seen to flower. So there are plenty of bamboos from which to make a choice for your garden.

Fargesia murielae dana is widely planted. This example has flowered since 1995. Fargesia 'Simba' is a seedling from this bamboo.

Adding colour

   Nowadays colour plays an important role in the garden, and generally speaking more flowering plants are used than in the past. Now that most people do not have room to indulge in avenues, lakes, grottos, and open-air sculpture galleries, they seem to throw themselves wholeheartedly into using colour. It is worth remembering, however, that a plant is going to be in flower for three months at the most, and that for the rest of the year you will be looking at the foliage and the shape of the plant itself.

The rose: queen of flowers

   The history of the rose goes back millions of years, with fossil evidence dating from 30 million years ago. The rose probably originated in Asia. It is known that Emperor Nero had discovered the scent and colour of roses because during festivals he had the streets, temples, and palaces strewn with thousands of rose petals. He did, unfortunately, have one difficulty: the old roses had a very short flowering season, but the Romans solved the problem by importing rosebuds from Egypt.

In the Middle Ages the rose was associated with the Virgin Mary and you can still come across the rose carved in wood and stone, and in the stained glass of the rose windows in churches and abbeys. There was not a wide choice of species available. Only *Rosa alba*, *R. gallica*, *R. canina*, and *R. damascena* were planted. It was not only the scent was important since the rosehips and rose petals were used for culinary and medi-

Rosehips are really a bonus after the flowers. These belong to Rosa nitida *which is suitable for making low hedges.*

cinal purposes. There were two new discoveries in the Middle Ages: the moss rose, *Rosa moschata*, with its musk scent and sprays of flowers, and the Provence rose, *Rosa centifolia*. The development of trade with China in the second half of the sixteenth century led to the importing of Chinese roses. These had a longer flowering season and a wider range of colours but were not so hardy.

The hybrid tea roses

The cross between an eastern and a western rose took place by accident on the French island of Bourbon. There was a hedge of Chinese roses, *Rosa chinensis*, growing in a garden next to a hedge of Damascene roses, *Rosa damascena*. The result was a hybrid, the first long-flowering, hardy rose: the Bourbon rose.

A second famous cross, between a Chinese rose and a musk rose that was flowering in South Carolina, was introduced to the trade by the Parisian rose grower Louis Noisette. The noisette rose was a free-flowering, very fragrant rose but unfortunately it was not hardy. Back crosses were made of Chinese with Bourbon roses and later with noisette roses. These produced roses with the fragrance of China tea, but again, these crosses were not hardy. Further crossing took place: between Bourbon and French roses. The results were hardy roses but with a shorter flowering season. New crosses produced the remontant roses, which flowered twice a year and bore large, scented flowers. Finally the breeders achieved the hybrid tea roses.

At the end of the nineteenth century the grower Pernet-Ducher produced a sensation: by using the yellow rose, *Rosa lutea*, from central Asia he was able to introduce the colour yellow into the hybrid teas. That was the origin of modern yellow roses. The hybrid tea roses are characterized by pointed buds, large flowers, and a long flowering season.

The polyantha roses probably originated from crosses with the Chinese dwarf rose. These polyanthas have large heads of small flowers. Cros-

'Mme Caroline Testout', bred in France by Ducher, was introduced in 1890.

sing polyantha roses with hybrid teas produced the floribunda roses, which have heads with larger flowers.

The old roses hold their own

Most old roses date from before the end of the last century. They have been out of fashion for many years but now they are back in favour again thanks to their beautifully shaped flowers and heady perfume. The buds of the old roses are rounder than those of the modern roses and they open out into cup-shaped flowers with some smaller petals in the middle. Sometimes these are curved towards the centre so that the flower looks like a ball. With some other cultivars the petals are so angled that the flower looks as if it is divided into four, or quartered. During the last forty years very old roses have been crossed with modern roses, enabling the beneficial characteristics of each to be combined. These new "old" roses have an old-fashioned flower shape, bloom throughout the summer, and are often more resistant to disease than the old roses themselves.

Hybrid teas, polyantha roses, and standard roses are all grafted, that is they are grown on the rootstock of a wild rose. Nowadays there are also roses (including many Meiland roses) that are grown on their own rootstock so that the stock does not produce any wild suckers.

Looking after roses

Although the newest varieties of roses have been bred with many good qualities, they do nevertheless demand a lot of attention. They like a fertile, well-drained, damp soil that is certainly not acid but does not contain too much lime. Light to medium clay soil suits them well.

This has a fairly loose structure and has a pH of 6–7 which is ideal. The structure of heavy clay, on the contrary, is too solid and the soil is poorly drained. You can improve such soil by digging sharp sand into the topsoil before you plant the roses.

If you want to plant roses on clay, dig and manure the soil before the winter, because the frost will help to break up the clods of earth to produce a good tilth. On heavy, wet soil roses should be planted in the spring.

Roses have other problems on sandy soil. It is true that sandy soil is easier to work but the water soon drains through, taking the plant nutrients with it and leaving the roses too dry. To make sandy soil suitable for growing roses you should work 200 to 300 litres (40 to 60 gallons) of compost per 10m² (12yd²) into the topsoil. On acid sandy soil raise the pH by spreading lime or ground limestone on the surface. Never

The rose garden at Penshurst Place in Kent, England.

apply lime and manure at the same time. Calcareous soil, which is mainly found in areas with chalk and limestone, can be made more acid by adding peat. Peat soil itself is often too acid for roses and although you can add lime to it you will probably still have to cope with an excess of water in the ground.

On all soils roses need additional food. It is preferable to apply this in organic form. Well-rotted stable manure does not provide enough nutrients on its own but should be augmented by adding concentrated organic fertilizer.

It is generally better to use organic fertilizer and compost because these improve and maintain the structure of the soil more than inorganics.

Planting roses

Like deciduous shrubs roses are planted after the leaves have dropped and before they begin to sprout again. November offers the advantage that the soil is not too heavy or wet.

Dig a generous hole 40 x 40 x 40cm (16 x 16 x 16″) in which the roots can be spread out in all directions. Place the rose in the hole so that the graft will be about 3cm (1″) under the soil surface. Fill in the hole gradually with the soil you have dug out and loosened. Take care that any organic manure does not come into direct contact with the roots. At this stage put in a stake for standard roses, which will avoid damage to the roots. Fill up the hole completely and tread the soil down well. After spring planting the

Rosa 'Mozart' flowers for a long time, reaches a good 1m (3'3") in height, and is extremely prickly!

roses must be watered. As the soil settles round the rose stem more soil should be added.

Combined in borders

V Nowadays roses are often combined with perennials in borders. In that way the rather stiff form that characterizes most rose bushes is less obvious. It is better to use perennials that do not take a lot of nourishment out of the soil and that are surface rooting. Low species of milfoil, *Achillea*; rock rose, *Helianthemum hybridum*; stonecrop, *Sedum*; various species of thyme, *Thymus*; and veronica species such as *Veronica incana* and *V. rupestris* are all suitable. There are other possible combinations where the bare underside of the roses is camouflaged with, for instance, *Gypsophila*; lavender, *Lavandula*; lavender cotton, *Santolina*; peony, *Paeonia*;

Tip

Look for a sunny position where the wind can blow freely through the leaves. This may seem rather exaggerated but it isn't. A rose that is fixed flat against a wall will be the first to suffer from aphids. Always train climbing roses up a trellis that is fixed to the wall or fence with a gap behind it. The air will be able to circulate round the branches and among the foliage.

and *Delphinium*. With these combinations the roses will begin to suffer in a year or two from the spreading roots of the perennials which are competing for food.

The perennials then have to be dug up and split and the ground must be well manured before they are replanted among the roses. Other combinations are possible depending on your personal taste and feeling for colour. You must, however, always watch for competition between roses and the plants round about them.

Plant the rose you have chosen towards the back of the border to make it easier to camouflage the unattractive lower part of the bush. You must, of course, choose taller roses in this context.

Why should a rose need to be in flower the whole summer?

Tip

Allow plenty of room for the rose that is planted among perennials. In a very close planting moisture hangs on the leaves during wet weather, making the roses in particular more susceptible to disease.

After all there is plenty of choice among colourful annuals and perennials which can take over from the roses when they have finished flowering.

I would make a special plea for the roses that have particularly attractive foliage. After all, you have to look at them for eight months of the year. *Rosa glauca* (syn. *Rosa rubrifolia*) has beautiful purplish-grey leaves which go very well

Symphony in pink: Rosa 'Albertine' with foxgloves. The hydrangea in the foreground echoes the colour of the foxgloves.

Plant roses towards the back of the border. The plants in the foreground hide the ugly base of the rose bushes.

with perennials such as bear's breech *Acanthus*; *Astrantia major*; cornflower, *Centaurea montana 'Caerulea'*; and water avens, *Geum rivale*.

The very healthy *Rosa moyesii* var. *fargesii* 'Geranium' takes up a lot of space and only bears blood-red flowers for about three weeks but from August until late November it has lovely orange hips.

The romantic look

The fashion for one rose per stem has now passed. Formal rose beds, too, are "out" and most garden owners naturally want flowers throughout the summer. The English rose grower David Austin has tried to unite the fragrance, colour, and shape of old roses with the characteristics of modern roses such as a long flowering season and disease resistance. The rose 'Heritage' is one example. It has magnificent scented pale-pink double flowers. The shape is a little stiff and the bush does grow taller than the height given in many catalogues, but this is not a frequently voiced complaint.

Before you buy your roses, look round a nursery or rose garden to see how the different roses grow in reality. The illustrations in catalogues always look wonderful but they are taken just when the flower is at its best. Do the petals really fall off when the flower is over, or do they hang there on the bush like bits of brown wadding for weeks afterwards? Does the pretty pink colour persist during flowering or does it fade to white or become dark pink? Do the flowering branches become top heavy so that they overhang and you can no longer look into the heart of the rose?

Shrub roses are also being planted widely. These have a rather open, more natural growth form and are extremely suitable for planting with perennials. In this group the flowers are mainly single and in pastel shades, such as the very well known *Rosa* 'Ballerina'. The few yellow varieties deserve to be mentioned here. *Rosa* 'Golden Wings' is a brilliant lemon yellow: an upright, 1.5m (5′) high rose, with single, rather larger

flowers and a delicious scent. A sturdy specimen like this is better planted towards the back of the border. *Rosa* 'Windrush' blooms even more profusely. It is rather paler than 'Golden Wings' but has fuller flowers and can serve as a support for summer-flowering clematis. *Rosa* 'Nevada' is a single, large-flowered, almost white shrub rose. Strictly speaking it only has one flowering period but it does produce smaller crops of flowers intermittently until September. It has an arching growth form and can reach a height of 2m (6′7″). The branches of *Rosa* 'Sally Holmes' fan out and bear heavy bunches of large creamy-white single flowers which give the impression of being double. *Rosa* 'Pearl Drift' is the shrub version of the climber *Rosa* 'New Dawn'.

Cluster-flowered bush roses also do extremely well in borders. *Rosa* 'Iceberg' and lavender or

'Bonica' is a long-flowering shrub rose. It grows to a height of 90cm (36″).

'Little White Pet' is a dwarf shrub rose that covers the ground well.

box has become a common combination used. *Rosa* 'Bonica' is an other double cluster- flowered rose; it is a very tough, healthy 90cm (35") high rose, branching low down. Other possibilities are the use of roses for ground cover in large beds or at the front of a border. The miniature remontant, or perpetual-flowering, *Rosa* 'Snowball' has white, double flowers. It looks good in association with *Heuchera micrantha*

'Palace Purple', which has purplish-brown foliage. The leaves of 'Snowball' are a shiny dark green and last until late in the year. This rose can also be used for a low, open hedge. *Rosa* 'The Fairy', with its large, bright pink clusters of double flowers, gives a fairy-tale look to the garden. It is also highly recommended for growing in containers.

Reach for the sky

There is an enormous choice of climbing rambler roses. They do not climb themselves but have to be tied up. The smallest of the rambler roses are capable of reaching a height of about 2.5m (8'2") which means that most garden fences and walls are really too low for them. In that case you will have to train them horizontally, which will encourage flowering. Roses in fact like being trained in this way against a wall

> ### Tip
> Ground-cover roses generally do not grow taller than 60cm (24") and the name suggests that they will cover the ground so that weeds do not have a chance. In practice, however, weeds do manage to grow. If the shrubs are very thorny, such as 'Snowball', weeding among them can be a painful business. An extra thick mulch will keep the weeds at bay here.

do not unless a number of conditions are fulfilled. Make sure that there is plenty of fertile, well-aerated soil round the roots. If that is a problem because rubble and sand is going to work its way up from the foundations, plant the rose about 50cm (20″) away from the wall. This will prevent the roots from becoming too hot, which roses dislike. Naturally there must be a gap of about 5cm (2″) between the wall and the rose to allow the air to circulate. Keep enough room to be able to water the rose because all that foliage loses a lot of water through transpiration.

It is not a bad idea to plant a rose against a north-facing wall; several roses do very well in this position, such as the very familiar *Rosa* 'New Dawn', which otherwise does not have as long a flowering season as is sometimes claimed. In the height of summer it certainly needs about four weeks breathing space before it can resume flowering. The well-known repeat-flowering yellow climber *Rosa* 'Golden Showers', which also has double flowers, is suitable for a north-facing wall. It has very healthy foliage and fewer thorns.

There is more space over arches, arcades and bowers; you can let the taller climbing roses grow over these, for example, *Rosa* 'Mermaid'. After a slow start it eventually grows much taller than 'Golden Showers'. 'Mermaid' has lemon-yellow flowers with golden-brown stamens and a delicious scent. Give it a sheltered position, in sun or half shade, because it is sensitive to severe frosts. In many gardens these days rose arches are used as gateways. Often the roses are combined with clematis, either because the two will flower in succession or because they create a beautiful effect together.

One of the best climbing roses is 'Bantry Bay'.

Try this winning combination of 'Pink Ocean' and the large-flowered clematis 'Rouge Cardinal'.

Tip

Only put in arches that are tall and wide enough for roses. Remember that the roses can spread and will not follow the exact line of the arch.

Working among such thorny stems is not a pleasant job. It is a good idea to plant only the summer-flowering clematis varieties which are less time consuming. They flower entirely on young shoots and have to be cut back each spring to 50cm (20″) above the ground.

Ramblers for trees

These are roses that grow particularly wild and strongly and flower abundantly, but only for a short time. It is not unusual for them to reach a height of 5, 6, or 7m (16, 20, 23′). It is better to reserve these very natural looking roses for that ordinary little shed, or that unsightly outbuilding. Many people have given up growing *Rosa* 'Mme Alfred Carrière' which can be found in catalogues under both the remontant climbing roses and the rambler roses. It does get out of hand and a pergola of normal proportions can soon disappear under its exuberant growth.

Ramblers seem to feel at home growing against trees. It is a good idea to attach the rose to the trunk. There is a dilemma here: is it better to train the rose round the trunk in a spiral or should it be attached straight up the trunk until it reaches the first branches of the tree? Make no mistake, roses can quickly become rampant in a tree. This is not really a problem, except that you do need to take out the dead wood with thorns. Proper pruning or occasionally taking out an old branch doesn't work because the rose has not becomes completely tangled up with the tree. But a rambler looks splendid, for instance in an old fruit tree that no longer crops well but still has an attractive gnarled shape and nice bark.

Rosa longicuspis is a species climbing rose. It does well in trees, but only flowers once.

A pear tree for example has beautiful white blossom and then a good month or so later it is flowering again, or so your visitors think! It is, however, the scented *Rosa* 'Seagull' whose bunches of white flowers have yellow stamens.

Other rambler roses include *Rosa* 'Bobby James', *Rosa* 'Wedding Day', and the species rose *Rosa longicuspis*. There are many more that look very similar: they flower abundantly during the season, and have lovely cream or white-and-yellow centres. They all grow to about the same size.

The roses just mentioned combine the best characteristics of both old and new roses. On page 129 you will find lists of the best roses of each type.

The year given is that in which they were introduced.

Gallica roses

Rosa gallica is the oldest of the cultivated roses. In contrast to other old roses the Gallica roses have strong colours, varying from deep pink to red, mauve, and violet; the flowers, which are double or fully double, are followed by round hips. The small, open shrubs have pliable, arching branches which are covered in small spines. Most Gallica roses are scented.

Rose	Colour	Height	Comments
'Belle de Crécy' 1848	pinky red to mauve	1.5m (5')	
'Cardinal de Richelieu' 1840	light to dark mauve	2m (6'7")	
'Officinalis'	light red	1.2m (4')	known in 13th century
'Tuscany Superb' 1848	velvety dark red	1.5m (5')	
'Versicolor'	light red white striped	1.2m (4')	

Damask roses

Rosa x *damascena* is itself a very old cross. It is a sturdy shrub with overhanging branches and many large thorns. The flowers are generally bright pink and very fragrant.

Rose	Colour	Height	Comments
'La ville de Bruxelles' 1849	old rose	1.5m (5')	long flowering season

Rosa gallica *'Versicolor' is a very unusual, striped rose.*

'Rose	Colour	Height	Comments
Madame Hardy' 1832	white	1.5m (5')	disease resistant
'Marie-Louise' 1813	intense pink	1.2m (4')	branches droop to the ground, need support

Alba roses

Rosa x *alba* has a robust, bushy, upright growth form and typically matt, grey-blue foliage. It has white or pink flowers. Many Alba roses are satisfied with a north-facing situation and generally can grow well on poor soil. Most of them are fragrant.

Rose	Colour	Height	Comments
'Alba Maxima'	creamy-white	2m (6'7")	the Jacobite rose, also suitable for a hedge
'Félicité Parmentier' 1834	fresh pink to white	1.2m (4')	scented, also for a hedge
'Great Maiden's Blush'	pale pink	1.5m (5')	grey-green foliage
'Königin von Dänemarck' 1826	deep pink	1.5m (5')	quartered flowers, grey-green foliage
'Madame Plantier' 1835	white	3m (9'10")	use as climbing rose

Centifolia roses

Rosa centifolia has an open growth form and very thorny branches, which bend under the weight of the flowers. The shrubs look somewhat untidy, but they are redeemed by the flowers, which were beloved of Flemish and Dutch flower painters. These roses are best planted among other shrubs.

Rose	Colour	Height	Comments
'Blanchefleur' 1835	white	1.5m (5')	full double and quartered flowers
'Centifolia' before 1600	pink	2m (6'7")	the hundred-petalled rose or 'Provence Rose' or 'Cabbage Rose'
'Chapeau de Napoleon' 1826	deep pink	1.3m (4'2")	bloom looks like syn. 'Cristata' Napoleon's tricorn
'De Meaux'	pink	1m (3'3")	pompom flowers
'Fantin Latour'	pink	1.5m (5')	

Moss roses

The *Rosa moschata* roses have a lax, upright growth; the branches have hairy stems and the foliage has a bronze tinge. The growth of glands on the sepals resemble moss and give off a resinous scent. The flowers vary in colour from pink to mauve.

Rose	Colour	Height	Comments
'Comtesse de Murinais' 1843	soft pink to white	1.75m (5'9")	quartered blooms with green moss on sepals
'Mousseline' 1855	warm pink	1m (3'3")	flowers in June and October; also in pots
'Nuits de Young' 1845	mauve-red		mossy buds, scented
'William Lobb' 1855	violet-red	2.5m (8'2")	can be used as a climber

'Souvenir de St. Anne's' is a very fragrant, modern Bourbon rose.

Bourbon roses

The Bourbon rose takes its name from the island of Bourbon in the Indian Ocean, now known as Réunion. Apart from the flowers, the bushes look more like hybrid teas. These types also flower more than once. Many of the old roses are fragrant.

Rose	Colour	Height	Comments
'Boule de Neige' 1867	white	1.2m (4')	ball flower
'La Reine Victoria' 1872	lilac pink	1.5m (5')	cup-shaped flower
'Honorine de Brabant'	dark pink with soft pink	1.8m (6')	stripe and spotted
'Louise Odier' 1851	deep pink	1.5m (5')	cup-shaped flower
'Madame Isaac Pereire' 1881	pink-lilac	2.5m (8'2")	cup-shaped, quartered flowers
'Variegata di Bologna' 1909	white/scarlet	1.5m (5')	striped flower; as climber to 3m (10')

Hybrid perpetual roses

Hybrid perpetual roses are direct forerunners of the hybrid tea roses. Since at that time repeat flowering was the most important aspect of these roses, no thought was given to the shape of the bush. The best ones are lifted overleaf.

Rose	Colour	Height	Comments
'Baronne A. de Rothschild 1868	silver pink	1.5m (5')	broad, scented bowl-shaped flowers
'Frau Karl Druschki' 1901	white	1.8m (6')	flower has shape of hybrid tea, very large, fully double, healthy
'Mrs John Laing' 1887	warm pink	1.2m (4')	cup-shaped flowers, very scented
'Reine de Violettes' 1860	violet to mauve	1.5m (5')	fully double quartered flower, most beautiful in autumn, almost thornless

English roses

The English rose grower David Austin has combined the natural growth form, flower shape, and fragrance of the old roses with the repeat-flowering characteristics and the wider choice of colour of modern roses. The English roses are more shrubby in form. Below is a small selection from those available:

Rose	Colour	Height	Comments
'Abraham Darby' 1985	apricot	2.5m (8'2")	cup-shaped
'Fair Bianca' 1982	white	90cm (35")	cup-shaped, myrrh-scented
'Graham Thomas' 1983	yellow	1m (3'3")	old-fashioned flower shape
'Heritage' 1984	light pink	1.5m (5')	flowers in bunches
'Pretty Jessica' 1983	pink	60cm (24")	scented, for small garden
'The Pilgrim' 1991	soft yellow	1m (3'3")	fully double rosette-shaped flower, very strong
'Windrush' 1984	light yellow	1.2m (4')	very strong, single flowers, profuse, scented

Shrub roses

Some shrub roses including species roses, such as *Rosa glauca*, have been mentioned in the section on hedges. The name is descriptive: shrub roses have a natural growth form. They look more like shrubs as far as shape is concerned and that is how they are usually classified. In the mid 1980s the public began to turn away from the large-flowered roses which were becoming ever bigger and more colourful. People wanted to go back to pastel colours and more natural-looking roses. Of course these also have to be sturdy and disease-resistant. Interplant, part of the Darthuizer Nurseries in the Netherlands, has developed, among others, the following shrub roses which are also known as Dart's hybrids.

Rose	Colour	Height	Comments
'Eyeopener'	deep red	70cm (28")	ground cover
'Fleurette'	salmon pink	1.2m (4')	very healthy foliage
'Lavender Dream'	lavender pink	70cm (28")	flowers until late in the autumn
'Rosy Cushion'	bright pink	1m (3'3")	broad shrub
'Smarty'	pale pink to white	1.4m (4'7")	arching branches, striking stamens
'White Fleurette'	white	1m (3'3")	natural shape, flowers until the first frosts
'Rush'	white with pink edge	1m (3'3")	free-flowering
'Sally Holmes'	creamy-white	1m (3'3")	many clusters
'Smarty'	white	1m (3'3")	broad shrub

The group known as "shrub roses" also includes roses which not only have lovely flowers, but also an attractive shape, decorative foliage, and/or can be useful for planting among other shrubs. Others are eminently suitable for planting among perennials in the border. Their origins differ.

Rose	Colour	Height	Comments
'Ballerina	bright pink with white centre	1m (3'3")	no scent, also standard, continuous flowering
'Fruhlingsgold'	soft yellow	2m (6'7")	delicious scent, flowers once, sometimes limited second flowering
'Golf'	white	1.2m (4')	yellow stamens, flowers June to mid-October
'Kathleen'	white-pink	1.7m (5'7")	arching, long flowering, pale orange hips
'Mozart'	pink with white centre	1m (3'3")	flowers until first frost, small hips
'Nevada'	creamy-white	2m (6'7")	large single flowers, and second flowering

'Blanche Double de Coubert' is an old rugosa *hybrid from 1892. The immaculate white flowers smell delicious.*

Climbing roses

Climbing roses, like ramblers, have no way of attaching themselves to walls and fences although they can cling to the branches of trees and shrubs with their thorns. They may have large or small flowers, and grow to various heights. The following have been chosen for their long flowering season.

Rose	Colour	Height	Comments
'Altissimo' 1966	bright red	4m (13')	single flowers, clusters
'Bantry Bay'	clear pink	3m (9'10")	scented
'Blush Noisette' 1817	pink-lilac	4m (13')	scented, few thorns, sheltered places, tolerates shade
'Clair Matin' 1960	clear pink	3m (9'10")	clear pink with white highlights, chocolate brown stamens
'Climbing Iceberg' 1968	white	5m (16'3")	double, clusters
'Compassion' 1974	peach	3m (9'10")	large double flowers, scented
'Golden Showers' 1957	bright yellow	3m (9'10")	stiff upright, semi-double flowers
'Pink Cloud' 1952	pinkish-red	3.5m (11'4")	flowers profusely, also north-facing wall
'Zepherine Drouhin' 1868	fuchsia pink	4m (13')	scented, north-facing wall, mildew!

'Danse de Feu' is a 3m (9'10") high climbing rose which has abundant scarlet, double flowers.

This single, pale pink, modest rose 'Dainty Bess' is, surprisingly enough, a hybrid tea.

The rambler roses, which flower only once during the season, produce very long, flexible stems, which means that in small gardens they are only suitable for growing against a shed or an old, gnarled apple tree. The following are relatively small.

Rose	Colour	Height	Comments
'Albéric Barbier' 1900	creamy-white	5m (16'3")	large flowers, scented, some second flowering
'Albertine' 1921	salmon-pink	4m (13')	large flowers, scented
'Blue Magenta'	violet	4m (13')	small flowers
'Bobbie James' 1960	white	10m (32'6")	small flowers, scented hips
'Climbing Cécile Brunner'	pink	6m (19'6")	small cluster rose
'City of York' 1945	cream	3.5m (11'4")	small cup-shaped flowers, scented
'Francis E. Lester' 1946	pinkish white	4.5m (14'7")	small flowers, scented, orange hips
'François Juranville' 1906	apricot	6m (19'6")	apple scent, large flowers, susceptible to mildew
'Gloire de Dijon' 1853	amber	5m (16'3")	between pink and yellow, large flowers, scented
'Veilchenblau' 1909	mauve, white centre	4m (13')	small flowers, scented, half shade

Large-flowered bush roses

One of the most recent offspring of the rose family is the hybrid tea rose, which has been bred by crossing tea roses with perpetual roses. They are referred to as large-flowered bush roses and they have been bred simply for their flowers. The following are lovely, sturdy roses from this group.

Rose	Colour	Height	Comments
'Alexander' 1972	orange		suitable for cutting
'Blessings' 1967	salmon-pink		red-brown foliage, cut rose
'Dainty Bess' 1926	pure pink	90cm (36")	scented, open upright
'Dame de Coeur' 1958	red		strong and healthy
'Just Joey' 1972	orange-bronze		large flowers
'Metro' 1991	creamy-white	90cm (36")	nicely-coloured foliage
'Peace' 1945	soft yellow with pink	1.2m (4')	very large flowers
'Peaudouce' 1985	soft yellow		lightly scented
'Pristine' 1978	pale pink		cut flower
'Super Star' 1960	vermilion	1.2m (4')	cut flower, thorny
'Troika' 1971	orange		good cut rose
'White Wings' 1947	white	1.2m (4')	open growth, single flowers, scented, brownish-red stamens

Cluster-flowered bush roses

Cluster-flowered bush or floribunda roses produce large sprays of flowers in which the individual, fully double flowers can be just as large as those of the hybrid teas. Polyantha roses, which have smaller flowers, are also included.

Rose	Colour	Height	Comments
'Amber Queen' 1982	apricot	50cm (20")	reddish-brown leaf

'Bonica' 1982	pink	90cm (36″)	fully double flowers, very strong, natural growth form
'Coppelia' 1976	bright pink	1m (3′3″)	cup-shaped flowers, blooms profusely
'Daylight' 1991	yellow	50cm (20″)	reddish-brown leaf
'Fragrant Delight'	copper	1m (3′3″)	fully double, very fragrant
'Lady of the Dawn'	soft pink	70cm (28″)	
'Leersum 700'	apricot	1m (3′3″)	double flowers in loose clusters
'Maria Mathilda' 1970	pure white	1m (3′3″)	double
'Memento' 1978	vermilion	70cm (28″)	
'Nirvana' 1980	soft pink	90cm (36″)	very large flowers
'Pernille Poulson' 1965	dark pink	1m (3′3″)	very strong
'The Queen Elizabeth' 1954	pink	1.5m (5′)	very strong, large, and large-flowered
'Iceberg' 1958	white	1m (3′3″)	

Patio roses

Patio roses are included under miniature roses, the ancestry which can be traced back into the distant past. The flowers are no larger than 3 to 4cm (1 to 1 ½″) across, which makes them very suitable for growing on terraces and balconies. The following are completely hardy miniatures that do not exceed 40cm (16″) in height.

Roses are also offered as standards. The height

The elegant 'Iceberg' with its pure white, double flowers is used a lot in the border.

Rose	Colour
'Cinderella' 1975	white to pink
'Minirette' 1981	pale pink
'Little Flirt'	light red with yellow
'Pink Reflection' 1979	white to creamy yellow
'Suntan' 1991	orange brown
'Zwergkönig' 1990	dark red

of the stem varies. For a cluster-flowered rose it is usually 80cm (32″) while for a climbing rose it is generally 1.25m (4′). Standard climbing roses are otherwise known as weeping roses. Many of the modern roses that have been mentioned are also available as standards.

Perennials, part of the colour palette

Perennial plants, or perennials, play an important part in most gardens. What exactly are they? The category includes all those plants

When you see so much yellow together, you may be sure that the border is situated in full sun.

that produce leaves and stems in spring and summer, then flower, perhaps set seed, after which most of the parts above the ground die off completely in the autumn. The part of the plant below ground remains still alive because it puts out shoots again the following spring. A perennial is herbaceous, whereas a shrub has shoots that become woody before the winter. For that reason deciduous shrubs always have a clump of twigs throughout the winter.

Among the perennials there are a few that remain evergreen.

At first sight there would seem to be no problems with perennials. So many different genera and species are available now that it is quite easy to have a colourful display in the garden in every month of the year. The difficulty is knowing which plants to choose.

Cow parsley, mugwort, ox-eye daisy, and even the common nettle are examples of plants that

are native to western Europe and are perfectly well adapted to the climatic conditions. Most perennials, however, come from other parts of the world where they may have been used to high altitudes, warm coastal regions, or steppes. If they are faced with totally different conditions they may fail to thrive or even die.

When you are choosing perennials you need to take into account their specific needs as regards amount of sunshine, type of soil and amount of water. Look at shelter, microclimate, etc. If your trees and shrubs provide the green element in the garden and determine the main structure, you can add colour to it with perennials. Are you going to choose a certain month in which part of the garden design receives particular emphasis, or are you going to repeat a long-flowering perennial in a particular colour at various places in the garden?

You can also choose a broad sweep of planting

Tip

The planting scheme for a border is often drawn up separately on paper. Remember that the arrangement of perennials must not be seen in isolation but in relation to the whole garden design, the house, and the surroundings.

in the border. Perennials offer many different possibilities.

The origins of the border

Until the beginning of the twentieth century it was usual to plant perennials as an edging round the lawn or as a narrow border round the house. The plants were set at intervals and the bare soil between them was kept weed-free by regular hoeing. Creating depth, interplay, and colour combinations were ideas with which the nineteenth-century gardeners as a whole did not get involved. It is true that there were works of art: carpet bedding using succulents, and pyramids of geraniums (*Pelargonium*).

It was the English gardener Gertrude Jeckyll who at the end of the nineteenth century began combining perennials in groups. She was originally a painter and she approached the garden more from the point of view of the plants. From 1890 onwards she designed gardens in which combinations of perennials in long, broad sweeps played an important part. As well as being much wider than the edges round the lawns, these borders could have an irregular shape, and by no means all of them were planted beside a lawn.

Gertrude Jekyll was full of praise for the cottage

The combination of perennials is not seen in isolation in this garden but in relation to the surroundings.

Borders were once confined to small strips round the lawns. Nowadays they may be much wider and combine large patches of foliage with vibrant colour.

garden, a type of border garden of obscure origins. In the various separate parts of the cottage garden such as orchard, soft fruit garden, and kitchen garden there were also ornamental plants which flowered profusely. The owners of these gardens had probably been working as gardeners on a big estate for a long time and had come into contact with newly-imported seeds and plants that they needed to propagate. It is easy to imagine that a cutting or a few seeds found their way home. There was not much time to find exactly the right place and certainly no time to work to a particular plan. The ornamental plants were often set alongside the path leading up to the door or in a strip under the windows. The cottage garden acquired its haphazard yet luxuriant appearance through plants growing wherever they had been planted.

Waves of colour

Whereas the first herbaceous, that is perennial, borders were simply oblongs beds planted with perennials, often in rows, Gertrude Jekyll advocated using irregular groups of plants, of varying size and shape, alongside and behind each other. She believed that colours should flow into each other to create a pictorial effect. Foliage plants, with their various shades of green, also found a place in her borders. Her favourites were plants that grew in the cottage garden: they had, after all, proved to be tough. If you want to design a border in the style of Gertrude Jekyll, then typical cottage garden plants will certainly find a place there. Bulbs of wild hyacinth (*Hyacinthoides non-scriptus*) and *Scilla* are a must. The list should also include peony (*Paeonia officinalis*), catmint (*Nepeta* x *faassenii*), double-flowered soapwort (*Saponaria officinalis* 'Rosea Plena'), rock cress (*Arabis alpina* ssp. *caucasica*), bunnies' ears (*Stachys byzantina*), alkanet (*Anchusa azurea*), tansy (*Tanacetum parthenium* 'Aureum'), spurge (*Euphorbia chariacas* ssp. *wulfenii*), *Bergenia cordifolia*, sneezewort (*Achillea ptarmica* 'The Pearl'), *Iris sibirica* and *I. pallida*, lilies (*Lilium candidum* and *L. regale*), evening primrose (*Oenothera missouriensis*), foxglove (*Digitalis purpurea*), castor-oil plant (*Ricinus communis*), Canna lily (*Canna indica*), hosta (*Hosta sieboldiana* and *H. plantaginea*), crane's-bill (*Geranium himalayense* and *G.* x *magnificum*) bell flower (*Campanula carpatica*), mullein (*Verbascum phlomoides*), lupin (*Lupinus*), oriental poppy (*Papaver orientale*), clove pink (*Dianthus caryophyllus*), *Achillea fili-*

No cottage garden could be without bleeding heart and forget-me-nots.

pendulina, red valerian (*Cetranthus ruber*), hollyhock (*Alcea rosea*), cowslip (*Primula vulgaris*), *Delphinium*, *Acanthus*, forget-me-not (*Myosotis*), daisy (*Bellis perennis*), lady's mantle (*Alchemilla mollis*), iris (*Iris*), lavender (*Lavandula*), day lily (*Hemerocallis* 'Flore Pleno'), various species of clematis, including herbaceous varieties, and roses. Many spring and summer-flowering bulbs and tubers are also included, together with annuals and biennials.

So Gertrude Jekyll often used nasturtium (*Tropaeolum majus*) to cover plants such as gypsophila (*Gypsophila paniculata*) that had finished flowering. The everlasting pea (*Lathyrus grandiflorus*) could disguise the remains of early-flowering perennials and fill in the gap they had left. It is often said that Gertrude Jekyll used a lot of pastel shades. You will see from the summary that follows, in which many bright colours are included, that that is far from being the case.

The beautiful flowers and the length of the flowering season of perennials and annuals are not their only assets.

Among the perennials, annuals, biennials, and bulbs there are many with splendid foliage such as *Bergenia*, giant hogweed (*Heracleum mantegazzianum*), various species of *Rodgersia*, butterbur (*Petasites hybridus*), *Kirengeshoma palmata*, Christmas rose (*Helleborus* species), pirri-pirri-bur (*Acaena* species), barrenwort (*Epimedium*), the plantain lily (*Hosta* species), the toad lily (*Tricyrtis*), false hellebore (*Veratrum*), and *Euphorbia* species.

The grand ideal

You have the best view of a border when you look along it because then the plants that are not in flower and any gaps are not obvious. In Jekyll's time the borders seemed endless because there was plenty of space available. They had to be at least 2.4m (8') wide to guarantee a variety of plants and a flowering season lasting from early spring to late autumn. Although you can get away with making the border shorter, a width of roughly 2m (roughly 6′) is needed to achieve an interesting interplay between the colour and shapes of flowers and foliage. Gertrude Jekyll also broke the earlier rule that the tallest plants had to be placed at the back of the border to give a slope from back to front. She created a more natural effect by having several taller plants standing out among the lower ones. If some plants died during the season, then the gap could be filled straight away with bedding plants or plants in pots. Graham Thomas, who remembers Gertrude Jekyll's garden, wrote: "...to see in reality those wonderful borders of graded colour was like an entry into a new world, or walking through a static rainbow."

The position of the border

Groups of herbaceous perennials stand out well against a green hedge. Leave a wide gap between border and hedge unplanted to allow access to the back of the border for weeding and tying up, and to the hedge for pruning and removing any suckers. If a border is right up against the hedge the plants at the back will not grow well because the hedge will be taking a great deal of water and nourishment from the soil.

If there is not enough space for a hedge, then fencing or trelliswork can be erected and covered by climbing plants to function as a windbreak. Walls used to be employed as background. Although they offer complete shelter from the wind they can cause turbulence on the down-wind side. They do have the advantage of retaining warmth, which allows a wider range of plants to be grown.

In a true "Jekyll" border no soil was visible. Every cm^2 (in^2) was occupied by plants.

A strip must be left between hedge and plants to allow access for work on the hedge.

The mixed border

The herbaceous border still attracts a great deal of admiration but it is important to realize that a very great deal of work is involved in maintaining it: applying fertilizer to all the plants (each species has different requirements), replanting regularly, weeding, tying up, digging up, and splitting plants. From late spring until well into October the border will look magnificent, but for the rest of the year there is very little to see.

One solution is to have a mixed border. Perennials, annuals and biennials, and sub-shrubs are planted between and in front of the shrubs and trees and there is also a place for bulbs and tubers. The mixed border demands less work in the way of putting in supports and tying up. The shrubs will provide support as well as acting as a wind break. You can also take into account the ideal situation for all the flowering plants. This type of border has a longer flowering season and still provides interest during the winter.

The initial planting

The first requirement for a new border is the preparation of the soil. Since the planting is going to last for at least three years (after

> **Tip**
> A rather dull spring-flowering shrub can serve as the support for a herbaceous, summer-flowering clematis. What about a blue-flowered *Clematis x durandii* over your evergreen rhododendron?

that many perennials will have to be dug up, split and replanted) the soil must be dug to a depth of 40cm (16″) and manure worked in to the topsoil.

If your soil is heavy and wet, March and April are the ideal months for planting. Sandy soils have the advantage that they can be planted during September and October, so that the plants can begin growing before the winter. Plants put into heavy, wet ground before the winter may well suffer from frost heave: through alternate freezing and thawing they end up partly out of the soil and will not have taken root by the spring. The chance of renewed growth is then very slight.

Plants put in sandy soil during the autumn months have an advantage over those on clay soil. Planting can, however, be done in spring on sandy soils. Spring-flowering plants that are transplanted as bare-rooted plants are moved immediately after flowering. Container-grown plants that are offered for sale from March to October may be planted safely at that time. Make sure that the root ball is soaked well before planting.

Perennials for various purposes

There are some perennials that need no looking after. They seem to grow and flower by themselves. They never suffer from diseases, they never need any support, and they go on and on flowering. Look at the lists on the following pages where the plants are grouped according to their different characteristics.

Above: The root ball of plants that are supplied in a container must be given a thorough soaking before planting.

Centre: In loose soil a hole is first made with the hand before the plant is put in.

Below: After planting, the soil is firmed down round the plant.

You can cut armfuls of flowers from this perennial, Salvia.

Perennials for cutting

The following plants can be left to grow in the border. It is a pity to cut too many flowers from a colourful display, as this can affect the balance of colour or destroy a colour scheme completely. There are, of course, hundreds of plants available. There are often several species within a genus and many cultivars within a species, all of which may be suitable.

When a particular cultivar is mentioned below it is because it has proved in practice to be particularly suitable for cutting.

Name	Height cm (in)	Flowering months	Colour	Comments
yarrow				
Achillea 'Taygetea'	50 (20)	6–9	yellow	grey foliage
monkshood				
Aconitum carmichaelii 'Arendsii'	70 (28)	8–9	blue	moderate sun
Aconitum napellus	100 (39)	7–10	blue	moderate sun
lady's mantle				
Alchemilla mollis	40 (16)	5–8	yellow	repeat flowering, also light shade
wormwood				
Artemisia ludoviciana 'Silver Queen'	80 (32)	–	–	lovely grey foliage
aster				
Aster amellus	30–60 (12–24)	8–10	lilac-blue	many fine cultivars
Aster lateriflorus 'Horizontalis'	80 (32)	8–10	mauve-white	also light shade, small flowers
Aster pringlei 'Monte Casino'	70 (28)	9–11	white	also light shade, small flowers, needs adequate moisture
masterwort				
Astrantia major	50 (20)	7–8	white-pink	also light shade
yellow ox-eye				
Buphthalmum salicifolium	50 (20)	7–9	yellow	
clustered bellflower				
Campanula glomerata	60 (24)	6–8	violet-blue	fertile soil
milky bellflower				
Campanula lactiflora	90 (36)	6–8	light blue	also light shade and damp
turtle-head				
Chelone obliqua	90 (36)	7–9	lilac-pink	also light shade

Name	Height cm (in)	Flowering months	Colour	Comments
Dendranthema 'Clara Curtis' (syn. *Chrysanthemum rubellum* 'Clara Curtis')	80 (32)	8–10	pink	also light shade, fertile soil
globe thistle				
Echinops ritro	100 (39)	7–9	blue	
hemp-agrimony				
Eupatorium cannabinum 'Flore Pleno'	120 (48)	7–9	old rose	light shade, architectural plant
sneezeweed				
Helenium 'Moerheim Beauty'	100 (39)	7–9	reddish-orange	
Shasta daisy				
Leucanthemum x superbum 'Little Silver Princess' (syn. *Chrysanthemum maximum* 'Little Silver Princess')	100 (39)	6–9	white	also light shade, fertile soil
loosestrife				
Lysimachia clethroides	70 (28)	7–9	white	also in shade
mint				
Mentha longifolia 'Buddleja'	100 (39)	7–8	lilac-pink	all mints are invasive
bergamot				
Monarda didyma 'Cambridge Scarlet'	80 (32)	68	red	light shade, moist
obedient plant				
Physostegia virginiana 'Summer Snow'	70 (28)	7–10	white	fertile soil, also light shade

The globe thistle and Campanula *are both good cut flowers.*

Name	Height cm (in)	Flowering months	Colour	Comments
coneflower				
Rudbeckia fulgida 'Goldsturm'	60 (24)	7–10	yellow with dark centre	
sage				
Salvia x sylvestris 'May Night'	50 (20)	5–8	blue-purple	
Greek mallow				
Sidalcea 'Elsie Hugh'	80 (32)	6–8	satin pink	
Tanacetum coccineum 'J. Kelway'	90 (36)	6–7	beige to pink	also light shade, fertile soil
vervain				
Verbena hastata	120 (48)	6–9	lilac-blue	self-seeds widely

Perennials for ground cover

There is a group of plants that will more or less cover the ground with their foliage, so preventing light from reaching the soil. Seedlings of weeds, for example, are starved of light and die off. Ground-cover plants are often used instead of grass, because they too form a horizontal green surface. This group includes many evergreen species.

Name	Growth	Situation	Evergreen
pirri-pirri-bur			
Acaena	invasive	sun, half shade, dry	no
yarrow			
Achillea tomentosa	fast growing	sun, dry	no
bugle			
Ajuga	invasive	shade, half shade, damp	yes
alisons			
Alyssum	slow-growing	sun, dry	yes
pearl everlasting			
Anaphalis	fast-growing	sun, dry	no
cat's ears			
Antennaria dioica	slow-growing	sun, dry	yes
rock-cress			
Arabis	fast-growing	sun, dry	yes
Artemisia rupestris	fast-growing	sun, dry	no
wild ginger			
Asarum	slow-growing	shade, half shade, damp	yes
woodruff			
Asperula	invasive	shade, half shade, damp	no
Aubrieta	fast-growing	sun, dry	yes
Azorella trifurcata	slow-growing	sun, half shade, dry	yes
Campanula portenschlagiana	slow-growing	half shade, dry	no
Campanula poscharskyana	fast-growing	half shade, dry	no
mouse-ear			
Cerastium	invasive	sun, dry	yes
pink			
Dianthus	slow-growing	sun, dry	yes

Name	Growth	Situation	Evergreen
barrenwort			
Epimedium	slow-growing	shade, half shade, damp	some
bloody cranesbill			
Geranium sanguineum	fast-growing	sun, dry	no
avens			
Geum	fast-growing	anywhere, damp	yes
ground-ivy			
Glechoma hederacea	invasive	half shade, damp	no
Gypsophila repens	slow-growing	sun, dry	no
rupturewort			
Herniaria glabra	fast-growing	sun, dry	
hawkweed			
Hieracium	invasive	sun, dry	
Horminum pyrenaicum	fast growing	half shade, damp	
Houttuynia	invasive	shade, half shade, damp	no
dead-nettle			
Lamium	invasive	shade, half shade, damp	no
Leptinella squalida	invasive	sun, half shade, dry	yes
creeping-Jenny			
Lysimachia nummularia	invasive	shade, half shade, damp	no
catmint			
Nepeta racemosa (syn. *N. mussinii*)	slow-growing	sun, dry	no
Pachysandra	slow-growing	shade, half shade, damp	yes
phlox			
Phlox	slow-growing	sun, dry	no
Jacob's ladder			
Polemonium reptans	fast-growing	half shade, damp	no
knotweed			
Polygonum	invasive	half shade, damp	no
Primula juliae	slow-growing	half shade, damp	
lungwort			
Pulmonaria angustifolia	fast-growing	half shade, damp	no
pearlwort			
Sagina	fast-growing	sun, half shade, damp	yes
soapwort			
Saponaria ocymoides	fast-growing	sun, dry	no
Saxifraga cespitosa	fast-growing	sun, half shade, dry	no
London pride			
Saxifraga x urbium	fast-growing	shade, half shade, damp	yes
Sedum	fast-growing	sun, dry	yes
bunnies' ears			
Stachys	fast-growing	sun, dry	yes
thyme			
Thymus serpyllum	fast-growing	sun, dry	yes
Tiarella	fast-growing	shade, half shade, damp	no

Name	Growth	Situation	Evergreen
clover			
Trifolium repens	invasive	sun, half shade, dry	no
slender speedwell			
Veronica filiformis	invasive	sun, dry	no
Veronica prostrata	fast-growing	sun, half shade, dry	no
Vinca minor	invasive	shade, half shade, damp	yes
Viola labradorica	fast-growing	anywhere	no

Invasive perennials

Sometimes the planting that looked so good on paper can be spoilt within a year or so by the advance of certain very determined perennials. The following invasive plants need to be kept firmly under control.

Achillea millefolium	yarrow
Alstroemeria	Peruvian lily
Anaphalis margaritacea	
Anemone tomentosa	

This speedwell covers the ground and even climbs up perennials. It has driven many people to despair.

Artemisia ludoviciana 'Silver Queen'	
Campanula glomerata	clustered bellflower
Campanula takesimana	
Chelone obliqua	turtle-head
Convallaria majalis	lily-of-the-valley
Doronicum pardalicanches	leopard's bane
Fallopia sachalinensis	
(syn. *Polygonum sachalinense*)	
Helianthus superbus	sun flower
Lysimachia punctata	loosestrife
Macleaya	plume poppy
Nepeta sibirica	catmint

The pirri-pirri-bur likes half shade and dry soil.

The clustered bellflower is a species of Campanula *that spreads. It is pretty, but keep it within bounds.*

Petasites	butterbur
Physalis alkekengi var. franchetii	Chinese lanterns
Solidago (some species)	golden rod
Macleaya	pluimpapaver
Nepeta sibirica Petasites	hoefblad
Physalis alkekengi var. franchetii	lampionplant
Polygonum sachalinense	duizendkoop
Solidago	sommige soorten

Perennials for calcareous soils

A number of plants will not grow well, if at all, on soils with a high lime content such as those in areas with chalk or limestone under the surface. A similar problem can arise on reclaimed coastal soils which may have a layer of shells below the surface. The following plants are lime-tolerant.

Name	Height cm (in)	Flowering months	Colour	Situation
yarrow				
Achillea filipendulina	80 (32)	7–8	yellow	sun, damp
alisons				
Alyssum	25 (10)	5–7	yellow	sun, dry
rock-cress				
Arabis alpina ssp. caucasica	20 (8)	5–7	white	sun
aster				
Aster	30–125 (12–48)	6–10	no yellow	sun, occas. shade
Aubrieta	15 (6)	3–5	red, blue	sun, damp
Bergenia cordifolia	40 (16)	3–4	pink	shade, half shade
Campanula carpatica	25 (10)	6–9	blue	sun, half shade

Name	Height cm (in)	Flowering months	Colour	Comments
cornflower				
Centaurea dealbata 'Steenbergii'	60 (24)	6–7	reddish-pink	sun
Centaurea macrocephala	80 (32)	7–8	yellow	
yellow fumitory				
Corydalis lutea	35 (14)	5–10	yellow	shade, half shade, damp
leopard's bane				
Doronicum orientale	40 (16)	4–5	yellow	sun, half shade, damp
Doronicum pardalianches	80 (32)	5–8	yellow	sun, half shade, damp
sea holly				
Eryngium	60–80 (24–32)	7–9	blue	sun, dry
cranesbill	25–100 (10–39)	5–10	all except	sun, half shade, shade
Geranium			yellow	damp
Gypsophila paniculata	100 (39)	6–8	white	sun, dry
Gypsophila repens	15 (6)	5–8	white	sun, dry
rock rose				
Helianthemum	20 (8)	5–8	all	sun, dry

Left: There is ample choice from which to make a lovely herbaceous border.

Self-heal, although no higher than 25cm (10") stands out on any soil.

Name	Height cm (in)	Flowering months	Colour	Comments
rose of Sharon				
Hypericum calycinum	30 (12)	7–9	yellow	sun, half shade
Shasta daisy				
Leucanthemum x superbum 'Alaska'	80 (32)	6–8	white	sun, half shade
catmint				
Nepeta x faassenii	30 (12)	5–9	lavender blue	sun, dry
evening primrose				
Oenothera	5–60 (2–24)	6–10	yellow	sun, dry
self-heal				
Prunella grandiflora	25 (10)	6–8	violet-blue	sun, half shade
Pasque flower				
Pulsatilla vulgaris	20 (8)	3–4	violet	sun, half shade
stonecrop				
Sedum	5–40 (2–16)	5–9	all except blue	sun, dry
bunnies' ears				
Stachys byzantina	30 (12)	6–8	lilac	sun, dry

You will find more information on perennials and ways to combine them in the chapter on the various kinds of garden.

Annuals and biennials for extra colour

The terms annual, biennial, short-lived, bedding and container plants are often used interchangeably. The names really only refer to the way in which these plants are grown and used in the western European climate.

An annual plant is one that germinates, grows, flowers throughout the summer, sets seed and sheds it, and then dies away completely.

The biennial plant is sown in the first year, from May onwards, and develops a rosette of leaves during the first growing season. It then overwinters, ready to sprout from the rosette the following year and produce flowers. Seed forms from July onwards and then the plant dies. At first sight it may seems unnecessary to use annuals and biennials at all in the garden since the shape has already been determined by the woody species, and the roses and perennials are providing sufficient colour. The annuals and biennials do make the garden more exciting: they can add extra emphasis, a more personal note, to the design. Furthermore the picture can be changed completely from one year to the next: the plants

Nasturtium is a well-known annual which is best planted in the garden complete with pot. Then the flowers always appear above the leaves.

that are grown from seed are only there for a short time. In spring a number of mainly low-growing, bedding plants are generally on sale but the choice is in fact not very large. There are many more annuals for which seed is available and you can grow these yourself. The choice has become much wider in recent years. A few decades ago the annuals on offer were all in very bright colours. Since then pastel shades have been added to the range. The biennials were always easier to combine with shrubs and perennials because of their colours.

Annuals and biennials can be grown in a vegetable garden for cut flowers. They are also used in mixed borders and it is possible to create a border made up solely of annuals. Sow them before you have made definite plans for the garden. They will prevent the topsoil from blowing away and preserve the nutrients and soil structure. Biennials also make ideal filling for gaps: annuals or biennials can be planted in the space allotted to a growing shrub. The disadvantage is that some of them spread, seeding themselves in places where you did not intend them to grow. Annuals are, of course, ideal for containers. A balcony made of iron and concrete can be trans-

Diascia barberae *likes dry soil and prefers a sunny place.*

formed into a sea of colour. The plants can be sown in various different ways. Some need to be sown where they are to flower, some sown in seed trays to be pricked out later, and others need warmth to germinate. Sowing the seeds *in situ* is naturally the simplest and quickest way. Sowing is mainly done in the second half of April but in a cold spring it is advisable to wait until the first half of May. Never add fertilizer to the soil where you are going to sow annuals and biennials because if you do they will put on a lot of leaf but produce very few flowers.

Less well-known annuals
Bright red geraniums, orange African marigolds, white alyssum, and petunias are not the only choice. The following list gives some outstanding but lesser known plants that are suitable for sowing and planting in pots and containers.

An ochre-yellow Californian poppy. Californian poppies must be sown in situ because they have a tap root and do not like being transplanted.

Plant	Month for sowing	Height in cm (in)	Distance apart in cm (in)	Colour
Alonsoa meridionalis 'Pink Beauty' pimpernel	4,5	50 (20)	15 (6)	pale pink
Anagallis monellii	5	20 (8)	15 (6)	gentian blue
Anchusa capensis 'Blue Angel' African daisy	5	25 (10)	15 (6)	mauve-blue
Arctotis stoechadifolia var. *grandis* Swan River daisy	5	60 (24)	30 (12)	white with blue sheen
Brachycome iberidifolia 'Blue Splendour'	5	30 (12)	15 (6)	blue shades
Collinsia grandiflora	3–6	30 (12)	20 (8)	lilac and mauve-blue
Convolvulus tricolor 'Blue Tilt'	4–6	25 (10)	30 (12)	dark blue with white and yellow
Diascia barberae	2/3 in trays	30 (12)	25 (10)	salmon pink
Dicranostigma franchetianum	2/3 in trays	40 (16)	20 (8)	yellow
Echium vulgare 'Blue Bedder'	5	30 (12)	20 (8)	blue shades
Emilia coccinea Californian poppy	4–6	45 (18)	20 (8)	orange-yellow and red
Eschscholzia californica	3,4	30 (12)	25 (10)	orange
Lavatera trimestris 'Silver Cup' poached-egg flower	4,5	70 (28)	50 (20)	silvery pink
Limnanthes douglasii	3–5	15 (6)	20 (8)	white with yellow centre
Melampodium paludosum marvel of Peru	4,5	15 (6)	15 (6)	yellow
Mirabilis jalapa Venus's navelwort	4,5	60 (24)	40 (16)	white, pink, red, and yellow
Omphalodes linifolia cream cups	3–6	30 (12)	15 (6)	white
Platystemon californicus poor man's orchid	4,5	30 (12)	15 (6)	creamy yellow
Schizanthus x *wisetonensis* 'Disco' catchfly	5	40 (16)	35 (14)	mixed pastel shades
Silene rosa-coeli 'Candida' blue lace flower	4,5	45 (18)	25 (10)	white
Trachymene caeruleus	4,5	60 (24)	25 (10)	soft blue
Ursinia anthemoides var. *versicolor*	4,5	30 (12)	25 (10)	orange with dark ring
Verbena rigida 'Lilacina'	2/3 in trays	60 (24)	30 (12)	lilac-blue

Biennials resemble perennials

Biennials are even easier to grow than perennials. You really only need to sow them once because they will seed themselves in succeeding years, giving the impression that they are perennial. Biennials flower in the year following sowing. Their colours are less bright than those of annuals so they are easier to fit into the mixed border. Many of them are well known from the past when they were often grown in the kitchen garden for cut flowers. They do not like being moved and most of them are therefore sown *in situ* and thinned out once. The following biennials have been grouped according to the time of sowing.

Sow in May: hollyhock (*Alcea rosea*), Canterbury bells (*Campanula medium*), Scotch thistle (*Onopordum acanthium*), teasel (*Dipsacus ful-*

The biennial sweet William comes in many colours.

lonum), foxglove (*Digitalis purpurea*), honesty (*Lunaria annua*), mullein (*Verbascum bombyciferum*), clary (*Salvia sclarea*), caper spurge (*Euphorbia lathyrus*), and wallflower (*Erysimum cheiri*).

Sow in June: daisy (*Bellis perennis*), sweet William (*Dianthus barbatus*), and forget-me-not (*Myosotis sylvatica*).

The remainder are sown in July: heartsease (*Viola tricolor*), nodding catchfly (*Silene pendula*), Iceland poppy (*Papaver nudicaule*), and sweet rocket (*Hesperis matronalis*).

Ferns: perennials without flowers

Nowadays ferns are often neglected although, for decades, the stag's-horn fern, maidenhair fern, and the hart's-tongue fern were fashionable house plants. Do they really merit a place in the garden?

Ferns are primitive plants. They do not bear flowers but produce spores on the underside of the fertile leaves. It looks as if the leaf has been sprinkled with a fine brown dust (stag's-horn) or as if the plant is infested with scale insect (male fern). There is, however, nothing wrong: the plant is merely "reproducing".

There are certainly no flowers to catch the attention but ferns have a mysterious quality: in spring the new leaves unroll in their own special way, depending on the species, quite unlike the perennials. The whole shape of the plant and the growth pattern of the leaves are extremely decorative. It is sometimes said that ferns will flourish in places where other plants refuse to grow, for example in the shadow of trees, but this is not true at all, because all ferns have specific requirements. Almost all ferns need acid soil and sufficient moisture without actually standing in water.

A group of ferns will add style to any shady garden. If your garden has a small stream running through it with some mossy boulders, you simply cannot do without a few ferns.

Large and small ferns

Ferns like an open, woodland soil, which must be fairly acid, pH 5.5 to 6.5. Use leaf mould, mixed with pine needles, dead twigs, and roots.

There are many different genera, species, and cultivars among the ferns. It is often difficult for the non-expert to distinguish between them. It is certainly worth taking the trouble to grow some of the ferns in the following list.

Name	Height in cm (in)	Situation	Comments
maidenhair fern			
Adiantum pedatum	45 (18)	damp, shade	horseshoe-shaped leaves on long dark stems
lady-fern			
Athyrium felix-femina	70 (28)	damp, shade	
hard-fern			
Blechnum spicant	30 (12)	damp, shade	evergreen
bladder-fern			
Cystopteris bulbifera	50 (20)	damp, shade	likes lime
Dryopteris erythrosora	75 (30)	damp, deep shade	also in full sun if damp, evergreen
Dryopteris wallichiana	100 (39)	damp, deep shade	evergreen
ostrich fern			
Matteuccia struthiopteris	100 (39)	damp, deep shade	
sensitive fern			
Onoclea sensibilis	50 (20)	damp, light shade	if wet also in full sun, fertile fronds evergreen
royal fern			
Osmunda regalis	100 (39)	damp, deep shade	if wet also in sun, lovely fertile fronds
polypody			
Polypodium vulgare	25 (10)	dry, shade	likes stony soil
hard shield-fern			
Polystichum aculeatum	80 (32)	damp, shade	evergreen

Left: *Large individual clumps of ferns appear to advantage in the herbaceous border.*

Tip

Do not plant ferns close together: the decorative leaves will grow together and form a green mat and the shape of the ferns will be completely lost.

Tip

If your fern, after thriving at first, begins to languish, you can feed it using fish nutrients. Bury the remains of the fish such as fins, backbone, etc. round the base of the fern. If that is impossible because of cats, you can use dried fish meal which is odourless.

Thelypteris palustris *is a marsh fern that is only at home in permanently damp ground. Besides this, it also likes a position in full sun.*

Climbing plants to add height

Among the shrubs as well as among the annuals and perennials are climbing plants. These have one thing in common: they grow upwards. Most of them are equipped with such features as twining branches, tendrils on leaves and branches, aerial roots, and even thorns which enable them to attach themselves to supports. Some trailers simply have long branches–if you do not secure them to something they will flop to the ground.

The climbers have all kinds of uses. Supported by posts, netting, trelliswork, and trees they will soon grow upwards, thus forming a vertical green surface in your garden without taking up too much space on the ground or casting too much shadow. Vigorous climbers can overwhelm sheds, houses, and pergolas under their load of flowers and foliage. The Russian vine is notorious for this and has made many gardeners wary of climbers. It has brought down many a pergola under its weight, frequently invading the house itself.

It is important to choose the right climbing plant for a particular position. There are really modest climbers that will leave your house in one piece. You must, however, find out in advance how, if at all, the climber you are buying needs to be trained. The care of climbers will be dealt with later.

Painting with climbing plants

Climbers were not created just to grow up against a wall, fence or pergola. How about an area covering with everlasting pea, *Lathyrus latifolius*, or the annual nasturtium, *Tropaeolum majus*? Give a clematis or a climbing honeysuckle, *Lonicera*, space on the ground. You can kill two birds with one stone with the honeysuckle because not only does it make perfect ground cover but you can also enjoy its fragrance. This creates a very different impression from a bed planted with *Salvia* 'May Night' or *Hosta sieboldiana*.

If the wall of your house is an eyesore, give it a facelift with a climbing plant, for instance a Virginia creeper, *Parthenocissus*, with its magnificent autumn colours. If the garden is too small for a pergola the climber can grow up a pillar. With its tall yet narrow growth it can replace a tree to serve as the roof of the garden. The less vigorous climbing plants, such as various cultivars of clematis and several annuals, can be planted in a pot or container to decorate the balcony, terrace, or roof garden.

If there are no foundations in the ground the climbing plant may be planted closer to the post.

Here Clematis x durandii *serves to liven up a ground cover of periwinkle.*

Planting climbers

Climbers and trailers are often grown close to solid structures with foundations. The soil beside the foundations is often poor and may contain rubble, lime, and sand which many plants do not like. Next to walls and posts for pergolas that are cemented in you will need to dig a hole 60cm (24″) deep and 50 x 50cm (20 x 20″) at a distance of 50cm (20″) from the structure. Partially fill the hole with good garden soil or compost and set the climber at the same level as it was in the nursery. Any net or sacking is removed from the root ball and the hole is then filled in completely. Allow two weeks before you fix the climber to its support to give the soil time to settle.

It is often too hot for climbers up against the wall because they do not like their roots to be

baked. This applies especially to the clematis which likes its roots to be cool and damp.

Choosing a climber for a particular purpose

The kiwi, *Actinidia chinensis*, needs a large pergola because it can easily cover an area of 12 x 12m (39 x 39′). It needs warmth to be able to fruit well but this will only happen if you

> ### Tip
> To make sure that your climbing plant by the wall does not dry out you can sink a length of perforated drainpipe beside the roots. Fill the drain with gravel. Water and fertilizer can be applied via the drainpipe. This is better for the plant than giving the roots a splash of water now and again.

Birthwort has insignificant flowers in the shape of a pipe, hidden among the large leaves.

have both a male and a female plant. The kiwi plant has attractive oval leaves. The smaller relative of the kiwi, *Actinidia kolomikta*, is suitable for growing up trelliswork. This cannot support such a great weight and since this climber will take five years to cover an area of 1.5 x 1.5m (5 x 5') it is ideal for the purpose, because it does not grow very tall. It has broadly elliptical, pointed leaves, the upper side of which are creamy-white and pink, but these colours will only develop in a sheltered, sunny situation. The plant lends itself well to the patio garden.

Akebia quinata is somewhere in between. It has very decorative leaves with five leaflets and the branches twist together like a honeysuckle so that it often forms a bushy shrub at the top.In spring it has small purple-brown flowers which are not very striking. It will also grow on a north-facing wall and is suitable for growing up

Clematis macropetala *'Rosy O'Grady'*.

walls, fences, and small trees. Many species of *Ampelopsis* are invasive. They have pretty, deeply-cut leaves. One that is less rampant and is therefore suitable for trellises and pillars is *Ampelopsis glandulosa* var. *brevipedunculata* 'Elegans' with its small, irregularly cut ornamental leaves which are spotted and speckled in pink and white. The young stems and leaf stalks are pink. This *Ampelopsis* needs a sheltered situation in light shade.

Aristolochia macrophylla grows to enormous proportions. This shade-tolerant climber has pretty, heart-shaped leaves that resemble *Catalpa* leaves, and is beautiful for growing over a tunnel or pergola. Unfortunately it is not evergreen.

Berchemia racemosa has attractively veined, oval leaves. Following the unremarkable flowers the plant produces green fruits which turn red and finally black. It does not grow too vigorously and is suitable for sun and half shade.

Ceanothus x *lobbianus* is evergreen and hardy in a sheltered situation. With its blue flowers the plant is an asset to a trellis. It does not grow too tall so it will not hang over the fence and flower for the benefit of the neighbours!

The oriental bittersweet, *Celastrus orbiculatus*, is unsuitable for growing on a trellis but does have lovely autumn colours. The female plants bears striking yellow and orange fruit, providing there is a male plant there too. Give the pair of them space on a large pergola, tunnel or tree, but avoid drain-pipes and guttering.

Clematis alpina and its cultivars are less vigorous growers for sun and half shade. They flower in April and May after which they need to be pruned. *Clematis* 'Huldine' is a summer-flowering cultivar, with white flowers tinged with mauve. It grows rapidly. *Clematis macropetala* and its cultivars only reach 3m (10') in height and flower in April and May. They have small flowers followed by pretty seed heads.

Most people know *Clematis montana* and its cultivars, which are the familiar spring-flowering types of clematis. They grow very tall and are therefore ideal for pergolas. *Clematis vitalba*, the native traveller's joy or old man's beard, can be allowed to grow over trees and shrubs in the wild garden. Some gardeners plant it by an old shed over which it will spread in no time. The climber is very lovely, with its display of flowers lasting around ten weeks from June onwards. *Clematis vitacella* and its cultivars are less vigorous and can be pruned in the spring. They make good climbers for trellises, as do many of the summer-flowering, large-flowered cultivars. The clematis always prefers a cool root-run: the flowering stems, however, always seek the sun. *Clematis rehderiana* is a vigorous species that bears fragrant, tubular flowers in the autumn amongst pretty foliage. You can walk or sit under a scented roof. At 5m (16') it is also ideal for growing in trees.

The spindle, *Euonymus fortunei*, which is evergreen, can well reach 8m (26') and can cover a wall beautifully although it is less vigorous than the ivy. Like ivy, however, its young branches have aerial roots, while in the later stages the growth of both climbers is non-rooting. The variegated cultivars of the spindle grow more slowly and can also be used as a trailing feature in pots and containers on a balcony.

Ivy, *Hedera helix*, in all shapes and sizes, makes an attractive cover for trelliswork, and is evergreen. The climber is useful for providing shelter in sun and shade. Do give it a sturdy support, because eventually old wire-netting will not take the weight of the plant. There are few species but more and more cultivars. Ivy is also often used as ground cover.

The common hop, *Humulus lupulus*, has both attractive foliage and pretty seed heads, but it is invasive. It is a beautiful plant for the wild garden, because it is the host plant for the comma butterfly. An arbour covered with hops is lovely.

The climbing hydrangea, *Hydrangea petiolaris*, is a slow starter, but once it does begin to grow it needs plenty of room. It is therefore extremely suitable for a large wall. Training it over a pergola is rather more difficult, although it can look beautiful as a specimen shrub. It has very pretty foliage and coloured twigs. In summer the shrub can be lined up with a summer-flowering clematis.

The trailing shrub winter jasmine, *Jasminum nudiflorum*, can be kept in check against a trellis. It has yellow flowers in the winter but you do need to use the shears on it after it has flowered. There is a very nice honeysuckle that is not so rampant, *Lonicera japonica* 'Aureoreticulata', which has yellow-veined leaves. This climber is also suitable for a trellis. The vine, *Vitis vinifera*, has pretty foliage and is grown for its fruit. There are, however, other species with even more attractive foliage. They all grow rapidly. *Vitis vinifera* 'Purpurea' has three- to five-lobed dark red leaves throughout the season. This vine will tolerate some shade. In contrast, *Vitis coignetiae* prefers light shade but will also tolerate

Vines grow very vigorously and so need the support of a large pergola.

sun. For a vine it has a very large leaf which has brown hairs on the underside. It takes time to get established but once growth starts it is not unusual for it to reach a height of 15m (50′). It is suitable for walls and large pergolas. Virginia creeper, *Parthenocissus*, likes the sun. Since it grows vigorously it is best to use it to cover a large wall, pergola, or arbour.

Wisteria is absolutely lovely for an arbour, a pergola, a handrail (perhaps on a bridge), or a high wall. There are two well-known species: *Wisteria floribunda*, the Japanese wisteria, which twines to the right and only reaches 10m (33′), and the Chinese species, *Wisteria sinensis*, which twines to the left and can reach a height of 30m (100′). There are also plenty of roses. If you look around a rose nursery during the flowering season you will find many that are suitable for growing up a trellis.

Among the annuals, too, there are many climbers, almost all of which need a sunny situation, such as black-eyed-Susan, *Thunbergia alata*, orange with a dark centre, and *Ipomoea lobata*, with its orange and yellow flowers. *Plumbago auriculata* can be over-wintered indoors. It has pale blue flowers.

Both annual (*Tropaeolum majus*, orange-red and yellow) and perennial (*Tropaeolum speciosum*, red) nasturtiums are suitable for growing up a trellis. The perennial species prefers to be in the shade. You will need to give it some protection in the winter, otherwise you will lose it during even a moderate frost.

The hardy annual Canary creeper, *Tropaeolum peregrinum*, has yellow, fringed flowers. It can grow up to 4m (13′) high and is suitable for growing over hedges and up pillars.

Lathyrus latifolius is a perennial that grows well

Tropaeolum speciosum *scrambles up the yew hedge. This nasturtium needs protection in the winter.*

over a trellis, small hedges and low walls, and as ground cover. It grows to 2m (6′7″) so it can be kept in check in a limited space. A place in the sun or the shade makes little difference; it flowers abundantly. *Cobaea scandens* can cover a whole wall in a single summer. It has mauve flowers that resemble those of *gloxinia*. It does need to be sown in trays beforehand. There are some other climbing plants which are not hardy in western Europe, but can be over-wintered in a greenhouse or conservatory. Have a look for them in a good seed catalogue.

Bulbs and tubers

There are many spring- and summer-flowering bulbs and tubers. The best-known representatives of this group, like the annuals, have very bright colours. It is not so easy to decide where to plant them despite the

fact that in the spring there is very little colour in the garden. The bulbs are sometimes described as being "suitable for containers" or "for separate beds". But times are changing here too. The flowers are still very colourful but there are more subtle variations in colour between red, white, and blue.It is therefore easy to make a choice, especially among bulbs and tubers for naturalizing.

The "big three"

Everyone knows them: the tulip, daffodil, and hyacinth. Every gardener has a few examples somewhere in the garden, if only to be able to enjoy the return of spring as early as possible. The rich colours and the size of the flowers makes many people forget how cold, windy, or wet spring often is in practice. These three announce that the new season has really started and all sorts of things are happening in the garden. It is as if each year nature has kept its promise and everything is coming to life again. The garden is celebrating with colour.

Tulip

Tulip bulbs are planted from October to the end of November. A good rule of thumb is to plant the "big three" at a depth twice the height of the bulb. If there is no frost tulips can also be planted in January. Depending on the weather, the flowers will last one to two weeks. That seems very short, but thanks to a wide variation in the time of flowering between the species it is possible to have tulips in flower in the garden from the beginning of April to the end of May. It is better not to buy tulip bulbs of just one species for the private garden but to choose a big group from those which flower at various times. Tulips cannot tolerate too much water. They need a

The advantage of naturalized bulbs such as the bluebell is that they do not need to be dug up. While the foliage is still dying off, the ground is already taken up with summer-flowering plants.

Different ideas for using bulbs.

good, well drained soil but are otherwise not fussy about it, although they do need sun. The tulip bulb is an annual: that is the parent bulb dies off after it has flowered, but new bulbs develop round it. The formation and growth of these bulbs demands a great deal of energy so that immediately after flowering the pistil, the beginning of the fruiting body, must be removed. All the energy produced by the leaves has to go towards building up the new bulb that is developing underground. The bulb should only be dug up after the leaves have died down completely. After that the bulbs must be stored in a dry airy place until they are planted again in the autumn. Generally speaking tulips are lifted each year because of the build up of various diseases that occur in tulips (and hyacinths). The bulbs are replanted the following year in another place, or the top 20–25cm (8–10″) of soil is replaced.

Choosing tulips

The official list contains more than 2500 different tulips, so that choosing which to plant can be difficult. You will perhaps find the divisions according to flowering season of some help. The first tulips to flower are the early single and early double ones. The early single tulips do not generally grow any taller than 40cm (16″). The early doubles are rather shorter and the flowers are large in proportion. The Darwin hybrids, and Triumph and Mendel tulips belong to the mid-season group. Late-flowering tulips include

> ### Tip
> Do you want to leave the tulips in the ground but keep the soil free from the wireworms that spread disease? Immediately after the tulips have flowered plant African marigolds among the bulbs: there is no better soil disinfectant.

Parrot tulips are "in" again in a big way. This is 'Estella Rijnveld'.

some Darwin tulips, lily-flowered tulips, several late peony forms for cottage gardens, double late tulips, Rembrandt, and Parrot tulips. Then there are the dwarf species and hybrid tulips such as Kauffmanniana and the *Tulipa fosteriana* and *Tulipa greigii* groups. *Tulipa tarda*, *Tulipa turkestanica*, *Tulipa sylvestris*, and *Tulipa wilsoniana* are suitable for naturalizing.

Daffodils

Daffodils have possibly been known for longer than the other flowering bulbs: they are also native to western Europe. The flowering season varies between the different groups from the end of February to the end of May. There is, however, less variation in colour than among the tulips. Daffodils do have the tremendous advantage that they will also grow in shaded situations, besides which they are all suitable for

naturalizing and can therefore be left in the same place for many years. They can be planted from the end of September to the beginning of December, but the earlier they are planted the better they will flower. Immediately after the leaves appear above ground the bulb begins to develop a number of new bulbs which means that you are assured of an increase in the stock. It is advisable in this case, too, to remove the developing seed pod immediately after flowering. Daffodils appreciate damp soil, if possible with a good supply of humus. Too much water will cause the bulbs to rot.

Daffodils in various shapes

Daffodils are classified according to the shape of the flower. The trumpet-shaped daffodils are the best known group. The flower is characterized by the trumpet which is longer than the petals. There is only one bloom per stem. Large-cupped daffodils are sometimes trumpet-shaped but the trumpets are generally much smaller than in the trumpet-daffodils. Here, too, the flowers are borne singly. The same applies to the small-cupped daffodils of which only the flower is smaller. In the double daffodils there is no distinction between the trumpet and the petals since the solitary flower is made up of several layers of petals. This makes the flower heavier and more suitable for a vase than for the garden. The split-cupped daffodil has splits which vary in number and the cup may be fringed. The multi-headed daffodils are all the rage both in house and garden. In some cases the flowers, several to a stem, are beautifully scented. Jonquils, which prefer not to grow in the shade, are the most fragrant of the multi-headed daffodils. The long-stemmed *poeticus* daffodils, which are suitable for naturalizing, are also scented. There remain the low-growing species such as *Narcissus cyclamineus* with its single, nodding flower, and *Narcissus triandrus* with several scented flowers per stem.

Hyacinth

The hyacinth is very fragrant so you must try

The daffodil 'Ice Follies' belongs to the large-cupped group.

growing it indoors. You can literally bring a breath of spring into the house. In the garden plant them in a sunny place from the end of October until mid-December and protect them from frost with a good covering of leaves. Because of the structure of the flower hyacinths have a tendency to fall over. The larger the bulb the larger the flower head. If you are used to buying hyacinth bulbs for forcing with a bulb size of 16/17 or even 17/18, you will find 15/16 or even smaller satisfactory for the garden. Give them some support. Because each small flower forms a separate seed pod and the lower flowers open first, these will be setting seed while the ones at the top have yet to open. This means that the bulb will only be able to build up its food reserves at the last minute. After flowering the flower head should be removed, after which the bulb is left in place as long as possible. When the foliage has died off completely the bulb is lifted, dried, and stored in an airy place. If you leave hyacinth bulbs in the ground the flower heads will gradually decline in size over the years. The hyacinth multiplies by forming small bulbs, known as bulblets, round the original bulb. When you lift the bulb you can take these off and plant them out. Several years later they will have grown into full-sized bulbs.

Types of hyacinth

All the strains that are available commercially have one parent: *Hyacinthus orientalis* from south-eastern Europe and Asia Minor. In about 1550 the first *Hyacinthus orientalis* bulbs were brought into western Europe where they were grown and described. They were then exclusively blue in colour. This hyacinth, which does not look at all like the highly bred double and single forms, is still available. Then there are the multiflora hyacinths. These are heavy bulbs which

The hyacinth 'Bismarck', together with pansies. The heavy hyacinth flowers can easily bend over, so plant a smaller size of bulb or support the flower heads.

produce more than one flowering stem per bulb. The multi-floras can be left in the same place for many years without being lifted at the end of each season. There are also tulips, daffodils, and hyacinth bulbs available for growing indoors.

Planting bulbs

Bulbs will grow in any soil provided that it has enough humus and is fairly moist to dry. In the first instance fertilizer can be added to the soil in the form of well-rotted farmyard manure, compost, or leaf mould at the rate of one to two barrow loads per 10m² (12yd²).In existing gardens it is necessary to remove the surface-growing, woody roots to a depth of 30cm (12″) under shrubs and trees. This is not always possible without causing damage to the trees and shrubs. For this reason roots should only be removed at intervals round the tree or shrub.

Tip

Other rules apply if you are gardening on sandy soil. If you plant the bulbs in the newly dug soil to a depth of twice the height of the bulb you are in fact setting them much too shallow. The ground is still going to sink so that the bulbs often end up too near the surface. Here the rule is: plant them deeper!

Hyacint 'Ostara'

Name	Height in cm (in)	Situation	Comments
ornamental onion			
Allium species	15–150 (6–60)	sun	plant all ornamental onions deep
ramsons			
Allium ursinum	30 (12)	half shade	
Anemone blanda	10–15 (4–6)	sun	
wood anemone			
Anemone nemorosa	10 (4)	half shade	
Camassia cusickii	70 (28)	sun	also grows in wet soil
Glory-of-the-snow			
Chionodoxa	10 (4)	sun, half shade	
bird-in-a-bush			
Corydalis solida	10–15 (4–6)	shade, half shade	
crocus			
Crocus large-flowered	10–15 (4–6)	sun, half shade	
crocus			
Crocus small-flowered	5–10 (2–4)	sun, half shade	
Eranthis hyemalis	10 (4)	half shade, damp	
foxtail lily			
Eremurus bungei	100 (39)	sun, dry	ugly foliage, among other plants
dog's-tooth violet			
Erythronium dens-canis	20–30 (8–12)	half shade	speckled leaf
snake's-head fritillary			
Fritillaria meleagris	20 (8)	sun	also in wet soil
snowdrop			
Galanthus nivalis	10–15 (4–6)	sun, half shade	
bluebell			
Hyacinthoides non-scripta	20–30 (8–12)	half shade, damp	
summer snowflake			
Leucojum aestivum	30–50 (12–20)	sun	also in wet ground
spring snowflake			
Leucojum vernum	15 (6)	sun, damp	
grape hyacinth			
Muscari armeniacum	10–20 (4–8)	sun	
species daffodils			
Narcissus	10–50 (4–20)	sun, half shade	
star-of-Bethlehem			
Ornithogalum species	20–75 (8–30)	sun, half shade	
wood-sorrel			
Oxalis triangularis	20 (8)	sun	reddish-brown foliage
Puschkinia scilloides	10 (4)	sun	
Siberian squill			
Scilla siberica	10 (4)	sun, half shade	
species tulips			
Tulipa	10–30 (4–12)	sun	

The summer snowflake is a little taller and the flower is larger than in other species of Leucojum. *It is a must for any garden.*

Right: Anemone blanda *'White Splendour' is the largest and strongest of all the spring flowering varieties.*

Less well-known summer-flowering bulbs and tubers

These plants demand rather more work. You can plant the bulbs and tubers in a sunny, sheltered place at the end of April, but they must be lifted again before the first night frosts.

A warning about the summer-flowering bulbs and tubers: people who as a rule want to spend little time on the garden would do better to confine themselves to spring- and autumn-flowering specimens which once planted can then be enjoyed for years to come. To get the best out of the summer-flowering bulbs and tubers you will have to put in a lot of work planting, manuring, lifting, and covering.

Name	Height in cm (in)	Colour	Planting depth in cm (in)	Comments
Acidanthera bicolor	80 (32)	white with purple	5 (2)	also in pots
Crinum x *powellii*	100 (39)	pink	–	top of bulb must remain visible
montbretia				
Crocosmia x *crocosmiflora*	80 (32)	orange	5 (2)	can remain in soil in winter if covered
Cypella herbertii	60 (24)	yellow-brown	5 (2)	
summer hyacinth				
Galtonia candicans	150 (60)	white	5 (2)	nice in tub or container
Hymenocallis x *festalis*	60 (24)	white	10 (4)	also for pots
chincherinchee				
Ornithogalum thyrsoides	40 (16)	white	5 (2)	
tiger flower				
Tigrina pavonia	50 (20)	mixed	5 (2)	separate flowers only bloom for one day
Tropaeolum tuberosum	150 (60)	orange-yellow		
Zephyranthes grandiflora	30 (12)	pink	5 (2)	

The chincherinchee is a familiar plant. The flowers used to be dyed for the cut-flower trade!

Autumn-flowering bulbs

Just as you are not expecting anything more, crocuses begin to come into flower and it is not yet winter. This is not a freak of nature because what you are seeing are the autumn crocuses. Several good species are *Crocus goulymyi* (soft lilac), *Crocus medius* (purple), *Crocus nudiflorus* (deep mauve), and *Crocus speciosus* (violet blue). The meadow saffrons also flower in the winter. These include *Colchicum autumnale* (pale mauve-pink), *Colchicum byzantinum* (mauve-pink), and *Colchicum speciosum* (violet). *Sternbergia lutea* with its bright yellow flowers goes well with the vibrant autumn colours of the shrubs and trees. The autumn-flowering bulbs are planted in August at a depth of 5cm (2″) for crocus to 10cm (4″) for meadow saffron. They flower in September, October, and

Colchicum autumnale *'Waterlily'* and Colchicum autumnale *'Album'*.

Crinum x powelii *can overwinter outside in a very sheltered place providing it is well covered.*

Page 173: Zantedeschia rehmanii *'Carminea' is a container plant that can stand outside from May to October.*

4 Building materials in the garden

You will need to aside space in the garden for terraces, paths, fences, pergolas, drives, and walls as well as for plants. Unlike plants, which are dynamic –growing, spreading, adapting, and constantly changing – these hard materials are static, unchanging, and, once in place, they become fixed features. Static features need to be chosen very carefully since they will determine the look of the garden for a long time to come. Expense is also an important consideration be- cause the materials needed to build them will cost a great deal more than the planting scheme. So, what materials are available and what should you bear in mind when selecting them?

Using wood and stone

Wood and stone blend in extremely well with plants, and they can make plants look even more attractive. However, they

Metal railings with small pillars, usually associated with old buildings and gardens, can be found nowadays with new buildings.

can be over-used so that the static elements in a garden appear to overwhelm the dynamic ones. This is especially true when the material used does not suit the shape or building materials of the house. Sense of nostalgia inspires some people to lay a drive of bricks under the mistaken impression that because they are old they must be right, while the character of the bricks is totally out of keeping with a modern house which is built mainly of steel and concrete. In general, materials that are contemporary with the house itself are the most likely to harmonize with it. However, they do not have to be the original materials, which may no longer be available or may have become extremely expensive. Providing they are chosen carefully, modern versions of old materials will not look out of place alongside the older building material used in the construction of the house.

Wood and stone have the great advantage that, once in place, they will not alter in shape. A narrow wooden fence will remain narrow and a wall will not grow so that the drive becomes too narrow for the car. A hedge, on the other hand, will broaden out, and a hedge beside a drive will certainly need to be clipped regularly. Do remember, though, that wood and stone need regular maintenance and that their initial price will far outweigh that of the plants themselves.

Types of hard material

Hard materials include bricks, natural stone (as well as pebbles and gravel), and concrete. All hard materials absorb water and will remain damp. This is more the case with soft stone that has a rough surface than with harder types of stone which have smoother surfaces. Moss and algae very soon become established on damp surfaces. If you want to prevent a "green" path becoming a slide you will have to remove this growth regularly. There are various commercial preparations for getting rid of algae and moss. Choose the most environmentally friendly one unless youy prefer to

A path of natural stone. Stone setts are never all quite the same size, so they are always laid with gaps between them.

remove the growth by hand with a scraper or a knife. Space is often left between slabs or bricks to allow ground-cover plants to grow. However, for safety's sake, do not allow plants to grow on the main paths or steps: after rain, all plants become slippery.

Concrete slabs and pavers are cheap, but not as hard as natural stone and brick, so they will remain wet for longer. They are, however, available in many different shapes, sizes, and colours. Concrete blocks have been on sale in natural shapes for a number of years now: you may well have already come across these "cobbles." These are square concrete blocks which, after they have set, are put through a mill so that their sharp edges are been smoothed off. This gives them a more natural look. A further advantage is that the top surface is flat, which makes them good to walk on. Concrete slabs and pavers do not, however, seem to be colour fast. If you have gone to a lot of trouble to find a particular shade of slab to go with your house, it can be very annoying to find a year or so later that the colour has altered so your path and house no longer look right together.

Natural stone is also used for paving and comes in various shapes, sizes, and colours. It can have a rough surface as, for instance, on granite setts, or can be highly polished like marble. Although not always nice to walk on, natural stone looks attractive and is not out of place in a rock garden.

Brick keeps its colour, is hard, and comes in many shapes and sizes. It is more expensive than concrete but cheaper than natural stone.

There are so many different shapes and sizes of pavers and bricks that, when you decide to go ahead and build, you will scarcely know which

to choose. Go and have a look at what is on offer at stone merchants, garden centres, builders' merchants, and DIY stores, and try to get ideas from exhibitions and demonstration gardens. A special fabric called a geo-textile is often laid under gravel (at very little additional cost) to prevent weeds coming up from below. After a time, however, with the accumulation of

This path of smooth stone slabs is much easier to walk on than the gravel and cobbles which surround it.

Left: *These pebbles from river beds have been carefully chosen according to size and colour and then bedded in mortar. The result is dazzling.*

Right: *Gravel is a relatively cheap material to use for surfacing.*

dust, loose sand, and seeds, some weeds will germinate so you do need to keep gravel clean.

Types of wood

Wood is a natural material that looks right almost anywhere. Tropical hardwoods are naturally rot resistant but if you prefer not to use these, then pine from central and northern Europe is suitable. Pine absorbs timber preservative very well and the chemical penetrates deep into the wood, enhancing its resistance to rot. Deal (fir) is also widely used nowadays. It does not, however, absorb timber preservative as well and is therefore better used above ground. European timbers should have been well treated with preservative before use and will need regular maintenance. Ideally, timber should have been pressure-treated with the appropriate chemicals. It is also possible to treat the timber yourself by immersing it in, or painting it with, the preservative. This wood will not, however, last as long. Up to now, treated timber has not always been environmentally friendly. That old wooden fence that has fallen down and needs to be taken away should be regarded as chemical waste because of all the chemicals it contains. In recent years there has been an increase in the use of harder kinds of timber, including *Robinia*. This very hard timber grows extremely well in Europe and is used in the building trade. Split chestnut makes a long-lasting and more rustic fence. The development of less environmentally damaging stains and preservatives is now under way: there are various water-based stains and preservatives available and even some with a linseed base.

All wood, whether hardwood or not, will become damp and remain damp for a long time. Treat any wood that is to be walked on to prevent it becoming slippery. Nasty accidents may occur if it is not treated.

Paths and avenues

Paths are necessary for gaining access to the most important places outside the house. The most important paths will usually be surfaced because you need to go into the house with clean, dry feet. A path must be functional. In other words, it must lead somewhere. A winding path that leads from the kitchen door to the middle of the lawn and ends up 1.5m (5′) from the terrace is pointless. A path need not lead only to a door, but can guide you to a sculpture, a garden seat, or a view point, thus giving your garden perspective.

Width of path

The width of the path depends on its intended use. It must also fit in with the scale of rest of the garden. The access to the garage must be 3m (10′) wide or you will feel as if you are driving off the edge!
You will, more-over, want to be able to get out of the car reasonably comfortably (and with dry feet). Mistakes in layout may only seem small irritations at first but they will assume huge proportions later on.

Left: *Hardwood is preferable for load-bearing structures. It is also safe for making bridges.*

A path along which you only need to push the wheelbarrow can be 60cm (24″) wide, while you should allow at least 1m (3′) for the other main paths. It must be possible to wheel a bicycle or push the garbage can along them without having to squeeze through between the plants. When first laid, a path always looks wider than it will eventually become. First of all, the plants alongside it are going to grow taller, which will immediately make the path appear narrower. Secondly, the plants will grow towards, and frequently over, the path itself.
On paper, a path often looks too wide. However, you can quickly change its appearance by adjusting the height of the plants that grow alongside it. Tall trees will make a path look

Brick has been combined with natural stone and concrete for the surface of this path. Thanks to the uniform colour it does not look messy.

The colour of the sedum flowers picks up the red of the concrete blocks.

Stepping stones have been used in this garden to prevent people from damaging the ground cover, especially the moss. The stones are laid 64cm (26″) apart from centre to centre.

narrower; a path with a border of low-growing plants, on the other hand, will look more like it did on paper. When designing a "footpath," assume that at least two people will want to walk side by side along it, even when it is overhung with greenery and there has recently been rain. The surface of the path can be of brick, natural stone, or concrete.

Combinations of concrete and brick are also sometimes used. Small paths can be covered with wood chippings or bark. Boulder clay with sharp sand and shingle makes an excellent surface for both wide and narrow paths. Another possibility is fine rubble that has been well packed down. In that case the path must have a retaining edge.

It is not advisable to use pea shingle as this will quickly tread all over the garden, including the lawn, and in the end you will take it into the house caught in the grip soles of your shoes.

If you like stepping stones be sure to place them far enough apart so that you land on them and

not in between. According to a long-established
formula, the stones should be 64cm (26″) apart
from centre to centre.

A trick of the eye

You can use some tricks to make a path look
longer or wider. You can probably imagine that
a path 20m (65′) long and 80cm (32″) wide will
look much narrower than a path 4m (13′) long
and 80cm (32″) wide.

To make the latter appear longer, you can, for
example, use 20cm x 5cm (8″ x 2″) bricks for
paving. A surface of slabs 40cm x 60cm (16″ x

*The plants soften the hard lines of the path. Changing the
angle of a path also breaks up the line and livens up the
effect.*

*A path of boulder clay can include either coarse grit or
fine sand. It is advisable to lay an edging, as in the
picture.*

24″) would make the path appear much shorter. You can achieve the effect of extra length by including a pattern, for example a long stripe, in the paving.

Even the planting can help. A path will appear longer if you give it an edge of plants that have vertical flowering habits, such as salvia, delphinium, and mullein.

It is a good idea always to border a path with plants. Greenery softens the hard outline to some extent.

Changing the angle of the path also breaks up the line and livens up the effect.

If the path runs alongside the lawn it is better to lay it at the same height as the lawn to make mowing easier.

Stagger the decks a little and having all the gaps running in the same direction. This prevents path adjoining the terrace from looking very long.

Drainage

Bear in mind when you are laying the surface of the path that you will want it to remain as dry as possible. Slope it a little towards the garden so that excess water will run off. A gradient of 1 to 2cm per metre (1/2″ to 1″ per yard) is sufficient for a path that runs past the house. A path in the garden should, oviously, drain off to the lowest point.

The stones or pavers are usually laid on a bed of sharp sand at least 10cm (4″) thick. For a drive, the sand bed has to be 25cm (10″) thick and the paving is laid with a camber – that is, with the highest point in the centre between the car-wheels and the lowest point along the edge. This will prevent puddles.

If the sub-surface is heavier and less permeable, it is better to lay an extra, permeable layer of gravel or rubble under the sand bed. The layer of rubble needs to be tamped down with a plate

compactor. In small gardens, sharp sand is soaked with water before the paving is laid. The sand beds in well this way and, after drying out, is beautifully firm. After the paving has been laid the sand will not settle any further.

The alternative drive

A drive often consists of two rows of slabs with a worn strip of grass in between. A more attractive solution is to use grass-reinforced concrete – pavers with holes in which grass can be sown. The pavers are laid and allowed to settle for a couple of weeks be-

Paths and terraces are laid on a bed of sand ideally 15cm (6″) thick. When all the stones are level a layer of river sand is spread over them and brushed into the gaps. The whole area is then tamped down and over several weeks the remaining sand is gradually brushed into the gaps.

Here the drive, the path to the front door, and the path round the house have been made into one. The way the smooth concrete slabs have been laid makes the garden look wider.

fore the grass seed is sown in the holes. The result is a hard-wearing, green surface.

The drive and the path to the front door here form a whole. Constrictions have been introduced to make this long drive look shorter. Naturally less paving has been needed and it has avoided the whole of the front garden being paved.

The drive can also be completely paved. You might even enjoy making patterns with slabs and bricks, perhaps in combination with wood. It is preferable not to use more than two different materials and two different sizes because any more than this and your drive will become very noticeable.

In gardens that have little space for the children to play in you can lay the drive out so that games can be played on it (for example, hopscotch, cheques, and chess).
A further possibility is to plant ground-cover plants in between the two rows of slabs. This planted area will survive quite well if the car is not always parked in the same place.
Brick or stone are usually used for drives. It is not advisable to use treated timber.
Do not use bricks or slabs left over from building alterations.
These will not be proper paving materials and they will not be hard enough for the purpose. They will break up in a relatively short time through frost damage.

The terrace

Every garden should have a terrace because, from time to time, everyone wants to relax and admire what they have created. The best place to do this is somewhere out of the wind and that is why a terrace is usually laid beside the house – apart from the feeling of protection this gives you.Besides, you will have all your comforts close at hand: coffee pot, a magazine, the doorbell, telephone and so on. If you think these conveniences are not really necessary you may want to site the terrace further down the garden. Even so, make sure that it is easy to reach. In larger gardens, there is often a second sitting area giving a different view of the garden. A second sitting area also gives you the opportunity to sit at a different angle to the sun. You can protect the side of the terrace from the prevailing wind by planting a hedge of shrubs. To protect the terrace during the early years, before the shrubs have grown sufficiently, you can place a screen of rush matting behind them.
This rush material looks natural and is not expensive in comparison with wood or glass screens. Within four years or so this matting can be removed.

Sun and shade

When you are laying the terrace, do consider its position in relation to the sun. Some people prefer to have their terrace facing the sun so that during the cold winter months they can take advantage of what sunshine and warmth there is. If you do this, make sure you provide some shade. A small tree or large shrub situated near the terrace will shade part of it, for the benefit of people who cannot bear the hot sun. A parasol is not a suitable alternative because the shade it affords is not like the cool shadow thrown by a tree. A pergola, on the other hand, will serve the purpose well. You can adapt a pergola in various ways:

you can, for example, leave the spaces between the uprights open or fill the in with woven rush panels, wattle hurdles, trellis, or wire mesh with climbers growing over it. Until the climbing plants that are going to provide a shady "roof" are fully grown, you can cover the top of the pergola with shade netting. The material used for the terrace must be wind and weather proof. Hence, natural stone, brick, and concrete are obvious choices. Pressure-treated timber decking can also be used. A timber deck, or platform, is made from wooden planks that are screwed or nailed on to wooden beams, leaving gaps of 1cm (1/2″) between the planks. The decks are laid on a base of rubble and sand. It is advisable to place the decks in such a way that the air can circulate freely underneath. The deck is placed on a frame of hardwood beams to avoid direct contact with the ground. The combination of the space between the planks and the gaps between the planks and the beams ensures that the deck will dry out quickly after

In this garden a small tree has been planted in the terrace. Do not take the paving right up to the trunk but keep a circle of soil at least 60cm (24″) in diameter clear.

a rain storm. A wooden terrace like this often looks very attractive, but it is not suitable for families with young children. A deck can be very frustrating for toddlers, because too many treasures can fall down between the planks and be lost for ever. For a terrace that is going to be used a great deal it is better to choose a material that you can lay smoothly and without gaps. This will stop tables and chairs wobbling or sinking into gaps in the surface. If you are buying paving slabs with a pebble finish, make sure there are no broken pebbles on the upper surface. A child falling on sharp stone will undoubtedly gash his or her knee and it is not comfortable or safe to walk bare-foot on a sharp surface. Check too that the pebbles are set deep enough into the slabs so that they will not work their way out.

Grooved planks often provide a solution. They are less slippery less quickly and you can get a better grip on them. You can, however, soon lose small objects down the gaps.

Surface area and drainage

You need to allow at least 2m² (3yd²) sitting room per person if you are going to sit in one place and not move round with the sun. If you do not intend to move you need to allow 4m² (5yd²). Always lay a terrace with a slight slope away from the house and towards the garden. Allow a drop of 2cm (1″) for the first metre; a gradient of 1cm per metre (1/2″ per yard) is sufficient for the rest of the terrace.

The sunken sitting area

Unless you provide good drainage a sunken sitting area may give you a very unpleasant surprise: it needs to be well drained. On wet soil it is also a good idea to site a "sunken" area at a higher level. Walls made of sleepers, wooden posts, or moulded concrete posts against which the earth can be banked up will give the impression of a sunken area. Always put plastic sheeting between the earth and the wall to prevent soil being washed through the gaps.

Differences in level achieved, for example, through the creation of raised beds and sunken sitting areas, often make a garden look larger because it cannot all be seen at once. You can achieve a similar effect, however, partly through your planting scheme. It is not advisable to use differences in height in a garden of less than 100m² (100yd²) because they will make the garden appear smaller.

Retaining walls and steps

You can use retaining walls and steps to overcome differences in height. Because the wall is holding the earth back, it must be sufficiently solid and have good foundations. Remember that a retaining wall should not be too high; otherwise it will look out of scale. Furthermore, higher walls need more solid and deeper foundations. It would be better to span a height difference of 1.5m (5′) with two or three retaining walls and the same number of steps. And remember, you can plant up retaining walls to your heart's content.

The wall should slope at a gradient of 10 per cent towards the earth bank. This is to withstand the pressure of the earth behind it and also to catch more of the rainwater.

If you leave gaps in the wall here and there you can let plants grow in them. It is better to let the stone or brick under the gap project a little with a slope towards the back, so that the back of the stone or brick is lower than the front. All this will provide extra soil for the plants and help to maximize available moisture.

On most soils you can build low walls in what is called "running bond": bricks laid lengthways and one brick thick. On wet, soft soils you should not make the wall deeper than this or it will sink under its own weight. Low walls do not necessarily have to be cemented in place: they can also be laid "dry." However, they do

Here is a less familiar use of a retaining wall. Plants grow on this wall that you would hardly expect to find by a pool.

still need a foundation. Dig out a broad trench (always broader than the width of the wall from back to front). It can be shallower on heavy soils than on light ones.

You fill the trench with rubble which is then compacted. A layer of brick or stone is then cemented in place on top of it. After that has set the bricks or stone can be laid dry on top. All kinds of stone or brick can be used for this, even broken pieces. You can use a mixture of cow manure and clay to secure them in place. This will provide nutrients both for the plants you put in deliberately and those that seed themselves. For solid, low walls you can use concrete blocks. These do not need a special foundation: a layer of sand 5cm (2') deep is sufficient. Wood can also be used for retaining walls: just think of sleepers piled one on top of

A sloping retaining wall has been made out of broken slabs placed on top of each other.

another. These are fixed to each other by means of wire nails. You will not need any foundations provided the sleepers are laid on the flat side (25cm or 10"). Vertical sleepers and round wooden posts can also be used for retaining walls. Wood used vertically must always have at least one third of its length sunk in to the ground. Plastic sheeting always should be sunk in the ground behind retaining walls that are made of wood.

Walls and microclimate

Everyone is familiar with the concept of a walled garden. In such a garden the climate beside the walls is different from that in the middle of the garden, and this differs again from the situation immediately outside the walls. However small a garden, it will have a range of microclimates.

It is not always necessary to build walls to achieve an enclosed garden; you can also use the opportunities for planting offered by existing high walls, such as those of the house, garage, or garden shed. During the day the brick or stone warms up and this warmth is released gradually during the night. West and south-facing walls are ideal for plants that need extra warmth, such as roses, fruit trees, and a number of shrubs that are not reliably winter-hardy such as the evergreen species of Ceanothus. The preference here is for shrubs and climbing plants that can be trained against the wall by pruning. However, you must not plant the rootball too close to the wall. This area usually contains the poorest soil, mixed with rubble, brick, and pure sand. Close to the wall, tends to plants, they not receive any water because they are sheltered by the overhang of the roof. Moreover, they cannot develop roots properly because these must all develop on the side away from the wall. It is therefore a good idea to plant the shrub or climber 50cm (20″) out from the wall.

Walls facing the north and east are suitable for ivy (*Hedera*) and the climbing hydrangea (*Hydrangea petiolaris*).

A wall has one great disadvantage: it does not allow the wind through and wind blowing straight on a wall can have damaging effects. The space between two houses or walls often causes the wind to funnel through it. Shrubs and trees planted in front of and partly in this funnel will act as windbreaks and filters.

Steps

A step is a continuation of a path or terrace to reach a higher or lower level. Make steps of material that blends with the path or terrace. The transition from path to step must not, however, be so smooth that the difference in height is hard to see. The beginning and end of the step must be clearly visible.

Steps must be made of level and safe materials and it must not be possible for plants to grow between the slabs, stones, or brick they are made of because, after rain, greenery will make going up or down the steps a risky business. Plants growing along the sides of the steps, on the other hand, do look attractive because they soften the hard lines of the structure. The green fringe these plants create provides a transition to the planting in the garden.

The step formula
A step must be comfortable to walk on. There is a special formula to ensure this based on the fact that the average pace is 64cm (26″) long: twice the height of the riser, plus once the length of the step equals 64cm (26″). The ratio between tread and riser must be correct, other-

The edge of the steps is made very obvious by the use of two different materials.

The brick kerb has been painted to prevent people tripping over it.

wise the step will be uncomfortable to walk on. If, for exam-ple, the riser is 12cm (2 x 12 = 24cm) the tread must be 64-24 = 40cm. (2 x 5″ = 10″; the tread is 26-10 = 16″.) It is better not to have the riser more than 15cm (6″) high otherwise the steps will be tiring to use. Make the tread deep enough so that you can place your foot on it firmly. Sometimes the side walls of the steps are faced with stone or brick, especially where the earth has to be held back. Plants can be allowed to grow over these walls. All the materials that are suitable for paths and terraces can be used for steps. U-shaped concrete blocks are particularly appropriate, as well as wooden posts and sleepers. Wood and stone make a good combination and have the advantage of making the steps show up well.

It is extremely important to maintain the steps properly and to remove moss and algae regular-ly; plants can make steps just as slippery, and therefore as dangerous, as moisture.

Boundaries and fences

Fences are erected to mark off the division between neighbouring properties, to give a garden on an open site a more enclosed character so that it fits in more with the local surroundings, or indeed to shut those surroundings out completely. In the last case it is better to put up a solid fence and, of course, a fence serves its purpose immediately: hedges and shrubs take much longer.

It may be necessary to protect the garden (or the terrace) from the wind. A more open screen or group of shrubs will achive this purpose better than a solid barrier. A fence that is intended to reduce noise must be absolutely solid.

Always look for a material that will fit in with the house and garden, and do not put up a fence in the front garden just for the sake of it – only if it is absolutely necessary. Also, make sure the fence makes a suitable background for the greenery, because in most cases the planting is the most important feature of the garden. You can choose from stone, brick, wood, wattle hurdles, and chain-link fencing (whether plastic covered or not).

This last looks somewhat artificial and is generally only used if something has to be shut in or shut out: for example, round a deer enclosure or to keep rabbits out of the kitchen garden. On the other hand, a fence like this can soon be disguised with plants. There are both solid and open kinds of fencing.

Solid fences do not let the wind through and therefore cause turbulence. You can make a fence like this yourself with tongue-and-groove planking secured vertically or horizontally to posts or a framework. Depending on the choice of material, such a fence can be very long-lasting. Prefabricated panels are often made of treated deal (fir or pine).

Basket-weave fencing is extremely popular and the panels are relatively cheap. Ready-made wattle hurdles look good in the wild garden but unfortunately these natural heather or osier panels do not last more than three years or so.

Bamboo screens also deserve a mention here: they can be an asset in both the wild and the

You can buy ready-made trellis panels. They may be as open or as closed as you wish.

modern garden as well as among ornamental grasses. Brick and stone walls have already been men-tioned. Walls made of ornamental concrete blocks can be built quite a high without appearing too massive.

There is only the question of whether a concrete wall will fit in with your house and the other solid surfaces around it.

Sometimes it can be better that the wind is filtered, in which case an open type of fencing is more suitanle. Trellis work, which consists of laths secured to a frame, can be bought ready-made. It provides an ideal support for climbing plants.

Reasonably cheap fences can be made of chain-link, either plastic coated or galvanized. Plants can be allowed to grow up this. Nowadays, wooden garden fences 1m to 1.25m (3′ to 4′) high consisting of vertical wooden planks with pointed or rounded tops are supplied as kits. Other types may also be available with hori-zontal planks in wood or plastic finishes, but before you finally decide to buy remember that plastic attracts a heavy growth of algae. Other open-work fences include welded wire,

Right: *From the outset a bamboo panel offers sufficient protection.*

Below: *Welded wire does not provide enough support for heavy climbers. Keep the grid at least 5cm (2″) from the wall.*

either galvanized or not. All climbers will grow up such a fence as this, although some species of clematis have difficulty with the rusty wire of the non-galvanized type. Paling, preferably pine, can be either solid or open and is used in varying heights.

You can make straight as well as rounded shapes with this. Relatively speaking, you need a lot of wood for this type of fencing, so the cost mounts up. Slabs made out of concrete are also used as paling. Wood and plastic fences take up hardly any space and do not need foundations, although of course you can put these in just to be on the safe side.

Rush panels go well with open fencing when more protection is needed temporarily. This material has, however, a very short life. Loose

The arbour with its thatched roof fits in with its surroundings. In front of it there is a wild-flower meadow that only needs to be mown once a year.

> **Tip**
>
> Wood rots more quickly at the junction of air and soil. The wood has to be protected at this point. You can buy ready-made metal post supports suitable for use directly in the ground or in a foundation.
> There are even post supports that can be fixed on to concrete slabs or beams.

planks (of rough-sawn pine or of hardwood, for instance) can also be used with welded wire. The wood that has to support the fencing must be strong and durable.

Use posts made of either hardwood or pressure-treated timber. If treated timber is used it is advisable to put it on a base so that the post itself is set just above the ground.

Do remember that if your timber supports are not on a base they must be sunk into the ground

to one third of their length, which will increase the length of timber needed per post.

Arbours, pergolas, and tunnels

An arbour is often a small structure overgrown with greenery in which you can shelter from a shower of rain if it is warm enough to be outside – you can be out of doors and still be dry. An arbour usually has a lot of windows, either glazed or not, but it is possible to leave whole sides open. In hot countries an arbour affords protection from the scorching sun and wind, and it is possible for people sitting there to be relatively cool, to

The plane tree (Platanus x hispanica) *can be trained to form a roof. To keep the roof flat the plane must be pruned once in winter and at least once in summer.*

enjoy a cup of tea, and to take advantage of the garden. In cooler climates the sun is welcome and protection from the rain is much more important.

The arbour does not have to be an actual building because that would be too big for most gardens. You can make an arbour of metal poles or bars. A climbing plant (for example, a scented rose) is then used as a roof, because however open an arbour might be otherwise, a roof and climbing plants are its essential elements.

You can also make an arbour from various trees, as we have already seen in an earlier chapter. In the last few years the common plane, *Platanus x hispanica,* has been used for roofing arbours. This plane tree is healthy, grows strongly, and forms a thick foliage shedding few leaves during the growing season. It is an excellent tree to shelter under from either the sun or the rain.

Tip

Choose the tree for your arbour very carefully, because what looks nice is not always practical. The tree doesn't have any fruit that can bombard you, does it? What about honeydew which can become sticky? Do the leaves come out early and fall late in the season? Consider all these questions and ask for the right tree.

Parasol

Everyone is familiar with the round hole in a garden table that takes a parasol. The foot of the pole is sometimes anchored in a heavy base. Such parasols do not provide cool shade, although they do offer some protection from the rain. I mention this here because more and more attractive and, what is more important,

For a large area of canvas choose a neutral colour. This parasol harmonizes with its surroundings.

larger and larger parasols are coming on to the market. Obviously the larger the parasol is the more attention must be paid to anchoring it. Be careful, too, about the colour of the cover. In all cases consider choosing a colour which is an "extension" of the colours in the surrounding plants, and avoid a sharp contrast. A parasol will form a large area of one colour which could easily clash with the surrounding planting.

The leafy walk

Pergolas and tunnels are not dissimilar. The literal meaning of "pergola" is an arch covered with foliage. Originally designed to support vines, the pergola has developed into a walk or path. It can connect important parts of the garden, it can form a boundary, and it nearly always leads somewhere. You should really use it as a kind of link because a pergola can, as it

EA pergola often forms a link between different sections of the garden. It almost always leads somewhere: here to another part of the garden.

were, provide a thread that joins different elements to each other. It can also be used to enclose areas, for instance, beside a sitting area or as protection against prying eyes, wind, or too much sun. As a partition a pergola is not as obtrusive or massive as the kinds of fence and screens already mentioned. It also has the great advantage that it can introduce height and a vertical green feature without the whole picture being dominated as, for example, with a tree.

The eye is, as it were, drawn through the leafy walk, under which you can enjoy the play of light and shade to the bright point at the end. A pergola is usually made of wood or a combination of stone or brick with wood. It goes without saying that the construction must be solid and reliable. The uprights and the cross-beams are always made of hardwood or pressure-treated softwood, if not of iron or steel. The horizontal distance between the uprights depends on the space available and personal preference.

The pergola offers many possibilities for growing a variety of climbing plants. In recent years a combination of roses clematis has often been used. Uprights placed close together soon give the idea of a tunnel. If the planting in the garden is not yet mature, a bare pergola will look too high and too broad. After a year or two, however, this pergola that once looked "too high" will fit perfectly into the space. The same applies to the pergola as to paths: in a bare garden it should indeed look too big and obtrusive because the proportions will be just right when the garden is fully grown.

Tunnel, gateway, and arch

A tunnel is a pergola in which the uprights are placed closer together. The roof of the pergola is often of horizontal wood while that of the tunnel is rounded. The height, width, and length of both pergola and tunnel will depend on the space in which they are to be erected. Remember too that tall people will have to walk under the pergola and through the tunnel and that branches and flowers will hang down from the roof. It is not pleasant to be able only to walk under the roof and, of course, the same will apply to the width.

For a tunnel with thickly planted sides the minimum dimensions are even more important. Although you should be able to see less in a tunnel and although you should be able to plant the shrubs that form the sides of the tunnel as close together as you wish, in practice it is better to leave some gaps so that you see the play of light through the foliage.

A tunnel is usually made up of a single species, for example, a laburnum walk of *Laburnum anagyroides* 'Vossii', an alley of the hornbeam (*Carpinus betula*) or an arch of holly (*Ilex*). The simplest tunnel is a gateway or arch. These were

The laburnum must be trained over iron arches and pruned to the correct shape.

Right: *A gateway has been created by weaving several branches from the beech hedge together at the required height above the path.*

originally placed as entrances to the house or garden but very soon were used to create vistas or to serve as an open connection between various parts of the garden. Gateways and arches are made of wood, iron – wrought iron, that is – stone, or brick, and sometimes they are decorated with ornaments. Use materials that fit in with the other structures in the garden. The rose arches from the cottage garden can easily be fitted in to present-day, smaller gardens, like openings in hedges. They make people curious to see what surprise is in store for them at the other side!

Climbers

Climbing plants can cause headaches and sometimes even despair when it comes to attaching them to walls, pergolas, or fences. Their branches may wind themselves round each other, either to left or right, or there are green tendrils on the branches of a plant so that it can attach itself to the wall or fence with aerial roots or suckers. You need to use the appropriate support for each type of climber. You will also realize that if you attach a plant directly to the wall or fence with nails you not only do damage but you will have to loosen all the branches again when it comes to pruning. And you will have to secure them again afterwards, which often means making yet more holes. That is why many gardeners leave the plant attached to the bamboo cane that it was supplied with so that at least the plant has some support. It can always be tied up properly later. The result (with honeysuckle, for example) is

that the cane becomes tightly enmeshed with a bundle of twining stems. All the structures mentioned earlier, such as fences, pergolas, and arches, can be used to provide support. Special trellis panels, ring stakes, and link stakes can be used to support perennial plants. Tarred garden twine and raffia are indispensable for tying up plants. Sometimes metal wire, sometimes galvanized or plastic covered, is used for support. The precise method of fixing and its associated maintenance will be dealt with in the chapter entitled '*Maintenance – the hard work*'.

The children's play area

Depending on your family, there may be be space in the garden reserved for children. Besides, if you are going to have a lot of visitors with children you will need to make the garden attractive for them. I am always struck by how well the sandpit scores in the

Twining or trailing climbers can be trained up using garden twine.

playground popularity stakes. Good drain-age is important when you are making a sandpit. If the subsoil is properly drained it will be easy to excavate a place for the sandpit. The rim of the sandpit will then be level with the surrounding paving, and it will be easy to sweep sand back into it. Wood is the best material to use for the edge, because it is warmer to sit on than stone or brick. It is not pleasant, nor is it particularly healthy to sit on a cold surface. Provided the wood is well maintained and free from splinters, a child is less likely to hurt him or herself than on harder material. Generally speaking the sandpit is sited where it can easily be seen and it is therefore usually laid out beside the terrace. Later, if so required, it can always be turned into a small pond which will then be close at hand. In short, the best place for both now and the future is close to the terrace.

Plastic sandpits are available at garden centres. These come complete with a lid. You can also buy canvas covers for wooden sandpits. These lids or covers are not a luxury and will certainly prove their worth if there are cats in the neighbourhood. A sandpit should be filled with silver sand.

Other possibilities for play

A rope swing hung from the branch of a tree is naturally much more attractive than one with a metal or wooden frame. If possible use a tree near the terrace and the sandpit. You really need a tree because it will shade the play area during the heat of the day. The swing can also be hung from the pergola, provided it is very solidly constructed. If your garden does not offer enough opportunities for play, then you could consider adapting a path or drive where the children can play. You can lay the paving slabs so that the children can chalk on them and play hopscotch. Ball games, marbles, and skipping are other possibilities. If the garden is large enough, a sandy area surrounded by trees and stout, thornless shrubs where the children can build dens and play-houses will give endless opportunities for play. Whatever you make for children and however attractive you think it is, do leave something to their imagination. Not everything needs to be finished off completely.

More sand outside than inside the sandpit is no problem when the sandpit is sunk into on a paved terrace.

Nice to look at, fun to play on, and also providing a possible sitting area. With a good pair of hands and green fingers you will go a long way.

5 Garden ornaments

For centuries gardens have been decorated not only with plants but also with non-living things. Pots, vases, tubs, and statues are the obvious additions to plants but garden furniture should not be overlooked for its ornamental appeal. Water can also be regarded as an ornamental feature in gardens.

Water in the garden

Water was one of the earliest things used to make gardens look more attractive. As it is indispensible for all life, every important ci-

Right: An ancient design in contemporary terms: the well and the canal, the water supply for the garden.

Below: An old well has been given a central place in the garden. Originally grass was grown around a well to reduce dust in summer and mud in winter.

vilization developed in close proximity to water. The Chinese civilization arose on the banks of the Yellow River, the Egyptians along the banks of the Nile, while Persia owes its origins to the Tigris and Euphrates Rivers. Irrigation systems became highly developed and water was led to gardens through a system of tunnels and canals.

The Persians divided up their gardens into quarters, using water, the source of all life, as the centre point.

The essential water tank be-came a decorative feature in its own right. It was soon noticed that the water's surface in a "raised" tank reflected

more light than one at ground level and that the plants and fish in the water could be seen more easily. Besides, it was easier to scoop water out of a container raised up from the ground. However, there are problems with water tanks raised above ground level.

Fluctuating temperatures cause concrete and cement to expand and contract, while basins made of stone, brickwork, and cement can leak noticeably after a hard winter. Nowadays, various artificial materials can be used to make a waterproof lining for the pool, and the edge of the fabric can be hidden under a rim of projecting slabs or decorative stones.

The classical pool

 The classical pool always has a formal, often geometric, shape. The natural pro-

A classical pool. The Persians decorated their pools with ceramic tiles.

perties, of water reflecting, sparkling, splashing, and cooling are emphasized in its design. A fountain or water spout provides moving vertical lines that contrast with the water's still surface. This type of pool can be sited anywhere in the formal garden, which means that you do not need to worry about siting it in a lower or higher part of your garden. It must, of course, fit in with its immediate surroundings. The water with its statues and fountains, is the focal point of the classical pool, not the plants.

The informal pool

Most modern pools have lost their original function as water reservoirs, and creating an informal pool is a very different matter from creating a classical pool. Reflecting its surroundings is still an important element of an informal pool, but ponds, streams, and little waterfalls are purposely laid out to make it look as if the water has reached that part of the garden quite naturally. To achieve this effect, a water feature will be sited at the lowest point in the garden or part of the garden. A pool like this is

often surrounded by marginal plants and/or a bog garden. Much more emphasis is placed on the plants and the animal life in, on, and around the pond. However, never let your pool become so natural looking that it becomes overgrown all the way round; always keep one side open so that you look into it.

Also, be careful not to let more than a third of the water surface be covered with plants or you will loose the water's reflective quality.

Although extra ornamentation in the form of urns, statues on pedestals, vases, and carved fountains is not generally appropriate for informal pools, modern types of ornamentation, particularly features with organic shapes, can complement its natural look. More information on ponds can be found in Chapter 14, where there is a detailed description of how to make various types of water feature.

Ornaments and materials

It is a difficult matter to discuss garden ornaments, because so much depends on individual taste.

Some say that a garden should look nice on its own and that it does not need any additional ornaments; others say that, from time immemorial, statues, vases, urns, and even garden seats have added the finishing touch to a garden's overall effect. However, all would agree that whatever the decoration it must fit in with its surroundings.

In the oldest gardens in Persia and Egypt wood was used for arbours and pergolas, and the Chinese used stone for decorative features. Whatever the ornament, natural materials were always the starting point. In the West, however, taste was different, and natural materials were not always available. Cast iron, brick, and lead were the new materials used here. These were considered natural looking in the garden and a few years of weathering were thought to make them even more attractive. All kinds of tricks

Leave part of the water surface free of plants so that it can reflect the surroundings.

This concrete statue will age very quickly if it is smeared with yogurt.

were used to make new material look older than it was. Nowadays it is the turn of concrete and plastic to receive treatment to disguise their "unnatural" appearances. You can age *concrete* relatively quickly by smearing it with yogurt or buttermilk. It will look old even quicker if, after treating it, you place it near to where it will be smothered in exhaust gases or in a polluted atmosphere. You can even treat plastic so that it looks like bronze or wood.

Welded wire mesh is often used to support climbing plants, but galvanized wire is "out" because people think rusty wire looks more natural.

Sculpture can now be made from *polyester resin*, a synthetic resin that is indistinguishable from

Seats and statues

Most people have no trouble finding a suitable place in the garden for a seat, but often less attention is paid to how comfortable the seat is. The idea of a garden seat is that it should invite you to sit down, to tempt you to a particular spot in the garden. And if you are sitting there alone, there really ought to be something to be seen. A garden seat is often positioned in an alcove, nestling between hedges in an arbour, or with some protection behind it. There is an enormous choice in both materials and styles. What you choose will depend on your personal taste and the function you want the seat to fulfil. Do you prefer to have something that looks nice or does the look of it not matter as long as it is comfortable to sit on? Think about all the advantages and disadvantages of the material. Will the wood dry quickly or remain wet for too long after a rain storm? Although wrought iron looks very attractive, are the metal bars going to be imprinted on your back for the next three days after you've been sitting on the seat for an hour? Can the chairs be left out of doors summer and winter or are they so heavy that they have to be left outside anyway, whether or not they are weatherproof? How much time is going to be taken up in maintenance? A statue similarly attracts attention so do not hide it among the shrubs! Let it stand out in an area that has been planted appropriately so that it does not com-pete with the statue for attention. A restful planting scheme of vertical grasses, yucca, and foliage plants would be ideal. Whether you like classical shapes or prefer modern works of art, the possibilities are almost endless, and an abstract sculpture in which everyone can see something different will make a bold contribution to the interplay of shape and line in your garden.

Left: *This iron furniture, soft-green table, and chairs look attractive. It is, however, doubtful whether they are comfortable to sit on.*

This hardwood steamer chair can be kept out of doors. A cushion makes it very comfortable to lie on.

Stones and water, sundials, and gnomes

If you would like to have a water feature but a pond is out of the question, then a millstone or a bubble fountain will make a lovely addition to your garden. It's a simple matter to make provision for the water to be pumped round. Like a birdbath it should be sited in a quiet corner among shrubs and other greenery that will protect it.

Sundials will only tell the time if they are positioned in the sun. This is why a sundial is a typical ornament in the herb or rose garden. It would be out of place in a shady corner where a birdbath would be appropriate.

Most people think a concrete frog or duck looks nice on the edge of a pond, but everyone turns their noses up at gnomes. Yet in the seventeenth and eighteenth centuries these were frequently

A new millstone made of grey concrete is hollow inside and slightly hollowed out above.
The tank is filled with coarse gravel and the water is circulated by a pump.

used as garden ornaments. There was once fierce competition between statues of angels and other classical figures on the one hand, and gnomes on the other.

In the end the choice and position of garden ornaments come down to one thing: whether classical or modern in material or style, only you and the immediate surroundings will determine whether or not the feature is going to be appropriate for the place where you want to put it.

Above left: *A sundial needs to be placed in the sun.*

Below left: *This sculpture looks lovely in these surroundings.*

Pots, vases, and urns

Pots, urns, troughs, vases, amphoras, and containers in various styles and materials are used to decorate our gardens. Although urns were originally used to hold the ashes of the cremated dead, these decorative pots soon came to be used to propagate and grow plants. In areas with a low rainfall this method of growing plants is ideal. The pots are set close to the house or even on the windowsill where they will catch rain dripping from the roof. Whether beside a well, a water tank, on the terrace, or by the kitchen door, these pots are always situated close to a source of water because plants growing in earthenware should ideally be watered twice a day. This applies not only to the warmer parts of Europe such as the Mediterranean countries, which experience winter rainfall only, but also to regions that have cooler

Page 210: *These jolly gnomes fit in well here.*

climates.Some urns and pots are so beautifully shaped and so richly decorated that you really would not want to put plants in them at all! On the other hand, the shapes of urns and vases lend themselves toa covering of flowers and foliage. Sometimes the decoration of the pot become hidden under flowers. You can grow almost any kinds of plant in pots. Perennials, annuals and biennials, bulbs and tubers, and even trees are suitable for larger or smaller containers of the appropriate size.

A climbing rose has been deliberately trained over this lead urn. The dark colour of the urn emphasizes the light 'New Dawn.'

It goes without saying that a tree will need a very large pot or, preferably, a concrete tub.

Container plants

The introduction of many new plant species from the tropical and subtropical parts of the world has brought with it many problems. Many of these plants cannot survive in temperate zones because the winters are too cold and wet there.The differences between countries can be very great. It is impossible to overwinter a bottlebrush, *Callistemon citrinus*, or an *Abutilon megapotanicum* out of doors in most of western, central, and northern Europe, but in some parts of southern England these plants are unaffected by the climate and even increase in size each year. In France people used to put orange trees, in tubs outside in the castle gardens. (If you ask for "a little orange tree" you will usually be sold x *Citrofortunella microcarpa*, calamondin.) The orange, which is a native of southeast Asia, will die however during the cold winters in France and the rest of northern Europe, so a way had to be found to overwinter it safely. From the second half of the sixteenth century people began to build orangeries, glazed lean-to conservatories, against the walls of the house. Twice a year the plants, sometimes even trees, had to be moved into or out of the orangery. This job was made easier if the plants were grown in pots or tubs. Because these plants have to overwinter under higher temperatures than normal and as they are grown in containers, they are referred to as container plants. Whether a plant is classified as a container plant also depends on the country it is being grown in. For example, *Bougainvillea* is a container plant in Northern Europe while round the Mediterranean it is considered a hardy climber for pergolas and arbours.

There is more about pots and containers in Chapter 15 under "container gardening."

Container plants in winter

Before you succumb to the charms of a container plant, remember that it cannot remain outside during the winter but will have to be put somewhere else for protection.

In some countries nurserymen offer a "winter quarters" service: you take your plants along in late autumn and collect them again after the last night frost in spring. This takes some organizing on the part of gardeners and not everyone has so much time, effort, and money to spend on their plants. If you have a room that is cool and light during the winter, it will provide perfect winter quarters for your container plants.

In northern and western Europe Bougainvillea *must be treated as a container plant because it will not survive an average winter out of doors.*

Wooden barrels make outstanding containers. In this case the container plant, a hydrangea, can remain out of doors throughout the winter.

You can also put your plants in the conservatory providing you don't forget to water them occasionally.

The living room will be too dry and warm if you have central heating.

Casting an ornament

You can make casts of all sorts of attractive objects once you have the right materials available to do this. You will need:

- an attractive object
- a board, larger than the object
- liquid latex (available in a hobby shop)
- soft soap
- a soft brush
- cement
- sand
- water
- a measuring jug
- a large bowl (washing-up bowl or similar)
- small scoop or trowel

Method:

- Look for a simple shape that is not too big to handle. It can be anything, a statue, a fruit or a half-relief scene. Remove all the dust from it and put it on the board. With a fruit, put the least interesting side downwards.

- First of all make the mould. Using the brush spread the liquid latex in thin layers over the object (1). Each layer must be allowed to set before the next one is applied.
For a simple shape three to four layers will be sufficient. Very intricate shapes or very large objects will need more layers.

- To support the mould well it is advisable to cover a fairly wide strip of the board with latex (2). The brush can always be cleaned with water and soft soap.

- Remove the object and wait until the latex has turned a pale yellow colour (3).
The latex has now set and the mould is ready.

- A fairly shallow mould must now be supported on the board with sand (4). If the mould is large or rounded it is easier to make an imprint of the object in a bucket of sand so that the mould is supported all the way round. Put the rubber mould in the imprint in the sand.

- Mix the cement in a large container. Take one part cement to three parts sharp sand or silver sand (5) and mix the ingredients well (6).

- Make the mixture into a paste by gradually adding small amounts of water and mixing it in thoroughly. Do not add too much water at one go. The paste is ready when it is soft but does not fall off the trowel (7).

Put the mixture into the mould and tap the board or bucket quite hard at regular intervals to get rid of any air bubbles trapped in the cement (8 and 9).

- Leave the mixture to set for at least 24 hours. Keep it out of the sun (10).

- Your garden ornament is now finished.

You can make a second and third object with the mould, in fact as many as you want. If you want to keep the rubber mould you must dry it well after use and dust it with a thin layer of talcum powder.
If you want to "age" the new ornament quickly you can smear it with a layer of yogurt or buttermilk. If you want to colour it, use cement paint. Begin with a simple shape and if you get the taste for it, you can make more complicated items as your skill develops.

1. First make the mould. Brush thin layers of latex over the object. Each layer must be allowed to set before the next one is added.

2. Put a fairly broad strip of latex on to the board as well.

3. Remove the object and wait until the latex has become pale yellow. The mould is now ready.

4. A fairly shallow mould must be supported on the board with sand.

5. Mix the cement in a large bowl. Use one part cement to three parts sharp sand or silver sand.

6. Mix these ingredients well. Make a paste by gradually adding small amounts of water and mixing well.

7. *The mixture must be soft but must not drop off the trowel.*

8. *Transfer the mixture to the mould.*

9. *Give the board or bucket frequent sharp taps to remove air bubbles trapped in the cement.*

10. *Leave the cement to harden for at least 24 hours, out of the sun.*

11. *The final result: a splendid decoration for your garden.*

Part 3

*L*laying out
the vegetable garden

6 Food from your garden

People rarely consider a vegetable garden to be a thing of beauty; after all, there is practically nothing to see, particularly in the winter. A vegetable plot like that is better laid out somewhere at the back of the garden, out of sight. As you will no doubt have guessed by now this part of the book will try to prove that the opposite is true. By introducing structure into a vegetable garden and adding ornamental, eye-catching elements, you can create a vegetable garden that certainly is a pleasure to look at

Siting and arranging the vegetable garden

The right conditions are even more important for vegetables than for ornamental plants. After all, you want your vegetables to grow as well as possible because the end product must be healthy and, if at all possible, free of chemical sprays. What is the ideal position for vegetable crops, and how should the plot be divided up? Can things be grown all mixed up? Will certain plants need extra protection? Is it

This vegetable garden is enclosed by a border of flowering plants and shrubs.

wise to combine herbs and other ornamental plants with the vegetables?

Sunny and easily accessible

♣ If the area round the house has not yet been divided up, choose the sunniest and most sheltered plot because this is the most suitable for the vegetable garden. Most vegetables need six to eight hours of sun a day. It is also important that the plot is close to the house and easily accessible. The fun will soon wear off when the carrots you fancy for lunch on a rainy day can only be reached by crossing over wet grass, borders, and lawns. A well drained soil is the best for growing vegetables, and the soil's fertility can always be improved by the use of fertilizer. You will find a lot of information on this subject in the section "Improving the soil" in the chapter "A closer look at the soil."

Manuring the vegetable garden

♣ As crops are constantly being removed from the vegetable garden, compared with the ornamental garden, a great deal more plant nutrients will be taken up and removed from the soil. It is therefore even more important than in an ornamental garden to manure a vegetable plot well. With new crops there will be a need for supplementary fertilizers. You can also take advantage of the plant nutrients that the garden, or rather the plants, provide for free. Leguminous plants, such as peas and beans, develop nodules on their roots that contain bacteria. The bacteria absorb the free nitrogen from the air and this is taken up by the root nodules. You can take advantage of this extra nitrogen by growing leaf vegetables on the patch where legumes were grown. The foliage of the legumes is cut back and the roots are left in the ground. Sowing a green manure is one alternative to leaving a patch fallow, with the soil exposed to

This vegetable garden has everything for a festive meal: vegetables and cut flowers at Bingerden House, Netherlands.

wind and rain and liable to lose nutrients. Plants not intended as crops are grown as green manure. They help to preserve the structure of the soil by preventing the development of a hard crust. Furthermore, organic matter is being added and, at the same time, the deep root systems of plants such as lucerne and rye grass improve the soil's drainage.

The roots of leguminous plants have root nodules which fix nitrogen.

Leguminous green manures also add nitrogen to the soil. Green manures are mainly sown as a late crop that freezes during the winter, which is later raked off or dug in. However, to prevent fresh material (which will attract harmful soil-living insects) from being added to the soil, it is better to mow the green crop and return it to the soil via the compost heap.

Protection

♣ Most plants dislike wind, and wind damage can make a the leaves tough and hard. Vegetable crops therefore need protection on the north and west, since most winds come from these directions. Make no mistake, however: the drying east wind can also be a threat

The alder forms a lovely thick hedge, which keeps out the wind.

Is your vegetable garden alongside a busy road? Then plant a hedge of snowberry, Symphoricarpus. This is good at filtering and purifying the air.

especially in the spring when it blows fiercely. Leave the south side open to avoid shade, and remember that protection on all sides of a garden will increase the risk of damage from night frosts.

Sacrificing part of the vegetable plot to grow a protective hedge is not a popular solution with many people. A hedge seems to produce nothing but work and dead leaves and it takes up the space that could be better used to grow a couple more rows of French beans. Yet it is better to plant a hedge, even a narrow one, that has more to offer your vegetable plot by way of protection than an extra ten bags of French beans in the deep freeze.

The advantages of a hedge

♣ If your vegetable garden is alongside a road you will want to prevent deposits from vehicle exhausts landing on your crops. In that case a hedge can serve as a green buffer. Snowberry (*Symphoricarpus albus*), for example, is widely planted because of its ability to filter and purify the air.

Not every vegetable garden is alongside a road, but the wind blows everywhere. As a result, the nutrient-rich upper layer of soil can be blown away. A hedge can offer protection against this. It is better to plant a hedge as a windbreak on the north, west, and perhaps east side of the plot. A hedge will also help to keep the soil warm. In an open garden the warm and cold air currents mix together but warm air will always settle just above the surface. This is particularly beneficial in the spring when night frosts could damage young plants. A garden enclosed on all sides is at a disadvantage because the different layers of air do not mix so much, and the cold air will remain still and will sink to the ground. Reducing the wind's strength will also reduce the amount of evaporation.

The important layer of water vapour that exists in the air just above the plants will not be removed immediately. This is especially important in the case of winds off the sea which, because of their high salt content, have a marked drying effect.

Finally a hedge encourages animal life. It provides nesting sites for birds which, among other things, will eat harmful insects. Other useful creatures such as predatory mites, ladybirds, and ichneumon flies find a home in a hedge.

Thus planting a hedge creates a special microclimate in your garden.

The disadvantages of a hedge

♣ There are of course disadvantages in having a hedge. For example, it takes up space and uses water and plant nutrients. You can prevent the roots from encroaching on your garden in their search for food by cutting through them each year and by digging a trench which you fill with manure. The roots will then not have too far to go.

A young hedge will take water from the crops at first but, once it is properly established, its roots will bring up food and water from deeper down in the soil.

Hedges throw a lot of shade so, certainly in small gardens, it is advisable to plant them only on the north and west sides.

That hedges are a source of disease is a greatly exaggerated suggestion. There are certainly a few pests and diseases that overwinter on some shrubs: the black bean aphid overwinters on the spindle, wheat rust on barberry, and fireblight is at home on, among other shrubs, hawthorn and medlar.

However, these drawbacks can easily be overcome and the balance is certainly in favour of a hedge as a windbreak.

Hawthorn, privet, hornbeam, beech, tree of life, field maple, and yew are suitable for narrow, closely clipped hedges. Hawthorn and privet are also resistant to winds off the sea.

A hawthorn hedge provides nesting sites for birds.
Various species of birds eat harmful insects.

Although the fences are narrow and keep the wind out, conditions here are unfavourable for vegetables because the fences cause turbulence and draughts and throw too much shade.

If your garden is so small that you really cannot spare a strip of ground for a hedge, you will have to rely for protection on a screen of, for example, rush matting, posts, windbreak netting, a fence of willow branches, wooden laths, sleepers, and brick.

Whatever kind of screen you choose make sure it is not completely closed: a solid barrier causes turbulence and down-draughts.

Tip

What about a hedge of red- and blackcurrants, raspberries, sweet corn, petit pois, marrowfat peas, or stick beans? These will not encourage bird and insect life but they are produc-tive.

Dividing up the space

Allow on average 50m² (60yd²) per person for the vegetable garden and a further 25m² (35yd²) for potatoes. You will then be able to have food from your garden the whole year round. If the vegetable garden forms part of the ornamental garden and you want to make it an ornamental vegetable garden, you will probably choose attractive crops and not grow the whole range of vegetables. Crops such as potatoes, leeks, and onions are not something to go into raptures over from an aesthetic point of view. Exact measurements and quantities will then be less important and dividing up the plot will depend on the total effect you wish to create.

Even if your garden is not very big paths will be necessary for access. You need to be able to reach the plants from the main path (at least 60cm (2') wide) and, in larger gardens, via side paths. For practical reasons the crops are grown in beds no wider than 120cm (3'11"). This

You can use stick beans as a temporary hedge, which will offer protection to crops that like to grow in sheltered places.

Part of the vegetable garden: the bed for carrots and other rootvegetables. There are narrow paths between the slightly raised beds, these are advisable especially on wet soil.

Tip

Growing "warm" crops on a slope is certainly worth the effort.
Remember that the bottom of the slope is colder and damper than the slope itself, since cold air sinks. Hence there will be a "cold foot" to the slope.

width allows all the work to be done without having to stand in between the plants. On wet soil it is advisable to deepen the path somewhat and to pile the soil that was dug out to make the path on to the beds. Excess water will then drain off.

The part of the garden that lies in half shade should be reserved for strawberries, endive, beetroot, rhubarb, celery, Swiss chard, red-, white-, and blackcurrants. Crops that demand extra warmth and sunshine can be grown without glass on a slope. A south-facing slope with extra protection on the north east will benefit more from the sun. Try growing tomatoes laid on the slope, in the same way as you would grow cucumbers, courgettes, and melons.

Planting plan and crop rotation

The golden rule for everyone who has a vegetable garden should be "Every year I draw up a plan on paper taking account of crop rotation." Crop rotation means *never growing the same crop on the same patch of ground two years running.* If you grow the same crop again the following year it will take exactly the same nutrients out of the soil. The organic acids from the plants will also release new foodstuffs into the soil that other crops will be unable to make use of. Even if you add sufficient fertilizer the same crop will exhaust the soil, there will be a shortage of nutrients, and the crop will be weak and unhealthy. The roots of the plants will not develop well and production will decrease. This is known as soil exhaustion and it can occur with any crop. When you sow seed in the spring you will probably remember what was grown in that part of the garden the previous year, but what was there two or three years ago will be much more difficult to remember. Planning the layout in advance is a good way of overcoming this problem.

A planting plan is a map of the garden on which you mark the space allocated for the crops you intend to grow in any particular year. The crops can be divided into four groups on the basis of their manuring requirements and sensitivity to insects and fungi. First of all there are the brassicas and other leafy vegetables, such as spinach and lettuce. The second group includes the roots and tubers, such as beetroot, carrots, scorzonera, and onions. The legumes and vegetables that are actually fruits belong in the third group.

Potatoes, although tubers, form a separate group. If you do not want to grow potatoes you could perhaps sow annual cut flowers and/or herbs. Whatever you decide to grow this bed must also be included in the rotation scheme.

Fruit trees are permanent planting but other fruit crops, such as currants, brambles, rasp-

Peas and beans are both pulses and so they are grown in the same bed in the vegetable garden.

berries, and rhubarb should be moved every ten years. Perennial herbs should be moved after five years. You could build a terrace among these crops to provide instant pick-your-own fruit for summer outdoor parties.

Four-year or eight-year rotation?

♣ If you keep to this scheme of crop rotation the bed will be taken up in the first year by leafy vegetables, and in the second year by root crops. Potatoes are planted in the third year and in the fourth year fruits and legumes.

Although certain vegetable crops belong to a particular group they do not always have the same nutrient requirements: so leeks, which are included under the tubers, and celeriac are hungry crops while carrots, onions, and chicory

Carrots and onions are root and bulb crops that make the same demands on the soil. Planted together they are more resistant to diseases.

require very little. The leafy crops such as cauli-flower, headed cabbage, and spinach need a lot of feeding while lettuce, endive, sprouts, and curly kale can manage with considerably less. When you also take into consideration the fact that some diseases can remain in the ground for more than four years, for example clubroot in cabbage, there is something to be said for dividing the garden into eight plots and dividing up the crops into Leaf I and Leaf II, and Root I and Root II, and so on.

Intercropping

Intercropping involves growing various crops after (early, main, and late) crops and alongside other crops, often in rows.

This promotes variety in the plant and animal life in the soil. The result is often an improvement in the quality, scent, and flavour of the vegetables. With good combinations various diseases occur considerably less frequently and some combinations produce an increased yield. You do not have to plant the crops side by side in rows. To make the whole picture more attractive, you could, for example, grow a low plant with a compact leaf growth as a border round a rather taller one (beetroot with a border of carrots).

Plants are influenced by their neighbours. Tall plants shade lower-growing plants and sometimes their roots become intertwined. They can even compete with each other for water and nutrients.

Tall plants can, however, provide shelter for warmth-loving, lower crops. For example, broad beans serve as outstanding protecting for courgettes. All plants secrete particular plant acids which mobilize nutrients, and neighbouring

Strawberries and lettuces make good neighbours.

Jut forget this combination straight away: planting peas and onions together is asking for trouble.

vegetables can make use of these. A great deal is still unknown about the way plants influence each other.

You will find a few tried and tested combinations in the tips included in this chapter. You will also read more about companion planting in the section on herbs and vegetables later in this chapter.

If you do use intercropping you must make sure that the plants do not hinder each other. The soil will be used more intensively which does not only mean extra work but also more manure. The best results will be obtained if alternate rows of the different crops are sown in the

A space-saving combination: tomatoes and lettuces.

plot. You must, of course, still take crop rotation into account when using interplanting methods.

Step-by-step planting plan

♣ You must write the following down on paper and think about them, taking into account aspect, rotation, combinations, and division. You will then not forget anything when you actually start to plant:

– Make your plan of the garden to scale.
– Make a list of the crops you want to grow.
– Divide up the crops into groups: leaf, root, potatoes, and fruit (possibly 2 x leaf, 2 x tubers, etc.).

- Write down beside each vegetable how large an area it will need.
- Check on a sowing/harvesting calender whether two crops can be grown next to each other.
- Allocate the vegetables you want to grow to the most appropriate beds (it will be obvious that some may have to be crossed off your list).
- Fill any remaining space with herbs, flowers, or a green manure.
- Combinations of plants from the same group are ideal, for instance carrots and onions.
- It is better not to grow vegetables from the same family twice within one year because of disease. Remember, for example, that the crucifer family, includes the various brassicas, radish es, and members of this family that are green manures.
- The vegetables' various requirements for manure.
- The growing time of a crop, particularly in connection with succession.
- Any space-saving combinations, such as lettuce (which does not make great demands on nutrients) grown between climbing beans.
- Companion planting of crops that are mutually beneficial to each other.

Sowing

♣ Seeds can be sown directly in the place where they are to grow. However, in a vegetable garden that must look attractive and must be planted up all the time, some gardeners sow the seed elsewhere. You could sow them out of doors in a cold frame or in seed trays indoors. You will read about how to do this in the section "Maintenance – the hard work" in the chapter entitled "Various jobs." Seeds can also be sown in seed beds in the vegetable garden.

Sowing *in situ* is done either broadcast or in rows. Seed sown broadcast is scattered on a patch of ground straight out of the packet. This

method is used less frequently nowadays because of the difficulty of distinguishing between the germinating crop and germinating weeds. Also, the weeds cannot be hoed up and have to be hand weeded. Regular thinning of the seedlings is also a difficult job. An exception to this is made for purslane, spinach, turnip tops, and carrots.

Sowing in rows. Before sowing the soil is first loosened and, if necessary, watered.

Above: *Here carrot and celery seed are being mixed to see if the combination works well.*

Centre: *The seed is sown as thinly as possible in the drills.*

Below: *A rake is used to cover the seed carefully. Then the soil is bedded down firmly.*

When you sow seeds in rows the distance apart will depend on the crop. You will find information on this on the back of the seed packet.

Seeds and their secrets

♣ A gardener may only use a very little seed of some vegetables. The amount of seed in the packets from different seed firms does vary, and there may be more seed in the packet than you are going to need now. Leftover seed, if stored well, can be sown next season. However, it is useful for planning purposes to work out whether the seed has a sufficiently high germination rate. This will then avoid the unpleasant surprise of bare patches. You can test the germination of seeds as follows: put a number of seeds on a saucer between two layers of blotting paper. Water the whole saucer and put it on one side in a warm place. If about half the seed has germinated after a week the seed is still worth using. Sometimes you will see after a variety the name "F1 hybrid", for example Chiko F1 hybrid. This means that you can expect a crop which grows uniformly, in this case a Chinese cabbage with long, tight heads. F1 (*filius* is Latin for son) is the first generation after the crossing of two pure breeding lines. All the positive characteristics of several parents and grandparents have been bred into this offspring. To speed up the germination of seed that is slow to germinate, you can pregerminate or chit the seed. This process involves soaking the seed in lukewarm water for 24 hours, changing the water after 12 hours. Pour off the water and sow the seed. You can also mix the seed with damp

Tip
F1 hybrid seed is often expensive. Do not, however, be tempted to save seed from F1 hybrid plants because the next generation will have a very variable appearance and quality. Negative characteristics will come to the fore again.

sharp sand. This is put on one side in a warm, damp place until the seedlings begin to show. They are then planted very carefully, including the sand.

Using glass and plastic

♣ You often see in vegetable plots garden frames, greenhouses, and (sometimes) movable small plastic structures.

The ordinary, low cold frame is made of concrete or wooden walls with intermediate slats that support panes of glass 80 to 150cm (32 to 58″) wide. Each frame is sited as far as possible with its long axis east–west, which means that with the low side facing south the contents of the

This cold frame is rather higher than normal. This gives more opportunities for growing crops but the walls will also produce more shade.

frame will benefit as much as possible from the available light. A double frame, which has a rather higher central division (that is, 50cm (20″)), is placed north–south so that both sides receive the same amount of light.

Plants for both the vegetable and ornamental garden can be grown in frames. As a frame is warmer and more sheltered than outside, sowing can be done earlier in a frame and crops will perhaps be harvested earlier. Also, fresh crops can be started later in the year. Crops will ripen in a frame that would not do so outside. In autumn and winter the frame can be used as a storage place and a clamp for winter vegetables. There is nothing to stop you using the frame for extra decoration.

You could change the dimension to suit your needs and use it as a container for flowering annuals and biennials.

Perennials, and small trees, or shrubs are other possibilities, but you will not be able to use your

cold frame for its original purpose in the vegetable garden if you do this.

Light, air and warmth

♣ Plants in a cold frame enjoy the advantage of the sun's rays passing through the glass, while the sun's warmth is not dissipated so quickly. This, however, means that the chances of disease are usually increased because the plants are not exposed to varying weather conditions. The vegetables also remain rather soft. To achieve optimum growth the plants need ventilation, watering, and shading at the right time. The temperature will obviously be lower in cloudy conditions than in sunshine, and little sun combined with high temperature results in fast-growing, weak plants. If the lights, or panes, are raised to provide ventilation in such circumstances the temperature will drop. The humidity in the frame can also become too high and if no steps are taken there is a great risk of fungal infections and rot. Ventilation removes the surplus water vapour and lowers the humidity. If you want to put plants that have been raised in a frame out in the

In the greenhouse use water at the temperature of the greenhouse. Make a habit of refilling the watering cans again after watering and of putting them back in the greenhouse.

open, you have to acclimatize them gradually to the conditions outside. This hardening-off process consists of increasing the ventilation little by little until finally the lights are wide open, even at night. It is best to let the wind provide the ventilation. Do not suppose, on the other hand, that it is always too damp inside the frame, since plants growing in warmer conditions need more water. It is better to water the young plants lightly at regular intervals than to give them a lot of water now and then. If you water infrequently the fluctuations in temperature and humidity will be too great. If conditions are too dry, growth will be held back, and remember never to water in full sun.

Shading

♣ When the temperature in the frame becomes too high, mesh fabric shading can be used to keep out the sun. During long sunny spells ready-to-use shading washes, which do not wash off in the rain, or a solution of whitewash can be painted on to the glass. If you want to protect the frame against cold you can lay rush matting or old blankets over the top. Because the cold frame and greenhouse are used intensively it is advisable to replace the top 10cm (4") of soil annually with good garden soil or compost.

Plastic as an aid

♣ In recent years the use of plastic has expanded enormously. It has plenty of practical possibilities for the amateur gardener. One of these possibilities is a plastic greenhouse of treated timber with a reinforced plastic cover.

A glimpse inside a home-made plastic tunnel. For all the advantages that such a tunnel offers, you must remember that hoeing and weeding is very awkward under plastic.

Left: *The young peas are protected with perforated plastic film.*

Right: *When the peas are larger the film can be removed.*

Storm-proof yet light, such a greenhouse costs about 60% less than a conventional glass house. Foundations are not necessary and the temperature within is maintained evenly because, in sunny weather, the sunlight is tempered by the – often greenish – plastic. Unfortunately, the plastic only lasts about ten years or so. After that you are left with environmentally unfriendly rubbish.

Tunnels are very cheap to make. You can use bicycle rims and transparent plastic sheeting, but spring steel and electric conduits can also be bent into shape. Tunnels are easy to put up and take down, so that they can be moved even during the growing season, and included in the rotation scheme. They can advance the growing season by as much as six weeks.

The great advantage in using the so-called floating mulches, which are made of plastic or fleecy film, is that ventilation and watering are not necessary since the film is porous and expands as the plants grow. However, for toma-

Tip

Use brand-new, absolutely clean film especially for the early and late crops of leafy vegetables so that the plants can obtain maximum benefit from the light. If it is not clear or it is dirty the light will not penetrate to the crop and the nitrate level in the leaves will rise enormously.

Tip

If you want to protect individual plants against slugs or you want to keep young plants warm and protected, then the ordinary litre (2 pint), or better still 2 litre (4 pint), plastic bottles provide an answer. Cut off the bottom and put the tube over the plant.

toes the special covers hold too much moisture, in spite of the perforations, and the high humidity encourages disease.

You need to use a piece of film that is bigger than the actual seed bed to allow for the upward growth of the crop underneath it. Make sure that the film is firmly fixed down at the edges. A crop that is grown under film or fleece can be harvested fourteen days earlier than one grown outside. The material is very delicate and so will last only two years at the most.

Plastic seldom enhances the look of the vegetable garden, so it is advisable to avoid the use of this material if you are mainly concerned with the ornamental appeal of your vegetable garden.

Growing tips

• *Strawberries* like a deep, loose, humus-rich and moisture- retaining soil. Do not, however, plant them too deep because that will hinder regrowth and the formation of buds. It will also increase the chance of fungal infection. Planting must be done with great care.

Make a reasonably large hole and make a small mound in the centre over which you spread very carefully the roots of the strawberry plant. Then cover the roots with soil and firm it down well. This ensures that the heart of the plant is above the soil's surface. Give sufficient water during the time of growth. Strawberries have lovely leaves and are not out of place in a border around herb and vegetable beds.

• *Endive* should only be sown around the longest day. The soil needs to have warmed up if its cultivation is to be a success. If you sow endive in cold soil it will readily bolt later.

The same applies for *Chinese cabbage, loose-leaf lettuce, radicchio,* and *pak choi.* Sow them in situ and do not transplant them, otherwise they will quickly bolt. Radicchio, pak choi and *curly en-*

These antique glass cloches can easily be moved and can protect a single plant or a patch of seeds.

dive are useful plants for the ornamental vegetable garden.

• *Dwarf beans* have a shorter growing season and you can harvest them earlier than *climbing beans* which, however, give a better yield and suffer less from fungal diseases. The *French bean* is the most sensitive variety which does not always succeed, especially on damp, acid soil. Try one of the much stronger *runner beans* as a trouble-free alternative. However, this must be harvested young.

Cold and wet are the beans' greatest enemies. In wet years the seed sometimes will not germinate because it rots. On the other hand in dry conditions the seed can shrivel. To be certain of germination in both situations you can treat the seed beforehand with salad oil or liquid soap: the oily layer will prevent the seed from drying out and will also keep it from direct contact with moisture.

The *scarlet runner* is the prettiest of the bean family and makes an attractive feature in the vegetable garden. The *soya bean* should be sown in place in mid May. The bushes, which have long velvety leaves, reach a height of 60–70cm (24–28″).

• Anyone who has grown *cabbages* will know all about clubroot. This is caused by a slime mould which affects the roots of all crucifers It develops growths within the roots which prevent the plant taking up sufficient nutrients and water from the soil. The plant wilts and the foliage has a greyish colour. The roots also de-

velop tuberous swellings. This fungus prefers light, acid soil and can survive in the ground for many years. Use at least a five-year rotation and try to raise the pH of the soil by adding lime. A spring crop can be attempted on infected soil since the fungus only becomes active above 160°C (600°F). If you still want to grow cabbages without waiting several years, then you can grow them in a large bottomless pot filled with alkaline compost. Sink the pot in the soil up to the rim.

Nice brassicas are *red cabbage, broccoli, Chinese broccoli*, and the greenish yellow *cauliflower* 'Romanesco.' *Purple sprouting broccoli* can also fit into the colour scheme of your vegetable

If you plant the cabbage in fresh soil in a pot you will kill two birds with one stone: there is hardly any chance of clubroot and the plant can be moved at any time to another part of the garden where its lovely foliage will provide an extra feature.

Tip

Lovers of sweetcorn: if fodder maize is being grown within 200m (218yd) of your supersweet sweetcorn there is a good chance that cross pollination will take place. The sugar content of your sweetcorn will then be very disappointing.

garden. Sometimes let the cabbages bolt: each plant will provide a bouquet for the garden table. Cabbage flowers are visited by the small and large white butterflies, which lay a great many eggs on the leaves.

• Sweetcorn must be wind pollinated so the rows need to be 75cm (30″) apart. The seeds are big enough to be sown individually in the soil 25cm (10″) apart. A thick layer of compost between the rows will prevent the roots drying

Left: *The male flower appears at the tip of the sweetcorn plant.*

Centre: *You can see the female flower in the leaf axil.*

Right: *The corn cob, which develops after pollination. The cob is ripe when the silks are totally dry and brown.*

out and provide extra nutrients. You can usually harvest two or three cobs per plant. A good way to tell if they are ripe is by the dark colour of the silks round the cobs. You can easily break the cobs from the leaf axils by hand.

• Because the roots of *leeks* need a lot of oxygen and develop best in loose soil, to produce the desired long white shank leeks are planted very deep. Make a shallow groove along the row and make deep holes, as much as 18cm (7″) deep, at intervals with a dibber. Drop the seedlings into the holes. Do not firm the soil in the holes but leave the small plants loose in their holes with their centres open and bare. This way the roots will acquire sufficient oxygen. The holes will slowly fill up with earth washed in by the rain. In a dry period water the furrows and the holes will thus gradually fill up. Some people prepare a thin paste of cow manure and dip the roots in this before planting. The plants stand straight up and go on growing immediately. Do not make the paste too thick or it could have the opposite effect.

• *Radishes* must have moist conditions while they are growing. A constant supply of water will mean they will grow without interruption. Radishes grown under an erratic watering regi-

me will be dry and bitter. Manure is not required but a good quantity of compost can be added. A damp soil surface discourages the flea beetle. If you have no compost, spread some lime or wood ash because flea beetles hate them.

Besides, the soil for radishes should be on the alkaline side. Bolted radishes produce a cloud of white to pale lilac flowers on which a mass of white butterflies will descend. People sometimes deliberately leave some radishes to flower in a corner of the garden to tempt these butterflies away from the cabbages.

• A lime-rich compost is a good basis for all *lettuce* varieties. An investigation of your soil will show whether further fertilizer is necessary. Be careful when applying nitrogen and do not apply it as a top dressing because this will cause an unnecessary increase in the lettuce's nitrate content. Headed lettuces bolt easily for various reasons.

First the variety sown may not be right for the season. There are certain varieties suitable for the earliest sowing, including 'Lakeland,' and others for summer and autumn sowing. An exception to this is the variety 'Marvel of Four Seasons,' a melt-in-the-mouth lettuce with reddish-brown crinkled leaves that can be sown at any time of year. Lettuce also bolts if the soil temperature is too high when it is sown.

Finally, transplanted lettuce bolts more easily than that grown *in situ. Crisphead lettuce, cos lettuce*, and *butterhead* come in red and yellow colours and the leaves are decorative. Clumps of *lamb's lettuce* (no relation to the lettuce) can be used as edging.

• *Broad beans* need a windy position because the more freely the wind can blow through the rows, the better the seed sets.

Plant broad beans in deep, loosened soil at a distance of 10–15cm (4–6″) apart with rows 70cm (28″) apart. It does not matter if you have to shorten the tap root when you transplant the beans since plants with shortened roots remain

New Zealand spinach is a delicious crop, and ttractive to look at. It can also be grown in pots.

smaller and will flower earlier. For this reason some gardeners chop through the tap root with the spade even if the beans are not being transplanted.

• The roots of *Belgian chicory* can stand some frost providing they are left in the soil. However, they are very vulnerable if they have been dug up and lie on top of the soil. Therefore leave the roots in the ground that you do not need immediately for forcing indoors.

Belgian chicory is usually dug up in October/November. After the roots have been dug and perhaps allowed to ripen outdoors, the foliage is trimmed to a few centimetres (inches) above the root.

The growing point must be visible. Chicory sown early is very likely to bolt. The plant will then flower in the summer which is not the intention but the flowers are a beautiful shade of blue so you could perhaps deliberately sow a couple of plants too early.

• The greatest threat to *carrots* is the carrot fly, which prefers to lay its eggs in loose, open soil.

This is how Belgian chicory grows in the garden during the summer. It looks like a leafy vegetable.

After the chicory has been dug up it is left on the surface for a day or two.

Before it is replanted for forcing the foliage is cut off 4cm (2") above the root. The growing point must be clearly visible.

Since the carrot fly can emerge about the end of April, you must make sure that the seed is sown and the soil well firmed down before this.

Try to sow the seed very thinly to avoid having to thin the seedlings later, because each time the soil is disturbed and extra air enters it is to the grubs' advantage. Remove weeds between the rows by hand in good time and avoid hoeing. When you do finally begin to harvest never pull out the thickest clumps first.

This will expose the upper surface of neighbouring roots just where the root fly is going to lay her eggs. Pull out your meal step by step and tread the soil down hard afterwards.

You can edge various beds with carrots because the fine leaves form a straight, thick border.

Vegetables for the ornamental garden

♣ There are many vegetables that are striking because of their shape, flowers, and/or colour. These can therefore be used outside the vegetable garden. In many cases you will not be able to harvest these crops since that would spoil the effect.

Artichokes and cardoons have lovely leaves and flowers. They introduce height into the vegetable garden and border. Beetroot has very decorative foliage with scarlet leaf ribs. Red and yellow *Atriplex* have nice seed heads apart from their decorative foliage.

The bright red rhubarb can be planted for its flower heads (they can be eaten young!) and its red leaf stems. Swiss chard has bluish leaves that are crinkly and indented; it also produces wide branching heads of white flowers.

The onion is perhaps not so nice, although the Egyptian or tree onion is interesting with its pear-shaped bulblets. These soon sprout in the air and the stems twist into all kinds of shapes. The tree onion grows well in sun and shade and its bulbs make flavoursome onions.

Winter purslane and summer purslane are species that flower freely (white and pinkish white) and self-seed freely. They are attractive, low-growing plants that are sometimes regarded as weeds.

The leaves of courgettes are indented and have silvery flecks. These plants do not produce trailing stems. If you want to grow them in containers you will need to give them plenty of water. You will be rewarded with pretty foliage and edible, yellow flowers.

Protecting crops in the vegetable garden

♣ In Part 4 you will find more about animals, welcome and unwelcome, in the garden. You will see that there are many draw-

Courgettes have large, edible flowers and leaves with silver-grey flecks. This is not a disease! It is a characteristic of courgettes.

backs to pesticides, chemical or natural, and that the use of these is very often far from necessary. If nature is given time, a disease will not develop into a plague and the balance will be restored. In the vegetable garden it is difficult to wait, because you want to eat the vegetables, not the parasites.

If you do want to intervene, then use the least damaging means. Often home-made remedies are sufficient against various diseases and pests. The following are intended particularly for those that attack the vegetable garden.

– Infusion of stinging nettles: you pick a large bunch of nettles and let them stand in a bucket of water for 24 to 36 hours; then sieve the infusion, dilute it two to ten times with water and spray it over the affected crop. The dilution depends on the crop and the insect that is to be eradicated.

You can use a nettle infusion against all kinds of insects, including aphids. In many cases it will be necessary to repeat the treatment. If nettles stand in water for more than 36 hours they begin to smell unpleasant. After about eight days this liquid manure can be applied as supplementary feed to the base of plants, for example to newly planted brassicas. Diluted it is used as a foliar feed, as a compost starter, and as a spray against young caterpillars.

– For slugs you can sink small pots containing a little beer up to their rims in the soil around the threatened plants. Slugs, which love beer,

Left: A whole colony of aphids. Although the pests can be got rid of with an infusion of liquid manure made from nettles it is more sensible at this stage to pull up the plant and destroy it.

Centre: Caterpillars will strip a cabbage plant in no time. Act when the caterpillars are still small.

Right: The cabbage root fly cannot lay her eggs on the roots of the plant if she is prevented from doing so by a collar.

You can anticipate a lot of slugs, especially in wet years. You can remove them by hand or bury pots of beer among the crops. The slugs will drown in the beer.

fall in and drown. Putting broken egg-shells round the plants has no effect at all on the slugs.
– The carrot fly, onion fly, and cabbage root fly are kept away by using mesh. The carrot fly and cabbage root fly can also be attacked with dried tansy leaves applied at a rate of 1gm (a pinch) per m² (1.2yd²).
– The maggot of the cabbage root fly will not have a chance if a collar is fitted round the stems of cabbage seedlings.
– The onion fly can be kept off onions by interplanting the rows with carrots. The same pattern will keep away the carrot fly.
– Anti-insect mesh reduces the amount of light reaching the plants because of its fine structure.
You need to sow the protected crop a week

earlier than an unprotected if you want it to keep pace with your planting scheme.

- By sowing clover under cabbages you can avoid many insect attacks. Harmful flies and butterflies will no longer be able to recognize the contours of the cabbage and will fly on. Grass clippings have the same effect. Spread a thin layer between and under the cabbage plants each week.

- Chamomile tea is used to prevent damping off in seedlings, which is caused by fungi. Soak 5gm (1/4oz) dried or 10gm (1/2oz) fresh flowers for a day in 1 litre (2pints) water.

Grey moulds spread very rapidly under damp conditions. Keep sufficient space between raspberries and spray them with horsetail tea.

African marigolds discourage eelworms. They clear the soil and keep it in top condition for tomatoes. Here you see the small-flowered Tagetes patula.

The seeds and the young seedlings are moistened with this infusion.

- To increase the resistance of crops to fungal infections you can spray them with horsetail tea. You let 30gm (1oz) dried horsetail, *Equisetum arvense*, boil in 1 litre (2 pints) of water for a quarter of an hour; then after letting it steep for at least 24 hours dilute it with water (one part liquid to four parts water).

Stir well and spray it on. Do spray before signs of infection appear and repeat the application every three weeks.

- Creatures living in the soil, such as leatherjackets and cockchafer grubs, can be treated with a mixture of sawdust, bran, and molasses or syrup.

Mix it well and spread it between the plants in the evening. The mixture makes the in sects so lethargic that they become an easy prey for birds. All soil-living insects are attracted by fresh green material in the soil, so never dig in a fresh green manure.

- African marigolds and nasturtiums appear to give off substances that, when absorbed by neighbouring plants, make them unattractive to white fly. Sow them in the vicinity of tomatoes, cucumbers, and gherkins.
- Harmful nematodes, including eelworms, occur fairly frequently. A good crop rotation is desirable and can be supported by planting African marigolds in places affected by nematodes. The species *Tagetes tenuifolia* works well.

The Tagetes Polynema can easily reach a height of 2.5m (9'6"). The seeds are marketed on seed tape: very handy for using as a hedge!

Giant among the African marigolds

♣ The giant among the African marigolds, *Tagetes* 'Polynema,' has only recently been brought on to the Dutch market. According to researchers, the development of *Tagetes* Polynema means that the problem of the eelworms which attack the roots of crops has been solved. These African marigold attract 97% of the eelworms, which subsequently die. This is definitely not a small plant, because it can grow to 2.5m (8'2") which makes it especially suitable for use as a windbreak in a private garden. The roots go down to a depth of 1.5m (4'11") in the soil which is cleared of eelworm to that depth. 'Polynema' also acts as a source of nitrogen which is released into the soil the year after the plant is grown. You should let the crop grow for at least three months, then cut off the foliage, leaving the roots in the soil. Chop it up and leave it on the ground for a fortnight. Next dig the dead material into the ground. To be sure of success keep the ground in which the plant is growing free of weeds. The area where the African marigolds were grown will remain free of eelworms for three years. This is a comforting thought when you remember that eelworms are the indirect cause of fungal, viral, and bacterial diseases because when these creatures damage the roots they provide access for these diseases. Apart from using it as a hedge you could also include this plant in the crop rotation scheme for your vegetable garden. You have the opportunity to prevent many diseases in an environmentally friendly way and to provide a large part of the nitrogen requirements of your vegetable crops.

Flea beetles, mice...

♣ Flea beetles are so called because they can jump relatively large distances. They can completely ruin a crop of leafy vegetables and radishes. Keep the ground moist; they detest moisture. Interplanting rows of cress will also elp because flea beetles love it and will head for that, leaving the leafy vegetables and radishes alone. You can trap them using a piece of wood smeared with syrup, lime or wallpaper paste, just as long as it sticks to the wood, and wave this above the crop. The flea beetles will jump up and become stuck fast. You are not growing crops just for the mice to eat. Present them with an alternative diet of three parts flour with one part lime and 1 part sugar. Stir in enough water to produce a paste. Let it dry and then crumble up the solid mass.

Finally another tea: wormwood tea can be used against various insects and slugs. Boil 100gm (4oz) wormwood in 1 litre (2 pints) of water for 20 minutes. The whole must be left to steep for

Not everyone has the room for a standard fruit tree.

24 hours after which it is sieved, diluted and used as a spray. You may need to repeat this treatment after a week.

Fruit for every garden

There should be some fruit in the garden whether you have a vegetable garden or not. A pergola covered with a vine, or red- and blackcurrant bushes used to form a boundary hedge will provide you with fresh fruit. Many fruit trees and bushes look so attractive that they fit into any garden design, whether vegetable or ornamental.

Where to grow fruit crops

In the past standard fruit trees were planted 7m (22'9") or more apart in the orchard. Nowadays gardens are often of more

modest size and there is no separate fruit garden. Gardeners can now benefit from the development of the practical half-standard, bush, and spindlebush fruit trees, and the modern apple and pear varieties which can be easily pruned into all kinds of shapes. These can be included in small gardens so that it is now possible for apples, pears, cherries, plums, and peaches çome to full maturity. Most kinds of fruit like light and sun. The shape the fruit tree will grow into will determine its position in the ornamental or vegetable garden. For practical reasons it is best not to plant an apple, pear, plum, or cherry tree beside the terrace. Falling fruit will be a nuisance and insects such as wasps will be attracted to the ripe fruit. It is not sensible to plant fruit trees in the border either. The fallen fruit will rot away among the plants before you have the chance to remove them. The sturdy medlar, on the other hand, has fruits that are only good for eating when they are rotting. It is not a problem if these fruits lie in amongst the border for a time. A lot of fruit can also be grown against the pergola, wall, trellis, or fencing trai-

A pear cordon is being grown here against the railings of the vegetable garden. To encourage growth in the rods, the growth has not been tied in during the first year. The branches will only be tied in horizontally in the autumn.

> ### Tip
> In cooler regions fruits from warmer climate must have a sheltered position against a wall. Pruning will have to be adapted to suit the plant.

ned into such forms as cordon or fan. Some species that originate from more southerly regions must be given a sunny, sheltered situation. You often see fruit trees such as peach and vine trained against a wall. Bush fruit types can also be grown extremely well in hedges. This makes them useful plants for both the ornamental and the vegetable garden.

Suitable soil

Fruit trees grow best on well-drained, preferably humus-rich, and not too dry soils. Well drained clay and loam are very suitable. The humus content and therefore water-holding capacity of sandy soils can be increased if necessary (see Part 4 for improving and manuring the soil).

A few useful terms

By their very nature, one variety of fruit tree will grow more strongly than another. If a strongly growing variety is planted in fertile soil it can grow too strongly, while a weak variety grown on poor, infertile soil will grow too weakly. For apples and certain other fruit trees this problem can be overcome by choosing a good rootstock. For strongly growing varieties ask for the rootstock M-9 and for weak-growing varieties ask for M-26. Fruit trees such as plum, apricot, and Mirabelles are also grafted on rootstocks. Many countries, including Great Britain, have certification schemes for fruit trees and soft fruits. The British list includes apples, pears, plums, and cherries. If you buy certified stock you will know which rootstock was used and you can be certain that the variety will be true to type.

Pollination

♣ Trees and bushes do not produce fruit unless the flowers are pollinated. Some kinds of fruit will only produce a crop if there is a tree or bush of another variety nearby. If this is the case you must plant two spcimens, for example two apple trees, two pear trees or two Mayduke cherry trees. This double planting will allow the flowers to cross-pollinate. There are exceptions to this rule. Always ask your supplier if your fruit tree is self- or cross-pollinating.

There are also dioecious plants, for example the kiwi, where male and female flowers are borne on separate plants. For plants such as these at least one male plant must be sited near one or more female plants.

Only female kiwi plants can bear fruit. There must be a male plant nearby.

Pruning fruit trees and bushes

♣ There are many methods of pruning, and fruit trees or shrubs must be pruned to achieve the desired shape. This is especially important in the early years of growth. After that, most fruit trees are pruned to maintain their shape and to promote fruit production. Once you understand what sort of wood flowers and bears fruit on the tree or shrub, the rate of growth, and whether the fruit needs a long or short time to ripen, pruning will no longer seem to be so difficult. It is important that the sun can penetrate to the heart of the bush or tree, because sunlight is vital for large, well-ripened fruit and it will keep the tree healthy.

Blackcurrants fruit on young wood

♣ The blackcurrant fruits on the youngest wood and can thus be pruned from November to March. Before the buds open in the spring they swell up enormously. If you leave the pruning until it is too late you can easily knock a few buds off the branches. The best time for pruning, however, is November.

To obtain a well-shaped bush prune the branches of the young bush (often only one or two) above an outward-facing bud or eye. The strongest branches will grow from these buds, from the centre towards the outside. Four or five branches must be allowed to develop with side wood.

These framework branches should not be left to grow for more than three years. Each year the side branches that have borne fruit should be cut back as low as possible. The newly formed shoots that face outwards from the bush are left in place.

This maintains a good shape and allows light to penetrate into the centre. The young branches of the blackcurrant are recognizable by the pale colour of their wood. The blackcurrant can be

> **Tip**
> If you find it difficult to tell the difference between old and new wood, you can always harvest blackcurrants complete with their branches and take the berries off elsewhere. You will have then pruned the bush.

used in various ways in the garden: it can be grown in isolation in the vegetable and ornamental garden or it can serve as a hedge for shelter or to mark a boundary. It can also be grown along wires in which case it will take up less ground space. The blackcurrant has attractive foliage. If you grow it as a hedge between your garden and next door's, only prune it in the spring.

Raspberry, blackberry, and Japanese wineberry

♣ All the branches of the summer-fruiting raspberries that have borne fruit are cut down to ground level immediately after harvesting. If you forget to do this no harm will be done by pruning in the spring. The new stems, which formed during the previous growing season, are left intact, and these will fruit the next time round. If you grow raspberries along wires you should not leave more than seven stems per metre (39″) length, and you need to cut off the surplus young stems. The autumn-fruiting raspberry bears fruit on the branches that formed earlier in that year. Nothing could be easier: all the fruiting stems are cut down to ground level after the harvest. With this type of raspberry keep ten to twelve stems per metre (39″) length

With these raspberries only seven stems were left per metre (39″) length in the following year. Raspberries must be pruned after harvest.

Stems that have borne fruit are cut back to ground level. Leave the young stems seven to the metre (39″). Here pruning has been left until the spring.

in the new year. Of course, you should leave in place the sturdiest stems on both types of raspberry since these will produce the best fruit. Raspberries can be grown along wires or as free-standing bushes in the vegetable garden. You can use them as a shrub or hedge, but they are less suitable as features in the ornamental garden because of the way they need to be pruned.

The blackberry looks somewhat like the raspberry. It also flowers on young wood and has long branches that need support. In October, remove the branches that have fruited and any dead wood. Do not tie up the young branches because they are very frost sensitive. It is better to lay them on the ground and cover them with leaves, straw, or old rush matting. The shrub will then survive the winter undamaged. In spring, tie the thorny varieties to wires 30cm (12″) apart; for the thornless ones 15cm (6″) apart is sufficient. You can plant the blackberry in ornamental and vegetable gardens, against posts, wires, and wire netting. It also grows well over pergolas and against walls.

The Japanese wineberry also fruits on the youngest branches. It is pruned exactly like the blackberry and trained like the thornless variety. It could be used in the border, but remember that your hair and threads from your clothes will

Brambles produce very long branches and are therefore especially suitable for covering arches, walls, and pergolas. In October when they have finished fruiting the dead wood is removed.

Redcurrants fruit on old wood, that is on shoots which grow on old wood. Keep no more than five well spread-out framework branches on a free-standing bush.

be caught on the thorns while you are weeding the ground round it.

Red- and whitecurrants and gooseberries

Red- and whitecurrants fruit on older wood. Pruning is better left until February or March. When pruning the currants you need to make sure that the light can reach the centre of the bush. Each year several of the very oldest branches are cut back as far as possible. As a rule young shoots at ground level are cut off but occasionally a young shoot is retained to replace an old main branch. Keep no more than five framework branches on a bush. The best berries grow on one-year-old shoots that are growing outwards from a main branch. These shoots (from 10cm to no more than 20cm (4″ to 8″) are saved. Long side branches are shortened to 1cm (1/2″). Redcurrants grown as a hedge will receive more light. Three main branches are kept per metre (1.2yd) length.

In ornamental and vegetable gardens red- and whitecurrants are planted as free-standing bushes and as a sheltering hedge. They are also grown along wires fixed between posts.

Depending on the vigour of their growth, fruit trees and bushes are either pruned hard or lightly. A fertile, moderately vigorous redcurrant cultivar such as 'Stanza' can be pruned hard. A good grower such as 'Rotet,' however, is pruned lightly. The gooseberry fruits on both new and old wood. You should retain seven framework branches. Towards the beginning of March all the side wood is removed up to a height of 40cm (16″). The remaining side branches are thinned out to a distance apart of 10cm (4″); the strongest branches will give the best fruit. Side branches that are growing inwards or downwards are cut short. Plants that always suffer from mildew

Do not leave too many branches on the gooseberry. The branches have wicked thorns and a crowded bush makes it difficult to pick the fruit.

> **Tip**
>
> The branches of the gooseberry bush tend to grow close to the ground. When you are shapingm the bush remember this, and prune the main branches to an inward-facing eye.

in the summer need to have all their branches clipped in the winter. However this will mean losing some of the flowering wood. Do not manure gooseberries that are sensitive to mildew too heavily because this will encourage the disease.

Because of their prickly stems gooseberries are often banished to far corners, but they still need to be in the sun. They can, with appropriate pruning, be trained along wires to form a screen. Standard gooseberries are also suitable for the ornamental or vegetable garden.

Grapes: pruning in winter

♣ The vine fruits on side shootsthat are at least one year old. Vines are usually grown against a wall or building as a fan or cordon. This means that, after planting the vine's single stem is cut off at a height of 1m (3′3″). Pruning is done in November and December when the vine is resting. If pruning is done in the spring when the sap is rising the cuts will bleed, and this flow is very difficult to staunch. The eyes below the cuts sprout and, depending on the shape (fan or cordon), one or more shoots – known as canes – are retained as main branches and tied up. In the growing season, side branches that will bear the fruit develop on these canes.

The branches that have borne fruit are pruned beyond two to five eyes, depending on the variety.

A large knob sometimes develops after repeated pruning over a number of years; this can be cut

Above: *Pruning the vine in summer. Long shoots are broken off at the second leaf beyond the bunch of grapes.*

Centre: *The result of the pruning: more sunlight can reach the grapes.*

Below: *Side shoots on which no grapes are growing can be broken off completely.*

> **Tip**
>
> Always prune vines in the winter leaving a stump of wood about 3cm (1") above an eye. This will prevent the highest eye from shrivelling.

> **Tip**
>
> When the grapes in a bunch are not yet touching each other they may need to be thinned out. Do this with a small pair of scissors and try not to touch the grapes, even with your hair, because even this can damage them. Remove about a third of the fruit.

When the branches of trained fruit trees are tied directly to the wall there is a strong chance of damage and therefore of disease.

off in December, to leave one branch with several eyes. Bunches of grapes will grow on the sprouting buds. With outdoor vines you keep only the first two of these, and the remaining sprouting buds with any developing bunches of grapes are broken off. Breaking off avoids the risk of bleeding, since these shoots are in fact still green and have not yet become woody.

Because the shoots become very long, the fruit-bearing shoots are shortened to the second leaf after the last bunch. Any side shoots that may still develop can be broken off. Pruning before harvest allows more sun to reach the grapes, which will improve their sugar content and colour.

Vines can be planted in either the ornamental or the vegetable garden. Both foliage and fruit are decorative. In spite of all this pruning, a vine will still need a lot of space. It is suitable for high

> **Tip**
>
> Fruit trees must not be tied up directly to a wall or fence. This causes damage and, besides, walls become far too hot and leaves and fruit will become scorched and shrivelled. Always fix a frame to the wall first.

or broad walls and fences, pergolas, arbours, and summerhouses in sheltered positions. The kiwi is pruned in the same way as the vine and it requires a similar situation. Always remember to plant a male plant beside a female one!

General rules for pruning fruit trees

♣ Make sure that three or four main branches are spread out per layer and do not allow these to grow directly above each other. Keep the tree open to allow maximum light penetration. The more a branch is at an angle or the more vertical its direction of growth more vigorously it will grow, the thicker it will become, and the later it will bear fruit. Horizontal branches flower and fruit earlier. Pruning so that only eyes that are pointing outward and downward shoots are retained will promote horizontally growing shoots. Never prune branches and twigs that are already growing horizontally or downwards. These grow less vigorously and the branches begin to produce fruit earlier. Cut off completely twigs and branches on the upper side of fruiting branches, even if they are showing flower buds. Always prune above an eye that faces outward from the tree.

Take the young shoots from the trunk in good time. At this stage you can just break them off with your fingers.

The branches growing upwards are cut away because, once in leaf and flower or with fruit, they will completely shade the branch below. This will stop the sun from reaching the centre of the tree and will prevent the fruit from ripening. Shoots arising from the trunk that are not needed as main branches must be removed at an early stage to avoid making large wounds later.

Stone fruits

Cherries, Morello cherries, plums, and peaches are preferably pruned immediately after the harvest because the wounds will heal over more quickly at that time of year. If pruning is done in the winter, their resting

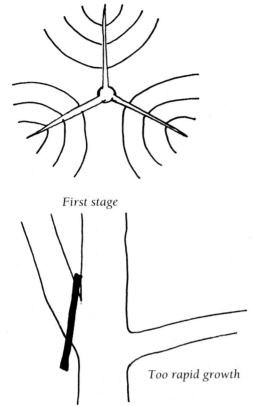

First stage

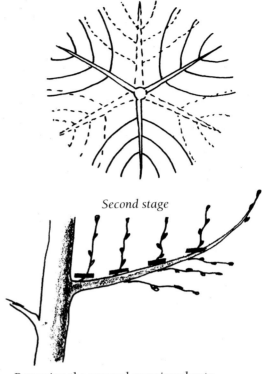

Second stage

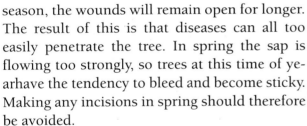

Too rapid growth

Removing the upward-growing shoots

season, the wounds will remain open for longer. The result of this is that diseases can all too easily penetrate the tree. In spring the sap is flowing too strongly, so trees at this time of yearhave the tendency to bleed and become sticky. Making any incisions in spring should therefore be avoided.

Plums bear fruit on young and older wood. Pruning is limited to removing dead wood and to thinning out surplus fruiting wood. Make sure that enough light can reach the heart of the tree since branches in the shade can easily die off. It will be necessary from time to time to remove some branches from the crown of the tree. Always treat large wounds on stone fruit trees with a *flexible* wound paint.

Morello cherries bear practically all their fruit on one-year-old branches. These grow naturally on the outside of the bush. Older wood often remains totally bare. To prevent a tree becoming bare with just a small fringe of cherries, from the outset cut out as deeply as possible all the wood

that has fruited. This will stimulate the formation of fruiting wood and at the same time limit the size of the tree. Peach trees also fruit best on one-year-old wood. Just like the Morello cherry

Morello cherries are happy with a northerly aspect. When the plant is being trained against a wall the heart of the tree also receives enough light. There is a greater chance that young wood will be formed regularly in the heart of a trained form than in a tree or bush form.

Peaches are pruned immediately after the harvest.

The cordon apple tree fits in well into a garden with a contemporary design.

the old wood has a tendency to become bare. In September, and not earlier or later, prune hard to encourage replacement shoots. Cut off the branches that have fruited just above a strong new shoot. Try to avoid cutting into thick wood because peach trees bleed easily. Of all these types of fruit the plum as tree, spindle or bush is still better planted in the border for practical reasons. The colour of the fruit warns you when you must begin picking. The peach is often planted against a wall for warmth but it is not a very attractive wall shrub. The Morello cherry can be trained and can brighten up a north wall. The birds leave these sour cherries alone for a long time. All these stone fruits do well in the vegetable or herb garden.

The apple tree as a cordon

♣ Apple and pear trees can be planted as tree, spindlebush or bush. If you do not have much space and yet want to plant apple and pear trees, you can keep them under control using special methods of planting, training, and pruning.

By planting young trees with their grafts upwards at an angle of 45°, growth is curbed and the formation of fruit is stimulated. Besides less branching takes place. The formation of spurs is promoted by shortening the side branches to a maximum of four buds between November and February. In the summer the two lower buds develop into flower buds. Again the branches above the flower buds are pruned. Behind the developing fruit new flower buds are formed and a whole system of spurs will arise.

The cordon must be securely tied at an angle of 450; otherwise it will have the tendency to grow in its original upright direction. If the cordon begins to grow too vigorously, untie it from the trellis and carefully bend it back at an angle of 450 or even rather less. Tie it up again and the cordon will be once more back in line.

At one time cordons were always grown against walls. They can, however, stand on their own feet to form a screen between two sections of the garden as a hedge in the summer and a trellis in winter.

Shrubs with edible fruit

♣ There are some plants classified as ornamental that also produce edible fruit. They are not only pretty but also good to eat.
- The black mulberry, *Morus nigra*, has dark red fruit. Never plant this near a paved terrace because the falling fruit will make dark red stains. In this respect the white mul-

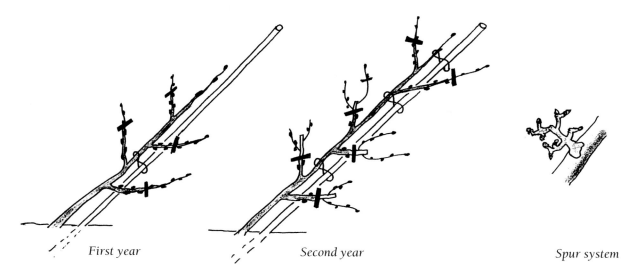

First year   *Second year*   *Spur system*

Pruning an apple cordon.

berry, *Morus alba*, is less of a nuisance. Both trees have large, decorative leaves and an umbrella shaped crown. The mulberry, which grows from 4.5 to 6m (14′7″ to 19′6″) high, likes a sunny, sheltered situation with a loose, deep, fertile, and also lime-rich soil.

— The walnut, *Juglans regia*, can easily reach a height of 20 to 25m (65 to 81′3″). Nowadays there are also bush forms. The broad, spreading tree form is not suitable for small gardens. This nut tree comes into leaf late and sheds its leaves early. The oval nuts must be picked up as soon as they fall. They do not fall at regular intervals and so quite a lot of work is involved to harvest them. Spread them out to dry well before you store them away in a box or crate.

— The medlar *Mespilus germanica*, which has already been mentioned, is available both as a shrub, 2 to 4m (6′7″ to 13′) and a tree which reaches approximately 6m (19′6″). The medlar has large white flowers that open in May. The fruits are only edible when they begin to rot. This tree, too, needs a sheltered situation.

— The almond, *Prunus dulcis*, (5 to 7m) (16′3″ to 22′9″) produces quite large pink flowers in March and April. In sunny, sheltered places it can produce large quantities of nuts.

— The hazel, or cobnut, *Corylus avellana*, can reach 6m (19′6″) in height. This shrub can tolerate a lot of shade and grows well on reasonably good, not too dry, soil. The male flowers, the catkins, appear in late January and February. Only the red pistils of the female flowers are visible. They are very frost-sensitive because they flower early. In the trade there are also varieties bred especially for their nuts, for example 'Cosford Cob,' 'Webb's Prize Cob,' and 'Pearson's Prolific.'

— There are various species of flowering quince, *Chaenomeles*. Its height of about 1m (3′3″) and its tangled growth make it suit-

These medlars are not yet ready; they are only good to eat when they are over-ripe.

Tip

Wash 500gm (1lb) of quinces well and cut them up. Add them to an enamel or stainless steel pan with 500cl (1pt) water and cook to a pulp; sieve and add 500gm (1lb) of sugar per 500gm (1lb) of pulp with the juice of a lemon. Stir the mixture and cook rapidly. Pour into clean, warm pots and seal with screw lids.

The rowan is a small tree with a light crown, so it is extremely suitable for a small garden. You will have to share the harvest of berries with the birds.

able for use in a hedge. The flowers, which are red, pink, or white, appear from March to May. The flowering quince needs a sunny position on fertile soil. In the autumn these shrubs are full of yellow, slightly damaged looking fruits. You can make delicious preserves from them.

- The quince, *Cydonia oblonga*, is a 4 to 5m (13 to 16'3") high tree which has large, pinkish-white flowers in May. The quince has large, felted leaves and the yellow fruits, which ripen in October, are suitable for making preserves. The quince grows on any soil, providing it is not too dry.
- In the autumn the orange berries of the rowan, *Sorbus aucuparia*, can be made into preserves and compotes.
  In spring the tree, which can reach 15m (48'9"), produces great heads of flowers. It is suitable for both sandy and clay soil.
- The elderberry, *Sambucus nigra*, has white flower heads in May and June. The black berries ripen in August. Although the shrub, which grows up to 5m high (16'3") can tolerate shade extremely well, for a good crop of berries it needs a sunny situation on fertile soil.

Above left: *The corkscrew hazel, Corylus avellana 'Contorta,' is also a nut tree.*

Below left: *The fruit of the flowering quince can be made into preserves. If you have fruit left over, use them in flower arranging.*

You can make elderflower syrup from the flowers. The berries are suitable for making syrup, preserves, and wine. Beware: not all species of elderberry are suitable for consumption; the red berries of *Sambucus racemosa* and *ebulus*, like the unripe berries of S. *nigra*, are actually poisonous.

- Roses that produce large rosehips, such as the hedgehog rose, *Rosa rugosa*, dog rose, *Rosa canina*, and eglantine, *Rosa rubiginosa* are species roses.
  In a sunny place on lime-rich soil these roses produce abundant crops which have a high vitamin C content and can be made into preserves and syrup.
- The mahonia, *Mahonia aquifolium*, an evergreen shrub which can thrive in the shade, has bunches of yellow flowers in spring,

The hedgehog rose, Rosa rugosa, *contains exceptional quantities of vitamin C. If you want to make preserves from the rosehips, that will keep it is important to remove all the pips.*

Be quick, otherwise the birds will get there before you. You can make preserves from mahonia berries in August. You may have read that they are poisonous. The roots are, but not the ripe berries.

followed by green berries which become blue later in the season. You can eat these off the bush or use them to make juice, or preserves. Like rose bushes they can be planted to form a loose hedge.

– Bilberries demand a damp, acid, humus-rich soil and a position in the shade. The bilberry, *Vaccinium myrtillus*, grows no higher than 40cm (16″). The blue berries, which are rich in vitamins A, B, and C, appear in the summer. The berries are eaten fresh or made into preserves and cordial. The cowberry, *Vaccinium vitis-idaea*, is a 25cm (10″) high evergreen bush, which is covered with red berries from September to November. These can be made into preserves. The American cranberry, *Vaccinium macrocarpon*, is a creeping, mat-forming plant with red berries 2cm (1in) across. They are made into preserves, compote, and cordial. These plants need not only an acid but also a very damp soil. Finally there is the blueberry, *Vaccinium corymbosum*. At a height of 1.5m (4′10″) it towers head and shoulders above other members of the family. The blue berries can be harvested between the middle of July and the end of August.

– The common juniper, *Juniperus communis*, which grows up to 2.5m (8′2″) high is an ornamental shrub with edible fruit. The fleshy berries only ripen in the second year. These blue-grey berries are used in sauerkraut and in recipes for braised meat.

– The wild strawberry, *Fragaria vesca*, cannot be left out of any summary of edible ornamental plants. It looks lovely in the vegetable or ornamental garden as ground cover or as an edging plant. It has tiny white flowers in May and June followed by red berries.

Herbs: the finishing touch

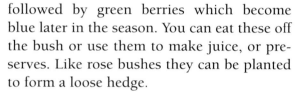 Herbs have been grown in private gardens throughout the ages, if not actually as cures then because of their pleasant scent. Nowadays herbs are mostly used to improve the flavour and aroma of dishes. In general they have beneficial effects on the digestion. With proper use, herbs can promote health and help build up resistance to illnesses. In the garden aromatic herbs attract a variety of insects, some of which are necessary for pollination; other harmful insects are kept at bay by herbs, while remedies to protect plants and to kill pests can be made from herbs. For this reason particularly it is sensible to make some space for herbs in the

This herb garden is in half shade. The herbs are combined here with old-fashioned flowering plants.

vegetable garden, and there is the additional be-nefit that many herbs also have pretty flowers.

A sunny position

Whether you want the herbs to form part of the vegetable or ornamental garden or whether you want to lay out a separate herb garden, it will make no difference to the herbs, providing they receive enough sun. They also seem to have a better aroma and more flavour if they are grown in poor soil. If you want to treat your herbs well plant them in well-drained sandy soil, to which you add a top dressing of a calcareous compost every three years as herbs like lime. It is not true that no herbs will grow in half shade. Ones that will include: mint species, parsley, celery, chervil, woodruff, and lovage. Re-member that some herbs, such as lemon balm

and mint, can spread rapidly. You can prevent this by planting them in a pot or a bucket with the bottom knocked out. This will keep their roots under control.

Acquiring herbs

When you are going to use herbs for sea-soning, you only need a very little each time. It is enough to have about three plants of each species, even for a large family. It is not a good idea to sow every herb you think you will need. It would be better to buy individual

> **Tip**
> If you cannot find out whether or not a herb likes dry and sunny conditions there is a way of remembering. The drier, greyer, and more needle-like the leaves, the more sun the herb needs, as well as a free-draining soil.

An exquisite place for herbs which in general like warmth and a lot of sun. A single flowering plant provides a frivolous note (Bingerden House, Netherlands).

plants, or even better to put in cuttings or a piece of a plant that has been split up.

A separate herb garden

♣ If you mention the words "herb garden" people's thoughts always return to herb

It is better not to plant mint, even the variegated ones, in open ground. They "run" all over the garden. A pot keeps them in their place.

gardens of long ago. An old-fashioned herb garden is laid out with two paths that cross each other. Smaller paths can be used to divide up these four areas into smaller beds. This arrangement of paths and beds has been perpetuated for centuries, purely because the paths allow access to the herbs in all weathers. Pave the paths or put down wood chippings so that, every day, you can have fresh herbs to add to your dishes.

Even a small herb garden may be too big solely for planting herbs. Combine the herbs with other "old-fashioned" plants. The last chapter gave an example of a herb garden for the shade in which various culinary herbs were combined with old, familiar ornamental plants such as attractive hedges of box, lavender, or evergreen shrub honeysuckle.

Box balls, used as a centrepiece, give such garden a geometric, formal appearance, which is much appreciated nowadays.

Herbs in the ornamental garden

♣ Not everyone has the available space to lay out a separate herb garden. Besides this may be unnecessary because many herbs are so pretty that they are not out of place in the herbaceous border. Many aromatic plants can be used to enclose the terrace or to make a nice edging for the path leading to the front door.

Tip

On a heavier, fertile soil make a sheltered and well-drained place for your herbs by raising one side, the north, to create a rier, warmer slope.

An edging of box or evergreen honeysuckle, Lonicera nitida and Lonicera pileata, on the north side will keep off the wind and allow the plants to enjoy the early spring warmth.

Flower, foliage, and/or scented herbs to consider for the border include lavender, oregano 'Herrenhausen,' clary, rosemary, lemon balm, *Artemisia abrotanum*, chives, hyssop, angelica, chamomile, sage, and *Atriplex*. Do not forget the red *Atriplex*. This provides a splash of red foliage in the border but then, of course, you must remember not eat it. In the border under the shrubs, woodruff can provide a beautiful green carpet.

Herbs in companion planting

In the vegetable garden various herbs grown in combination with vegetables, the so-called companion planting, can prevent certain diseases. You must be sure that the herb and the vegetable have a mutually beneficial in-

Many people know chives from the ornamental garden. You can eat the leaves.

fluence on each otherso that both plants grow well and discourage the spread of diseases. A combination of carrots and chives, leeks, and/or onions prevents an infestation of carrot fly. Chamomile and African marigolds prevent onion flies attacking onions. Horseradish has a beneficial influence on the yield of potatoes. Horseradish is planted at the corners of the potato beds the potatoes will encourage the potatoes to crop more heavily.

Many butterflies, and therefore caterpillars, avoid brassicas if strongly aromatic herbs such as sage, hyssop, and thyme are planted amongst them.

Elsewhere tomatoes are planted between cabbages. Celery and chamomile combined with leek prevent attacks by the onion fly. Garden cress planted among the radishes will discourage flea beetle. A good clump of chervil among the lettuces keeps the lettuces free of aphids. If you sow parsley among the lettuces you are asking

Angelica is a tall, biennial plant with decorative, deeply cut leaves and greenish-yellow flowers. It certainly deserves a place in the yellow-green shady corner.

for trouble; in no time the lettuces will be covered with aphids. When you are using herbs in companion plant-ing among vegetables it is better to sow the herbs because you will need many more than for culinary purposes.It is important to follow the growing instructions on the seed packets carefully because the sowing time and growing conditions of herbs differ widely.

Perennial herbs

♣ If you find it inconvenient to move perennial herbs as part of your crop rotation scheme, then you can set aside a central strip or bed in the vegetable garden where the herbs can have a permanent place. The vegetable crops will then be rotated around this herb patch.

Harvesting and drying herbs

♣ Foliage herbs have most flavour just before they flower, after which the quality deteriorates. When the leaves are used, therefore, it is better to harvest them before they flower. Sometimes plants have their flowers and buds removed to maintain their flavour and it is in any case wise to do this before the seeds form.

Harvest in the morning on a dry day. In August and September the seed heads of dill, aniseed, and other umbrella flowers are gathered while in the autumn the annual herbs are harvested. These are cut down to the ground completely. Only young stems and leaves are used from perennial herbs.

The herbs are first washed, taking care not to bruise the leaves. They are patted dry and laid out in a dry room.

It is better to dry herbs in a dark, dry, but well ventilated space. An attic or the room with the central heating boiler is a good place. Hang the herbs upside down wrapped in brown paper to keep them in the dark and free of dust. Herbs gathered for their seeds need something underneath them to catch the seeds or they will end up on the floor.

After about three weeks most herbs have dried nicely and will feel crisp. Strip the leaves from the stems, crumble them and store in well sealed, dark pots.

Herbs which loose their flavour

♣ There are some herbs that can only be used fresh, because they lose their flavour when dried. Such herbs include borage, parsley,

> **Tip**
> Use elastic bands to tie up your bunches of herbs. The herbs shrink during drying and the elastic, which shrinks with them, stops them falling down.

Tip
You can hang your herb rack in the light providing the herbs are in tins or pots of dark-coloured glass. This will preserve their quality.

chervil, cress, chives, and fennel. Do not let herbs cook too long or their flavour will be destroyed.

There are some herbs that lose their flavour completely if they are cooked, even if only lightly: dill, parsley, tarragon, borage, chives, hyssop, chervil, lemon balm, and horseradish.

Chamomile is one of the few herbs of which the flowers are used. This plant also deserves a place in the ornamental garden.

Butterflies and caterpillars hate the strong-smelling sage. They stay away so that the cabbages are spared.

Part 4

_M_aintenance:
the hard work

7 A closer look at the soil

Once your garden has been laid out or altered, it has to be maintained. The most obvious jobs are hoeing and weeding because weeds will keep on coming up and they will compete with your plants for food, water, and air. If you want to minimize the amount of work required to maintain your garden, you need to consider the natural conditions in your garden, including that of the soil. It is important for gardeners to appreciate the good and bad points of the soil and to know how soil can be improved.

Types of soil

In practically all countries there are noticeable differences in the landscape from one region to another. You can travel through areas of reclaimed marsh, through areas of blown sand, river valleys, pine woods, hilly or mountainous regions, oak woods, and dunes. All these have their own special vegetation, because the soil on which the plants depend is different in each case.

Sand

Sand is produced by the weathering of different types of rock. It consists of particles that vary in size from 0.05 to 2mm. Water drains quickly through the pore spaces between the sand grains, and it is not easily absorbed from below. The larger the particles the drier the ground. Sandy soil is recognizable by the minerals that can be seen sparkling in it. Pure sandy soils lack nutrients but, fortunately, they can easily be improved by the addition of clay in the

A sandy soil before cultivation.

form of clay minerals, such as bentonite and montmorillonite, or water-retaining gels which are available commercially, and by the addition of organic material.

Clay

Clay is also weathered rock, but this originates from granite. The clay particles are smaller than 0.016mm and are therefore very fine. Water only drains through the small pores in clay with great difficulty. This means that a clay soil can hold a great deal of water and is barely permeable. Once the clay has dried out, water only rises from below very slowly. Dry clay soil becomes hard and cracks; wet clay soil has pores that have been closed even further by fine particles that have been washed into the soil by rain. There is, however, an advantage in clay soils since the rocks from which they are derived contain many minerals that serve as food for plants. As the process of weathering is on-going the minerals continue to be released. The priority with a clay soil, is to improve its structure. This can be done by incorporating organic mate-

Clay soil remains moist for a long time. If you turn over an apparently dry lump you will find it still contains water.

If clay soil is dug before the winter the frost will break up the large clods. These disintegrate into smaller, easily tilled crumbs.

rial, adding sand (which can be heavy work), and by digging the ground before the frost.

Peat soils

❀ Peat consists for the most part of decayed plant remains. There are two kinds of peat soils: those deriving from raised bogs where the peat was produced by the decay of plants growing above water and those deriving from valley bogs produced from plants growing under water. Peat can hold a great deal of water and yet it still allows water to drain through. Peat above the level of the water table continues to decay and settle. Plants grow rapidly on this kind of soil, but they are less sturdy. The addition of minerals and lime will promote stronger growth. Peat soils suffer from an excess of water. Shallow-rooted plants are particularly at home on peat because of the high water table in these types of soil. Peat does, however, freeze easily because of the large amount of water it retains during the winter, and it is particularly sensitive to late-night frosts.

Marl

❀ Marl is the name given to a mixture of fairly coarse sand and clay, which is usually fertile, easily cultivated, water-retaining and into which plants can easily root.

Loam

❀ Loam consists of a balance of fine clay particles and very fine sand grains (0.002 to 0.050mm in diameter). Compared with clay, loam drains well and yet retains water, and it is very fertile. It is more than likely that the soil in your garden will have the characteristics of more than one soil type, since soil types rarely occur on their own.

The structure

❀ The way soil is made up, its structure, is determined not only by the various components of the soil, such as soil particles, water and air, but also by the relationship between these components. The structure is also continually influenced by the life in the soil, the quantity of organic material present, and the chemical properties of the soil. A soil with a poor structure would be one on which puddles of water remain after a shower of rain. This soil is not very permeable in itself, or there is an impermeable layer in the soil. On sandy soil this could be an ironpan or hardpan. On peat, a layer of wet clay could form a division between the topsoil and the subsoil. On new housing estates, an annoying layer of compacted layer of clay can often be found been covered with a layer of garden soil. In such gardens, you should even be prepared to find a layer of cement where the cement mixer stood during building work. There is also something wrong with the structure of your soil if it blows away during strong winds. Perhaps the soil does not absorb water after a dry period, or a hard crust forms on its surface. It is clear from the above that an imper-

meable layer must be broken through. However, a great many other soil problems can be solved by the repeated addition of humus.

Vertical drainage. The greatest force will be exerted if you stand right behind the post or soil augur.

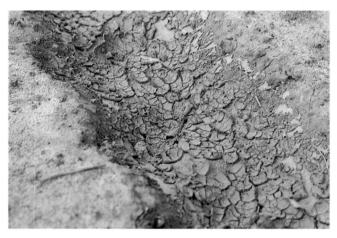

The delicate structure of this sandy soil has been destroyed by heavy tractor tyres. The capillary action has been lost, and a crust has formed on the surface.

Tip
An impenetrable layer can be broken through by using a soil augur to dig a 6cm (2") hole every 3m (9'10"). The hole is filled with gravel or clay aggregate.
The top 25cm (10") is filled with garden soil. Excess water can now drain away through the holes.

Horizontal drainage

Horizontal drainage can benefit soils that are always too wet. Somewhat above the highest measured water level (measure it in both summer and winter) dig trenches in the soil with a trenching tool to a ditch or gravel-filled soakaway. The trenches should be at a distance of 3m (9'10") apart and sloping slightly. Tile drains or perforated plastic pipes are laid on the floor of the trench, which is then refilled with earth.

If you use a spade and so make rather broader trenches, instead of pipes you can lay a 20cm (8") layer of gravel, clay aggregate, or bundles of

Making a turning movement (boring) will bring the hard layer to the surface.

After the hard layer has been pierced, the hole is filled with expanded clay aggregate or gravel.

The clay aggregate must fill the hole to within 25cm (10") of the soil surface.

The remainder of the hole is filled with garden topsoil.

brushwood. A plastic sheet is put over them and then the earth is put back. If the drainage system runs alongside trees or through a shrubbery, it is best to use closed PVC pipe at these points to prevent the trees' or shrubs' roots from growing into it.

Horizontal drainage obviously makes no sense unless the pipe drains out above the water table. The pipes must also be deep enough not to interfere with any work you do in the garden and must be below the root zone.

Humus

All the organic material that is left after plants and animals have decayed, the remains of animals as well as their manure, is known as humus. The remains of plants (such as leaves, stems, wood, sawdust, and roots) and the bodies of animals and small organisms yield dark brown carbon after they have been through a process of slow "combustion," or rather, decomposition. Besides carbon, all kinds of substances that plants need for growth are released into the soil.

This organic material forms a buffer in which nutrients are stored. Apart from plants, micro-organisms and all kinds of crea-tures that are too small to be seen with the naked eye feed on this store.

Dry, loose soil is easily blown away. Planting, adding organic manure, and covering it will improve its structure.

Humus acts as a binding agent in sandy soils, enabling them to retain more moisture. Humus is also an essential ingredient for clay soils since it loosens the soil, conducts water, and makes clay easier to work. Since humus is dark it makes the soil a darker colour, which enables it to absorb more warmth from the sun. This has a favourable effect on the growth of plants, both early and late in the season. This supply of food is continually shrinking and, in the course of time, it will have been used up. Humus must therefore be topped up continually.

Soil life varies with depth

Mice, moles and voles, slugs, earth-worms, mites, insects and their larvae, fungi, and bacteria assist in clearing up, and thus in the decay of, plant and animal waste. They live off this waste.

Organic material is broken down step by step. Soil organisms that eat fresh organic material live on and in the upper layer of the soil.

As these organisms need oxygen to live they are known as aerobic bacteria. By chewing, gnawing, or rasping they reduce the size of the waste, which sinks down further into the soil. Organisms living in anaerobic conditions feed on the waste from upper layers and decompose

Sieved compost added to a soil for a crop is kept in, and on, the top layer. The soil becomes darker in colour and, as a result, retains nutrients and the sun's warmth more easily.

it further. The droppings produced by this group feed organisms living at an even lower level. In this way plant nutrients are finally produced. In the intermediate stages of processing, the droppings are a cement-like type of material which sticks soil particles together, producing a crumb structure in the soil.

These worms mainly live on vegetation and manure in the compost heap.

Digging

As already mentioned, in the layer just under the surface of the soil, the decomposing, aerobic plants and animals are at work. At 5 to 20cm (2 to 8″) below ground, where there is less oxygen, very different organisms are active. Further down still, the soil contains even less oxygen.

The bacteria and fungi which live in the anaerobic layer will, literally, die of shock if they find themselves on the surface as a result of you digging your garden. Slugs and carrion beetles, on the other hand, will die from lack of food and light 20cm (8″) down.

You should therefore keep the layers in the same order when you cultivate the soil. As far as manure, compost, and so on are concerned, these are lightly worked into the top layer.

When the ornamental garden is being laid out or a new border is being dug, deep digging may be necessary to loosen the subsoil but the layers must not be transposed.

Soil, water, and air

Water is indispensable for all life on earth since most organisms consist largely part of water. A plant consists of as much as 70 to 90 per cent water. Nutrients are dissolved in and transported by water which also maintains the tension within the cells at the correct level. A plant transpires water, which can prevent it from "overheating."

As already noted, clays, humus-rich sandy soils, and peat retain a lot of water, while poor sandy soils behave more like a sieve.

Plant roots also need oxygen, and this is present in the pore spaces between the soil particles so

During dry periods regular watering is necessary to maintain growth.

Soil washes away easily from sloping surfaces that are not covered with vegetation.

Fallen leaves can be left under shrubs in the autumn. They act as a blanket against frost and are later broken down into nutrients that can be absorbed by the plants.

long as these are not completely filled with water. If a plant's roots continuously stand in water or the water level in the soil is raised, the plant will die off – not through drowning but through lack of oxygen.

By regularly adding humus, gardeners try to make naturally dry ground more moisture-retentive and to make clay soils somewhat drier.

A protective blanket for the soil

All soil tends naturally to be covered with vegetation. You only have to look at what happens when you have cleared the ground ready for planting or sowing and leave the soil to settle for a while. In a very short time it will be covered with a green haze.

Fresh seed is brought in from outside by the wind and by animals, and finds this a suitable place to germinate. You have to weed and hoe once more. By taking away these weeds you are impoverishing the soil, because after all the weeds will have taken food out of the soil in the same way that a vegetable crop does. Furthermore, wind, sun, and rain have a free hand with bare ground.

Rain washes away nutrients; sun dries the soil and changes its temperature; and wind causes erosion by blowing soil particles away as well as drying the soil out. Hence it is better to keep your soil completely covered. If you use organic

The stones set on edge prevent eroded soil from being washed away.

material to cover it, nutrients are added and weeds are discouraged. There are even more advantages in using a mulch: the soil remains evenly moist, there is less loss of heat, wind and water erosion are prevented, and the soil acquires a good crumb structure.

As a mulch you can use, for example, leaves, peat, grass clippings, wood or bark chips, compost, sawdust from untreated timber (not tropical hardwood), and coconut fibre.

> ### Tip
> Nitrogen is needed for the decomposition of a mulch which contains a lot of carbon (sawdust, straw, and wood chips). If this is not mixed into the mulch, nitrogen will be taken out of the soil initially. When you lay down the mulch it is better to incorporate some nitrogen.

There are some disadvantages in using a mulch all year round. Organic material attracts slugs, mice, and moles. You should therefore keep the mulch away from plants that have large, juicy leaves, such as *Hosta*. If you are gardening on wet ground, a mulch will keep the soil wet and cold for longer, especially in the spring. The chances of damage from late-night frosts will be greater here than on dry ground. You can cover the soil with ornamental plants (the so-called ground-cover plants).

Not all ground-cover plants prevent weeds since some weeds will still come up among them. This

> ### Tip
> Loosen the soil surface before you put down the mulch. This will aerate the soil and will create a direct contact between the upper layer and the mulch.

If you have a lot of wood from pruning, it can be processed with a shredder. Wood chips make an ideal mulch.

Bark and wood chips are particularly suitable for covering paths. It does not matter so much that extra nitrogen is being taken out of the soil here because you do not want plants to grow vigorously on a path.

can be a nuisance, especially if the ground cover you have chosen is a very prickly rose!

If you think a mulch looks untidy, plant shrubs and perennials closer together.

This will make the initial planting more expensive, but weeds will hardly have a chance of growing and the maintenance required will be less. Evergreen plants will naturally cover the soil all year round.

The fallen leaves from deciduous plants can be left round and between plants to provide protection for the soil in winter.

> ### Tip
> On heavy clay and peat soils which have a low water table, cracks can appear in the ground during dry summers. This can be prevented by keeping a layer of vegetation on the soil or by applying a mulch.

> ### Tip
> Gravel and stone chippings can be used as a soil covering. The soil underneath will be warmer for longer because the stones will have absorbed warmth from the sun during the day. Water can still penetrate. A mulch of chippings or gravel does not, however, add humus or nutrients.

Adapting the planting

❀ Most plants we grow in our gardens have come from different parts of the world. This means that they originally grew on different soils and were exposed to different climatic conditions. A plant will only thrive in optimum conditions. Busy Lizzie, *Impatiens sultanii*, does not like growing in full sun on dry soil and a rose growing on lime-rich soil shows it is not thriving by the yellow colour of its leaves. In circumstances that are less than ideal for a plant, there will always be organisms lying in wait to attack it and kill it.

You will then become aware of fungal infections, insects, and slugs. If you want to garden without employing too many artificial methods, the choice of plants must take into account the composition and nutrient level of the soil. So on

Busy Lizzies like shade and a lot of moisture.

Closely planted ground-cover plants keep out weeds, protect the soil, and maintain the humus layer.

Thyme likes dry and sunny conditions.

an acid, humus-rich soil which holds moisture, *Rhododendron*, bilberry (*Vaccinium*) , and creeping willow (*Salix repens*) do very well. It is best not to plant frost-sensitive plants on this type of damp soil because it takes longer to warm up in the spring and damage being caused by late-night frosts cannot be ruled out.

On the other hand, if you have a light-coloured, lime-rich, dry soil, which furthermore is dry, you have the ideal soil for plants such as thyme (*Thymus* , soapwort (*Saponaria officinalis*, lavender (*Lavandula*), evening primrose (*Oenothera*) , and acacia (*Robinia*).

Miniature landscapes

Not everyone wants to restrict their choice of plants to those suitable for their particular soil. The choice can be widened by changing the soil's conditions to some extent,

for example by introducing different levels into the garden.

A bog or pond can be created by making a lower area, and the excavated soil can be used for a raised section on which drought-loving plants can grow.

If you want to grow species from poorer soils in your garden even though your soil is fertile, you can also introduce height differences. The soil on a mound must never be manured. The nutrients in soil that has been heaped up will be washed down to a lower level, so that you will have both a nutrient-rich and nutrient-poor area.

A heavy, fertile soil can be made poorer by working a large quantity of sand into the upper layer.

On soils where the topsoil is fertile and the subsoil poor, you can bring up the nutrient-poor subsoil by deep digging.

Improving the soil

Soil organisms do not appreciate such disturbances. Besides, digging sand into clay soils or bringing up the subsoil is far from being light work. The time is long gone when armies of gardeners were available to carry out such task. Yet small modifications can still improve your soil.

Sandy soil can be improved by adding fine clay particles, such as bentonite. The organic material must also be topped up regularly by the addition of compost and perhaps manure.

Clay soil is helped by the addition of compost and humus. Organic material in the form of peat can be included, since the soil is naturally rich in nutrients. Peat must not be confused with a new material that is available for improving the soil. This is made from composted coconut

> ### Tip
> Peat should not be regarded as manure, although it can increase the humus content of the soil. Poor sandy soils retain more moisture after the addition of peat, and clay soils become more permeable. The peat does, however, lower the pH and the soil becomes more acid!

fibre, or coir and can be bought at garden centres. It is used as a medium for sowing seeds and striking cuttings, and also as a soil additive and mulch. It is loose and has an enormous moisture-holding capacity, as well as being free from metals, dis-ease spores, and weeds. The composted coconut fibres have a pH of 5.8 to 6.2 and do not there-fore make the soil acid. An important argument in favour of this by-product is that it removes the necessity for digging up peat bogs to obtain a similar organic product.

On soft peat soils, the addition of fertilizer and lime will promote stronger plant growth. In the years after your garden has been laid out, you can incorporate these materials into the upper layers of the soil among the plants. Peat and compost are put on the surface and raked in lightly.

All these organic materials must be topped up regularly as they are used up.

Compost

Using compost in the garden kills two birds with one stone. As you have already seen, compost is humus and it improves the structure and the water budget of the soil. It provides food for the organisms in the soil and it also provides nutrients for the plants. By the regular addition of compost the soil is, as it were, refreshed. In an ornamental garden where the planting is appropriate for the type of soil, fertilizing with compost should be sufficient.

If you make compost yourself you can obviously alter its composition. You could, for example, add manure from rabbits, guinea pigs, chickens, and birds to obtain a compost with a high nutrient content. Always make the compost heap in the shade of trees or shrubs to prevent it drying out too quickly. Dig out 10cm (4") of soil over a width of 1.5m (4'11"). Loosen the subsoil and cover it with a layer of twigs to aid drainage.

The compost heap is situated in the shade to promote decomposition and to prevent it drying out too rapidly.

Do not use any green wood from pruning because you will keep coming across it in the compost for ever and a day. Cover the twigs with a layer 25cm (10") deep of roughly cut-up kitchen and garden waste of plant or animal origin, preferably all at once. The waste should be sorted first. Spread over this a very thin layer of lime plus a layer of old compost or garden soil. The next layer is put on with a further addition of lime and soil. The heap is built up in this way to a height of 1.5m (4'11"). The top is then covered with a layer of straw, grass cuttings, or a piece of old carpet. You can give the heap a living cover by growing pump-kins, courgettes, or nasturtiums on it. Leave the heap for at least three months, after which it must be turned over into an empty space nearby. By turning the heap inside out you encourage decomposition. After a further three months the compost is ready for use. The lime is needed to speed up the process. The layer of soil introduces bacteria into the heap. A compost starter is sometimes used, especially when there is material such as wood in the heap which rots down only with difficulty.

The ratio of carbon to nitrogen

The material to be composted must have a parti-

You can cover the compost heap with grass cuttings.

cular carbon to nitrogen ratio, that is twenty parts carbon (C) to one part nitrogen (N).

It is there-fore advisable to add green waste, animal manure (rich in N), and fibrous material (twigs, dried plant stems, fallen leaves) rich in C to the compost heap in a ratio of 20:1.

Too much carbon and nothing much will happen in the heap; too much nitrogen will cause rotting and the release of ammonia.

If the carbon: nitrogen ratio is correct, all the waste will decay. An excess of straw will inhibit decomposition. A heap with too much green material will tend to smell.

Overview of C:N ratio of various kinds of animal and plant waste:

Organic waste	C : N
target	20 : 1
urine or liquid manure	0,8 : 1
blood	3 : 1
chicken manure	6,3 : 1
green waste	7 : 1
grass	12 : 1
stable manure	14 : 1
oat straw	48 : 1
wheat straw	128 : 1
fresh sawdust	511 : 1
rotted sawdust	208 : 1
kitchen waste	16 : 1
alder/ash leaves	25 : 1

Compost heap or bin?

Compost heaps can look neat and tidy that they do not have to be hidden away in a corner out of sight. If you have less space you can use a compost bin, although the material does not always rot down perfectly in a bin. A square bin of netting or untreated timber is more successful, and this looks neater and can be made as large as you want.

In a plastic or wooden bin the material on the outside rots down more quickly than with a heap, since the sides do not cool down so rapidly as in a heap. Keep a space the same size as the compost heap next to the heap so that the first heap can mature while the second one is being built.

Things not allowed on the compost heap

Never add potato peelings that have been treated with chemicals to inhibit sprouting, since the chemical acts as a growth retardant, the last thing you want in compost. Similarly, avoid orange peel that has been treated with a fungicide as this will kill the fungi that

Compost bins offer more protection and the wind cannot pick up any dry material. Compost at different stages can be kept separate (Bingerden House, the Netherlands).

are necessary for decomposition. You can add weeds that have gone to seed, but it is better not to risk the temperature in the heap being too low to destroy the seeds. Never put cooked food on the heap because it will attract dogs, cats, and rats.

Do not use the stems of brassicas, which could be infected with clubroot. You cannot get rid of the spores of this persistent disease. Do not add thick layers of grass or tree leaves, but always mix these with lighter material to allow air to penetrate. Heavy layers simply heat up and do not decay.

Grass will heat up in a compost heap and will not break down for lack of air.

Manuring the soil

A healthy soil is the basis for a healthy crop. Your first thoughts, therefore, must be given to the soil. By manuring, the soil's condition is maintained and, if need be, improved, and any lack of nutrients is corrected.

The action of the principal nutrients

Trials have shown that the following minerals are essential for plant growth: nitrogen, phosphorous, potassium, magnesium, calcium, and several trace elements. Many nutrients occur naturally in the soil and it depends on your maintenance policy whether

you will have to add a great deal or a little or none at all of these nutrients.

Nitrogen, shown by the letter N on ferti-lizer packaging, is necessary principally for the formation of protein and chlorophyll, thus for the green, growing parts.

Phosphorus , shown by the letter P, is important for the development of the roots, for the flowers, and the ripening of seeds and fruit.

Potassium is shown by K. This element influences the formation of carbohydrates, necessary for bulbs and tubers. Potassium also regulates the water budget of the plant and increases resistance to disease.

Magnesium, Mg, is needed for the formation of chlorophyll. It also plays an important part in the transportation of various nutrients within the plant.

Calcium is only a plant food to a very limited extent, yet it is indispensable for plants because calcium binds organic acids, such as oxalic acid, which would otherwise poison the plant. Calcium binds soil acids, is necessary for the formation of humus, improves soil structure, influences the uptake of nutrients, and promotes nitrogen fixation by bacteria.

Trace elements

For over a hundred years it has been known that very tiny amounts of other elements are needed for optimum crop growth. Even now, though, little is known about the exact working of these trace elements. It does appear, however, that both too much and too little can be harmful. For example, a shortage of

> **Tip**
> It is preferable to apply lime in the autumn or, on a dry soil, in the very early spring, and to mix it well into the soil. Never apply lime at the same time as organic fertilizer or with nitrate and phosphate fertilizers. Leave an interval of six weeks.

iron means that not enough chlorophyll is produced.

Adding trace elements is only justified if a shortage is apparent. This hardly ever happens in the ornamental garden.

Kinds of manure

There are various kinds of manure or fertilizer but they can be divided into two main groups, organic and inorganic or artificial manure. If you not only want to feed the plants but also to fertilize the soil, then choose organic manure. This can be further divided into non-concentrated organic manure (such as proper cow manure, horse manure, chicken manure, and so on) and concentrated organic manure including waste from slaughterhouses. You can use large quantities of the non-concentrated organic manures because the nutrient levels in these are relatively low. This manure contains the most organic material but few trace elements.

All animal manure must be at least six months old before it is used. Do not add it to the soil too early before the new growing season. To avoid leaching by the rain, you must work the manure into the top layer of the soil as soon as possible after spreading it.

This manure needs to be left in a heap for several more months. It must also be turned again before it is ready for use.

How much to add

On sandy soils in the spring and on clay soils before the frost, add 500 litres (100gall) stable manure per 100m2 (120yd2) of border plus 250 litres (50gall) compost. Special, very hungry plants such as roses should have 50 per cent more. In the autumn the border is covered with a 5cm (2″) layer of mulch.

In the vegetable garden use a basic rate of 500–600 litres (100–120gall) stable manure. Some crops will also need a supplementary feed to begin with.

Compost can also be used on its own. You will then need 600–750 litres (120–150gall) per 100m² (120yd²). In the vegetable garden you will also need to give a supplementary feed with a simple organic manure when starting a new crop.

Things are different for the lawn, which is, after all, a monoculture. Many nutrients are removed each year through regular mowing. Nowadays, special organic lawn fertilizers have been developed which contain, as well as nutrients, bacteria that can bind the free nitrogen from the air and micro-organisms that decompose cellulose. These micro-organisms have the ability to break down grass cuttings and prevent them forming a thatch. If you use this fertilizer, the grass cuttings must be left on the lawn as often as possible. Twice a year, in March and July/August, the fertilizer is spread on the lawn at the rate of 1kg (2lb) per 10m² (12yd²). This fertilizer is, however, not yet widely available.

Concentrated organic manure

If you cannot obtain stable manure, then you can use concentrated organic manures. These contain trace elements as well as high concentrations of nutrients and large amounts of organic material. Some of these you must regard as fresh manure. Fresh manure is too "sharp" and can scorch roots and the aboveground parts of plants. This manure must be mixed into the upper layers of the soil at least a fortnight before sowing or planting. Proprietary fertilizer mixtures are sold under various brand names. Widely used simple organic fertilizers are dried blood (13 per cent nitrogen and 85 per cent organic material), guano (bird manure, containing 14 per cent nitrogen), and hoof and horn, which contains 5 per cent phosphorus as well as nitrogen.

For a phosphate fertilizer you can use bone meal. This contains at least 18 per cent phosphoric acid together with 6 per cent nitrogen and 30 per cent calcium.

Apart from these concentrated organic fertilizers, additives are also available, such as ground oolitic limestone, ground dolomite, ground basalt, and bentonite. All concentrated fertilizers can be bought in powder or granular form.

Use a maximum of 15kg (30lb) mixed organic fertilizer per 100m² (120yd²).

Artificial fertilizer

Artificial fertilizer feeds the plant without benefiting the soil. The fast-acting fertilizers in particular give the plant a boost, which can cause it to outgrow its strength and fall prey to disease. The advantage of fast-acting artificial fertilizer for the vegetable garden is that any deficiency can be remedied quickly. Furthermore, it is easy to spread and the percentage and proportions of the various plant nutrients are known precisely. If you add too much the plant can be scorched by the high salt concentration. The risk of over-fertilizing is

> **Tip**
> If manuring has been neglected for years, drastic action will be necessary. Nutritional elements from liquid foliar feeding can be taken up directly by the plant via its leaves. This produces quicker results than most kinds of fertilizer, which are only absorbed by the roots.

obviously greater than with organic fertilizers. An excess of artificial fertilizer will leach out of the soil and damage the environment. Its manufacture, too, is bad for the environment.

As a basis you can use approximately 8kg (16lb) compound artificial manure per 100m² (100yd²).

Which manure to use?

The worse the soil structure the more important it is to choose a non-concentrated organic manure. The fact is that, in proportion, this contains the most organic material. If, on the other hand, your soil structure is good, you can then exclusively use compound, concentrated organic manures.

Acid and the soil

The terms "acid soil" and "acidity gradient" can be very confusing. In acid soil there is no naturally occurring limestone or chalk. The bacteria, which are necessary for the decomposition of organic material into nutrients that the plant can absorb, multiply with difficulty and work more slowly than in calcareous soil. An acid soil may also contain unrotted plant remains which will make it more moisture retaining but not more fertile. Ericaceous plants appreciate this acid, nutrient-poor soil.

The calcium level of the soil is expressed as the pH or acidity gradient. A pH of 7 is called neutral. Less than 7 (for example, a low pH of 6.5) is acid, and a pH higher than 7 (for instance, 7,5) is known as alkaline or basic: the soil is then calcareous. People talk about a low pH (for example, pH 4.7) when the soil is acid and thus has a high acidity gradient. If the soil is basic (for example, pH 7.9), then the soil has a high pH and the soil contains more calcium and is less acid. It has a low acidity gradient.

Each soil has its own ideal calcium level. For clay soil the pH must be about 7; for sandy soils it may vary between 5 and 6, although there are

Tip

Acid rain is caused by exhaust gasses that have combined with water vapour. These gasses, produced by industry, transport, and agriculture, act on soil as an acid fertilizer. At present, the only way to counter-act his is to lime soils that are affected by it.

calcareous sands in some places; for marl about 6.5; and for peaty soil the ideal pH is between 5 and 5.5. By adding lime to the soil the acids present are neutralized and nutrients are released. On heavy soil the lime binds the fine particles, making the structure more open. On average a dressing of 3kg (6lb) per 100m² (120yd²) is sufficient.

Which fertilizer to apply for the best effect depends on the nutrients that are already present in the soil. Since these are not visible to the naked eye, a soil investigation should be carried out to find which ones are lacking.

Digging

Obviously the soil must be worked if only to incorporate the manure. Surface digging is mainly done to work manure, compost, and suchlike into the ground and to loosen more compact soil so that more oxygen can penetrate. Make sure, however, that no weeds with tap roots are dug in or fresh green material. The latter attracts creatures in the soil, such as wireworms and leather-jackets. It is better to dig up all weeds that have not yet seeded and any green manure, and throw the fresh green on to the compost heap. Work manure and compost lightly into the surface layer of soil. If manure and compost are dug in deeper, much of the plant food will be washed down and lost.
It is better to dig clay soil before the winter and to leave the surface rough. Water freezing in the pores expands and will split the clods apart to

Turn over the topsoil sufficiently to bury the manure or to prepare the ground for a new planting season.

form crumbs. Sandy soil has a naturally loose structure that is very easily destroyed. It is more sensible to dig it in the spring when the manure is being worked in. Never walk over newly dug ground. Lay some planks over the surface to bring in manure or compost and to carry out any other work. If the garden, or borders, are completely overgrown, then you will need to use stepping stones or paths covered with bark chips to make a way between the plants.

Double digging

Double digging – three spits = 60cm (24″) – may be necessary to loosen the subsoil and to allow the plant roots to penetrate further into the soil. Try not to mix the layers and do keep the good garden soil at the top. A digging spade is the best tool to use in most cases, but for heavy clay soils it is better to use a standard fork because the soil will stick to it less and so the work will not be as heavy.

Tip

Use a digging fork to remove the roots of weeds. This is better than a spade which can easily chop through roots.

8 Tools and their uses

Which tools you will need for your garden will depend entirely on the size and layout of the garden and the way that you want to maintain it.

The basic tools

For normal work in the garden, more tools are needed than just a spade or a digging fork, shovel, and potato fork. There are certain jobs that are done in every garden, and all gardeners sow (with at least a hoe and a rake), plant (with a spade or trowel), weed (with a hoe or weed dibber), and loosen the soil (with a hand or powered cultivator). For the lawn, you will need a mower (manual or powered,) a pair of shears, a spring-tined rake, and perhaps an edging tool. For maintaining the hedges, clippers (perhaps electric). Finally secateurs and/or long-handled pruners and a pruning saw for the pruning. A watering can, garden hose, and material for tying up are also included under tools or accessories.

So with about ten different items you can look after your garden perfectly well. Remember also that, with good tools, the job is half done. Always buy these from an expert who can advise you, and do try them out before you buy them because no tool suits everyone.

Tools for digging

Actual digging is done with a spade, which has a steel blade. The harder the steel the higher the price. There are also spades with stainless steel blades that do not rust, but these are even dearer.

A row of the various tools needed for cultivating the soil. From left to right: a rake with bent teeth, a self-sharpening swing hoe, a Dutch hoe, a draw hoe, a spade, and a shovel. In the foreground there is a stainless-steel trowel.

A good spade is self-sharpening since its core is harder than the outside. The shape of the blade depends on its intended use. For example, for digging a spade with a blade not more than 15cm (6″) wide and 25cm (10″) long is adequate.

The blade must be slightly curved and slightly rounded at the bottom edge. This will then slide into the soil, as it were. The shaft is enclosed by the sleeve, which must be in one piece with the blade. If the shaft sleeve is riveted it is liable to break off. A shaft made of ash should be about 90cm (36″) long, depending on the height of the person who is going to use it the most. The shape of the handle can vary, and choice depends on personal preference.

A shovel, which has a broader blade, is used exclusively for picking up, moving, and spreading material, such as manure, garden waste, sand, and gravel.

The blade is almost dish-shaped so that it can pick up material, and curved so that not too much bending is involved. It is not made of hard steel.

A digging fork with flat or triangular-shaped tines made of hard steel is lighter to use than a spade. It is used for digging, planting, and lifting on heavy soils, and to remove weeds that have invasive roots. It is a little easier digging with a fork between plants because it will cause less damage than a spade.

A potato or manure fork has bent, widely spaced tines. This is used for picking up coarse material such as manure, weeds, and other waste.

The potato fork is "the" tool for raking up and collecting garden waste. It is also used a great deal for spreading and breaking up manure.

It is better to remove perennial weeds with a fork than with a spade, which can easily cut through the roots.

Loosening the soil

The soil can be loosened and sometimes weeds removed as well by using a cultivator, either powered or manual, and various kinds of hoe. Which tool is best will depend on the type of soil.

The powered cultivator

The powered cultivator has blades that break up the surface layers of soil to produce a crumb structure. It is useful on heavier soils that are very difficult to dig by hand. Wet soils should not be rotavated because they will become compacted.

Unfortunately all those blades also chop up the roots of perennial weeds, which then multiply, and they do no good to the various creatures living in the upper layers of soil. It is not advisable to use this machine on sandy soil because this soil's structure is very easily destroyed. A powered cultivator is not necessary for small gardens.

A cultivator has recurved prongs. You can cultivate the soil with one, three, or five prongs, as you choose.

The cultivator is the ideal tool for tilling the surface.

Manual cultivators

A manual cultivator has one, three, or five re-curved prongs on a shaft and is dragged through the soil. There are also models in which the prongs can be removed by means of a wing nut. The cultivator has a working breadth of up to 35cm (14″. This is an ideal tool for cultivating the topsoil, for example, for mixing in compost that loosens and aerates the soil. It is an ideal tool for larger areas of soil, for instance in the vegetable garden.

There is a smaller version which is used mainly on clay and loam. This has three curved prongs set close together, and it breaks up the topsoil to a width of 10cm (4″). It is dragged across the soil. You can also buy it with a short handle so that you can kneel down and use it among the plants.

Hoes

The Dutch hoe is pushed along just under the surface of the soil. It has a sharp steel blade that cuts off weeds under the ground. The back of the blade must be slightly raised when you are holding the top of the shaft at chest height. This is an ideal tool for light soils, but you must avoid overshooting and damaging the plants. On loam and clay soils it is easy to smear the soil and thus compact it. On these heavy soils, therefore, it is better to use a rake.

The draw hoe has a steel blade that is attached to

Tip

The rake (with eight to sixteen teeth) tends to be used for everything, yet it is only really intended for levelling the soil when you are going to sow or plant. Be careful when you use the rake among shrubs and perennials because, before you know it, these will have been raked on to the surface! You can use the rake to break up clods in clay soil. Moreover, you can make furrows and press the seed in with it. The rake is not suitable for sandy soil because it destroys the structure.

a shortish shaft by a curved neck. You can hoe weeds up effortlessly while loosening the soil at the same time.

Larger clods are also broken down into crumbs. Because it is drawn along, it is light to use on heavy soils.

Lawn rakes

A spring-tined rake is used for collecting fallen leaves and grass cuttings. You can also use it to rake up leaves and weeds among the border plants (you should never use a normal rake for this because it damages the plants). If you leave fallen leaves among plants in the border, it will then be easier to remove the weeds from these difficult areas.

The spring-tined rake has flexible teeth made of steel, bamboo, or plastic which are attached to the shaft in a fan shape. Some models can have their width adjusted by means of a wing nut. A flat-tined lawn rake is useful for raking up leaves both on paving and on hard surfaces, such as gravel. If you want to remove grass cuttings (although this is no longer necessary if you use the new fertilizer described in Chapter 7), a bamboo lawn rake is the best tool. This will also remove fallen leaves.

The lawnmower

The lawnmower is naturally the first item that comes to mind in connection with lawn care, and there are various kinds, including the cylinder mower, rotary mower, and the mechanical scythe. The latter is used for grass verges and wild gardens. It is especially suitable for cutting long grass which can then be made into hay, because the mechanical scythe does not chop it into short lengths.

The cylinder mower gives the best results, but is only suitable for very flat lawns. You have to discipline yourself into using it weekly, because longer grass does not cut well and can jam the machine.

A rotary mower, as the name implies, has a blade which rotates horizontally. This deals effectively with tall and coarse grass. It does not give as neat a result as a cylinder mower, but you can skip the mowing once in a while.

The various mowers can be powered by a petrol, diesel, or electric motor. All powered mowers are noisy; the electric motor is slightly less so but it has the disadvantage of being attached to a cable, which can be a problem if there are trees in your garden.

Petrol-driven motors should not be used at an angle, which makes them unsuitable for slopes. Mowers with a two-stroke engine can work on the slant because they have no sump, but older, two-stroke engines are often difficult to start.

A hover mower is suitable for uneven surfaces and slopes and will cut under trees and shrubs without difficulty. The finish to the lawn is, unfortunately, not as nice as with a cylinder mower.

Almost all mowers can be fitted with a grass box. If you buy a rotary mower avoid one with a detachable grass box on the side, because the weight of the grass can cause the machine to tilt and cut on the slant. Some rotary mowers have a rear box.

Before you go to the garden centre or agricultural engineers, think about what you want the machine to do.

What sort of ground – how much uneven ground, such as the sides of ponds and ditches and slopes – has to be mown regularly? How big an area is it. How much time do you want to spend on mowing? How often must you mow? How good do you want the lawn to look? You must also take into account how easy the mower is to use and, of course, safety.

It is also important to know what the arrangements are for servicing and whether spare parts are readily available.

Tools for lawn care. From left to right: battery-powered edge trimmer, brush cutter, plastic grass rake, petrol-driven lawnmower, half-moon edger, hand mowing machine, manual aerating fork.

Care of the lawn

The new lawn fertilizers that contain, in addition to organic fertilizers, bacteria which can break up cellulose and also fix nitrogen have made lawn care a little easier. If you apply this fertilizer twice a year, you will see the moss and thatch disappear like snow in summer (you will need to leave the grass clippings on the lawn as often as possible for this to happen). This treatment works best on light soils. You should still also be able to use a scarifying rake on your soil.

The scarifying rake has teeth like knives, and sometimes side teeth as well. You must drag the rake through the turf to open it up and to cut the grass roots. All the dry material (such as moss and thatch) is removed and the soil is aerated. This stimulates growth in the damaged roots and blades of the grass. This so-called "aeration" of the soil should also be carried out where a total lawn-care fertilizer is not applied twice a year. Aerators or slitters make holes through which air, water, and nutrients can penetrate to the grass roots. You can also use a garden fork for this.

Moss

If moss is growing on your lawn, it is usually assumed that the soil is acid. However, grasses like a mildly acid soil, and liming will weaken them.

Moss usually appears where there are such problems as compacted soil, a pH that is too high caused by too much or too little fertilizer, or too much shade. The situation can be improved by reducing the pH, thus making the soil more acid, and raking out the moss and sowing the bare patches. You can buy lawn seed mixtures suitable for shade.

Lawn edges

The edges of the lawn can be trimmed with shears, although many gardeners find this a boring job. Alternatives are paved paths and edges over which the wheels of the mower can run.

You do not need to kneel down to use all shears, since some have long handles. There are both mechanical and electric edging tools that you can use standing up.

A half-moon edger has a rounded blade for cutting the edges of the lawn. This is generally used twice a year. The edges can also be trimmed with

a spade. A strimmer is used by gardeners who have a lot of areas the mower cannot reach, for instance round trees or under shrubs.

The strimmer has an electric motor and a nylon cord that cuts through the grass.

Bare patches

The lawn can be damaged in various ways. Gardeners often hope that smaller bare patches will be sown by seed from the surrounding area, or that the existing grass will grow over them.

Experience shows that weeds usually get there first, which is a good enough reason to repair these patches yourself. Remove the top 5cm (2″) of soil, which is full of grass roots. Fill the hole with a mixture of garden soil, compost, and a little peat.

The soil should be about 1cm (1″) higher than the surrounding grass because fresh soil always sinks.

Sow seed on the bare patch and cover it with a thin layer of soil. If you sow in September, the soil will still be warm and early-morning mists will keep it damp.

The seed will germinate in about a week. If you use turf to fill the patch you prepare the soil in the same way, and the sod should be slightly proud.

Weed seedlings have come up in the dry, yellow patches.

The weeds and the old turf are removed.

The open patches are filled with good soil, which is firmed down.

Fresh grass seed is now sown and covered with a very thin layer of fine soil.

Finally, fill the gaps between the sods with a mixture of compost and peat. Keep the new turf damp until it is growing well.

Small tools

In the border, small plants need to be planted out or put in to fill gaps. In a mature border there is not much room left to work with a spade, so a small trowel will be easier to use. It must, however, be sturdy and not bend. A good trowel is therefore made of hard steel (at least the blade).

The handle can be made of metal or wood. A garden line with stakes is handy in the vegetable garden to ensure straight rows for sowing or planting. You can easily make one yourself with two pointed stakes about 35cm (14″) long joined with string or plastic cord. A dibber is also useful.

This can be made with a stake, again about 35cm (14″) long, pointed at one end, with a T-shaped handle at the other.

Garden twine is useful for tying up plants. Flexible ties are used for woody plants. The trunks or branches of these plants can then increase in thickness without the tie cutting into them.

Tools for pruning

The most important tool for pruning is a pair of secateurs. These are available in many different models. Make sure that the blades are made of stainless steel. The so-called anvil secateurs, in which an upper blade cuts against a hardened anvil, are the best known type.

These need less effort than the two-bladed by-pass secateurs which do, however, make a cleaner cut. The handles can be made of steel (heavy), aluminium or plastic (lighter).

Look carefully at the safety catch on the secateurs, which should not be able to spring open when the tool is not being used. The spring should be given a drop of oil now and again.

Check that the secateurs are comfortable. It makes a big difference which pair you buy whether you have small or large hands. There are also left-handed secateurs on the market.

The long-handled pruner is a pair of secateurs with long handles which give additional leverage. Some models have a ratchet mechanism which makes them lighter to use. These pruners are ideal for pruning thicker branches and thorny or prickly shrubs.

A pruning saw, either folding or not (with a slightly curved narrow blade) is useful for manoeuvring among shrubs and tree branches.

On the ground from left to right: grassclippers (sheep shears) also useful for clipping box bushes, long-handled pruners with anvil, hedging shears with wavy edge, secateurs, and adjustable (in the direction of cut) edging shears.

Against the door you can see a pruning saw and tree pruners with an anvil on a long pole for pruning the branches of trees.

The teeth must be aligned with the handle so that the saw cuts as you pull it towards you.

A pruning knife is not strictly necessary but is useful for trimming up an untidy pruning wound or a broken branch. Hedges are trimmed with hedging shears. There are dozens to choose from.

If you look at hand-operated hedge trimmers, there is one noticeable big difference in their blades. These may or may not have a wavy edge. The wavy-edged blade is more practical if you

have a hedge with thicker wood. Thicker blanches do not slide away from the blades so easily. You can buy most pruning tools with wooden, plastic, or aluminium handles.

Tip

If you do not have edging shears, then hedging shears can be used. These trim small lawns and the edges of the lawn extremely well.

Tools in use

Even the best tools will become unusable if they are not looked after. After use, all tools should be cleaned with a stiff brush and then oiled. It is better to hang them up for storage, because that avoids wear and they will stay sharper.

The wheelbarrow

Manure, compost, soil, garden waste, and tools can be moved in a wheelbarrow. A wheelbarrow is not strictly necessary in a small garden, where you can move the waste in a bucket.

Barrows have either one or two wheels. With the latter the weight remains on the wheels when it is moving, whereas with a single wheel the weight is taken by the arm and shoulder muscles. Look for a light model with broad tyres.

Watering can and garden hose

The watering can is indispensable for watering the odd pot or a seed bed when you do not want to uncoil the hose. Choose an oval shape for preference with an extra long handle to avoid bumping it on your legs and hence wetting your feet!

Buy as long a hose as you think you will need

Several hoses, connected to a water tap in the middle of the garden, are often more useful than one long garden hose.

and no more, because it always has to be uncoiled and coiled up again. It is often handy to buy several sections of different lengths and join these together as you need them. Invest in a good reel because it will prolong the life of your hose.

Watering

 Water is essential for plants. Plants lose water all the time by transpiration through their leaves. Bare soil in the sun and over which the wind blows also loses water through evaporation, unlike soil that is completely covered.

Roots can take water out of the soil in the evening and once the sun has moved off the plants. In the upper part of the soil there is a supply of water which is regularly replenished by rain. Part of the rain is held in the soil and the rest sinks down to the groundwater.

When to water

On warm days, plants can lose more water by transpiration than can be taken

up by their roots, and so leaves and stems begin to wilt. Wilting is a good thing for plants, because the total surface area of the plant is reduced and the risk of drying out totally is lessened. As the air cools down after sunset, the air humidity rises. The following morning the wilted individuals of yesterday are standing up straight. Nothing needs to be done at this point but if the following day the plants are still limp, there is clearly something wrong. They have not been able to recover as their supply of water has been used up, and you must do something to help. It is better to water during the evening, after the sun has gone down, because the least water will then be lost through transpiration. The intention in watering is to bring the available water up to the right level. Spraying the soil and the plants with the hose for half an hour will not help. Only the top few centimetres (inches) of the soil are wetted so, only the roots in the upper layer can take up the moisture. The deeper roots have nothing to do and so become lazy. Besides, deeper-rooted plants and those with tap roots will still not be able to reach the water. If you are not able to water for a day or two, all your plants will dry out.

During a dry spell it is better to water occasionally for several hours so that the whole of the upper layers – about 25 to 30cm (10 to 12") – becomes damp. This is preferable to giving a little water now and again. The roots are then encour-aged to seek water at greater depths.

Humus plays a role in watering

Whether or not you should water and for how long depends on the composition of your soil. Clay soil retains water longer than sandy soil. A good proportion of organic material (humus) is another factor that determines how water re-tentive your soil is. Humus helps sandy soil to retain water, while humus makes pure clay soil more permeable. After the supply of water has been replenished, it must remain available for the plants for as long as possible. A

Separate spray and misting heads can be place on stands at various positions in the garden. The angle is adjustable and the water reaches a long way, which makes this pulse-jet sprinkler suitable for larger gardens.

great deal of moisture is immediately lost by evaporation from the top layer of soil. Water falling on the surface closes the pores, and narrow openings develop through which the water is drawn up. It then evaporates on the surface. If after watering or a shower of rain the surface is loosened with a hoe, the connection between the moisture underground and the wafer-thin surface layer is broken, and hence evaporation is prevented.

It is even better to cover the soil between the plants with a mulch, which will prevent the soil forming a crust and will also stop the wind drying it out.

Ways of watering

A watering can with a rose is useful for watering seedlings, and you will avoid puddles forming by moving it from side to side. The fine drops prevent the soil forming a crust.

When using the garden hose, the finer the spray you use the less the surface soil is compacted. There are innumerable sprinkler heads for hoses which deliver the water as drops or as a fine mist. A sprinkler that can be fixed to a post is handier than one that you must hold, standing in the garden for hours. There are many types of sprinkler including the pulse-jet type, which reaches a long way and is suitable for larger gardens. You can also lay an underground system with sprinkler heads protruding above the ground at intervals. This can be controlled automatically by a humidity sensor on a time clock so that the system is only activated when the humidity in the vicinity of the sprinkler drops. Above-ground misting systems can also be installed which can be connected to the mains supply or an underground supply. Check with your local water authority for regulations on the use of hoses and sprinklers.

An oscillating sprinkler waters a rectangular area. Most water falls on the edge of the rectangle; however, this problem can be solved by moving the sprinkler regularly.

Weeds

In a very short time, bare ground becomes covered with plants. Where have they all come from? They have germinated from seeds that have been spread by the wind, birds, and animals. The type of soil and whether it is dry or moist, in sun or shade, sheltered or exposed will determine which seeds germinate. Docks do not grow on lime-rich soil and poppies grow on soil that has just been disturbed or turned over. "Weeds" are plants that are growing in the wrong place. Weeds only grow in soils and

under climatic conditions that suit them. In Indonesia the hibiscus is a weed and in the British Isles the stinging nettle. Farmers regard the cornflower as a weed while gardeners think it is a lovely plant for the border.

You can attack the weeds with the hoe and rake. There are weeds that can be easily hoed up, but others spread underground by means of a root-stock and it is these that cause the greatest problem.

Beating the weeds

Most people prefer to fill the garden with plants that have been brought from distant lands, and therefore from different conditions and soils, than with the native plants, the weeds.

Weeds have to be removed to prevent them smothering the ornamental plants and impairing their development. A newly planted flower border must therefore be weeded every week. Weeds are pulled out by hand when they are still very small and before they have used up too many of the nutrients.

You can hoe in shrub borders, but be careful to avoid the roots of the shrubs and any bulbs. In the vegetable garden, where the plants are usually grown in rows, the hoe is almost always used. It is better to hoe on a sunny, dry day.

That way you can let the weed lie on the surface. These will dry out and do not need to be raked up. You can save a lot of hoeing and damage by planting ground-cover plants under shrubs, although there will still be some hand weeding to do.

Hoeing in damp weather is a hopeless task. You have to remove every weed, preferably with a spring-tined rake, or it will grow again immediately.

Seep hoses are flattened garden hoses with holes in them. They function well among lower-growing plants. The hose is moved when a section of border has become well watered.

The hoe can be used to remove weeds from among and under shrubs

When is it best to weed?

The most frequent hand weeding has to be done immediately after planting. The young plants have not yet grown together and need all the nutrients they can get. Never give weeds the opportunity to run to seed because, if they manage to seed, they will spread in spite of your frantic hoeing. Remove the weeds in the autumn, too, just before the winter. You will notice the results of this in the spring when you will have fewer problems with weeds than your neighbours.

If you are not able to hoe or hand weed at a particular time, cut the flowers and seed heads off these pests in good time so that at least they can-

It is impossible to hoe among plants in the border. You have to hand weed here to protect the plants as much as possible.

If you do not remove or hoe every sprig straight away you could be in for a nice surprise. Here Euphorbia amygdaloides 'Rubra' *has sown itself abundantly.*

not seed themselves. Hoeing and pulling up perennial weeds will also keep these under control.

Remember that plants can only grow and spread because of their chlorophyll. Without this they will die.

Tip

Sometimes, a piece of ground where a lot of perennial weeds are thriving can be planted with potatoes before it is finally laid out. These provide a tall, close canopy that smothers any weeds growing underneath it by depriving them of light.

The natural look

If you have a garden in which the ornamental plants have been chosen carefully and, as far as possible, fit into the local environment, it is possible to minimize the amount of maintenance you will have to do.

However, this will limit your choice of plants. In a natural garden, plants that grow strongly and become invasive must be controlled; plants must be matched with each other as far as vigour is concerned.

The penetration and strength of the light will change over the years, as will the composition of the soil.

The plants' growth of will adapt to the changed conditions; some plants will disappear and new ones will emerge.

In present day gardens, most annual and biennial weeds disappear after a number of years because the soil is turned over and hence disturbed less frequently.

A corner of the wild garden.
You can see a great variation in plants.
Those that are too vigorous are kept in check.

By using old stones to make various levels, you can create different micro-climates. This makes a more varied plant growth possible.

Looking after border plants

🌱 In the first weeks after the border has been planted, everything looks orderly: neat clumps of green 25 to 45cm (10 to 18″) apart. The soil in between is still immaculate and beautifully black.

After a couple of rain showers, the plants' growth explodes. A green haze appears, but fortunately the ornamental plants are growing rapidly as well. The plants can support themselves up to a height of about 40cm (16″) but after that they need some help to stand upright.

Tying up

🌱 Some plants must be tied up. They must have support if they are not to be flattened by rain and strong winds. After such a beating it is almost impossible to force them into a nice shape again.

As a rule, plants should be tied up by mid-May. Bamboo canes, pea sticks, and metal and plastic supports can all be used.

Bamboo canes are used for tall plants with long flower stalks. Canes are naturally rather obvious, so they are stuck in behind the plant.

Plants are secured to a frame with jute twine, flexible ties or garden twine. The twines will rot within a year, while the flexible ties expand with the woody stems.

Light-coloured bamboo canes can be camouflaged by tying a few shoots flat against them. Then several stems are loosely tied to the cane with raffia or garden twine.

Occasionally the stems are tied one by one, as is the case with delphiniums. Plants with several long heavy branches – 200 to 300cm (6 to 10′ – which might be exposed to the wind qualify for this method of tying up.

For tying up bushy plants you can use *pea sticks*. These are twiggy branches cut from trees and shrubs.

Any kind can be used. A point is made at the bottom with a knife, and the branch is pushed into the soil close to the plant. If you put a couple of pea sticks round the plant it will grow through them naturally. After a time the dark supports will no longer be visible. If you do not have sufficient wood from pruning, ask for some "waste" from the public parks department or conservation service.

If pea sticks are not available at all, bushy plants or groups of plants can be supported by several bamboo canes arranged round the group. The whole group is held together with twine or raffia, which is tied loosely.

Low edging plants can also be supported by pea sticks to prevent them from growing over the edge. After a time you will not be able to see the supports.

Various types of metal or plastic *plant supports* are available in shops and garden centres. Rings and half rings are well known. Plastic rings are a green colour that does not always match the green of the plants and so these usually remain visible.

The metal versions are less obvious. Dark green lacquered metal supports and plant pins are nice to look at and, if some of the support remains visible, they can add an extra dimension to the border.

Support for climbing plants

Climbing plants must be supported and trained, but these plants will may need some assistance to climb. Each form of support uses a different kind of material.

There are a number of plants that cling on by means of aerial roots and suckers. These can climb walls and wooden fences without any difficulty, so you do not need to do anything. You must, however, make sure that Virginia creeper and ivy do not slip through under the roof tiles or grow indoors through a gap in a window frame.

If you let them grow against netting they will do quite well, but you will have to help them to weave through it.

Metal plant supports can be made in the shape of a half circle. They are very useful for keeping taller, bushy plants in order.

These plant stakes can be extended by means of a hook and eye. They keep edging plants unobtrusively within their beds.

Self-supporting climbers include:

Campsis radicans	trumpet creeper
Euonymus fortunei	spindle tree
Hedera helix	ivy
Hydrangea petiolaris	climbing hydrangea
Parthenocissus	Virginia creeper
Schizophragma	Japanese
hydrangeoides	hydrangea vine

There are also plants that twine, either clockwise or anticlockwise. If these are growing up a thin, taut string or round a smooth post, they will slide down. For a pergola the first stems must therefore be led upwards with rough material or round a tube of coarse chicken netting. As soon as the stems have reached the horizontal beams they will go their own way.

Wire netting, trellis-work, or steel welded mesh must be fixed to walls and fences. In the border use pea sticks or metal plant supports. Thanks to a combination of vertical and horizontal supports, twining plants will have no difficulty in growing upwards. Twining plants include:

Actinidia-species	
Akebia-species	
Ampelopsis-species	
Aristolochia durior	birthwort
Celastrus	staff vine
Humulus lupulus	common hop
Humulus japonica	Japanese hop
Ipomoea purpurea	morning glory
Lonicera-species	honeysuckle
Fallopia baldschuanica	
Wisteria-species	

Birthwort, Aristolochia durior, *grows rapidly and needs more than a 2m (6'7") fence. Here it is using its twining stems to climb up the antarctic beech,* Nothofagus antarctica.

During the course of evolution, parts of leaves and stems have developed into tendrils for attaching themselves to anything they touch. They cannot grip on to walls or fences and a thick post is too much for them, but they can hold on to the thinner wood of shrubs or to netting round posts. Fine and coarse netting, welded mesh, wooden trellis-work, bamboo, pea sticks, and even shrubs can all be used as supports. Plants which are easy to support include:

Bryonia white bryony
Clematis-species
Cobaea scandens (annual) cup-and-saucer vine
Lathyrus latifolius everlasting pea
Lathyrus odoratus (annual) sweet pea
Passiflora caerulea passion flower
Tropaeolum perigrinum Canary creeper
 (annual) creeper

Left: *The Virginia creeper attaches itself with suckers.*

Tropaeolum speciosum (perennial)
Vitis-species grape vines

A number of climbing plants do not actually climb. They have long trailing branches and have to be trained by being tied to supports. The materials suitable for supports have already been described in Chapter 4 on building materials. Remember not to fix the climber directly to the wall or fence, and use flexible ties for preference. The trailing plants include:

Ceanothus lobbianus
Chaenomeles flowering quince
Escallonia-hybrids
Forsythia suspensa
Jasminum nudiflorum winter jasmine
Pyracantha
Rosa rose
Rubus-species bramble

The grape vine takes hold of everything, including itself, with its tendrils.

Tip

There are only a few self-supporting climbing plants, so supports must be fixed to the wall. Use copper or stainless-steel hooks and eyes because steel, even galvanized, eventually begins to rust. Streaks of rusty water do not look attractive on a light coloured wall.

Modifying the behaviour of plants

Extending the flowering season

Some plants form seed as soon as they begin to flower. This is a pity, because all the plant's energy is put into forming seed and the flower buds are abandoned, more or less. The tiny flower buds that are already present in the leaf axils do not develop any further.

The flowering season of yarrow and globe thistle can be extended by removing the old flowers in good time.

If the old flowers are removed, the flowering season will be extended.
This is recommended for the following plants:

Achillea	yarrow
Aster	Michaelmas daisy
Campanula	bellflower
Coreopsis	tickseed
Delphinium	
Echinops	globe thistle
Gaillardia	blanket flower
Helenium	sneezeweed
Helianthus superbus	sunflower
Hemerocallis	day lily
Lupinus polyphyllus	lupin
Phlox	
Potentilla	
Rudbeckia	coneflower
Salvia x superba	ornamental sage

Flowering can be delayed until after the holidays with Heliopsis *by cutting the stems back by half at the beginning of June.*

Postponing flowering

Most perennials flower in the summer and you can expect a burst of colour in July and August.

If only the flowering period could be more extended! That can be done with group of plants which includes some that easily fall over or are flattened. You can cut back part of the stems by half.

The shortened stems begin to branch and broaden out straight away. The plant as a whole, therefore, becomes more rounded and more stable. The stems that were not cut will then grow on to flower first. When these have finished flowering, blooms appear on the newly branched stems.

The following plants are suitable for this treatment:

Golden rod becomes more bushy and stands up better if the stems are cut back by half at the beginning of June.

Aster	Michaelmas daisy
Buphthalmum salicifolium	yellow ox-eye
Campanula lactiflora	milky bellflower
Helenium autumnale	sneezeweed
Heliopsis helianthoides	
Lysimachia punctata	garden loosestrife
Monarda didyma	bergamot
Nepeta sibirica	catmint
Phlox paniculata	
Salvia x superba	ornamental sage
Solidago	golden rod
Veronica	

Preparing for the holidays

Remove as many flowers as possible before you go away on holiday – not only the ones that are over but also the ones that are fully open – otherwise while you are away they will finish flowering and produce seed. If you remove all the flowers there is a good chance that the plant will flower again when you come home. The blooms of perpetual-flowering roses are removed in a particular way.

The flowering head is cut back to the first normal leaf. Rose leaves consist of five separate leaflets, but immediately under the flower head the rose leaves have only three or fewer leaflets. After this pruning, give the rose an application of manure so that it can gather its strength for the next burst of flowers.

Winter protection

Frost-sensitive plants need protection in winter. Cover is available naturally in the form of their own dead leaves and stems. Fallen leaves from trees and shrubs provide extra cover. The sight of plants that have collapsed in autumn and winter goes so against the grain for many gardeners that they must have a great autumn clear out. A big mistake! To prevent plants freezing you can cover them with leaves, fir branches, moss, or reeds. You must provide winter protection for the following frost-sensitive plants:

Acanthus mollis can be killed off by severe frosts. Protect it with a light covering of leaves.

Acanthus	bear's breeches
Alstroemeria	Peruvian lily
Anemone x *hybrida*	Japanese anemone
Cortaderia	pampas grass
Crocosmia	montbretia
Eremurus	foxtail lily
Fuchsia	fuchsia
Gunnera	
Incarvillea	
Kniphofia	red-hot poker
Lavatera	tree mallow
Penstemon	beard tongue
Thalictrum (except *Th.* *aquilegifolium*)	meadow rue
Yucca	Spanish bayonet

> ## Tip
> Never cover the plants with peat because their lower leaves can rot under it, and too thick a layer can smother the plants.

The plants that are most susceptible to frost are the evergreen perennials. If the temperature is below freezing during the day as well as at night, they are likely to dry out and die. When the sun shines, they will try to take up water from the frozen soil to replace moisture lost from their leaves by transpiration. A light covering of fir branches or reeds is therefore laid over these plants to protect them as far as possible from the sun and the drying wind.

The yucca is a perennial plant which appreciates winter protection.

9 Various jobs

Sowing

🐌 Perennials, annuals and biennials (including vegetable crops), trees, shrubs, and even ferns (the spores), bulbs, and tubers can all be sown, but in practice it is chiefly annuals and biennials, vegetable crops, and sometimes perennials that are propagated by seed. Seeds behave in very different ways. Some are very large and others are as fine as dust. There are some seeds that can take weeks, even months to germinate. Others come up in a couple of days and some have to rest for a while after they have been collected. Some such as Christmas roses, must be sown immediately or they will not germinate. Some seeds, like sweet cicely, need cold stratification, which means that they will only germinate after they have been exposed to real or simulated winter cold.

Tip
If there is no frost during the winter, you can put seed that needs cold pretreatment into the deep freeze for a short time.

Some seeds must be sown indoors or in a warm greenhouse to germinate, while others can be sown either in or out of doors. The advantage of sowing in a warm environment is that plants needing warmth can be sown earlier, which means the plants will flower earlier.

On the other hand there are plants which do not need extra warmth for germination or which do not transplant well.

The seed of the Christmas rose must be sown almost immediately or it will lose its viability.

Indoors in propagators

🐌 There are many kinds of propagators available, with or without openings for ventilation in their covers. These propagators look attractive but they are not really necessary. Containers can be made from household items, such as plastic cups and egg boxes, as well as plastic and porous pots. Plastic and expanded polystyrene pots are warmer and retain more moisture than porous, clay pots. Whatever you are using, make sure that it has drainage holes in the bottom.

Assuming you are using a seed tray 50 x 40 x 90cm (20 x 16 x 4″) you will need approximately 15 litres (1 gallon) of sowing medium. This medium should not contain too many nutrients, it must be clean and well aerated, and it must be able to hold moisture. There are ready-to-use composts in the shops but you can make your own by mixing 2 parts of compost with 1 part of sharp sand. A mixture of 1 part leaf mould and 1 part sharp sand is also satisfactory –this remains moist for longer and contains even less nutrients. If you have no compost but can obtain peat, you can sow in a mixture of 3 parts

peat to 1 part sharp sand. Remember that peat contains no nutrients and the young seedlings will have to be pricked out into a richer compost very soon after they have germinated.

Mix the compost well and fill the trays to about 1cm (1/2″) below the rim. Firm it down well, especially round the edges where it will dry out more quickly. If you are sowing fine seed, seive the last portion of the compost (1cm – 1/2″) through a coarse sieve over the contents of the container. The surface is then smoothed down with a piece of wood. Finally, the container is filled to within 1cm (1/2″) of the rim. Moisten the compost well with a plant spray. Coarse seed should be placed about 4cm (2″) apart which means that they will not then need to be pricked

Sowing in trays: trays, packets of seed, sand, and compost are ready.

Mix well two parts damp compost and one part sand.

Fill the egg boxes with the sowing compost.

Press the compost down well, especially round the edges.

Sow several seeds together in a group (African marigold seed is used here). After germination the strongest seedlings will be kept.

Depending on the size of the seed, it is covered with a thin layer of sieved sowing compost.

In the end no seed is visible.

The whole tray is now made damp with the spray. The egg boxes with their lids closed are put in a warm place. The lid is removed immediately after the seedlings have begun to come up.

out. Fine seed should be sown as thinly as possible. Mixing it with a little dry sharp sand before sowing will help to prevent you sowing it too thickly. Sow the seed as deep as its own diameter.

This means that some seed does not need to be covered at all. Press the seed in lightly with a piece of wood.

Tip

If all that fiddly work drives you mad and you cannot get the seed in the right place, use pelleted seed. Seeds of various summer-flowering plants are available in the shops wrapped in a coating which aids germination. These look like fertilizer pellets.

Germination in the dark

The pots and trays should be placed near the window, but not in strong sunlight, at a temperature of about 18°C (64°F). Cover the trays with a sheet of glass or plastic to prevent them from drying out. The cover must be turned over each day to avoid the drops of water which condense on the glass falling on the seed and possibly causing them to rot.

Immediately after sowing lay a newspaper over the glass because germination takes place more rapidly in the dark. The newspaper must be removed as soon as the seedlings appear, otherwise they will become drawn and thin.

Some seeds are supplied on a tape on which the seeds are the correct distance apart. This makes sowing in rows very easy. After the ground has been loosened you simply spread the tape out on the soil.

The seed tape is covered with a thin layer of soil. Keep it damp!

Seed trays can also be placed on a shelf in a cupboard or in a dark room, providing it is really dark and you keep a careful eye on the temperature. When the small plants are big enough to handle with your fingers, the seedlings that are too close to each other must be thinned out. In the end they should be about 4cm (2″) apart.

Spraying and turning

The glass must be removed when the plants begin to touch it. You will notice that the compost dries out quickly now and it is necessary to start spraying. A watering-can gives too powerful a jet for young, tender plants. Young plants have a tendency to grow towards the light and,

before you know it, all the leaves and stems are leaning one way. To stop your plants growing at a permanent angle you must turn the tray regularly, preferably once a day. It is all too easy to forget to do this. To makes things easier, you can put a mirror or a piece of card covered in aluminium foil behind the trays on the side away from the window. The light falls on the shiny surfaces and is reflected towards the plants. They then have no reason to grow towards the window.

Hardening off

When the plants are about 10cm (4″) high they should be put into small pots to begin the process of hardening-off. If you have a cold frame, they can be put in there. If not, they can be put outside in the late morning and left for several hours. Each day they can be left outside a little longer but remember that, until May 20, they must be brought indoors at night. This hardening-off is of crucial importance. If it is neglected there will be a lot of casualties among your young plants.

Sowing in open ground

Seeds that do not need sowing indoors can be sown directly in open ground. Many vegetable crops and annuals such as marigold (*Calendula officinalis*), *Cosmos bipinnata*, cornflower (*Centaurea cyanus*), and various dried flowers, such as straw flower (*Helichrysum monstrosum*) and *Xeranthemum anuum*, are examples of these. Plants which form a taproot, such as Iceland poppy (*Papaver nudicaule*), Californian poppy (*Escholtzia californica*), and larkspur (*Consolida ajacis*), are sown directly where they are to grow.

Sowing in open ground means careful preparation. The patch of ground where you are going to sow should not be in the shade and, for flowering plants, should not be heavily manured because the plants will simply produce a lot of leaves and few flowers. If the garden is on poor

Californian poppies have a taproot, and so they do not tolerate being moved and must be sown in situ. A group like this must be sown in good time.

sandy soil it is better to work a 3cm (1 1\2") thick layer of compost into the top layer of soil. On heavy clay some sand is mixed into the top layer. Since the soil needs to have warmed up before sowing outside, seeds are not put in until after 15 April or, in a cold spring, only after 1 May. Vegetable crops which are sown directly *in situ* need a well manured soil.

Sufficient moisture

Rake the topsoil after it has been loosened and broken up finely. Make sure the soil is moist. If it is not it must be watered for several hours before sowing. If you do this just before sowing, the soil particles will stick to each other and it will be difficult to rake the seed in. Seed can be sown broadcast, or in drills which is by far the easiest method from the point of view of weeding. When the soil has been raked level mark

furrows in it a good hoe's width apart. The depth of the furrow depends on the kind of seed and the type of soil. Here again try to sow the seed as thinly as possible; very fine seed can be mixed with sand. After sowing, the furrow is covered lightly with earth. Out of doors seed is also sown at a depth equal to its size. The very finest seed is just mixed into the topsoil with the rake. The ground is watered again after sowing and firmed down to ensure good contact between seed and soil. To avoid drying out, the rows are covered with jute or rush mats or black polythene. These will also stop the birds pecking the seed. The covering is removed as soon as the seeds germinate, and they will now need to be watered in dry weather. Seeds that have been sown too thickly will need to be thinned out. Do this on a rainy day. Planting distance varies with the species but is always stated on the back of the seed packet.

You could perhaps plant out the thinnings somewhere else in the garden except plants with a tap root. With the extra room, the remaining seedlings will quickly grow, branch out, and flower abundantly.

There is more about sowing vegetables in Chapter 6 (se p. 227).

Taking cuttings

Plants grown from seed often different from the parent plants because they have inherited characteristics from both. If you want plants which are exact replicas of their parents, you can take cuttings. After sowing, taking cuttings is the most usual method of propagation.

Cuttings are young parts of the mother plant that are cut off and stuck in the ground where they will form roots and grow into new, separate plants.

For the purposes of the amateur gardener, cuttings can be divided into summer and winter cuttings.

Various types of cuttings

Both summer and winter cuttings can be taken from different parts of a plant. These are as follows:

- a tip cutting is taken from the tip of the shoot, which includes the terminal bud or growing point.

  The shoot is cut immediately below an eye or bud where, in summer, there is a leaf and, in winter, the leaf scar.

- a stem cutting does not include a terminal bud but has more eyes. It is always cut below an eye.

  For some species it is not necessary to take the cutting immediately under an eye; a leaf-bud cutting can be taken.

  This can be done with, among others, camellia and clematis.

- a nodal cutting is a stem cutting with only one bud and one node (a bud out of which a new stem will grow, beside the eye).

- a cutting with a heel has a small piece of older wood or wood from a previous shoot attached to it.

  The remaining piece of bark should not be too large because once in the ground, it will bend or roll up and may become an entry point for infection.

  This type of cutting is mainly taken from woody species that may take a long time to root.

Summer cuttings

Perennials in particular are propagated by means of tip cuttings which are taken in spring and summer. Softwood shoots about 10cm (4″) long are cut with a sharp knife from the plant and then trimmed below an eye, that is, where leaf and stem join.

The stem is slightly thickened here, which prevents rotting.

Check carefully that you have removed any flowers or flower buds because, if these develop, they will take a great deal of energy which the shoot can ill afford to lose when making roots.

Remove the leaves from the lower part of the cutting up to a third the way up. Now put the cutting in a jar of water to let it have a long drink.

You can use the same sort of containers for cuttings that were described earlier for seeds. A mixture of equal parts of peat and sand is suitable. Fill the container with the cutting compost and press this down well to 1cm (1/2″) below the rim. Space the cuttings out well and push them in up to the lowest leaf, making sure they are firm. The leaves must not be touching the compost!

Water them with a very fine spray and preferably cover them with a plastic lid. Keep the trays indoors or in a greenhouse or frame and out of the sun.

Once a week mist the cuttings. Wipe the condensation off the plastic lid each morning. Softwood cuttings are susceptible to rot because they are taken from the soft shoots of the plant. It is essential therefore that they root as quickly as possible.

This will best take place with a soil temperature of 21 to 24°C (70 to 75°F). It is better to keep the bottom of the cuttings warm rather than their tops.

> **Tip**
>
> The earlier in the year a softwood cutting is taken the earlier it will root.

Depending on which month you set the cuttings, they will need to be hardened off before they are planted out into open ground.

Winter cuttings

Woody species can be propagated by hardwood cuttings. A hardwood cutting consists of a section of ripe wood, without leaves, from a tree or shrub.

> **Tip**
>
> The bottom of softwood cuttings may be dipped into a fungicidal powder which can prevent fungal rot. Softwood cuttings must not be treated with a rooting powder.

The length of the cutting varies from 15 to 25cm (6 to 10″), depending on how far apart the buds are. Winter cuttings are taken during the winter months – between November and March – and can be put immediately outside in the ground in a sheltered, cool place.

Initially they are set side by side in bundles up to two thirds of their length set in the soil. They will then form a callus out of which the roots will later grow. In the spring these cuttings are planted out in open ground. Cuttings which are taken late in the winter, say February, can be placed in their final growing positions straight away.

Experience shows that it is better to take cuttings from species that are frost-sensitive early in November. In any case, it is better not to take cuttings during or immediately after a frost.

How to take a cutting

The cutting is taken just below an eye or bud because roots form most readily at this point. Besides, the tissues by a bud are not as tender and are therefore less vulnerable to the fungi that cause rot.

Unripe parts should be discarded. The upper end of the cutting is trimmed diagonally above a bud.

Make sure that the upper end of the cutting has been trimmed so that water cannot run into the bud below.

Wounding the cutting

In professional nurseries, winter and summer cuttings are often wounded although this is not necessary with species that root easily. Sometimes it can even be harmful, for example with very soft cuttings, because it encourages rot.

Wounding the cutting involves removing a sliver of bark from the outer side, a little deeper than the actual bark itself. The length of the sliver can vary from 1 to 3cm (1/2 to 1 1/2″). The lowest eye can be removed. If the wound is too deep, right down to the wood, there will be an increased likelihood of rot. It is often enough just to strip off or pull away needles, leaves, or side shoots from the cutting.

In many species, however, root development is encouraged in cuttings that have been wounded. There are various explanations for this. New roots develop on the cut surface of the cutting,

Cuttings of redcurrant: cut twigs the thickness of a pencil from the bush. The top three are perfect. The bottom two twigs are on one-year-old wood which will not root. This must first be removed.

The cuttings are trimmed at an angle above a bud (eye) to prevent water running into the bud.

and wounding exposes a larger area suitable for root growth. Another explanation is that more water, and perhaps more growth regulators, can be taken up by the cutting. The new roots may also find it easier to grow from a layer that is not as hard.

Some cuttings that are difficult to root can be treated with hormone rooting powder. The powder is applied by dipping the cutting into it to a depth of 1 to 3cm ($\frac{1}{2}$ to $1\frac{1}{2}$″).

Roots develop along the whole length of the cutting that has been in contact with the powder. The powder must not come into contact with the leaves or buds because that will delay the eyes from sprouting. The cuttings do not need to be moistened beforehand because enough powder will stick to them as they are.

It is advisable first to make holes in the compost where the treated cuttings are going to be planted so that the powder does not rub off.

Winter cuttings can be put directly in the ground. The soil must be loosened to a depth of 30cm (12″) and, on heavy soil, the nursery corner should be treated with sand.

On light sandy soil the surface layer is firmed down well after cultivation. The cuttings are al-

The cuttings vary in length from 20 to 25cm (8 to 10″). More than one cutting can be made from longer twigs. The cuttings are cut off straight across, immediately below an eye.

The cuttings are pushed into the ground for two thirds of their length at least 10cm (4″) apart. Press them in well.

most always stuck in upright (the right way up!). On very wet soil they are stuck in at an angle so that water will drain away from the wound; this prevents the cutting from rotting away. The depth to which the cutting is pushed in will depend on the length of the cutting, the species, and the type of soil. On peaty soil a third of the cutting is pushed in; on sandy soil about two thirds.

If you want to propagate a shrub as a standard, all the leaf buds except for the top three are removed.

The cutting is then pushed into the ground up to the remaining buds. The soil round the cutting is firmed down and watered. This assures good contact between the soil and the base of the cutting.

During the first months after planting the area around the cuttings is carefully weeded by hand and hoed. You will soon be able to tell whether or not your cuttings have rooted: they shoot and sometimes even flower. *Buddleja* species in particular can form little bushes that flower as early as their first summer with shoots 1m (3'3") long. In the autumn, after the leaves have fallen, the young shrubs are dug up and planted in their final positions.

Shrubs that can be propagated from winter cuttings include the following:

An x against the name of a shrub indicates that it should be wounded or treated with powder, or both.

Tree or shub	Wounded	Rooting powder
Acanthopanax	x	x
Acer negundo and *A. lobelii* (maple)	x	x
Actinidia	x	x
Aesculus (horse chestnut)	x	x
Aralia	–	–
Buddleja (butterfly bush)	x	–
Callicarpa	x	–
Campsis (trumpet creeper)	x	x
Caragana	x	x
Chaenomeles (flowering quince)	x	–
Chamaecyparis (cypress, summer cuttings)	x	–
Clematis	x	x
Cornus alba	–	x
C. sanguinea, C. stolonifera	x	x
Cytisus (broom, summer cuttings)	–	–
Deutzia (the fast-growing species)	–	–
Elaeagnus (oleaster)	x	x
Euonymus europaeus (spindle tree)	x	x
Diervilla	–	–
Forsythia	–	–
Ginkgo (maidenhair tree)	x	x
Hedera (ivy)	–	x
Hydrangaea paniculata and *H. arborescens* 'Annabelle'	x	x
Juniperus (common juniper)	–	x
Laburnum	x	x
Larix kaempferi	x	x
L. decidua	x	x
Lavandula angustifolia (lavender, summer cuttings)	–	–
Ligustrum ovalifolium, L. quihoui	x	–
Ligustrum vulgare (liguster)	x	–
Metasequoia glyptostroboides	x	–
Parthenocissus (Virginia creeper, cutting without suckers)	x	–
Philadelphus (mock orange)	x	–
Picea (all species)	–	–
Pinus	–	x
Potentilla fruticosa	x	x
Ribes (currant)	–	–
Salix (willow)	x	–
Sambucus (elderberry)	x	–
Sciadopitys Japanese umbrella pine, stand three days in water)	–	–

Skimmia	–	x
Stachyurus	x	x
Symphoricarpus (snowberry)	x	–
Tamarix (tamarisk)	x	x
Taxus (yew)	–	x
Thuja (red cedar)	–	–
Thuja (tip cutting)	x	–
Thuja cutting with heel, side shoots)	–	–
Thujopsis	x	–
Tsuga	x	x
Vaccinium corymbosum (blueberry)	–	–
Viburnum tinus	x	x
Viburnum opulus and *V. sargentii*	x	x
Weigelia	x	x

Cuttings of sub-shrubs: before you put the cuttings in open ground the soil must be loosened and raked.

Cuttings from sub-shrubs

Sub-shrubs can be propagated by cuttings taken at the end of the summer. Sub-shrubs are low-growing, woody species that are treated like perennials. It is difficult to draw a line between the woody shrubs and perennials because various plants that are in fact woody die back during the winter. *Lavatera*, *Fuchsia*, *Lespedeza*, southernwood (*Artemisia abrotanum*), and *Perovskia* all belong to this group.

The cuttings are easy to strike in a cold frame and you could also try them in a sheltered place in the open garden. This spot should be a corner sheltered from cold winds and out of strong sunlight. Both outdoors and under glass the soil must be well loosened. Compost mixed with sand should be worked into the top layer.

Cut out weak shoots

You can take cuttings from many herbs, such as lavender, rue, sage, and rosemary. *Veronica* (Hebe), heathers, and some evergreen shrubs such as box and *Rhododendron* good results from cuttings taken at the end of

The best cuttings are taken from ripe shoots that have not flowered. Any flowers are cut off.

The cuttings, about 10cm (4″) long, are cut at an angle below a leaf.

The leaves are stripped off the cuttings up to half way.

Cuttings ready to put in: l. to r. lavender, box, Salvia officinalis 'Purpurea', and Salvia officinalis.

August. Take cuttings from the very end of the branches where no flowers have developed. Cut any flowering shoots back as far as the leafy part of the stem. The cuttings should be 10cm (4″) long. The weak, young tops are cut out of cuttings that have not yet completely ripened or that have flowered. These weak tops should certainly be removed if flower buds are still likely to appear. The cuttings are trimmed at an angle, below a leaf. Remove all the leaves from the lower half of the cutting, then put the cuttings

The cuttings are stuck in the ground side by side. They must not touch.

The cuttings can be protected and kept moist under a plastic cloche.

next to each other in the ground up to the level of the leaves. They must not touch each other. Firm the soil well to maintain contact between soil and cutting.

Rooting powder

Rooting powder can promote root development with certain cuttings. Ask your supplier for a rooting powder for outdoor use. Before you push them into the ground, make a hole so that the powder is not rubbed off.

Use a watering can with a very fine hose to moisten the cuttings but avoid soaking them. Then put the lights on the frame. During the day the frame must be ventilated and the cuttings protected from strong sunlight.

Plastic cloche

If you are rooting cuttings in open ground, a plastic cloche will be very useful. An old umbrella could be used as a frame for a transparent cover.

Plant the cuttings in a circle and put the umbrella cloche over them like a dome. You only need to water the cuttings if it is extremely dry, and never do so in winter. The cuttings in a cold frame, however, need to be watered occasionally to prevent them from drying out.

Propagating clematis

At the end of July or the beginning of August you can propagate clematis by means of internodal cuttings. Find a young shoot with well developed and unblemished leaves. If the leaves are not yet fully developed, the cutting will concentrate first on developing its leaves and only later will it put out roots.

Clematis has pairs of opposite leaves. You make the cutting by snipping the stem just above one pair of leaves and 2 to 3cm (1 to 1 1/2″) below the next pair. You can therefore make a number of internodal cuttings from just one stem. One leaf of the pair is removed to reduce the surface

Clematis cuttings: long shoots are cut off in late July or early August. In fact several cuttings can be made from one long stem.

The cutting is cut off immediately above a pair of leaves and 3–4cm (1 1/2 – 2") below a pair of leaves. One leaf is then removed to reduce transpiration. The cutting is now ready.

area for transpiration (to prevent the cutting drying out) and to enable you to put more cuttings together in a given space. Again, the leaves should not touch each other. Use the same cutting compost you used for sub-shrubs. Clematis cuttings have the best chance of rooting in a cold frame. The cuttings can be planted out the following spring, after having been hardened off.

Layering and division

In the autumn and in March and April, woody species that are difficult to grow from cuttings can be layered. There are various ways of doing this, but the simplest method is to bend a branch from a shrub downwards and to fix it in the soil with a wooden peg or iron pin. The remaining part of the branch is bent upwards in a curve. This should be bound upright to, for example, a bamboo cane. Roots are encouraged to form by twisting the branch a half turn when you bend it into shape. If you are afraid the branch will crack, you could as an alternative scrape some bark from the undersurface of the part of the branch that will be in contact with the soil. The soil for layering must be fertile. Humus-rich sandy soil is recommended for this type of propagation.

New roots will form where the branch touches the ground. Only detach the new shrub from its parent when the roots are well developed. The time it takes for roots to develop varies greatly from shrub to shrub and, in most cases, happens within two years, but the rooting process can take longer, even up to five years!

If this way of acquiring new plants takes so long why bother to layer shrubs? One of the reasons

Layering shrubs: first note where the bent stem touches the ground.

The leaves are removed from the stem of the Weigela where it touches the ground.

A portion of the bark is scraped off the underside of the branch.

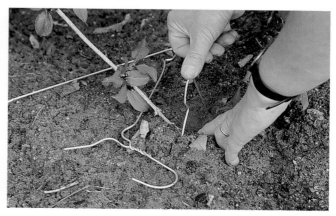

The branch is fixed down with a metal hook, in this case part of an old coat-hanger.

Make sure the hook is pushed firmly into the ground because the branch must remain in contact with the soil!

is that almost all plants can be propagated by layering, including plants that cannot be propagated by cuttings.

Tie the bent stem upright to a cane.

Dividing and replanting

When perennials have been growing in the same place for several years, they should be lifted – that is, taken out of the ground. You do this for various reasons: the plant may have spread out and has begun to smother weaker plants; or the plant may no longer be as attractive as it was, perhaps be-

Dividing perennials: digging round a clump of water avens, Geum rivale.

The clump is divided with a knife. Make sure that it is divided up to leave about five shoots and sufficient roots on each section.

This plant has made eleven new plants.

The young plants are planted out or heeled in immediately after being divided up.

cause it no longer produces the same number of flowers. Dividing the clumps and replanting them in separate portions can rejuvenate them, and the perennials may then last another three to four years or so.

Plants which flower early in the year can be divided immediately after flowering. If, however, they flower in early or mid summer, it is better to wait until the autumn. Autumn-flowering plants are best divided in the spring, because the plants could freeze before they have become fully re-established, especially on clay soils.

Large clumps are divided into small pieces and you use the younger, outer shoots for replanting, discarding the oldest part in the centre.

Try to divide the plants carefully using your hands, damaging as few roots as possible in the process. Very often the crown cannot be pulled apart and you will need to use a sharp knife. You must cut very carefully so that each bunch of roots still has five little shoots attached to it.

Do not let the clump dry out when doing this. It is better to heel them immediately side by side into a newly dug bed. Heeling-in is the same as planting except that as many plants as possible are put into the ground close together. Dry clumps have great difficulty in taking up water, and plants that are too dry when planted will dry out further, in spite of watering. Because the plants will be growing in the same place for a number of years, the soil should be well fertilized before planting: about a barrowload of manure per 10m² (12yd²). On sandy soil, well rotted stable manure is preferable while on clay soil, manure with a high straw content gives the best results. On both types of soil mix a further half barrowload of manure into the top layer.

Animals welcome and unwelcome

Apart from your plants, your garden will provide shelter for other forms of life, some welcome and some not. Whether you are happy with these extra guests will depend on how they treat your plants and how you feel about them. Do they damage your plants by burrowing and gnawing them, or do they simply give you the creeps?

If you think about a garden as a community of people, plants, and animals in which even scavengers have their particular tasks, then the terms beneficial and harmful that are usually applied to such cretures are simply being used from a human point of view. Always remember that amateur gardeners do not depend for their livelihoods on their gardens. If you take deliberate action by attacking a particular animal, you are interfering in a more or less ordered system in which everything has its own place.

Chemicals are on the humans' side because there are countless chemical means to protect your crops or to get rid of an apparent enemy. You must, however, ask yourself whether it really is necessary to spray and destroy like this?

If you permit a rich animal life to live in your garden, you are not only doing yourself a service but you are also contributing to a richer environment.

Many commonly used insecticides are not selective. They kill not only harmful insects but also those whose presence is entirely beneficial. Slug pellets, for example, not only kill slugs but are also poisonous to mammals and are harmful to humans. Selective insecticides have the least damaging effect on the environment, because organisms other than the target ones are spared. And remember always to read the directions for use very carefully.

Making your garden attractive for animal life

You can attract as many organisms as possible – many useful ones alongside the harmful ones – by having as great a variety of plants as possible. Use various species of trees and shrubs, those that have catkins and flowers as well as those that produce fruit. Plants with single flowers are a must for butter-

Birds do not only polish off seeds and harmful insects: blackbirds are also very fond of red currants.

flies, bees and bumblebees. These insects cannot find nectar and pollen in the double-flowered species that are grown more and more these days. There may be a small corner somewhere in your garden that does not need to be hoed and pruned. The birds in particular will appreciate this corner. A water feature in your garden will certainly attract these consumers of unwanted seeds and caterpillars. Finally, do not be too tidy: try to keep the soil covered with plants as far as possible.

Welcome guests
Birds are attractive to look at and help to get rid of all sorts of pests. Starlings, among other birds, live on caterpillars, beetles, and leather-jackets, while great tits eat countless numbers of caterpillars and insects.

You can attract birds by providing nesting sites. Birds particularly like nesting in thick hedges, ivy (blackbirds and wrens), and conifers (gold-crests, among others). Birds prefer shrubs with berries, except the berries of *Callicarpa, Gaultheria*, Guelder rose, and snowberry which they dislike. Nest-boxes can be put beside these shrubs. Some birds love the seeds of sunflowers, Michaelmas daisies, *Linaria*, cosmos, and thistles. Water is indispensable for all birds. They can survive the winter with rotten apples, stale bread, and such like, and fat is acceptable at any time of the year. Remember that birds are easily scared away. They are terrified of cats and do not like netting and birdscaring tapes.

A nest-box for tits
A nest-box is best made of pine or deal 1.5 to 2cm ($^3/_4$ to 1″) thick. The back section, however, should be more sturdy, preferably oak. You will also need long nails (extra long for hanging the box up) and glue to assemble the parts and make the box watertight. When it is complete the nest-box must treated only externally with

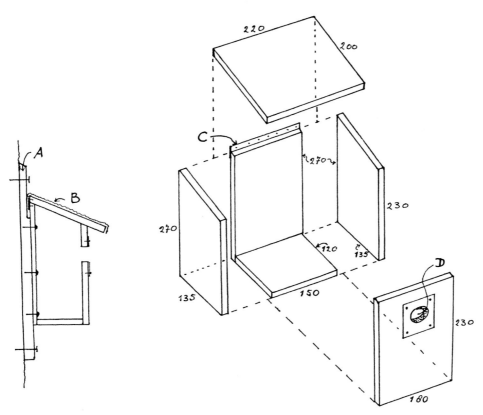

The construction of a nest-box for tits. A: hanging plank, 40cm (16″) long, 2.5cm (1″) thick; B: roofing felt; C: hinge; D: opening 2.3cm (1 1/8″) diameter.

varnish or wood preservative. The roof is covered with roofing felt secured with felt tacks. The nest-box must be completely watertight. The roof overhangs and often slopes to prevent rain getting in. You must be able to lift the roof off the box, and real DIY enthusiasts could design the bottom so that it can be opened easily for cleaning after use. The bracket should not be horizontal but slope upwards at an angle of 45 degrees to prevent the wind blowing the box off. Whatever type of nest-box you are making, the distance from the bottom to the entrance hole (which varies in diameter according to species) must be at least 17cm (7″) or the young birds will come out of the box too soon. Do not put a perch in front of the hole because it could provide a foothold for predators. A zinc or aluminium plate can be fixed round the hole for extra security. This will prevent woodpeckers and rodents making the hole bigger to get in.

Not enough nesting sites in your garden? You can buy all kinds of nest-boxes.

The cat from next door

Cats, especially those "from next door", chase away a great many birds. Cats love catmint, *Nepeta*, and will roll in it and eat it. They also find peat attractive. They can be deterred by spreading coffee grounds in appropriate places. Throwing water over cats will get results, if only temporarily.

Hedgehogs

Hedgehogs do a lot of good work at night. They live off insects, slugs, and fruit, among other things. They like a quiet place with plenty of leaves or other vegetation. Always check a bonfire before lighting it because there may be a hedgehog curled up in it.

Moles

Moles live on creatures in the soil, such as leather-jackets, wireworms, and worms. They loosen the soil and help to aerate it. They burrow through the soil and push it up into the familiar mole hills which can be a great nuisance on a lawn. Plants can dry out because roots in mole runs are no longer in contact with the soil. Moles can be particularly active in gardens that have a rich soil fauna. They can be prevented from burrowing under the lawn by sinking wire netting in the ground vertically to a depth of 40cm (16″). If they must be removed, it is best

Rabbits can make good pets and also provide good manure.

to catch them with a mole trap. The biennial caper spurge, *Euphorbia lathyris*, is reputed to drive moles away. It is preferable not to use chemical remedies against moles because these often contain strong poison which can also be dangerous to your pets.

Tame and wild rabbits

Tame rabbits in a run or a specially made rabbit hutch produce droppings which are very suitable for the compost heap. Tame and wild rabbits that run free through your garden are, however,

---

Tip

Are there a lot of rabbits where you live? Then there is nothing else for it but to plant herbaceous (biennial and perennial) species in the garden that they do not like. They leave the following plants alone: monkshood (*Aconitum*), alkanet (*Anchusa*), lords-and-ladies (*Arum*), angels' trumpets (*Datura*), foxglove (*Digitalis*), viper's-bugloss (*Echium*), spurge (*Euphorbia*), stinking hellebore (*Helleborus foetidus*), hogweed (*Heracleum*), iris (*Iris germanica*), catmint (*Nepeta*), Solomon's-seal (*Polygonatum*)

very keen on eating all kinds of plants, especially fruit trees.

You can protect the bark of fruit trees by putting a wire netting cage round the trunk or a special rigid tubular guard.

If you have a small pond in your garden you will, with a bit of luck, have frogs too. The common frog is not very aquatic outside the breeding season. You may come across frogs and toads in the garden.

Snail shells vary in colour. They clear up weaklings among the plants.

Frogs, toads, and newts

Bogs and pools of water attract frogs, toads, and newts. These eat slugs, insects, and small fish. For frogs in particular, a pool should have a gently sloping bank. If the bed is covered with fine clay this will make it naturally watertight. Too much vegetation should be avoided, and the southern edge should be kept bare.

Chickens

Free-range chickens are a valuable asset but can be a nuisance because they scratch the soil in search of leather-jackets, worms, and insect larvae. They do the least damage if the space they roam in is about ± 20m² (± 24yd²) for the larger breeds. They should also be provided with a patch of grass to feed on. The species with feathered legs (Brahmas and Cochins) do not dig up plants.

Slugs and snails

Slugs and snails are scavengers. They process diseased and rotten leaves into food for other organisms. Generally they first clear up all those plants that are not thriving because they are in an unfavourable position or soil, or because they have been newly planted. Snails not only live on plants but also on algae, which is why they are often seen on tree trunks. Of the various species of slug, the most damage is done by the netted slug which is to be found on all kinds of plants and fruit. However, not all slugs live on plants. The great grey slug, for example, which is about 10 to 15cm (4 to 6″) long and is grey with dark flecks, lives on fungi. It is very difficult to keep slugs off thyme and hyssop. The slugs' natural

---

Tip

If you want to use slug pellets, you must ensure that these poisonous things are used dry (7 pellets per m² (1.2 yd²) is sufficient). Also, use them in a slug trap. They must never be left behind in the garden afterwards. They are also poisonous to mammals.

predators natural predators are thrushes, hedge-hogs, toads, and ground beetles. If you crush the clusters of slug and snail eggs in the soil this will prevent a massive expansion of the slug and snail populations. The eggs look like small translucent balls, from 0.1 to 0.5mm across. Slugs can be caught in beer traps. You can also spread out large leaves, such as rhubarb, to entice them.

Sooty mould is parasitic on the honeydew secreted by aphids. When the aphids have gone the mould will disappear of its own accord.

Aphids

Aphids live on plant juices. From this they exude a sweet fluid which is, in turn, attractive to ants. This fluid also functions as a growing medium for fungi, such as the black sooty mould. Aphids can also transmit virus diseases. Despite all this trouble, it is often not necessary to spray aphids in the ornamental garden. It may make more sense to cut the plant back or to attack the aphids with a powerful jet of soapy water. The natural enemies of the aphids include ladybirds, larvae of hover-flies, ichneumon flies, birds, and spiders. An environmentally friendly infusion of stinging nettles and soft soap dissolved in alcohol is not very poisonous but it does not work selectively. Sage bushes also seem to discourage aphids.

Ants

Ants do not generally cause harm but they can be a nuisance. A good patch of marigold will drive them away, and they do not like lavender, mint, tansy, or wormwood either.

Bees and bumblebees

There are many plants from which bees take nectar. As they are doing this they are helping to

A swarm of bees with the new queen has settled in a willow tree.

The swarm is cooled with a water spray to make them less active.

The swarm is shaken into a hive. Cigarette smoke avoids stings.

The result: the swarm has a new home.

pollinate flowers that will later form fruit. To keep the bees' flight path clear, plant a tall crop just in front of the opening to the hive so that they are forced to fly upwards immediately. Special bee plants include willow, maples, box, heather, ivy, various herbs, asters, golden rod, and flowering brassica species, especially broccoli.

Butterflies

Butterflies can be found on food plants, and many of the plants attractive to bees are also attractive to butterflies. Other notable butterfly plants are the butterfly bush and *Sedum spectabile*. If you remove all the caterpillars in your garden, fewer butterflies will appear. If you plant a spindle tree, *Euonymus europaeus,* there is a good chance of spindle moths and caterpillars appearing. These shrubs are eaten bare every year but, whether or not they have been treated with insecticide, they will become green again. They will not, however, produce any berries. If you cut off the webs completely the shrub will not become totally bare.

Flies and midges

Both flies and midges are discouraged by the nut tree, and flies do not like elderberry bushes at all. An open compost heap with scraps of cooked food is an open invitation to flies. Midges also do not like the smell of mint.

Earwigs

Earwigs can be caught in plant pots stuffed with shavings or straw that have been placed upside down on canes among the plants. Earwigs not only eat plants but also small creatures, including aphids.

Woodlice

You find woodlice in dark, damp places. They have a preference for dead or rotting material so are often found in the compost heap. In a neat and tidy greenhouse they will still survive on seedlings. By leaving a couple of pieces of dead wood in your greenhouse you will keep the woodlice away from your plants. The woodlice's

natural predators are harvestmen and nocturnal hunting spiders.

Earthworms

Earthworms cannot be praised enough. They make the soil more open and fertile and their excreta, which you often see in the garden as the familiar coiled wormcasts usually between slabs or in the grass, make first-class manure. Wormcasts can even be bought in some shops! In the compost heap worms work wonders by turning garden and kitchen garbage into a rich dark soil.

Froghopper or spittlebugs

You probably are be familiar with cuckoo-spit, in which the green larva or spittlebug lives in a patches of spit-like foam. This relatively harmless creature lives on plant juices. If a plant is covered in cuckoo-spit, a strong jet of water will help to remove it.

Leaf miners

On lilac, privet, and holly you sometimes see leaves with tunnels or cysts in them caused by the larvae of various flies. These flies lay their eggs on the leaves and, after hatching, the larvae eat their way round between the layers of tissue. You will be able to see these if you cut open a tunnel or cyst.

The spread of leaf miners can be prevented by picking off the affected leaves and burning them. Never throw them on the compost heap.

Admittedly it does not look very nice, but these leaf-rollers are not doing the rose much harm. It is flowering freely and the damage is limited to a few leaves.

Leaf-rolling sawflies

At the end of twigs in particular, you will sometimes see leaves that have been rolled up and spun together. If you pull them apart you will find small brown or green caterpillars, which quickly start to make looping movements. They nibble flower buds of all kinds, but especially roses, fruit trees, holly, and many hedge plants.
A combination of climbing roses and old fruit trees almost always attracts leaf-rollers. Their numbers can be reduced by killing the caterpillars or by cutting off the spun leaves.

Mildew: leaves covered in a greyish-white powder.

Fungi

Fungi in the garden include not only powdery mildews on, for example, asters but also toadstools.
• Sooty mould is particulary prevalent on roses in the ornamental garden. The chances of roses being affected are much less if you ensure that they are growing on a nutrient- and lime-rich soil. You could also plant varieties that are less susceptible to sooty mould.
• Mildew is recognizable as a greyish-white powder on leaves. In occurs particularly in *dry* summers on plants that had not grown sufficiently well before they formed their flower buds. From the middle of June you often see white powder appearing on goldenrod, aster, phlox, and roses, which are very vulnerable to it although newer strains are more resistant. The attack can be lessened by moving the plants to a new location and cutting off all the affected leaves. Selective, biological sprays based on sulphur are available in garden centres.
• Fireblight, which is in fact caused by a bacterium, is dreaded by fruit growers and tree nurserymen because whole plantations or orchards can be destroyed by it. Be on the alert if, during summer and autumn, flowers and shoots suddenly Shrivel up while the leaves do not fall but remain where they are, dark-coloured, hanging on the branches. Very susceptible species include the tall medlar, *Cotoneaster*, the hawthorn *Crataegus*, and *Photinia*. Others that can be affected are firethorn, ornamental crab apple, apple, quince, pear, and the *Sorbus* species (rowan and whitebeam). In some countries the very susceptible species may no longer be planted in some areas to protect fruit crops and tree nurseries. Affected trees must be cut back hard or even pulled up and the diseased material must be burnt. The pruning tools you have used on the affected trees must be disinfected with spirit before you use them on any other trees or shrubs. The gardener must wash thoroughly afterwards, as should be the clothing he or she wore.
• Toadstools: if untreated white wood is used in

the garden or dead wood is left lying about, there is a good chance that in a little while all kinds of pretty or not so pretty toadstools will appear. These can vary from sulphur tufts and ink caps to the common oyster fungus and dryad's saddle. These wood toadstools generally feed off dying wood and do not attack healthy wood. An exception to this is the coral spot (*Nectria*), which occurs widely on dead branches but can also spread on to living wood. Coral spot can be recognized by the many tiny orange-red spots and pimples on dead branches. Affected wood should be removed and burnt.

If your garden is not kept too tidy, all sorts of pleasant surprises could be in store for you.
In all events, all kinds of plants and animals will be more at home, and there will be much more of interest for anyone visiting your garden to see.

If in the height of summer the ends of the branches shrivel and the leaves do not fall but hang like limp flags on the branches, you had better phone experts, for example the Plant Health Department of the Ministry of Agriculture, who can tell you whether or not you have a case of fireblight.

Do not "spring clean" your garden in the autumn. The fungi (toadstools) will then flourish!

10 Pruning: a necessary evil

If your garden were allowed to grow completely wild and you were prepared to let nature have a free hand, there would be no need to prune. Trees and shrubs would have free rein to grow, flower, set seed, and die.

Most gardeners want more than this. They want to encourage that slow-growing shrub which is growing lop-sidedly to grow more vigorously and to become more shapely.

Pruning can also stimulate flowering and fruit production, and it rejuvenates old, woody species.

General rules for pruning

There are a few general rules for pruning which apply to all woody species:

- Remove one of two branches that are rubbing against each other, or bend one so that the branches no longer hamper each others' growth.
- Branches that are touching the ground should be totally or partially cut back.
- Where branches are growing close to each other at the same level, remove all but one.

  A branch that makes a tree or shrub unbalanced should be removed or shortened.
- The suckers (wood that grows from below

> **Tip**
> A branch that has been pruned almost always produces new shoots just below the cut.

ground) must be completely removed as soon as they appear.

Branch, shoot, and twig

There is often confusion over the names of the various parts of a tree or shrub. In chronological order they are as follows. A *shoot* is this year's growth, which appears in spring and early summer.

When a branch is cut off the new shoots sprout immediately below the cut.

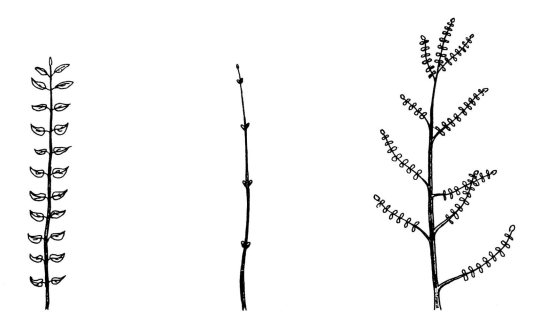

From left to right: shoot, twig, and branch.

It is leafy, herbaceous (green and pliable), and unbranched. At the end of summer the shoot becomes woody and is then referred to as a twig.

A *twig* is a woody shoot in its first winter. In the case of deciduous shrubs, this will be leafless while the twigs of an evergreen shrub will, of course, still have leaves. After the first winter the twig grows longer and produces side shoots. A branch then develops.

As *branches* age they produce more side shoots (spring and summer) and side twigs (winter). Shrubs can consist of one-, two-, or three-year-old branches, or even older ones. Shoots and twigs are never older than one year.

Pruning trees

The structure of the tree

A tree consists of a trunk with branches growing out of it. The trunk grows faster than the side branches. The terminal bud at the end of the branch usually causes the branch to extend. However, this is not the only place where shoots can appear. Buds lower down will

also grow into shoots. Most shoots (which will later become twigs and branches) develop in the crown and the outer edge of the tree, because the strongest growth is at the ends of branches and is in a vertical direction.

Pruning

With young trees, surplus twigs and branches are removed early so that the remaining twigs and branches can develop normally. In the first few years formative pruning is required to ensure that the crown develops into a regular shape. Care is needed to make sure the leader grows in proportion with the rest of the branches.

Choose the best branches for the crown; they should spread out in all directions and in a regular shape. If branches cross each other remove all but one, together with any branches that are growing towards the centre of the tree. Cut branches back to an outward-facing bud or "eye." With species that have opposite buds, one bud is removed to prevent the branch forking. Most trees may be pruned in winter and spring. Old trees are only pruned when their crowns have become so broad and heavy that there is a danger of branches breaking off. Some trees may

It takes a long time for a large wound to heal over. Meanwhile there is a serious danger of rot setting in and diseases entering the wound. Prune in good time so that the wound will only be small.

need their leader pruning back to a lower, well developed bud because their leader is too long and weak. Trees such as ash (*Fraxinus*), bean tree (*Catalpa*), horse chestnut (*Aesculus*), and maple (*Acer*) should not have their leader shortened. Trees which produce few shoots in the early stages of their growth such as walnut (*Juglans*), wingnut (*Pterocarya*), and tree of heaven (*Ailanthus*), are not pruned. With the

---

Tip

Be careful when you prune! In some trees the flow of sap is so strong in spring that pruning could cause the tree to bleed to death. Examples include birch (*Betula*), maple (*Acer*), walnut (*Juglans*), tulip tree (*Liriodendron*).

---

beech (*Fagus*), you need to be careful not to remove too many branches at one time because the tree may suffer from scorching. If the trunk is suddenly exposed to the sun, the bark in the affected areas comes loose; so wind and rain can damage the wood underneath. You can protect the trunk with a layer of whitewash or by wrapping it in jute sacking. The lime (*Tilia*) is also susceptible to scorching.

Pruning trees in special forms

- Weeping forms mostly need thinning. The drooping branches are cut back to an outward-facing eye in such species as birch (*Betula*), and willow (*Salix*).
- Columnar forms are pruned to an inward-facing eye.
- The pollarded tree: if old trees have to be cut back severely, you can pollard them. This

Right: *The suckers that grow from below ground must be removed as low down and as early as possible.*

• 330 •

The branches of the plane tree are cut of at the same height and bent outwards, to create a canopy of green foliage in summer. Each year the young twigs are removed from the old wood.

drastic method of pruning is only used if absolutely necessary. The following trees can be pollarded: elm (*Ulmus*), maple (*Acer*), sweet chestnut (*Castanea*), plane (*Platanus*), horse chestnut (*Aesculus*), ash (*Fraxinus*), oak (*Quercus*), poplar, (*Populus*), wingnut (*Pterocarya*), willow (*Salix*), lime (*Tilia*), and false acacia (*Robinia*).

Pruning conifers

Most conifers will only tolerate trimming: in April or May the tops of the branches are taken off with a sharp knife. If this is done from the outset, the tree or shrub will remain green and thick. The red cedar, *Thuja*, recognizable by its erect top, and the Leyland cypress x *Cupressocyparis leylandii*, tolerate pruning better than most other conifers. The yew, *Taxus*, can be cut back hard but will always sprout again. It grows very slowly and is very poisonous. Firs (*Abies*), and spruces (*Picea*), must never have their tops cut unless one of two leaders needs to be removed.

Shrubs

All the characteristics of trees to a lesser extent can also be seen in shrubs. Shrubs, or bushes, do not, however, produce one leading stem and they branch just above the ground. They are planted in the ornamental garden because of their attractive flowers, fruit, or foliage, and the time and method of pruning must take account of this.

Pruning shrubs

Spring-flowering shrubs
Shrubs which flower before 1 July do so on wood that grew the previous year and the year before that. After flowering all the branches that have borne flowers are cut back as far as possible, preferably to just above the ground. One-year-old, unbranched twigs are left. If only a few young shoots have come up from ground level, the branches that have flowered are then pruned to the lowest young twig. Never cut off spent branches at 1m (3'3") or higher because a whole cluster of new shoots will appear from here, leaving the lower part of the shrub bare.
This applies, for example, to:
Forsythia
Philadelphus (mock orange)
Kerria (jew's mallow)
Spiraea thunbergii
Spiraea arguta
Ribes-species (flowering currant)
Tamarix tetrandra tamarisk

Summer-flowering shrubs

For those shrubs that flower after 1 July, all the twigs and branches are pruned in March or April. Each shoot that forms in spring and early summer has the potential to flower because these shrubs flower on young wood. The twigs of the butterfly bush (*Buddleja*) can be cut hard back. *Hypericum, Spiraea* x *bumalda,* and *Potentilla* are all examples of shrubs which are cut down to within 10cm (4″) of the ground in March.

In the case of *Hydrangea paniculata,* the thick twigs are shortened drastically and the thin ones are removed altogether.

Bedding roses and hybrid tea roses must always

Hypericum androsaemum is pruned in spring. You will then be able to enjoy the berries in autumn and winter.

Below: *Potentilla fruticosa is cut back in spring to within 10cm (4″) of the ground.*

be pruned above a low outward-facing bud. Leave three to five heavily pruned twigs. Suckers must be pulled off as far below the soil as possible, rather than cut off. *Hydrangea macrophylla*, the hydrangea with the rounded flower heads, is an exception to this pruning rule. Each year a third of the oldest branches are cut hard back.

In late spring cut the dead flower heads (above a pair of sturdy buds) from the branches that have flowered the previous year. The dead heads protect the young shoots against frost.

Shrubs that fruit

Shrubs that flower in spring and bear fruit in autumn need only be thinned out. After they have flowered a few of the old branches are taken out, as well as any crossed branches or those that rub against each other.

The younger branches are left to produce fruit in autumn.

Examples include:
Cotoneaster (the fertile snowball species)
Viburnum
Berberis (barberry)
Chaenomeles (flowering quince)
Ligustrum (privet)
Rosa-species

Shrubs with attractive stems

The twigs are the most colourful part of these shrubs; the flowers and fruit are insignificant in comparison.

These shrubs are pruned hard in March or April to allow new, brightly coloured shoots to grow during summer.

Examples include the dogwoods:

The flowering quince, Chaenomeles, *is pruned after it has flowered. Only the old branches and those that are tangled are removed to avoid interfering with the fruit crop.*

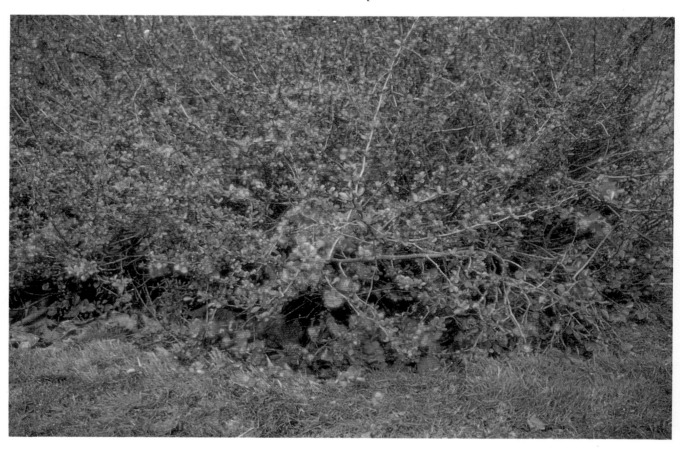

Cornus alba 'Sibirica', red
Cornus alba 'Kesselringii', purple
Cornus stolonifera 'Flavirimea', yellowish green

Prunus species

These shrubs are not pruned until the beginning of July because the sap flows very freely in spring. In the case of *Prunus triloba* all the twigs and branches are shortened to about 3cm (1 1/2″) after flowering.

Shrubs and sub-shrubs that must not be cut back to bare wood

Both spring and summer-flowering species come into this category. The spring-flowering shrubs are pruned after flowering, leaving some greenery below the cut because that will encourage old wood to sprout again.
Examples include:
Alyssum
Cytisus (broom)

Erica (bell heather)
Iberis

Shorten the branches of the summer-flowering species in the spring, again leaving some greenery below the cut. Examples include: *Calluna* (heather), *Hebe* (veronica), *Helianthemum* (rock rose) *Lavandula* (lavender), *Santolina* (lavender cotton), and *Thymus* (thyme).

Climbing plants

The early-flowering clematis, honeysuckle (*Lonicera*), and winter jasmine (*Jasminum nudiflorum*) are thinned out after they

Heaths often look attractive even when the flowers are over. Do not prune them too late or a great many new shoots will develop. Cut them back hard, but always leave some green shoots below the cut.

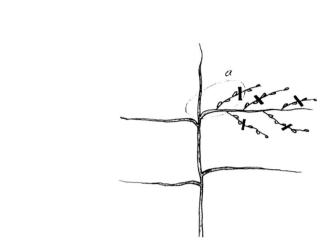

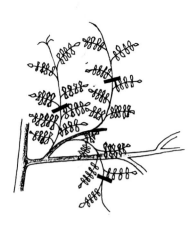

Pruning Wisteria *in February and in summer. Right: detail of summer pruning.*

Pruning the perpetual-flowering climbing rose. Left to right, one-year-old, two-year-old, and three-year-old wood.

have flowered. The branches that have flowered may be removed. In addition, from time to time an old branch can be removed completely from older shrubs. Summer-flowering clematis, passion flower (*Passiflora caerulea*), *Polygonum*, and honeysuckles that flower after 1 July, for example *Lonicera japonica*, are pruned hard in spring. With *Wisteria* you need first to shape the framework. Long growths are cut back each year to 75cm (30″); the laterals are shortened by a third each spring. Once the framework is established the one-year-old twigs are cut back to two or three eyes. To promote flowering you must also cut back the new shoots to four or five eyes in July.

Climbing roses are pruned in the spring. Long one-year-old, green or greenish-brown unbranched twigs are left because they will produce the most flowers.

Two-year-old branches also flower well but the side twigs on these – recognizable by last year's dead flower – must be shortened to two eyes (about 3cm (1 1/2″)).

Three-year-old branches that bear the pruned branches from last year must be cut off as low down as possible.

Topiary and training

Although the main aim of pruning ornamental shrubs is to enhance flowering and to rejuvenate, today a shrub's shape is also an important factor in garden design. Shrubs that were once regarded as hedging shrubs are now used to create living sculptures, al-though they can still, of course, be planted as hedges.

How a shrub grows

Each branch, twig, or shoot ends in a terminal bud, the growth point. This contains growth hormones which light converts into growth inhibitors. Think of plants grown in the dark: weak and straggly stems. If you never prune a shrub, most new shoots will develop from the terminal buds, while the buds behind them will be discouraged from developing. If the terminal bud is removed the brake on the development of the side shoot is removed, and these will quickly develop below the cut.

Stretch a line between canes before you start to prune. Check with a spirit level that the hedge is straight.

Plants whose leaves grow close together seem to have strong powers of regeneration and it is these that are used for hedges, shapes, and figures.

When should a hedge be pruned?

How often a hedge should be pruned depends on its purpose. If you want it to become a tall, closed hedge in a short space of time and you feed it well, you will have to prune it several times a year. Fertilizer as well as pruning will stimulate growth.

Hedges containing vigorous shrubs, such as privet, flowering currant, Leyland cypress, and dwarf cypress, must also be pruned several times a year. As a rule of thumb prune once a year

While the hedge is developing it is cut once before the longest day. A second trim follows in late July or early August.

towards the end of summer. If the hedge is still growing strongly and its shape is fast disappearing, prune once when the new shoots have formed, up to the end of May, and once at the end of July or the beginning of August. Never prune if there is a danger of frost.

Prune new shrubs more often

A different pattern of pruning is followed in the first few years after a new hedge has been planted. Fast-growing, deciduous hedges tend to grow upwards and develop few side branches. If they are pruned only once a year gaps soon develop lower down. After the shrub has been planted, cut it back to a third of its height, even though this may leave a hedge only 20cm (8″) high. In the second spring after planting, cut the leaders back to half their length and prune the laterals regularly. In the third year, one third of the upper part of the

> ### Tip
> It is better not to use shears to cut the evergreen cherry laurel and other hedging shrubs with large leaves because damaged leaves turn brown. Use secateurs instead.

hedge is pruned, and so on. Once the hedge has reached the desired height, clipping it once a year is often sufficient.

The evergreen honeysuckle, *Lonicera nitida*, and box, *Buxus sempervirens*, should be cut back by half after planting to make them fill out at the bottom. Other fast-growing evergreen hedging shrubs are cut back by half in the first year after

It is better not to clip large-leaved hedging shrubs with shears because any damaged leaves will turn brown. Take out protruding branches with a pair of secateurs.

> **Tip**
>
> All hedges must taper upwards (beech hedges especially appreciate this). You can then be sure that the lower branches are receiving enough light.
> The disadvantage is that the hedge is very wide at ground level.

planting; in the second year only a third of the total length of the branches is removed. From the second year onwards the sides of these hedges are also pruned. Hornbeam and beech form many laterals low down, and the leaders are cut back to two thirds of their length after planting. The side branches are also cut back to some extent. In the second year take off a third of all the newly formed branches both on top and at the sides. In the following years, work is

A living green carport: the hornbeam, Carpinus betulus.

limited to annual pruning at the end of summer. It is quite in order to prune the hedge in spring when it has reached the desired height. It will then, however, make so many new shoots that you will need to clip it several times a year to maintain its shape. The idea of letting a climbing plant grow through a hedge is very attractive but not practical. When you want to prune the hedge at the end of July, the climber will be in full growth and/or flower. In addition, a woody climber can damage a hedge.

The coniferous and slow-growing evergreen hedging plants are left untouched in the first year. From the second year onwards the sides

> **Tip**
>
> If you want to use sub-shrubs for a hedge, prune them hard no earlier than the middle of May, and leave a little greenery below the cut.

Hawthorn lends itself well to pruning into a dome shape.

are trimmed during summer. The tops of these hedges do not need trimming until they have reached the height you want. Once that happens an annual trim is sufficient. An exception is the Leyland cypress.

Topiary

The simplest shape to create in a hedge is a recess, niche, curved upper edge, or buttress. You can create these architectural features in your hedge when it has grown as tall as you planned. In the past it was usual to plant two rows of shrubs side by side to make a thick, broad hedge that stood out in comparison with the other elements in the garden.

The most successful shrubs for this purpose are those that sprout well from old wood and that have been used for topiary for centuries: yew (*Taxus*) and holly (*Ilex*), and box for lower green shapes. A further advantage of these shrubs is that they only need pruning once a year. Most of the shapes already mentioned can be cut out of the hedge as it stands, but if you want to make a buttress you will need to have in place already one or two extra plants.

"Windows" are more difficult to shape. Because the hedge needs to close up again above the window, you can try to bend the shrubs in an existing hedge sideways so that you can very carefully push in a frame.

You must then cut away those parts of the branches that curve inwards (into the middle of the "window") and tie the remainder to the frame. Then tie these branches to each other over the top of the frame. Another method is to fix a frame on a pole above the hedge which is then allowed to grow round it. However, it takes much longer to achieve the effect this way.

Frames for square windows are always best fixed on stout poles in the hedge. For battlements, balls, and spikes, allow several branches to grow

Tip

The framework can also be made out of wire and bamboo canes. You can prune the branches through the gaps in the frame to encourage the growth of side shoots.

up through the top of the hedge. If you want to give the impression that the ball is separate from the hedge, tie the branches together with tarred twine or flexible ties.

For balls, cones, etc., you can either make a framework out of coarse wire netting or buy one ready made. Let the branches grow a little to begin with so that you can prune them first; then place the wire framework over the whole shape. All these features can be created either in a pot or in the ground.

It is difficult to train a feature to grow out of the hedge on a single stem because you need to let one leader grow through the hedge and then cut it off exactly above the centre point of what will become the ball. Once this is done, you can begin to shape the ball.

If you want a ball 50cm (20″) in diameter on a trunk 1m (3′3″) high, cut off the leader at 1.27m (50″). All the lateral branches are left at a length of 1m to 1.27m (39 to 50″).

These form the lower surface of the ball. If you do not have a good eye for shapes or a steady hand, you can make a framework of the correct shape and fix this on a stout pole to guide you.

Domes and toadstools are other possibilities. In this case the leader is cut off just below what will be the upper surface of the dome.

Tip

It is even possible to have a different species of shrub growing in the hedge which can be used to create a dome, cone, or ball when the hedge has reached the desired height.

Topiary in pots

If you want to produce a ball on a single upright trunk in a pot, you must never clip the main stem completely bare while you are growing it. Each year the leader grows taller and side shoots grow on this, which are shortened a little in spring.

The following spring the side shoots below the new extension are pruned a little, and the laterals which were pruned the previous year are now cut off close to the trunk.

Complex shapes and animals

It is not too difficult to make several layers out of a cone shape, and you can use a number of evergreen shrubs for this.

There is less danger here of the upper surface of each layer turning brown because the layers are tapering.

First of all you grow a complete cone shape and then begin the pruning. Before you start, you need to decide whether or not you want it to stand on a plinth and, again, this can take different forms.

First cut the plinth to the shape you want. Remove all side branches for 30cm (12″) above the plinth.

You now shape the first layer. The branches are growing upwards at an angle so they must first be secured horizontally by tying them to the trunk below the layer with tarred twine or flexible ties.

Again, the second layer is formed about 30cm (12″) above the first, and so on. Each time the lower branches of the layer have to be bent hori-

In topiary the distance between the layers must be sufficient for the upper surface of each layer to receive enough light. If they do not the upper surfaces will turn brown.

zontally and secured to the trunk. The diameter of each layer must be less than the one below it to produce a definite cone shape. The underside of each layer will remain bare of leaves because no light reaches them.

However, the upper surface will remain green if there is a reasonable gap between it and the layer above, and if the layers decrease in diameter towards the top of the cone.

To make a spiral you can begin with an existing cone. Yew and box are recommended for this. You will achieve better results, however, if you clip the shrub into a spiral shape as it grows.

Older evergreen shrubs or conifers with small leaves are the most suitable for making animal shapes. Box and yew are ideal. An animal on a base or in a pot looks better than an animal on the ground.

It is very difficult to trim these shapes by eye; you should train the branches along wires and keep them in check by pruning. It is best to make a framework of wire netting or thin gauge wire.

Choose an animal that has a definite shape, such as a swan (neck), a rabbit (ears), or a bird (wings and tail), and avoid detail in the shape. Like the simple shapes in the hedge, one or more branches are allowed to go on growing.

The wire figure is fixed to a stout pole and pushed into a base. A couple of branches are again allowed to grow on.

Tie them together with tarred twine or flexible ties and lead them over the outside of the figure. Let several branches grow inside the shape and prune them to encourage plenty of side shoots. You can anchor a shape in a pot with bamboo canes.

Tip

Draw the spiral on the existing cone with wet chalk. You can then see if the curves look right.

Topiary animals will attract more attention if they stand on a base.

Some shrubs and trees grow naturally into ball shapes, for example the ball acacia *Robinia pseudoacacia* 'Umbraculifera'; *Prunus fruticosa*; maple *Acer platanoides* 'Globosum'; ivy *Hedera helix* 'Arborescens'; and *Hedera colchica* 'Arborescens.'

These only need a light pruning. In the case of trees in particular, this can be done in two ways.
All the branches above the graft are often cut short, which means that for months you will be looking at a strange bunch of twigs.
The other system is to cut one branch right down to the graft and to shorten the other branches by half.
This will at least leave a framework of branches for the winter.

Tip
Give your topiary space. Most evergreen shrubs prefer growing as single specimens and hate plants touching them or the remains of prunings left on their foliage. Where the light is excluded the leaves will turn brown and drop off.

Evergreen seats

If you can make a topiary animal shape you will find making a green bench or chair no problem at all. The seat can be made out of a plank of wood supported on two concrete blocks.
Decide what height is the most comfortable for sitting. Position the bench in the garden and plant evergreen shrubs or slow growing conifers along the back and sides. These shrubs should be ones that naturally grow upright. You could also fill in the front of the bench with greenery. Make sure that the seat does not become too deep, from the back to the front.
The back of the seat will grow rapidly for the first couple of years as it will be stimulated to do so by regular pruning. You cannot really lean back on it, but a cushion will make it more comfortable.

A lime avenue

Lime is generally used for stilt hedges, although hornbeam, plane, elm, horse chestnut, and maple can also be used. The limes, *Tilia platyphyllos*, *Tilia* x *europaea* 'Pallida,' and *Tilia* x *europaea* 'Zwarte Linde' are the ones most frequently used.
The Caucasian lime, *Tilia euchlora*, which is sometimes used for stilt hedges, has branches that have a strong tendency to droop and so a great deal of pruning is involved if you want to maintain a tidy shape. *Tilia* x *euchlora* and *Tilia tomentosa* and their cultivars do not drip honey dew.

There are various ways of training lime trees. The best known are the espalier or pleached lime, and the hedge. The espalier form is trained rigidly and is more or less symmetrical. The branches are usually held horizontally although there is a variation in which the branches grow upwards at an angle. The hedge is simply a free form that is maintained as a hedge.

If you want to make a stilt hedge with pleached limes, it is advisable to begin with trees that have trunks with a minimum circumference of 14 to 16cm (5″ to 7″) measured 1m (3′3″) above the ground. You can then make several layers straight away.

Depending on the height of the first branch and the length of your lime avenue, plant the trees 2.7 to 3.6m (8′11″ to 12′) apart.

A screen of pleached limes with a tall beech hedge in the background. A low beech hedge has been planted between the limes.

> ### Tip
> If you are able to tie in all the laterals from your lime tree immediately, it is more attractive if the last lateral consists of one side branch while the main stem is bent over and used as the opposite lateral.

You can train the branches along a bamboo framework or tie the branches to wires. The wires are fixed to very strong posts at each end. The height of the posts depends on the height of the highest lateral. As a rule the wires are fixed 40cm (16″) apart.

At the place where you want to have your lowest lateral, bend two opposite branches and tie them to the wires with flexible ties. About 40cm (16″) above this, look for a further two branches that are close to the wire and secure them as before. About 40cm (16″) further up, yet another two

branches are fixed to the wires. If there are no more branches to fix to the next wire, the leader is cut off just above the last laterals.

New shoots will grow below the cut and these can be secured along the wire as laterals the following year. The branches between the laterals are cut off.

Pruning and training pleached limes

How you prune the limes from now on will depend on the final shape you aim to achieve. Do you want the laterals to look like ropes covered in greenery, or do you want a closed screen? Do you want to create a flat screen or do you want a more massive block?

Here are some general tips for shaping and maintaining pleached limes. The outer ends of the laterals must point upwards a little to maintain their growth. As long as the laterals are growing towards each other the terminal shoots must never be cut off.

Each winter, long side shoots on the laterals must be shortened or even removed. Leave all the short side shoots. The closer they are to the main trunk the faster the side shoots will grow. The lowest lateral will tend to grow less strongly, so the side shoots on it are pruned less.

You can encourage growth in the lowest lateral by pruning more vertical side shoots from the laterals above it. There is no need to remove the shoots which are growing downwards because they will hardly grow at all. Finally, you can allow the laterals that touch to grow into each other.

After your living framework has been created, you can prune pleached limes into a normal hedge. They will not, however, produce as much side wood as, for example hornbeam, which is better for this purpose.

Designing with trees

The leafy walk

You must be able to walk comfortably under a walkway. The width must be about 2.5m (8'3"),

with the height one and a half times the width. Arches and cross pieces are needed for support. Wood looks the most natural but iron is more durable.

Wisteria floribunda can be trained vertically up a post before being trained horizontally at the correct height. Usually six branches (framework branches comparable with the laterals of the lime) are secured flat against a screen.

In winter all vertical branches are clipped, and the horizontal ones are trained like a spider's web. In summer the surplus vertical shoots are removed.

A walkway can also be formed from lime trees. Choose a species that does not drip honey dew, such as *Tilia* x *euchlora* or *Tilia tomentosa*.

The lime trees here have been trimmed into a hedge. An opening allows access to the front door.

Part 5

*P*ractical

examples

11 The border

 Chapter 3 gave you some information about the origins of the border and about the perennials that are planted there. This chapter takes a more detailed look at the subject and tells you how, by following certain rules, you can create your own ideal border.

The layout of the border

 The best place for a herbaceous border is in full sun. Site the border where you can look along it, not directly at it, from the place where you will spend most time looking at it. If you look directly at a border, you will see the flowering plants in separate groups with gaps between them, or plants that have already finished flowering or have not yet come out. Looking along a border gives the impression of a seamless whole.

A third of the border in flower at the same time

 Everyone would like their border to be in flower the whole year round. A border like this, however, would have to be huge: you

Paths laid out throughout the garden allow access to the borders, even in wet weather.

The paths are almost invisible during summer.

wil only get the impression of a sea of colour if a third of the plants in the border are in flower at the same time. Present-day gardens are often too small for a layout like this, and one solution is the mixed border: for example, shrubs combined with perennials and annuals. Different parts of the garden can be emphasized at different seasons. You could set a group of summer-flowering perennials against a background of shrubs that flower in early summer, while another corner could stand out in spring with an ornamental crab apple surrounded by spring bulbs and ferns.

If your garden is large and you want to limit the amount of work you need to do, you could also plant a shrub border containing something of interest throughout the year. This type of border has the advantage of looking attractive during winter, in contrast to the herbaceous border, which has little to offer apart from the odd evergreen plant.

Make a design on paper first

It is a good idea first to design the border on paper. You have already drawn a plan of your garden at a scale of 1:100 or 1:50 (1:60), and the position and shape of the border have already been recorded. You can now enlarge the border on graph paper at a scale of 1:20 or 1:25

(1:30). Draw the immediate surroundings of the border at the correct scale and look at your shadow chart (Chapter 2) to find out which part of the border is in full sun. Make sure that you have seed catalogues and books containing lists of plants arranged according to area of spread, colour, and height. If you want to lay out a border with perennials that flower in early and full summer, choose those that flower in May, June, July, and August. Set about it like this:

• Divide the border into beds of various shapes and sizes. Make the central group the largest. Write the chosen months of flowering in pencil so that you have enough space to fill in the names of plants later and so that you can change your choice of plants if necessary.

• To achieve the desired effect, you must use several plants in each bed or in a group. How many will depend on the height and spread of the plants. If you put marguerites in a bed, a group of three to five gives a pleasant effect. However, you need fifteen plants of thrift (which is much lower growing) to achieve the same effect. Put in an average of six to seven plants per m² (1.2yd²).

• Never make a group or bed smaller than 50 x 50cm (20″ x 20″). Perpetual-flowering plants are recommended for small herbaceous borders. You

Polygonum amplexicaule *and* Lavatera, *which are both in flower for more than three months, make a very good combination.*

can achieve effective contrasts by alternating the shapes of flowers; the broad flowers of sneeze-weed, *Helenium*, will look better beside the pointed sage, *Salvia*, than the flat clusters of yarrow, *Achillea*.

• Plant the border in such a way that a number of new plants are coming into flower behind those in full flower or in front of those that have finished flowering.

• Put the tallest plants at the back of the border and the smallest at the front, with the medium ones in between. A single, taller specimen plant among the lower-growing plants will give your border a certain distinction.

Tip

The "Top Twenty" perennials (in flower for more than two months): *Acanthus spinosus, Aster frikartii* 'Mönch,' and *Aster* 'Wunder von Stäfa,' *Astrantia major* 'Lars', *Calamintha nepeta* ssp. *nepeta, Chamaemelum nobile* 'Ligulosum,' *Cimifuga ramosa* 'Atropurpurea,' *Coreopsis verticillata* 'Moonbeam,' *Gaura lindheimeri* 'Whirling Butterflies,' *Geranium* 'Ann Folkard,' *Geranium nodosum, Helleborus orientalis, Kalameris incisa* and *Kalameris incisa* 'Alba,' *Lavatera olbia* and *L. thuringiaca, Polemonium caeruleum* 'Lambrook Mauve,' *Polygonum amplexicaule* and its cultivars and *Salvia verticillata* 'Purple Rain.'

• In a large and especially a long border, repeating the same combinations of plants gives a restful impression.

An informal garden with mixed borders

The planting scheme we have designed has been used to divide up a rather long, narrow back garden into different areas: one beside the white mulberry tree, which is next to the terrace at the south end of the garden; another where the lawn narrows by the weeping pear tree; and an area under the plane tree, surrounded by shrubs, which backs on to the adjacent woodland garden. The boundary is marked here by a mesh fence covered in ivy. The flowing lines of the design make the garden look bigger. The different areas are separated by evergreen shrubs so that the pattern of the garden is maintained, even in winter. Care has been taken to ensure that for seven to eight months of the year, several different plants are in flower at the same time. On the east side an ivy-covered wire mesh fence hides the conifer hedge, which is bare in places. The compost bin and garbage can are also hidden behind this fence. In the second area a path covered in wood chippings winds through the border to give easy access on both sides. The paving is laid in a curving pattern to reflect the overall design of the garden. Old bricks have been used and a row of bricks has been laid along the edge of the lawn. A space 50cm (20″) wide has been kept clear alongside the two conifer hedges to make border and hedge maintenance easier.

A view along the right-hand border. At the end of September the show is far from over: there is still plenty to see.

Planting

The first terrace is just outside the house and is paved with bricks.

B Terrace at the bottom of the garden (concrete slabs and bricks)

C Lawn

I *Platanus* x *hispanica*, plane tree
II *Pyrus salicifolia* 'Pendula,' weeping pear tree
III *Morus alba*, white mulberry

a *Abelia* x *grandiflora*
b *Buddleja davidii* 'Black Knight', butterfly bush
c *Lavatera* 'Barnsley'
d *Pieris japonica*
e *Viburnum bodnantense* x 'New Dawn'
f *Rhododendron aberconwayi* and *Rhododendron yakushimanum*
g *Hydrangea macrophylla* 'Nigra',
h *Taxus baccata* 'Fastigiata', yew
i *Taxus baccata* 'Repandens', yew
j *Hibiscus syriacus* 'Mauve Queen',
k *Callicarpa bodinieri* var. *giraldii*
l *Rubus thibetanus* 'Silver Fern', ornamental bramble
m *Buddleja davidii* 'Pink Delight', butterfly bush
n *Amelanchier lamarckii*
o *Hydrangea paniculata* 'Unique'
p *Clethra alnifolia*, sweet pepper-bush
q *Ceanothus thyrsiflorus* var 'Repens'
r *Ficus carica*, fig
s *Hedera helix*, ivy
t *Clematis* 'Hagley Hybrid'

1 *Hosta fortunei* 'Hyacinthina', plantain lily
2 *Astrantia major*, masterwort
3 *Pachysandra terminalis* 'Youngii'
4 *Anemone tomentosa* 'Robustissima',
5 *Eupatorium rugosum*, hardy age
6 *Liriope muscari* lilyturf
7 *Verbena bonariensis*
8 *Salvia sclarea*
9 *Euphorbia martinii*, spurge
10 *Agastache foeniculum*, Mexican giant hyssop

11 *Heuchera micrantha* 'Palace Purple' alum root
12 *Helleborus argutifolius*
13 *Euphorbia amygdaloides* 'Purpurea', spurge

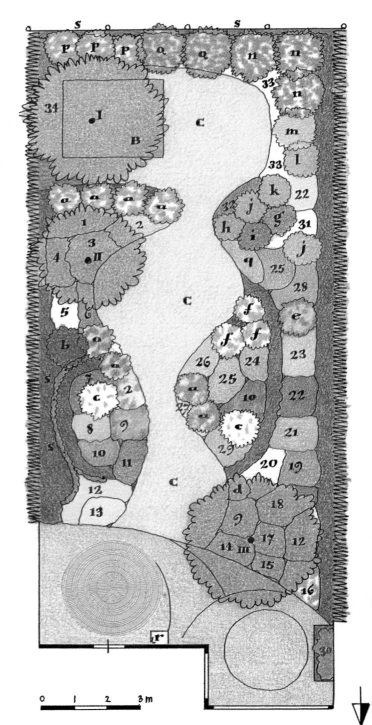

14 *Alchemilla mollis*, lady's mantle

15 *Pulmonaria longifolia*, lungwort

16 *Tellima grandiflora* fringecups

17 *Lysimachia punctata*, loosestrife

18 *Anemone vitifolia* 'Honorine Jobert'

19 *Aster novae-angliae* 'Andenken an Alma Pötschke'

20 *Hosta plantaginea* var. *grandiflora*, plantain lily

21 *Polygonum amplexicaule*

22 *Cephalaria gigantea*

23 *Macleaya cordata*

24 *Foeniculum vulgare* 'Bronze Giant', fennel

25 *Polygonum campanulatum*,

26 *Bergenia cordifolia*

27 *Dicentra formosa*, bleeding heart

28 *Helianthus salicifolius* sunflower

29 *Tradescantia andersoniana* 'Leonora',

30 *Origanum laevigatum*, marjoram

31 *Cimicifuga ramosa* 'Atropurpurea'

32 *Astilbe pumila*

33 *Geranium phaeum* 'Album', cranesbill

34 *Aster divaricatus*, aster and *Euphorbia amygdaloides* 'Purpurea', spurge

A rhapsody in blue surrounded by box hedges

Behind the farm house, a small formal flower garden has been created within a large, deliberately informal garden. Trees provide more shade on the eastern than the western side so that in the large border shade-loving plants can be included.

The two gardens are not exact mirror images: they are not the same size and one is more shaded than the other. However, the use of the colours blue, white, and yellow in both, and the use of the same broad lines in each, create a similar effect.

A   Paving with old bricks

B   Box hedge

C   *Rosa* 'New Dawn' over an arch

a   *Rosa* 'Iceberg,' standard 2 x

b   *Buxus sempervirens*, 2 x, box ball

c   *Potentilla fruticosa* 'Eastleigh Cream',

d   *Caryopteris clandonensis* 'Heavenly Blue'

e   *Ceanothus thyrsiflorus* x *repens*

lanting

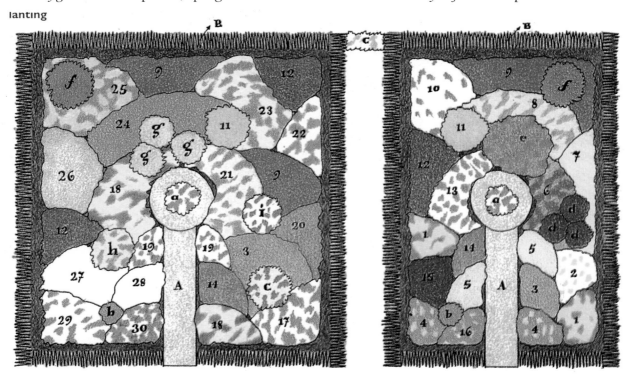

f   *Hedera colchica* 'Arborescens', 2 x, ivy
g   *Euonymus fortunei* 'Vegetus' 3 x
h   *Corylopsis pauciflora*
i   *Fothergilla major*

1   *Euphorbia martinii*, spurge, 2 beds
2   *Rudbeckia purpurea* 'White Lustre'
3   *Ruta graveolens* 'Jackman's Blue', rue, 2 beds
4   *Epimedium perralderianum* 'Frohnleiten', 2 beds
5   *Salvia officinalis* 'Icterina', pineapple sage, 2 beds
6   *Lavandula angustifolia* 'Hidcote Blue', lavender
7   *Helianthella quinquenervis*
8   *Phlomis russeliana*
9   *Aconitum napellus*, monkshood, 3 beds
10 *Phlox paniculata* 'White Admiral'
11 *Humulus lupulus* 'Aureus', golden hop, 2 beds
12 *Anchusa italica* 'Dropmore',3 beds
13 *Salvia froskahlei*
14 *Geranium platypetalum*, 2 beds
15 *Catananche coerulea*
16 *Alchemilla mollis*, lady's mantle
17 *Polygonatum officinale*, Solomon's seal
18 *Epimedium versicolor* 'Sulphuricum', 2 beds
19 *Houttuynia cordata* 'Flore Pleno,' 2 beds
20 *Meconopsis betonicifolia*, blue poppy
21 *Aconitum septentrionale* 'Ivorne'
22 *Cimicifuga ramosa* 'Atropurpurea'
23 *Nepeta goviana*
24 *Matteuccia struthiopteris*, ostrich fern
25 *Symphytum grandiflorum*, comfrey
26 *Hosta* 'Krossa Regal'
27 *Anemone hybrida* 'Honorine Jobert',
28 *Geranium sanguineum* 'Alba', cranesbill
29 *Euphorbia amugdaloides* ssp. *robbiae*, spurge
30 *Aruncus aethusifolius*

> **Tip**
>
> If you are gardening on damp, peaty soil, the following perennials will do well: Aconitum, Alchemilla, Aster(s), Astilbe, Brunnera, Centaurea, Chelone, Dicentra, Digitalis, Eupatorium(s), Euphorbia, Galium, Geranium, Hosta(s), Iris sibirica(s), Lysimachia, Lythrum, Mecanopsis(s), Polemonium, Polygonum, Pulmonaria, Primula, Rudbeckia nitida(s), Solidago, Symphytum, Tiarella, Thalictrum, and Walsteinia.
> Those marked with 's' are liable to slug damage in very wet periods.

Anchusa italica lends a touch of delicate blue to the border.

12 A garden with heathers and a rock garden

In recent years, Heather gardens have gone out of fashion. People have the idea that such gardens are very expensive to create and that the plants do not live very long. Now it is high time that heathers were considered seriously again.

Looking after heathers

At one time many people planted heathers under the misconception that it would be expensive to begin with but that, after a while, the plants would look after themselves.

In this narrow front garden heather is combined with other plants. You will find the list of plants on page 356.

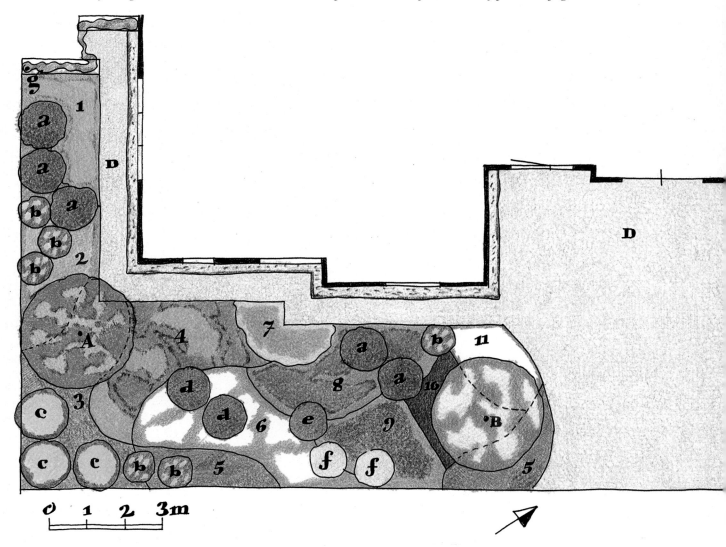

Unfortunately, things do not work out like this. Heathers and heaths must be clipped every year, and some green shoots must be left immediately below the cuts. If heathers are not pruned at all they age rapidly, becoming woody and bare. Pruning them at this stage will kill them completely. There is also the question of how many plants to put in per m² (1.2yd²). Six plants per m² (1.2yd²) should be sufficient, although twice that density is sometimes recommended. This difference in density can be explained by the fact that heathers and heaths form roots on the surface, and these suffer if the sun reaches them. If you use the lower density of planting, and cover the ground in between the plants with bark, wood chips, peat, or cocoa shells, you should have no problems. Also, avoid hoeing between the plants because this also damages the roots.

A heather garden on sandy soil

A heather garden can look very attractive if the heathers are combined with other shrubs and perennials to give some variety. Many ericaceous plants are evergreen.

The diagram shows a front garden in which ericaceous plants have been given a prominent place.

aller evergreen shrubs have been planted to increase privacy, and the boundary between the garden and the pavement outside has been indicated with low, evergreen shrubs to avoid the need for a hedge or wall.

Two screens (woven panels, trellis work, or wooden/concrete sections) have been erected at an angle on the way through to the back garden. This ensures privacy and stops the wind funneling through the gap. Wisteria has been trained over them.

For a garden approximately 15 x 9m (approximately 50' x 30'), the planting scheme can include the following, which together make a good combination:

A *Tamarix pentandra (ramosissima)* 'Rubra'
B *Pyrus salicifolia* 'Pendula', grafted at 2.25 m (7'4"), weeping pear tree
a *Nandina domestica*, 2 groups
b *Symphoricarpus x doorenbosii* 'Mother of Pearl', 3 groups
c *Hedera helix* 'Poetica', ivy
d *Viburnum tinus* 'Eve Price'
e *Caryopteris* x *clandonensis* 'Heavenley Blue'
f *Ilex crenata* 'Convexa'
g *Wisteria sinensis* 'Caroline'
h *Taxus baccata*, yew
1 *Gaultheria procumbens*, checkerberry
2 *Daboecia cantabrica* 'Robin', St Dabeoc's heath
3 *Santolina chamaecyparissus* 'Edward Bowles', lavender cotton
4 *Erica carnea* 'Kramers Rote', alpine heath
5 *Lavandula x intermedia* 'Grappenhall', 2 groups, lavender
6 *Calluna vulgaris* 'Long White', heather
7 *Panicum virgatum* 'Rehbraun'
8 *Erica cinerea* 'Atrosanguinea', bell heather
9 *Euphorbia martinii*, spurge
10 *Liriope muscari*
11 *Erica darleyensis* 'White Glow'

Combine heathers with other shrubs and plants.

Most ericaceous plants prefer a sunny position in a slightly acid, peaty, or humus-rich soil. If sandy soil is on the acid side, it can be made suitable for lime-loving plants (such as lavender and lavender cotton) by adding compost and giving an annual dressing of lime.

Ericaceous plants and conifers for the heather garden

All the plants mentioned below are evergreen and, unless otherwise stated, prefer a sunny position.

Name	Height cm (in)	Flowering season	Colour	Situation	Comments
bog-rosemary	100 (39)	4-5	white	damp	sheltered situation
Andromeda japonica	100	4-5	white	damp	sheltered situation
Andromeda polyfolia	30-50 (12-20)	5-7	pink	damp	sheltered situation
bearberry	20 (8)	4-7	white		red berries
Calluna Arctostaphylos uva-ursi					
heather					
Calluna vulgaris					
C. v. 'Alportii'	50 (20)	9-10	pink	dry	
C. v. 'C.W. Nix'	60 (24)	9-10	reddish-pink	dry	
C. v. 'Gold Haze'	50 (20)	9-10	white	dry	golden-yellow foliage
C. v. 'H.E. Beale'	60 (24	9-11	bright pink	dry	
Cassiope tetragona	20 (8)	4-5	white	damp	golden-yellow foliage, protect in, winter, shade tolerant
leather-leaf					
Chamaedaphne calyculata	30 (12)	4-5	white	damp	shade-tolerant
broom *Cytisus x kewensis*	30 (12)	4	cream	dry	
St Dabeoc's heath					
Daboecia cantabrica	40 (16)	7-9	white, pink	dry	sheltered situation
Erica carnea	20 (8)	2-4	pink	dry	lime tolerant
E. c. 'C.M. Beale'	30 (12)	11-3	white	dry	
E. c. 'King George'	30 (12)	12-3	scarlet	dry	
E. c. 'Winterbeauty'	20 (8)	12-3	deep pink	dry	compact
Dorset heath					
Erica ciliaris	40 (16)	7-10	pink	dry	quite large flowers, grey hairs on branches
E. c. 'Alba'	25 (10)	7-10	white	dry	
E. c. 'Pygmaea'	15 (6)		rose pink	dry	creeping
E. c. 'Rosea'	20 (8)	6-9	scarlet	dry	compact
cross leaved heath					
Erica tetralix	60 (24)	5-6	pink	damp	

Name	Height cm (in)	Flowering season	Colour	Situation	Comments
Cornish heath					
Erica vagans	30 (12)	7-9	mauve-pink	dry	
E. v. 'Lyonesse'	30 (12)	8-10	white	dry	
E. v. 'St. Keverne'	35 (14)	7-9	salmon-pink	dry	
checkerberry					
Gaultheria procumbens	20 (8)	6-9	white	damp	red berries, shade tolerant
Gaultheria shallon	75 (30)	5-6	white	damp	black berries, shade tolerant
dyer's greenweed					
Genista tinctoria	100 (39)	6-9	yellow	dry	deciduous
Hebe armstrongii	60 (24)	6-7	white		bronzegreen foliage
Hebe buxifolia	60 (24)	6-7	white		protect all hebes in severe winters
juniper					
Juniperus communis 'Hornebrookii'	50 (20)			dry	ground cover, broad
J. horizontalis 'Wiltonii'	30 (12)				broad, forms very thick mats
J. media 'Pfitzeriana Aurea'	100-250 (39-98)			damp	shade-tolerant, becomes very broad
J. sabina 'Tamariscifolia's'	80 32)				fine needles, preads out
sheep laurel					
Kalmia angustifolia 'Rubra'	100 (39)	5-7	rose-pink	damp	
Kalmia polyfolia	40 (16)	5-6	pink	damp	hates lime
labrador tea					
Ledum groenlandicum 'Compactum'	50 (20)		white	damp	
dwarf pine					
Pinus mugo var. *pumilio*	150 (59)			dry	broad
Rhododendron					
R. hirsutum	80 (32)	6	pink	damp	half shade
R. impeditum	50 (20)	4	violet	damp	half shade
R. williamsianum	100 (39)	4	pink		half shade
Taxus baccata 'Repandens'	50 (20)				shade tolerant
T. b. 'Summergold'	100 (39)				golden-yellow
cowberry					
Vaccineum vitis-idaea	30 (12)	5-8	white	damp	red berries, shade tolerant, prefers sandy loam

Taxus baccata 'Repandens' grows no higher than 50cm (20") and tolerates shade well. It makes a welcome addition to the heather garden in difficult situations.

Rock gardens

At the end of the last century, it was very fashionable to have rock formations in gardens, particularly if these were natural looking.

The intention was that they should contrast with the rest of the garden. This fashion did not last very long: gardeners began to prefer instead something that fitted in better with the contours of the garden itself.

Outcrops of rock in a garden were turned into rock gardens, and in those gardens without such outcrops, artificial rock made a good substitute.

If you do make a rock garden, remember that it will probably not blend into the landscape unless you live in a hilly region.

The contrast between a rock garden and the natural landscape will be most pronounced in flat areas. Why should people want to make a rock garden in an area like that?

A rock garden offers the opportunity to grow plants that do not thrive in the conditions in "normal" gardens, namely, the alpines.

The term "alpine" was originally given to plants that were discovered growing in the Alps early this century, but it has now been extended to plants from other mountainous regions.

Growing conditions

In the mountains, the greater the altitude the smaller the plants and the closer to the ground they grow for protection against the bitter winds.

This also enables them to take advantage of the warmth retained by the rock. When you are designing a rockery you need to recreate the alpine

Pinus mugo var. pumilio just like the yew, has its own special character. This small tree is very suitable for the heather garden.

habitat as far as possible. To begin with, choose a part of the garden that is open and sunny, but avoid a flat, exposed situation and provide shelter from the north and east wind. Although in the wild these plants are not protected throughout the year, they benefit from the protection of a thick layer of snow in winter.

A group of shrubs that gives the impression of mountains in the distance makes a good background for a rock garden. Dig out the soil from a large enough area in front of the shrubs to make a natural-looking slope.

Preparing the site

 Although a lot of soil has been removed, do remember that a rock garden stands

Left: A variety of plants in a rock garden.

or falls by the amount of drainage it has: rock plants will not survive wet winters. The drainage must be improved especially in heavy and wet sub-soil.

The site must also be completely cleared of weeds.

Choice of materials

Many countries lack abundant supplies of natural stone, and so all the material for a rock garden has to be imported. Garden centres have a wide choice, although many people opt for the pure white, polished Carara marble.

This has the disadvantage that it can attract green algae and soon looks dirty. Tufa, which is yellow when cut but soon turns grey, is very

It is possible to transform your garden into a rock garden even in a very flat region.

During the winter the rock plants are protected by snow.

suitable for the rock garden. It can also be obtained in interesting shapes.

It is light to handle and can be drilled to make pockets for plants.

Volcanic rock looks rather dark on its own and needs to be combined with other kinds of stone. Pumice can be used but tends to be expensive; slag from blast furnaces is a cheap alternative. Sedimentary rocks, such as sandstone and limestone, are ideal. Cobbles are too smooth for the plants to root in, but they can be used to form a dry stream bed.

Flagstones can be used as stepping stones and can also be built up into low retaining walls.

Building the rock garden

Sedimentary rock, as its name suggests, occurs naturally in layers and, obviously, these rocks are often covered with soil. To reproduce this look in your rock garden, lay the stones with the broadest face uppermost.

Begin building in layers from the bottom of the slope upwards so that each stone forms the base for the one above. Set the stones that have the most attractive faces outwards.

Avoid creating a too regular effect. Set the stones securely into the ground, sloping down towards

This rock garden, built up from layers of limestone, is a lovely example of patience, precision, and creativity.

the back so that water will run into the soil round the plants. If the stones are laid horizontally, the water will run away and the whole rock garden will dry out. Leave gaps between the stones to accommodate the plants.

Make a good hole for each one and fill it with a mixture of garden soil, sand, and peat. Set the (preferably young) plants in the gap and fill it completely with more of the mixture.

When you have finished all the planting, cover the soil with a layer of gravel or stone chippings and water the plants well. To begin with you will need to water the plants regularly in dry weather to encourage them to grow.

A number of plants grow in rock crevices and they can be put in during the construction of the garden. First, fill the crevice with damp peat and then put in the pot-grown plants without disturbing their root balls.

Place a stone over the upper end of the crevice to prevent heavy rain from washing away the soil.

Alternatives to the rock garden

If you would like to grow a few alpines without redesigning your whole garden, you could make an alpine feature. The retaining wall of a sunken sitting area could provide a home for *Aubrieta, Arabis, Cerastium,* and *Iberis.* If you do not mind not having a scrubbed and pristine terrace, you could plant a few alpines between the paving slabs to soften the hard edges. Raised beds, that are actually little more than tables and in which deeper-rooted plants have no chance of thriving, can accommodate many rock plants. Wrap up the raised bed well in winter because frost can easily penetrate it. Raised beds protected by walls are more resistant to frost.

Androsace is very suitable for a rock crevice.

This feature is built of granite pillars filled with tufa.

> ### Tip
> Rock plants like to grow with their roots in gravel, so even if your garden is well drained put in some hard core under the stones.

> ### Tip
> *Erigeron karvinskianus, Aubrieta deltoidea, Saponaria ocymoides, Sedum acre,* and *Silene maritima* grow well in rock crevices.

Then there is the gravel or scree bed. The plants grow in a layer of gravel or grit mixed with clay. If you site the bed in the sun, plants such as *Onosma alborosea, Dianthus alpinus, Campanula cochleariifolia, Edraianthus graminifolius, Phlox subulata,* and *Morisia monanthus* will thrive there.

A home-made trough

Troughs and containers look rather like raised beds and in both you must provide adequate drainage. Winter protection will be necessary. Old troughs are very heavy and are difficult to come by, but you can make them yourself.

You need two cardboard boxes (one 15cm (6″) taller, wider, and longer than the other), a couple of laths, short sections of drain pipe, cement, peat, sand, and water, together with a large sheet of plastic on which to work.

It is better to make a large trough of reinforced concrete in a wooden mould. You will also need a piece of plastic-covered wire mesh to prevent frost damage.

To make a container using the cardboard boxes, stand the sections of drainpipe upright in the larger box. Then lay a couple of laths on the bottom of the box.

Make a mixture of two parts cement, two parts peat, and three parts sand. Mix it to a stiff paste with water. Pour it into the larger box until the laths are just covered. Set the smaller box on the cement base and fill the gap between the two boxes to form the walls.

Press the mixture well down with a wooden spoon. Finally, smooth the upper surface and let the cement dry well before you remove the mould. Wait several weeks before setting the

container in its permanent place and planting it up.

A wooden mould is generally used for larger troughs. Fix wooden planks together with screws to make two wooden chests, and place the wire mesh in the layer of cement.

If all this sounds too complicated, you can buy a modern imitation stone trough at a garden centre and roughen the outside with a coat of cement paint mixed with sand.

Adding a little paint here and there will give you a container that contrasts with the plants you are going to grow in it.

You can make a trough like this for yourself, and it will be much cheaper than any you could buy in a garden centre.

13 Making the most of a small garden

In many gardening books you will find garden designs that are very attractive but are only suitable for larger-than-average gardens. For this reason, this chapter gives some ideas for small gardens.

The mixed garden

In this example (shown in the plan on page 368), there is an area paved with flagstones between the house, workshop, and the neighbouring house, with a large archway leading to the street. This paved space is also used as a sitting area. The owners wanted more plants in their garden and also wanted to be able to sit in the shade. The garden is a little more than 9m (29'3") long at the most, and varies in width between 5.20m (17') and 8m (26').
The "wish" list looked like this:
- the workshop must still be easy to reach,
- the ugly (low) concrete wall must be removed,
- grow a wisteria up the west-facing wall,
- include perennial plants that have a natural look,
- be able to sit in the shade.

First of all, a green trellis was attached to the concrete fence, and ivy (a), and honeysuckle (b), *Lonicera* x *brownii* 'Dropmore Scarlet,' were planted beside it. It was an easy matter to plant the wisteria against the west wall.
For the rest, it was a case of making the most of the available space. In front of the workshop the sitting area is in full sun but, after midday, anyone sitting in the garden can move towards the archway which, together with the house, pro-

vides shade. The original sitting area by the archway was rather larger.
The garden as a whole appears larger because the borders on either side have been extended and are joined by a pergola (II).
This avoids giving the impression of a shoebox with a coloured border round the walls. The pergola (II) provides the garden with a roof and adds height to the design, fulfilling the function of a tree.
'The pergola has only been included to give the garden a solid feature and it has initially not been planted up. One upright, however, has *Akebia quinata* growing up it to see what the effect will be like. Later on, the other uprights can be covered with specimens of the same species to keep the picture simple.
Several ornamental crab-apples, (*Malus* 'Golden Hornet' in pots) have been included. If they are properly looked after they can be left in the same pot for many years, in this case ten. The paving consists of bricks set edge on.

The walls and borders here are closely planted.

The pergola, bamboos, and climbing plants on the walls introduce vertical lines into a small garden.

Ten years later, the same planting is still there but not necessarily in the same place: in a border plants tend to "run." In the border on the eastern side (e), you can see ivy, *Hedera helix*, and honeysuckle, *Lonicera x brownii* 'Dropmore Scarlet.'

Despite a luxuriant planting scheme there is still space for two terraces.

The perennials:
Digitalis purpurea, foxglove
Acanthus mollis bear's breeches
Pennisetum alopecurioides
Macleaya cordata, plume poppy
Althaea rosea, hollyhock (biennial)
Euphorbia lathyrus, caper spurge (biennial)
Polemonium caeruleum, Jacob's ladder
Anthemis nobilis, chamomile
Astrantia major, masterwort

The following plants grow in the border next to the house (f) on the western side of the garden:
Alchemilla mollis, lady's mantle
Salvia sclarea, sage (biennial)
Aster lateriflorus 'Horizontalis',

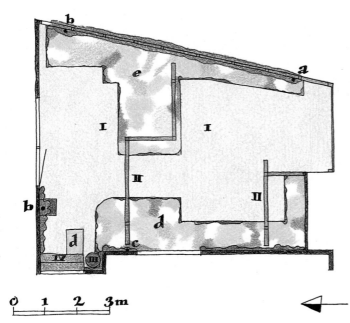

0 1 2 3m

Helleborus niger, Christmas rose
Geranium macrorrhizum 'Album', crane's-bill
Corydalis lutea, yellow fumitory
Hosta sieboldiana, plantain lily
Campanula persicifolia 'Alba', bellflower
Ligularia dentata, leopard-plant
Aconitum carmichaelii, monkshood
Astilbe 'Vesuvius'
Anemone tomentosa 'Robustissima', Japanese
   anemone
Malva moschata 'Alba', mallow
Sinarundinaria nitida, bamboo
Koeleria glauca
Sasa pumila, lbamboo (invasive)
Astilbe chinensis var. pumila
Lysimachia nummularia, creeping Jenny
Aruncus sylvestris, goat's beard
Polygonum superbum, knotweed

A sunken sitting area

The owner wants to make big changes to an existing garden that has a large holly tree at the back of it, worn grass surrounded by a narrow flower bed, and a terrace paved with slabs, together with a path (two paving slabs wide) leading to the garden shed. The whole

garden is enclosed by walls, partly concrete and partly brick. The owner has clear aims: he wants a garden that will need little maintenance, a large part of it paved; a sunken area for a table and four chairs where he can enjoy the evening sun; privacy for the dining room without erecting fencing, which casts a shadow; no grass but, instead, a lot of evergreen plants, summer-flowering plants and climbers. All this has to be fitted in to an area 6.25 x 11m (20'3" x 35'9"). The most important item on the "wish" list is the largest possible sitting area.

The owner was anxious that even using concrete bricks instead of paving slabs the terrace would look monotonous. A good solution was to make a second terrace at a lower level. Before the paving could be laid, a layer of soil 10cm (4") deep had to be replaced with sand. An extra layer of soil was excavated to form the sunken sitting area. This soil was not removed from the garden but used in the border, which was 15cm (6") higher than the terrace and path and 30cm (12") higher on the two sides of the lower terrace.

A pergola was erected to give the house privacy and to give the sitting area a more cosy, enclosed feeling. It also softened the lines of the new brick wall. In this garden *Rosa* 'Bantry Bay'

In a small garden, 20cm (8") is often adequate for a sunken sitting area. Do provide good drainage!

flowers longer and more abundantly than *Rosa* 'New Dawn', while *Rosa* 'The Fairy' provides a long-lasting, colourful feature. The remaining plants were chosen from those that have attractive foliage, including a number that are evergreen. The following plants found a place and made an attractive combination. The plants from the "old" garden were, for the most part, transplanted into pots.

Rosa 'Bantry Bay'
Rosa 'New Dawn'
Akebia quinata
Actinidia kolomikta
Clematis macropetala
Lonicera japonica 'Hall's Prolific'
Rosa 'The Fairy'
Lavandula angustifolia 'Hidcote', lavender
Prunella grandiflora, , self-heal
Campanula portenschlagiana, bellflower
Euphorbia amygdaloides 'Rubra', spurge
Polygonum campanulatum
Helleborus argutifolius
Anemone tomentosa 'Robustissima', Japanese anemone
Heuchera micrantha 'Palace Purple'
Aster divaricatus

The honeysuckle, Lonicera japonica, is semi-evergreen and is growing here against the wall in complete shade. It grows straggly and needs to be kept tidy.

A large strip of this garden is in the shade throughout the day, so an appropriate planting is needed, such as Hosta and Aster divaricatus. Sun-loving plants would have no chance of surviving here.

Helleborus orientalis
Ajuga reptans, bugle
Hosta fortunei 'Hyacinthina', plantain lily
Geum rivale, water avens
Blechnum spicant, hard-fern
Asarum europaeum, asarabacca
Sagina subulata, heath pearlwort

Involving the children

 Do your children enjoy gardening, or are they still at the age where they play in the sandpit or on the swing spending the whole day close to mum and dad?

Whatever age they are, the days are over when a well kept garden meant that there were only boring jobs for the children to do. Nowadays parents are convinced that children, too, should be able to enjoy the garden. There should, for instance, be space to play with a ball.

For children who are interested in growing things – and many children are if they are only allowed to get on with it fairly independently – you can plan a very exciting corner in the garden.

Of course it is much more interesting to be able to grow what you want in your own garden, and a few square metres (yards) of your own is more convenient than your parent's great big patch. Give the children their own little garden, if need be screened by a low hedge or woven fence panels. Make sure this is in a good position, in fact a position you already had your eye on, so that whatever they plant or sow will grow well. There is then a good chance that gardening will become one of their hobbies.

Children will naturally want to be able to choose their own site for their garden. A good place is by the terrace or under the bedroom window, because you can keep an eye on progress from there. You will be able to tell straight away whether your mother will be cross about the state of your garden and whether you need to hoe or weed.

Remember that all gardeners like to have a good view of their gardens from the different rooms in the house.

Made to measure

The size of the children's garden will depend on the size of the whole garden, the number of children, their ages, interests, and what they want to do with it. If your children are interested in gardening, reckon on 10m² (12yd²) for each child, excluding a play area for younger children.

Remember that a six-year-old, whose attention span is limited, will be capable of looking after less garden than a ten-year-old.

Tools for adults have handles that are too long for children. Provide them with suitable tools: hand trowels and forks are ideal.

Big hits with children

– New *carrots* you have grown yourself always taste better than bought ones.
  Suko finger carrots are a very early, sweet variety.

– The tops of *main crop carrots* can be cut off and put in a saucer of water to sprout. Within a few days there will be a cluster of bright green leaves.
  You can also try this with the tops of celeriac.

– *Radishes* are soon ready to harvest. Sow at intervals of fourteen days.

– *Cress* is another fast-growing crop that is fun to sow in the shape of a name or initials. It can be cut in a few days and eaten in sandwiches with cream cheese, or with sugar and lemon juice. If it is allowed to grow to about 8cm (3″) it can be mixed raw into mashed potato.

– It is better to buy *lettuce* plants. Nowadays there is a wide choice of leaf shape and colour.
  Plant them out at least 30cm (12″) apart to dis-couraged fungal infection.

– Try growing *tomatoes*. Buy a sturdy plant of a cherry tomato variety that does not need to have its side shoots pinched out and that will give a heavy crop.

– There are both edible and ornamental varieties of *pumpkin*.
  One plant per m² (1.2yd²) is sufficient.

– Try the variety of *dwarf beans* called 'Purple

Teepee,' which crops well and has pods held high and dry above the leaves, reducing the danger of fungal diseases.

— *Climbing* beans are fun to grow; make a wigwam of bamboo canes to support them. If you make the frame extra large it will also serve as a wigwam for the children. Put in three plants per cane.

Scarlet runner beans have large, showy flowers which make a good cover for the wigwam. They can also grow up the fence.

— Children can make a living screen to shelter the garden out of *sugar-sweet corn* and *ornamental maize*. A couple of red- currant bushes will also protect the garden, though they take up a lot of space.

On the other hand, the children will enjoy the berries, and so will the birds; you will need to cover the bushes with a net at harvest time.

— It is easy to grow *flowers for Grandparent*. Most cut-flowers self-seed without difficulty. Asters can be obtained in various heights and colours; there are double varieties of marigolds in all shades of yellow and orange; the biennial Sweet Williams flower quite early and make fine bouquets for June birthdays; pinks have a delicious scent and they can be grown as perennials.

— Competitions to grow the tallest *sunflower* are very popular. Some varieties will easily reach 3m (9'10").

Sunflower heads (with the seeds in them) can be kept until the winter when the birds will appreciate them if you hang them in a tree.

Dangers lurking in the garden

There are many plants that are poisonous to a greater or lesser extent. Some of these have medicinal uses in which the toxic ingredient is used in minute quantities to promote healing.

Attractive foliage, lovely flowers, to say nothing of the beans, you can have all this with the scarlet runner, which is not difficult to grow.

Eating the flowers or a few berries of these poisonous plants can be harmful. Small children will put almost anything in their mouths, and they naturally find berries very attractive.

The following list gives a measure of the toxicity of these plants:

Latin name	Common name	Toxicity	Poisonous parts
Conifers			
Juniperus sabina	Sabine jupiter	xx	all parts
Taxus	yew	xx	all parts except the seed coat
Thuja	western red-cedar	xx	all parts
Deciduous trees and shrubs			
Aesculus	horse chestnut	x	seed, bark, leaf
Amelanchier	snowy mespil	x	seed, fruit edible in small quantities
Andromeda	bog-rosemary	xx	especially the fruit
Berberis	barberry	x	especially the root, not the ripe fruits
Buxus	box	x	all parts
Cytisus	broom	xx	all parts
Daphne	mezereon	xxx	especially the berries
Euonymus	spindle-tree	xx	especially the seed
Genista	dyer's greenweed	xx	all parts
Ilex	holly	x	the fruit
Laburnum		xxx	especially the ripe seeds
Ligustrum	privet	xxx	bark, leaf, especially the berries
Mahonia		x	roots, not the ripe berries
Prunus laurocerasus	cherry laurel	x	all parts
Prunus serotina	black cherry	x	seed, bark, and leaf; flesh of fruit edible
Rhamnus	buckthorn	xx	bark, leaf, fruit
Rhododendron		xx	leaf, flower and honey
Sambucus	elderberry	x	leaf and unripe berries
Symphoricarpus	snowberry	x	the berries slightly
Perennials			
Aconitum	monkshood	xx	especially the tuber
Adonis		x	all parts
Agrostemma		x	especially the seeds
Anemone	pheasant's-eye	x	especially the sap
Aquilegia	corncockle	x	all parts
Arum maculatum	lords-and-ladies	xxx	especially the berries
Atropa belladonna	deadly nightshade	xxx	especially the berries
Delphinium		xx	especially leaf and seed
Euphorbia	spurge	xx	the milky sap
Helleborus	Christmas rose	x	all parts
Lupinus	lupin	xx	especially the seeds
Pachysandra		x	all parts
Trollius	globeflower	x	all parts
Vinca	periwinkle	x	all parts

Both the leaves and berries of the ivy, Hedera helix, *are poisonous.*

Latin name	Common name	Toxicity	Poisonous parts
Climbing plants			
Aristolochia	birthwort	x	all parts
Clematis		x	all parts
Hedera	ivy	xx	especially berries and leaf
Lonicera	honeysuckle	xx	the berries slightly
Wisteria		xx	branches, pods and seeds
Annuals and biennials			
Datura	angel's trumpet	xxx	especially the seed
Digitalis	foxglove	xxx	all parts
Heracleaum	giant hogweed	xxx	especially the sap
Lathyrus	everlasting pea	xx	especially the seeds
Ricinus	castor oil plant	xxx	especially the seeds
Solanum	nightshade	xx	especially the unripe berry

Latin name	Common name	Toxicity	Poisonous parts
Bulbs and tubers			
Colchicum	autumn crocus	xxx	all parts
Convallaria	lily-of-the-valley	xxx	whole plant
Fritillaria	crown imperal and fritillary	xx	especially the bulb
Galanthus	snowdrop	xx	bulb and leaf
Hyacinthus	hyacinth	xx	all parts
Iris		xx	all parts
Narcissus	daffodil	xx	all parts
Polygonatum	Solomon's-seal	xx	especially the berries
House plants			
Agave		xx	especially the rootstock
Amaryllus		xx	especially the bulb
Anthurium		xx	the young leaf and the flower spike
Clivia		xx	rootstock and the leaf
Codiaeum		xx	the milky sap
Dieffenbachia		xxx	all parts
Euphorbia	crown-of-thorns	xx	the milky juice
Hoya	waxflower	x	not the nectar
Gloriosa		x	all parts
Monstera	Swiss-cheese plant	x	leaf and stem
Nerium	oleander	xxx	especially the leaf
Philodendron		x	all parts
Zantedeschia		xxx	especially the leaf and the tuber

Apple pips contain amygdalin, which is poisonous, but eating an apple complete with pips poses no danger as the quantity of toxin is far below a lethal dose. A case has been reported of a man who died after eating a cupful of apple pips.

A garden for the whole family

A garden of 100m² (120yd²) must be one in which the whole family feels at home and one in which all are free to enjoy themselves. Small children must be allowed to roam all over it.

This does not just mean that a play area in the sun is included but that there are paved paths to ride bicycles along. And what could be nicer for

children than a fruit tree or some fruit bushes in the garden?

> **Tip**
>
> In the unlikely event of someone showing symptoms of poisoning – varying from abdominal pain to convulsions – take him or her to a doctor or the nearest casualty department immediately.
> Meanwhile, try to induce vomiting by putting your finger down his or her throat, or by giving a glass of lukewarm water with either a teaspoonful of salt or mustard stirred into it. When he or she has vomited, take him or her to a doctor and take a piece of the poisonous plant with you.

The fritillary is poisonous, though it looks harmless enough.

Information on the design of the garden

A garden was designed with plenty of scope for the children to play (see the plan on page 376); since it is surrounded by walls, it was laid out as a patio garden: the whole garden can be used for play or as a sitting area. Paths and two terraces have been created using cobblestones and bricks set edge on, although bricks alone would have been sufficient. The bricks on the paths and terraces are laid in various patterns.

The choice of planting and the position of the borders have made it possible to site a second, separate terrace, which is not visible from the kitchen and living room. A plane tree provides shade for this second terrace.

The arbour or, if you prefer it, the pergola with a swing, is an important element. The beam from which the swing hangs is placed east-west on the south side. Climbing plants growing up the vertical supports (leave 40 x 40cm (16″) free on the inner side) provide tall greenery and soften the hard lines of the design.

The garden has been designed to have something of interest at all seasons of the year. In spring the apple and pear trees are in flower against the fence on the south side, followed by fruit in late summer and autumn. On the opposite, shaded, side there is a group of plants that flower in spring and autumn. Here the garbage can and compost bins are hidden behind a screen of ivy growing up wire netting secured to posts.

The border beside the second terrace and the group of plants next to the kitchen are in flower in summer. A group of foliage plants has a place beside the patio doors, with a climbing plant, everlasting pea (Lathyrus latifolius 'Rubra') growing up the wall. This plant grows extremely

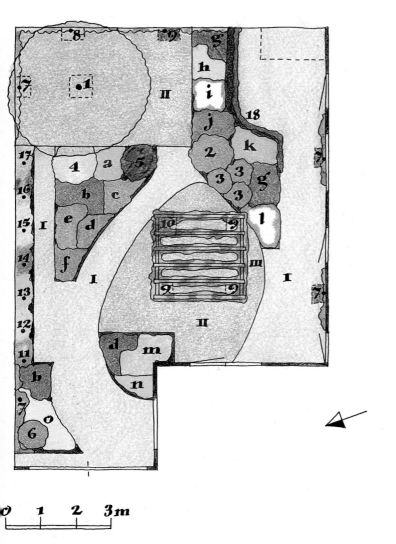

Apple and pear trees are grown as cordons against the fence. You can enjoy blossom in spring and fruit in autumn.

tend to grow upright and, after one season, they will probably be at an angle of 600; the main stem will then grow faster. Untie them and then secure them again, if necessary at a steeper angle, to inhibit their growth.

The parts of the garden

I Paving with yellow bricks laid edge on (tones with II)
II Paving with cobbles 10 x 10 (bronze tint)
III Arbour with swing

Planting

1 *Platanus acerifolia*
2 *Kalmia latifolia*
3 *Hedera colchica* 'Arborescens'
4 *Lavatera* 'Barnsley'
5 *Nandina domestica*
6 *Sinarundinaria nitida*
7 *Lathyrus latifolius* 'Rubra'
8 *Jasminum nudiflorum*
9 *Rosa* 'Golden Showers'
10 Vine 'Boskoop Glory'
11 Apple 'Jonagold'
12 Apple 'Golden Reinette'
13 Apple 'Golden Delicious'

well in shade and is repeated in shaded places throughout the garden to provide a restful motif. Another feature that is repeated is the rose, which grows over the pergola as well as against the fence beside the second terrace. The vine 'Boskoop Glory' is growing up one post of the arbour.

Its foliage provides shade and the children can swing and enjoy the grapes at the same time.

A word of warning: it is important to plant the apples and pears at an angle of 450 and secure them in that position immediately. The trees will

14 Apple 'Elstar'
15 Apple 'James Grieve'
16 Pear 'Conference'
17 Pear 'Doyenne de Comice
18 *Hedera helix*

Perennials

a *Polygonum campanulatum*
b *Agastache foeniculum*
c *Origanum* 'Herrenhausen'
d *Heuchera micrantha* 'Palace Purple'
e *Rudbeckia purpurea*
f *Salvia verticillata* 'Purple Rain'
g *Euphorbia amygdaloides* 'Purpurea'
h *Hemerocallis* 'Stella d'Oro'
i *Helleborus argutifolius*

j *Aster macrophyllus*
k *Anemone tomentosa* 'Robustissima'
l *Houttuynia cordifolia* 'Flore Pleno'
m *Salvia officinalis* 'Icterina' + *Meconopsis cambrica*
n *Corydalis lutea*
o *Epimedium versicolor* 'Sulphureum'

Materials for the pergola, arbour, and swing
If the uprights are put directly into the foundations:
– 4 PVC pipes 100cm (39″) long and 20cm (8″) diameter,
– cement and sand
– 4 posts (uprights) 9 x 9cm (4 x 4″) and 300cm (9′10″) long,
– 2 beams 9 x 9cm (4 x 4″) and 270cm (8′8″) long,

Every child would love to have a play house like this one.

A pergola and a swing are combined here. To the left in the background is a wall of ivy, which hides the bins.

– 2 beams 9 x 9cm (4 x 4″) and 252cm (8′3″) long,
– 4 cross-beams 7 x 7cm (3 x 3″) and 270cm (8′8″) long,
– strong bolts to fix the beams to the uprights,
– hooks for the swing.

It is better to cut grooves in the cross-beams and glue them to the beams. It is also possible to fix metal post supports in concrete for the uprights. A play house is obviously the last word in a garden for most children. The example in the photograph on page 377 may give you an idea for a ready-made house or one you can make

This seat cannot be seen from the living room. It is screened by the tall plants in the border to the right.

yourself, although it does not have to be as elaborate as the one illustrated. Children will happily make play houses for themselves out of old timber (but beware of splinters!) and used car tyres.

A festival of flowers

The owners of this garden (see photo below and on page 378 below) were tired of looking out on grass. Because they were keen on flowers and mainly interested in perennials, they wanted a large summer-flowering border. In addition, they wanted a second terrace, (preferably not overlooked) and prefered the garden shed to be screened by plants. Their grandchildren must also be able to take their cycles from the house to the gate. Finally, there had to be hard standing for their pots. The path is 2.25m (7′4″) wide, wide enough to turn on a bicycle. This connects with the terrace to give a sufficiently large sitting area. A large part of the terrace beside the house is taken up with plants in pots. Siting the herbaceous border in the middle of the garden in front of the living room windows has hidden the second terrace, which gets morning and after-

This beautiful border makes the garden look bigger because it extends more than half way across the paved area.

noon sun. It has also partly disguised the shed. The paving by the house has been kept simple because the border lends enough variety. A circle of bricks has been laid by the second terrace. The sun shines on the large border from the south and west, and it is shel-tered from drying winds and winter cold on the north and east sides. Plants that do not normally survive severe winters reappear in the border in spring as if nothing had happened. There are, however, problems with the planting in the narrow border along the northeast wall. Conditions are cramped and the soil is very dry. The rose 'Abraham Darby' did not thrive in the sunny border; it very soon became diseased and was dug out. The owner wants to replace it with a pyramid of ivy.

Possible planting scheme
Lavatera 'Barnsley'
Chaenomeles speciosa 'Moerloosei', flowering quince
Ceanothus lobbianus (small leaf, evergreen, blue flowers in summer, 2m (6′7″) high)
Anemone japonica 'Honorine Jobert' (shade)
Helleborus purpurascens, (shade)
Anemone tomentosa 'Robustissima' *Campanula lactiflora* 'Alba', bellflower
Arundinaria murielae, bamboo
Gaura lindheimeri
Tradescantia x *andersoniana* 'Zwanenburg Blue',
Euphorbia wulfenii, spurge
Polygonum amplexicaule, knotweed
Salvia verticillata 'Purple Rain'
Euphorbia amygdaloides 'Purpurea' (shade)
Verbena bonariensis
Heuchera micrantha 'Palace Purple'
Astrantia major, masterwort
Salvia sclarea, (biennial)
Rudbeckia purpurea
Scuttelaria incana, skullcap
Geranium endressii 'Wargrave Pink', crane's bill
Geranium wallachianum 'Buxton's Variety'
Santolina chamaecyparissus, lavender cotton
Milium effusum 'Aureum', wood millet (shade)
Symphytum grandiflorum (shade)

14 Ponds

A water feature in the garden is like an open fire in a room: you cannot take your eyes off it. The water always attracts attention, and it can be very educational. There are also practical reasons for having moving water. The sound of a fountain can distract attention from unwanted noise, for example from traffic.

A pond can, however, pose a danger to small children, and you must always be very attentive to safety measures.

Ponds are always attractive and they add another dimension to the garden, whatever their size.

Construction materials

There is a wide choice of materials from which you can build a pond, including flexible plastic or butyl rubber liners, preformed ponds, puddled clay, and concrete.

If the groundwater level is fairly constant and does not fall too low, a natural pond at the lowest point of the garden is the ideal choice. If you have a formal garden with an artificial pond that is perhaps above ground level, you must not use a flexible liner or puddled clay.

Drawings for a concrete and brickwork pond, plan above and cross- section below.

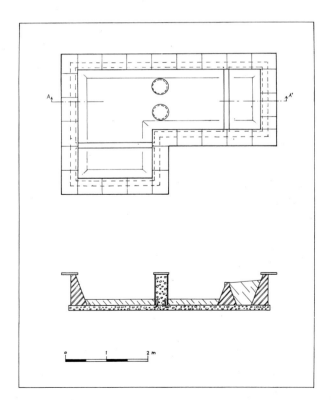

Right: *Ponds can also be constructed above ground.*

A brick and concrete pond

The base of this pond, 75cm (30″) below the water level, is made of reinforced concrete which does not shatter during hard frost, unlike plain concrete. The brick side walls are cemented on to this base.

The inside faces of the walls slope outwards at quite a steep angle to ensure that any ice formed is pushed up and so cannot force the walls apart. You can see from the drawing that two intermediate walls have been included to make basins that can be filled with soil to provide different depths of water.

The depth of the water will depend to some extent on the surface area. The water must not become too warm, but neither should it remain cold for too long. Deep water will take longer to warm up than shallow water, and in spring animals and plants will take longer to come back to life.

On the other hand, if the water is too shallow the temperature can rise too steeply. How quickly the water will warm up will depend on the size of the area exposed to the sun. In addition, fish and certain water plants need a minimum depth of 60cm (24″) of water to be able to survive the winter. In small ponds always allow for a section 60cm (24″) deep, and in larger ponds at least 75cm (30″).

This is what the concrete pond looks like.

Leave part of the bank free of plants so that you can see the water. Avoid giving the impression of a box.

The pond should have different depths of water to support a varied plant life. Think of natural ditches and ponds: the plants in the deepest water are quite different from those in the shallow water near the bank.

During the construction of the pond, two PVC pipes were sunk into the wet concrete base and securely anchored before being filled with concrete.

The upper surface of the pipes was covered with washed, round slabs with a gravelly surface. The edge of the pond was finished with a layer of similar, square slabs, laid to extend 5cm (2″) over the edge.

After that the base and sides of the pond were coated with bitumen to seal in the harmful chemicals in concrete and brickwork as well as to make it completely watertight.

Once the pond has been filed with mains water, it can be planted up with water plants. You can then put the bog plants you have chosen round the edges.

If you choose the right plants, the edges of the pond will soon be concealed. Large-leaved plants such as hostas are ideal.

The liner pond

§ The advantage of a liner pond is that it can be in whatever shape you choose. A good PVC liner is available in widths of 4m and 5m (13′ and 16'3″). Butyl liner is available in widths of 3.6m, 4.9m, 5.5m, 6.1m, 7.3m (12′, 16′, 18′, 20′, 24′).

It is not advisable to use the heaviest gauge for ponds more than 100m² (120yd²) because it is difficult to fold and, in addition, a liner for a pond of that size weighs more than 150kg (330lb). The liner can be supplied to size or you can use adhesive to make a large enough piece yourself. When the pond has been filled with water, the liner must not be under any tension.

You should lay it in position with some material to spare. You will also need extra liner for the edges. Allow 25cm (10″) more than you think you will need.

Clear away stones, roots, glass, and any other sharp objects from the pond, and put down a layer of sand, old carpet, or protective uderlay in the hole before you finally position the liner. It is possible to buy reinforcing material to cover the edge of the pond to prevent dogs, herons, and clumsy gardeners with rakes from pricking holes in the liner. This is, however, just as expensive as the best original liner material.

It is important that the edge of the pond is horizontal. After the pond itself and any shallow surrounding areas have been excavated, posts of treated timber are driven into the ground about

The shape of the pond is marked out with small posts and then excavated. The walls are smoothed out and sharp objects removed.

Connect the posts on the inner side with one or more planks, which are nailed on the pond side to the posts. The upper edge of these planks must be exactly level. The plastic liner is pulled over this edge and hidden under the soil behind it.

Finishing off the edge

Here the pond liner is doubled over behind the stones that sit on the bank of the pond.

All the soil, soft stones, roots, and plants which together form the edge of the pond will extract water from the pond. If you pull the liner up behind the soil on the edge of the pond to stop this syphoning of water, there will always be a visible edge between the pond's surface and the edge. The effect of this syphoning can be counteracted by controlling the water supply with a float. The pond is then automatically topped up again when it falls below a certain level.

a metre (yard) apart (depending on the shape of the rim) where the edge is to be laid. The tops of the posts must be more or less level.

The pond has now to be planted up.

You can hide the narrow edge of the liner that can still be seen above the plank by laying a border of stones or turves which projects slightly over the water. The border must be securely anchored. When you have pulled the edge of the liner over the posts and planks, you bury the back of the liner in the soil. Then put a layer of broken bricks or stones on the soil over which you put a layer of cement, extending this in a thin layer on to the liner.

Stones, bricks or turves are then pressed into this. A projection like this over the water will cast a shadow on the thin strip of liner. Small plants can be grown on the turf without them touching the water.

The edge can also be disguised by fixing a second plank with screws as high as possible over the liner against the top plank and the post. Naturally the timber must be treated or, better still, it should be of hardwood.

A third plank is fixed horizontally above the two planks and the posts. You could even let the turves hang over the edge into the pond. The sides will then become damp because water will slowly be siphoned out of the pond, and this will make an automatic water supply a necessity.

This pond is faced with azobe wood (African oak)..

The pond is fed by groundwater. During a long dry spell the water level can fall; the amount of fall will depend on the size of the pond and the level of the groundwater table.

An other option is to create a gradual transition from pond to garden by hiding the liner with stones. Flowering plants can be planted amongst these. The edge of the pond can be covered with alluvial clay, or draped with artificial grow mats into which plants will root.

There are endless ways of disguising the edge of a pond. Nowadays PVC covered with a fine layer of grit is available at specialist garden centres.

Filling the pond

As far as possible, you should aim to have soil at the bottom of your pond that is just like the soil found in ditches and natural ponds. The ideal substrate is one rich in nutrients but which contains little organic material.

If materials such as compost, leaf mould, animal manure, and artificial manure are present in large quantities in your pond, single-celled algae will multiply at an alarming rate. These algae convert organic material into nutrients which the plants can absorb.

This can be beneficial, but unfortunately the algae multiply making the water cloudy and full

This is a quiet spot, ideal for looking at the water and what is growing round it. There is also a good view of the fish and other pond life.

of green slime. It is better to use clay or loam for the pond or the special pond compost that is now available. If your garden soil is poor sand do not use this in your pond. Poor sandy soil contains too few nutrients for the plants and, besides, the sand will swirl about in the water.

You cannot put waterplants in sandy soil either, it will not settle, creating yet another kind of cloudiness.

The concrete pond described earlier has a layer of clay 15cm (6') thick in the deepest part; the shallow sections are filled with clay up to a depth of 55cm (22″), sloping up to the sides to give depths of water from 15 to 20cm (6″ to 8″).

Water in the pond

🦢 In most cases, ponds are filled with mains water. Clean water from a ditch or captured rainwater are, however, better because they contain fewer minerals. On the other hand, these are often rather acid and too soft for fish and plants to survive well.

The plants become slimy and the fish become covered in slime, which inflames their scales. Spring water can be used providing it does not contain too much iron.

You can fill and plant up a new pond from the middle of May onwards. If you use mains water, wait a few days to allow the added substances in mains water (such as chlorine) to disappear before you put in the plants.

The water will also have had a chance to warm up a little.

Life in the pond

🦢 What are you going to put in your pond? You should definitely include plants that will take light and nutrients from the algae, since the biggest problem with a pond is keeping the water clear.

Plants with floating leaves and particularly ones that live under water (such as Canadian pondweed, frogbit, water crowfoot, pondweed, hornwort, and water-soldier) compete well with the algae.

They also release oxygen into the water and provide cover for the fish.

If you always feed the fish at the same time each day, they will be waiting for you.

Some plants that have floating leaves and fine, hair-like roots are difficult to plant and keep in place.

One answer is to wrap a bundle of stems in a piece of sacking weighted with a stone and let this sink to the bottom at the desired position. The plant will float and roots will develop that will anchor it to the bed of the pond.

Deep-rooted plants with floating leaves and marginal plants must be treated in the same way as terrestrial plants.

Large aquatic plants which spread rapidly are often supplied in baskets or plastic-mesh planting crates, and it is advisable to plant these complete with the container.

This will avoid one species taking over completely. The container will also stop the goldfish rooting around in the soil and making the water cloudy. Finally, you can put a layer of pebbles on top of the soil at the bottom of the pond.

Bacteria that convert ammonium salts into nitrates and nitrites (both of which are indispensable for plant life) will cling to the pebbles. This will avoid the rotten-egg smell sometimes experienced in ponds.

If you want to be able to see the fish in your pond, only part of the water surface should be covered with leaves. Generally, a two thirds cover is sufficient.

If the whole surface is covered, no sunlight will penetrate and the submerged water plants will die and begin to rot. Try to follow the middle way by having a varied planting; alternate plants with floating leaves with those that have submerged ones and with marginals.

Animal life

 Wait about six weeks after planting before you put fish in the water. That will give the

Left: *The surface of this small pond is almost completely covered in leaves. The plants must be thinned once a year.*

plants a chance to become established and well rooted. If fish are introduced too early, they can damage the plants by stirring up the mud before the plants have had an opportunity to grow properly.

Goldfish and golden orfe are often put into garden ponds. Although goldfish stir up the mud they, like the golden orfe, can be seen easily. The common sticklebacks, bream, and carp are at home in a pond. Golden carp are sensitive to cold and will not survive a severe winter.

Grass carp will eat any plants and leave nothing untouched.

Just like fish, the ram's-horn snail will eat up dying plant remains. In addition, this snail is the great enemy of algae.

Frogs will return to the pond each year to breed, and their spawn will add interest to your pond's wildlife. Fish eat all kinds of animal life, including midges and their larvae. This makes fish an almost essential element in a pond with stagnant water.

> ### Tip
> Immediately after planting, a pond can develop an algal bloom. Add a bucket of water containing water fleas which you will find in a clean ditch. These creatures will set about the green algae and can often make the water clear again within twenty-four hours. If there are fish in the pond, you may have to repeat the process a few times because fish eat water fleas.

One fish per m² (39″) of the water surface is sufficient. Too many fish will mean too much waste matter; and a raised level of organic material will result in an explosive growth of algae which will cloud the water.

On the other hand, the algae do produce oxygen, which the fish will take advantage of. If the water does become cloudy, some fish should be removed while at the same time you should put in more plants with floating leaves.

Managing the pond

§ Once the pond has been filled and planted, in theory it should look after itself. If you do nothing, at some point your pond will reach a biological equilibrium: it will tend to dry out to become land again.

Almost every pond owner wants clear water in a natural-looking pond. There is an almost un-limited range of equipment to help in this, ranging from aerators, pond and biological filters, for use in or beside the pond, and sub-mersible and pumps for installing on dry land.

Your local pond specialist will be able to advise you. The latest gadget is a pond filter that con-verts ammonium into nitrates and nitrites and

then removes them. This will keep the water clear in ponds that only contain fish.

How many plants?

§ Most oxygen is released into the water by the submerged plants, and water with a high oxygen content is also more likely to be clear. Hence a number of submerged plants should be included; reckon on at least eight clumps per m³ (1.3yd³).

Try to ensure that, as quickly as possible, a third of the pond's surface is covered by leaves. If the waterlilies are slow to start, shade the pond with a good selection of plants placed along the pond's margin. A lot of fish will tend to make the water murky.

Depending on the species, do not exceed a maxi-mum of five fish per m³ (1.3yd³) for at least six

The water is pumped into the air by the fountain and, as a result, the oxygen content of the water is increased.

weeks after planting up the pond. The clearest ponds (without using pumps and filters) are those without fish.

The pond in winter

§ During the summer, the fish in a planted pond will find sufficient food themselves. People do, however, feed them occasionally, to attract them to the surface where they can be seen easily.

From November to April, however, the fish do not need to be fed at all. They are cold-blooded, and their bodies function very little at low temperatures.

What both fish and evergreen water plants need during the winter is oxygen. This can be provided by breaking a hole in the ice and putting a bunch of straw into it. Breaking the ice is not, however, the best solution, since it will disturb the fish and could damage the structure of the pond. A better idea is to put a ball in the pond before the ice forms; once the pond is frozen over, you can remove the ball and bale out some of the water to leave a layer of air under the ice. This will provide oxygen and also act as insulation. Put straw or a bunch of plant stems to keep the airway open.

Nets and mesh

§ You will need to prevent organic matter (such as leaves) falling into your pond during autumn.

If not, the water will become foul. Green and blue algae will multiply at an alarming rate. The same thing can happen with blossom in spring,

A wire is stretched between the iron pegs round this pond to keep the herons away. Later in the season, the pegs can be used to anchor a net over the pond.

and should birds drop bits of bread into your pond, these should be removed. Spreading a fine net over the water or protecting it with an old window pane will help.

Water and safety

Children as well as adults will enjoy the wonderful life of your pond. What happens to frogspawn?

How do pondskaters move over the water's surface? What exactly does the whirligig beetle do? Children are drawn to water and therein lies the danger, especially for small children. A child can drown in 5cm (2″) of water.

Children are curious and inventive and are unlikely to be discouraged by a fence; in fact, they may see this as merely an obstacle to be overcome.

If children are likely to play in your garden it is advisable to stretch a piece of mesh over your pond at a depth of less than 5cm (2″). This should preferably be strong welded mesh, supported on piles of stones and securely anchored at the edge.

The mesh need not be an eyesore. It can be cut to fit the shape of the pond and can be painted to camouflage it. Leaves will quickly grow through this mesh and so it will soon become almost invisible.

Aquatic plants

Plants with floating leaves			
Name	Flower colour	Flowering season	Depth of water in cm (in)
Aponogeton distachyos	white	5-8	50-120 (20-47)
Callitriche palustris floating water plantain	green	6-7	5-20 (2-8)
Luronium natans waterlily	white	6-9	10-30 (4-12)
Nymphaea alba	white	6-9	50-120 (20-47)
Nymphaea alba 'Froebelii' dwarf waterlily	dark red		30-45 (12-18)
Nymphaea alba 'Pygmaea alba'	white		20-50 (8-20)
Nymphaea tetragona fringed waterlily	white		10-30 (4-12)
Nymphoides peltata	yellow	6-8	20-80 (8-32)
Nuphar lutea	yellow	6-8	50-100 (20-39)

Left: Nymphaea 'Attraction', a beautiful waterlily, needs water 30 to 150cm (12″ to 59″) deep. It is also suitable for growing in a large tub if you can give it adequate frost protection in winter.

Name	Flower colour	Flowering season	Depth of water in cm (in)
Nuphar pumila	yellow	5-8	20-40 (8-16)
water-crowfoot			
Ranunculus aquatilis	white	6-8	10-50 (4-20)
water-soldier			
Stratiotes aloides	white	5-8	40-100 (16-39)

Submerged aquatic plants and plants with floating leaves and trailing roots

Name	Flower colour	Flowering season	Depth of water in cm (in)
waterfern			
Azolla mexicana	traces	7-8	80 (32)
Ceratophyllum demersum			30-50 (12-20)
Canadian pondweed			
Elodea canadensis	white	5-8	10-80 (4-32)
water violet			
Hottonia palustris	pink	5-7	20-40 (8-16)
frogbit			
Hydrocharis morsus-ranae	white	5-8	from 15 (6)
Lemna triscula			from 10 (4)
Myriophyllum spicatum			20-50 (8-20)
Potamogeton crispus			from 20 (8)
broad-leaved pondweed			
Potamogeton natans	white	6-8	from 20 (8)
Trapa natans		6-8	from 30 (12)
greater bladderwort			
Urticularia vulgaris	yellow	6-8	0-30 (0-12)

Left: *It is not always easy to keep the water in the pond clear but, if you can, the water plants will be reflected in it. The round leaves of the lotus give lovely reflections.*

Right: *Round ponds can soften the sharp outlines of a design in, for example, a formal garden.*

Tip

It is difficult to say how many fish your pond will support. This will naturally depend on the species and size of fish. If you put in fish 10cm (4") long, reckon on eight fish per m³ (39").

15 Plants in pots: containergardening

Pots, tubs, and other containers, as well as the plants in them, have already been considered in the chapter on garden ornaments.

This chapter contains practical details about growing plants in pots and containers and how to care for them in the longer term.

The pros and cons of pots and containers

Container plants are those that need to be brought indoors during the winter in order for them to survive. In western Europe this applies to plants from the tropics and sub-tropics. For centuries these plants have been grown in pots and containers that are decorative in themselves.

Many plants from annuals and bulbs to hostas and even trees, can be grown in containers.

The great advantage of a plant in a pot or container is that it can be moved. A gap in the garden caused by a failed plant can easily be camouflaged with a plant in a pot, and any empty spaces can be filled up. Balconies and roof gardens also look better if they are decorated with flowers

Terracotta pots with hardy plants in them must be protected from frost to prevent damage.

and foliage plants in containers. Generally speaking, plants in containers do not reach their full size, which can be a further advantage in terms of perspective. Plants in containers are also growing in conditions that are very different from those in open ground, so their care also has to be different.

To give the plants a good start and the best possible chance of thriving, begin with a special compost. It is quite wrong just to fill a pot with garden soil.

Compost for pots

Compost for container plants has special characteristics because the plants are growing in very limited space. The compost must retain sufficient moisture but must also have sufficient air so that the roots can breathe. In addition, it must be capable of providing plant nutrients over a long growing period.

You can use normal potting compost as a base. This usually consist of six parts peat, two parts leaf mould, and one part river sand. Commercially prepared compost contains enough nutrients and lime to last from four to six weeks.

You will need to add further ingredients for plants that have very specific requirements, such as cacti, succulents, and many alpines. These prefer a more open but at the same time heavier compost. You could use, for example, two parts compost with one part coarse sand or grit, and one part fine clay.

Most plants that are going to spend their entire lives in a pot or container also need a heavier and more nutrient-rich compost. This must be general-purpose compost suitable for a large range of container plants, since the group includes plants of many different genera and species. A suitable mixture would be two parts potting compost, two parts fine clay, one part well rotted stable manure (or dried fertilizer), and one part sharp sand. Perlite or vermiculite can be included to improve its moisture-holding properties.

Choosing the container

Whichever type of container you choose, make sure that it has sufficient drainage holes in the bottom. Fragments of clay pots, gravel, or something similar will prevent the compost washing through.

If the container is to stand on a flat concrete surface, it is advisable to raise it off the ground a little on special feet or blocks.

The most familiar plant containers are the red earthenware ones. These are on sale in all shapes and sizes and are often imported from southern Europe. A square shape, or one that slopes outward from the base, is ideal. Earthenware is porous and takes up water, which causes the compost to dry out easily.

In the summer plants in this type of container will have to be watered twice a day. You can conserve moisture by growing the plant in a plastic inner pot or by lining the earthenware with plastic. There will be few problems with plants that like dry conditions.

If the pot is exposed to the wind on a terrace or balcony, it is a good idea to weight it with a couple of bricks. If you want to leave porous earthenware out of doors during the winter, it must be bone dry or it will shatter in the frost. There are, however, some frost-resistant makes available.

Wooden tubs vary from the traditional to the modern. They are mostly larger than earthenware pots and containers, which means they are particularly suitable for larger spaces. They are often used for trees and shrubs. Choose hard

Tip
Whether or not your container plant is going to overwinter out of doors, always use a plastic inner pot in an earthenware pot. If the plant overwinters outside, the decorative terracotta pot can be brought indoors out of the frost.

wood and, if you are going to make a tub your-self, use treated pine because softer or untreated timber rots very easily. Never use creosote on the wood because this will kill off the plants com-pletely. A wooden container can be lined with plastic.

The advantage of *plastic* is that it is light, which makes it suitable for use in roof gardens (see below). Plastic containers must, of course, be well anchored.

Because plastic is not porous it will not shatter during the winter, and it will lose little moisture during the summer. The compost in the pot will be evenly moist and warm, and roots do not have the tendency to grow towards the pot wall in search of air. Nowadays plastic containers are available in many shapes and colours, and some look like earthenware.

Unlike earthenware, plastic does not weather so the pots never look old.

Another possibility is to use *rush or osier baskets*. These need to be lined with plastic to prevent water leaking out. Because baskets absorb water they rot fairly quickly. It is therefore a good idea to use them only for annuals so that each au-tumn the plants can be thrown on to the com-post heap and the baskets dried out and stored indoors until spring. That way they will last several years.

Concrete and artificial stone containers can be at-tractive but unfortunately they are heavy. Most of them are rather large and clumsy so they are more suitable for large spaces. If the concrete is frost-resistant the containers can be left out of doors throughout the winter.

You can use the deeper containers for shrubs or even trees. The combination of concrete and a

Tubs are once again available in traditional designs.
Make sure they are raised off the ground to increase their life.

hardy tree or shrub is particularly recommended because the container does not need to be moved at the beginning and end of the season. The shallower containers and troughs are suitable for plants such as cacti and succulents, which prefer dry conditions.

If you look around you will see that there are many more things that can be used as containers, ranging from basins and garden urns to teapots and clogs.

Whatever shape and whatever material you choose, there are two important points to remember:

– Containers made of copper, zinc, or iron must not come into direct contact with compost or roots, because plants cannot tolerate these metals and they will fail to thrive and will eventually die. Always line metal containers with a layer of plastic or use an inner pot.

– Unless you are going to use it as a water feature, every container must have one or more holes in or near the bottom for drainage.

The position

Plants in containers always occupy special positions. The aspect of the garden, balcony, or roof garden is important because the plants have to grow to their full potential within the confines of the pot or container. For instance, a northerly aspect means that the plants are going to be in shadow for most of the day. You can plant those specimens that need very little sunlight, such as fuchsias, hostas, and various evergreen shrubs.

Situations open to the west and southwest will be windy, and plants here must be resistant to wind and will need to be well anchored. Choose a low, compact planting. On the eastern side the temperature can fall well below freezing in winter.

For perennial plants or shrubs to have any chance of survival at all, you will need to provi-

Left: *Fuchsias are very much at home in a north-facing situation as they do not miss the sun.*

On the western side, this low planting of annuals has every chance of surviving.

de a sturdy, well anchored windbreak. Choose hardy plants or use to annuals.

It is possible to grow almost anything on the south side, but here water will be a great problem, especially with earthenware containers which dry out rapidly.

From balcony to roof garden

Most balconies, even those owned by non-gardeners, have a couple of pots of geraniums on them. These, however, have to be brought indoors in winter and space found for them in the house or apartment. Pots with *Rosa* 'Fairy' and lavender or *Lavatera* 'Barnsley' provide colour throughout the summer. It is also worth trying a redcurrant bush.

A tree in a large bucket gives shade and makes a suitable background for a small water feature in a half barrel. A garden on the balcony can soon get out of hand. The same applies to a roof garden when its owner starts to remove the gravel to make way for a small border of cottage-garden plants.

Rush screens, attached to welded mesh, will shelter the garden. Clematis will grow up the screens and the chimney. Before you know it, a garden on a balcony or roof has become a real garden in miniature.

Weighty matters

When you are laying out a roof or balcony garden, weight is a very important consideration. As far as possible use "light" materials: a great deal of weight can be saved in containers and in the growing medium. Plastic containers are the lightest.

Borders and edges can be made of lightweight blocks, but most weight can be saved in the substrate. Some 1m³ (1.3yd³) of damp soil on its own weighs approximately 1800kg (3960lb), and if you want a layer about 30cm (12″) deep in a pot or border, the weight will be almost 600kg (1320lb) per m² (39″). As well as the pots or containers, you must add to this the weight of the plants themselves. The gravel layer used to finish the roof weighs 2000kg (4400lb) per m³ (39″).

Permanent and variable load

The permanent load of a roof consists of the weight of the roof construction itself and the parts of the construction that bear down on the building.

In addition, the materials used to make the roof watertight must be included. Tell the architect before the plans for your house are completed if you intend to construct a roof garden. He or she will then take account of its weight in the construction of the roof. In this case the weight of the substrate and the plants will be included in the permanent load.

Furthermore you have to consider variable load, such as snow, people walking or sitting in the garden, water, and wind. Although not all of these items will apply, the architect will always consider them.

It is impossible to say precisely how much weight you may add to a balcony or roof because structures vary. In general you may add whatever weight you have removed.

If, for example, you remove the gravel from part of the roof, you can put something in its place that weighs as much or less than gravel because you will not be increasing the permanent load. An insurance company will investigate whether a roof's construction was sufficient to cope with the extra load if it starts to leak and causes damage because of the plants resting on it. Before you lay out a roof garden, consult an architect first.

In some areas there are regulations covering the height of planting and the total weight of balcony and roof gardens.

It is important to use light materials on a flat roof. Here lightweight tiles and building blocks have been used.

Tip

A semi-automated watering system can be installed and set to control the time and duration of watering.

This is useful when you go away on holiday, ut the system will not take account of the weather – it will water the plants even during a rain storm. The variable load will then increase enormously.

were used. They were half filled with expanded clay granules, and covered with a layer of potting compost. The clay granules were chosen because they reduced the total weight of the containers and contents by 25%. A small terrace area (12m²) (14.4 yd²) was paved with lightweight tiles. The gravel layer was removed and, to avoid damage to the roofing material, the

Honeysuckle flourishes against the sloping roof.

The plastic containers are half filled with clay granules. The sloping roof gives some protection from the wind, which can be considerable.

A lightweight garden on a flat roof

The flat roof is on the southwest side of the house. On the east side a small part is sheltered by a wall 1m (39″) high connected to the house. The rest of the balcony was initially completely bare.

Permission was sought to place several containers filled with perennials, various small trees in pots, and grow bags on it. Plastic containers which are light, frost-resistant, and chip-proof

tiles were placed on rubber strips. The low wall and the roof were covered with clematis planted in grow bags.The original welded mesh, fixed on the east and west sides, was inspected each year and the attachment points checked for strength. After seven years the mesh had to be replaced because it had rusted so much. Mean while, several small trees growing in pots have been removed, and a border of cottage-garden plants (low ground-covering perennials) established in their place.

Again, first of all the gravel was removed and an edge of lightweight blocks was used to make a bed 12cm (5″) deep. A geo-textile was laid under the compost to prevent roots damaging the roof covering. A very thin layer of compost like this will be very prone to drying out, especially when there is no water-holding layer underneath it.

A view of the container garden.

The container garden

❀ The owner of this small town garden has grow plants in the open ground. for many years The garden had a small border on the south side. Since he also grows a lot of tropical and sub-tropical plants, he finds it easier to grow them side by side in pots and containers. The whole garden has been paved and a canvas awning provides shelter for the plants during the holidays, in the winter, and during heavy rain. Because the garden is small and enclosed, all the plants overwinter successfully out of doors except the geraniums, which are taken into a cool room indoors.

Special compost

❀ Every three years all the plants are repotted in fresh compost. The gardener makes this up himself to a special formula. A third is

river clay, which is spread out into flat cakes with a rolling pin, partially dried, and then crumbled. One third is coarse sand and one third is completely rotted stable manure.

The plants are repotted in this mixture in the spring. No extra fertilizer is given in the first year. The following two years the plants are fed. Nowadays, pelleted fertilizers are available that are coated with a thin layer of wax. This ensures that the nutrients are gradually released into the compost.

The higher the soil temperature and the higher the humidity, the more nutrients are released. If you prefer an organic fertilizer you can use a mixture of dried blood, hoof and horn, and bone meal. A dressing of 40gm per 12l pot (1 ½oz per 21pt pot) at the beginning of the growing season will be sufficient.

Watering plants in containers is a precise business. Always feel with a finger whether the compost is still damp 3cm (1″) below the surface. If it feels dry water the plant. Never use ice-cold water because it will give the plants a shock that could kill them. Water should be at about 18°C (64°F).

Left: *The large sheet of plastic fixed to the fence breaks the wind and provides a micro-climate in which* Justicia, Prostanthera, Leptospermum, *and* Curcuma *(lilac pink) can even survive the winter.*

A path leads from the kitchen door to the back gate.

16 Vegetable and herb gardens

The earlier chapter on the layout of the vegetable garden, crop rotation and propagation has no doubt set you on the right path when it comes to growing vegetables. It only remains to choose between a traditional vegetable layout, which is designed primarily for the production of food, and the garden where, alongside vegetables, there is a place for ornamental plants and herbs.

A traditional vegetable garden

The design on page 405 shows a traditional vegetable garden 20 x 15m (65 x 48'9"). It is one that is often seen in allotments. If

In a traditional vegetable garden, cut flowers are often grown in a separate bed. Here cosmos are growing next to the peas which are supported with pea sticks.

it forms part of the garden next to the house, the shed may well be situated in another place and the compost heap will be hidden somewhere at the bottom of the garden. This garden faces south east and is sheltered from the north west by trees and shrubs immediately behind the vegetable garden. At the back of the garden there are large wooden compost and manure bins and a tool shed, which also provides shelter from the rain. In addition, part of the garden is sheltered from strong winds on the northwest and northeast sides by a hedge of raspberry canes, together with gooseberry and redcurrant bushes and the two plum trees. The plum 'Opal' shades the compost and manure bins.

Layout of the beds

The beds are 120cm (3'11"), except for the first two which are 1m (3'3") deep. The paths between the beds are just wide enough to walk along, 30cm (12") wide; the central path is 1m (3'3"), and the path round the garden 50cm (20"). The cold frame – 240 x 150cm (7'9" x 4'11") – can be used for germinating seeds and pricking out seedlings. The space round it makes it possible to work easily. It's a good idea to mark the corners of the beds permanently and number them to make crop rotation easier.

Planting plan
A Shed
B Sieved compost
C Manure heap
D Second-stage compost bin
E Compost heap
F Plum 'Opal'
G Redcurrants x 2

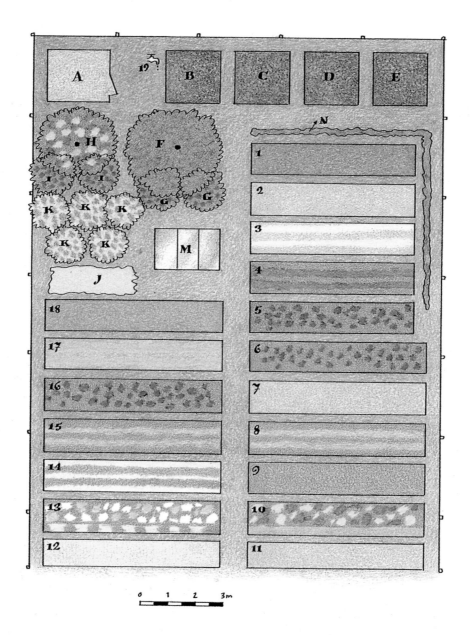

H Plum 'Victoria'
I   Redcurrants x 2
J   Spring onions
K Gooseberries x 5
M Cold frame
N   Raspberries
 1 Red cabbage
 2 Peas followed by endive
 3 Peas followed by fennel
 4 Early turnips followed by soya beans
 5 Strawberries and lettuce
 6 Strawberries and lettuce

 7 Late potatoes
 8 Broad beans and early potatoes
 9 Peas followed by French beans
10 Chrysanthemums and winter carrots
11 Spring cabbage followed by curly kale
12 Spring cabbage followed by sprouting broccoli
13 Chrysanthemums and celeriac
14 Peas followed by leeks
15 Broad beans and potatoes
16 Strawberries and lettuce
17 Carrots and onions
18 Tomatoes
19 Water tap

The Zinnia is a plant that has stood the test of time.
It should find a place in every vegetable garden.

The ornamental vegetable garden

The main aim of the vegetable garden is to produce food, but it does not have to be dull and can be designed to look very attractive. Although most crops grow to about the same height and very few are growing during winter, it is possible to include shrubs, climbers, colour, and other features to convert the vegetable into a pleasure garden. In this design (page 407) various vegetables have been included which not only taste good but also look attractive. In addition, an attempt has been made to avoid the garden's ornamental aspect conflicting with the rules of good husbandry. The curved paths may come as a surprise but they do add an extra element, without affecting access to the beds. Alongside the main path are scarlet runner beans, golden hop, and white sweet peas, all growing against tall canes which are placed in circles and tied together at the top. The garden is sheltered on three sides while the south side has been left open. The garden is 15m (48′9″) deep and 13m (42′3″) wide. The main paths are 1m (39″) and 60cm (24″) and the paths between the beds 30cm (12″). The beds are 1.2m (3′11″) wide.

Planting plan

1 Manure heap
2 Shed
3 Plum
4 Compost heap with ornamental pumpkin
5 Compost heap
6 Whitecurrants
7 Blackcurrants trained along wires
8 Red cabbage

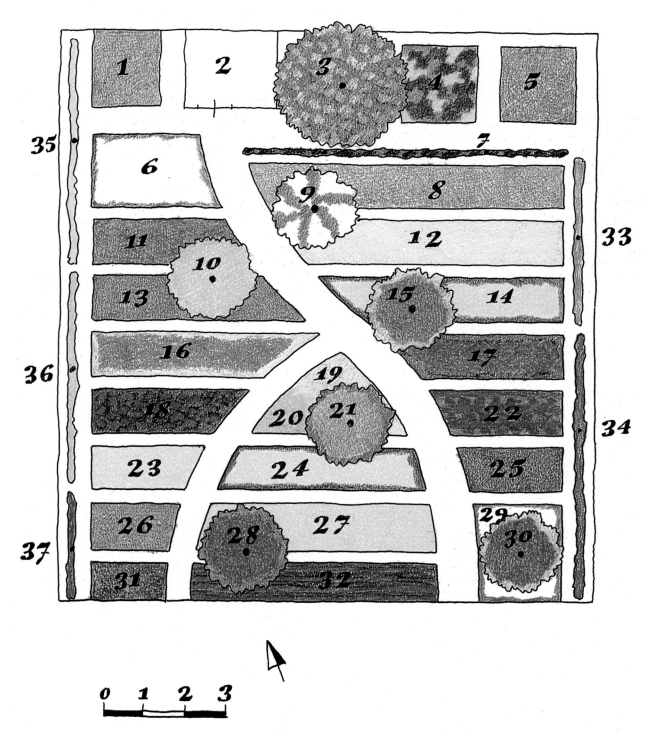

9 Sweet pea, *Lathyrus odorata* 'Cuthbertson White' (annual), with chamomile, *Matricaria* recutita (annual) within the circle
10 Golden hop, *Humulus lupulus* 'Aureus'
11 Medium dahlias with bronze leaves and red flowers, for example *Dahlia* 'Ellen Houston'

12 Green cauliflower, for example 'Romanesco'
13 Globe artichoke, for example 'Vert de Laon'
14 Early spinach, followed by yellow tomatoes ('Golden Sunrise')
15 Scarlet runner beans and celery within the circle

A pair of steps immediately becomes something special when it is decorated with pots of herbs and other plants (Bingerden House, Netherlands).

16 Peas followed by leeks
17 Rhubarb, for example 'Champagne'
18 Strawberries interplanted with curly endive
19 Variegated sage, *Salvia officinalis* 'Icterina'
20 Golden marjoram, *Origanum vulgare* 'Thumbles's Variety' (this variety does not scorch in the sun)
21 Golden hop round the edge, various culinary herbs within the circle. Never grow parsley and celery together!
22 Strawberries interplanted with oak-leaf lettuce
23 Butter beans, for example 'Boterkoning'
24 First spinach, then tomatoes followed by leeks
25 Pak choi
26 Endive

27 Butter beans
28 Scarlet runner beans with celery within the circle
29 Chinese garlic
30 Scarlet runner beans with celery within the circle
31 Lettuce 'Lollo Rosso'
32 Early spinach followed by beetroot
33 Supersweet sweet corn
34 Marrowfat peas 'Blauwschokker'
35 Supersweet sweet corn
36 Yellow raspberries
37 Raspberries

A herb garden for the shade

Most herbs need sun to grow satisfactorily but fortunately there are several that are suitable for shade. If there is a shaded corner in your garden, perhaps this old-fashioned herb garden could be the answer. The garden measures 4.40m x 4.40 (14'4" x 14'4"). The paths are 60cm (24") wide. You can plant privet or box for the low hedges. Beech does not grow so well in shade. In addition to several well

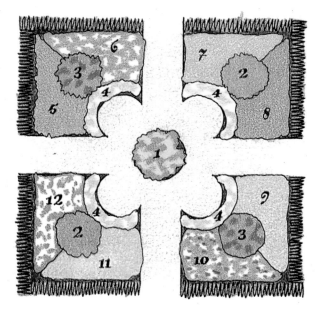

0   1m

known culinary herbs, old-fashioned flowers are included, as they were in the medieval monastery garden.

1 *Angelica archangelica*, angelica
2 *Campanula latifolia var. macrantha*, bellflower
3 *Aquilegia vulgaris*, columbine
4 *Galium odoratum*, woodruff
5 *Apium graveolens*, celery
6 *Convallaria majalis*, lily-of-the-valley
7 *Viola odorata*, sweet violet
8 *Petroselinum crispum*, parsley
9 *Allium schoenoprasum*, chives
10 *Fragaria vesca*, wild strawberry
11 *Dicentra spectabilis*, bleeding heart
12 *Anthriscus cerefolium*, chervil

Parsley has very finely curled leaves. It can be used as an edging plant in a shaded garden.

Index

Photo credits

Jan van Boekel, Rijsbergen, the Netherlands: page 115, 117, 348, 349

Gerard Borgonje, Raalte, the Netherlands: page 41, 360, 361, 362, 363, 364 la+ra, 365

Ben Dresen, Dongen, the Netherlands: page 107

Lida Geers, Dongen, the Netherlands: page 9, 23 ra, 36, 38, 46, 52, 53, 58 lb, 59 ca, 62, 71, 72, 73, 75, 77, 78, 79, 83, 85 ra, 87, 88, 91, 108, 109, 143, 159 ra, 174, 179, 180 lb, 183 ra, 184, 185, 188, 190, 195, 199, 201, 205, 214, 215, 217, 218, 219, 220, 221, 222, 223, 224, 225, 226, 227, 228, 229, 231, 232, 233, 234, 235, 236, 237, 238, 239, 241, 242, 243, 244, 245, 246, 247, 249, 250, 251, 252, 253, 254, 255, 256, 257, 258, 259, 262, 263, 264, 265, 266, 267, 268 ra, 270, 271 ra, 272, 273, 274, 275, 276, 277, 279, 280, 281, 282, 284, 285, 286, 287, 288, 289, 290, 291, 292, 293, 294, 295, 297, 298, 299, 300, 301, 302, 303, 304, 305, 309, 311, 312, 313, 314, 315, 316, 318, 319, 320, 321, 322, 323, 324, 325, 326, 327, 350, 351, 356, 359, 366, 367, 368, 369, 371, 376, 377, 378, 379, 382, 383, rb, 384, 385, 387, 390, 391, 399, 401, 402, 403, 404, 406, 408, 409

Martina Hop, Groningen, the Netherlands: page 214 b, 398

Arend Jan van der Horst, Baasdorp, the Netherlands: page 13, 14 rb*, 17, 18 lb, 18 b, 31 a+b, 32, 35, 42 r+l, 43, 47, 48, 59 b, 66, 69, 101, 102, 104, 110*, 119*, 138*, 141, 181 b+a, 186*, 189, 194, 202 cl, 209*, 211, 212*, 341 (* = garden design: Arend Jan van der Horst)

Mineke Kurpershoek, Amsterdam, the Netherlands: page 17, 23 l, 28 l, 33, 37, 44, 45 l, 49 r, 64, 68, 86, 121, 122, 123, 124, 128, 133, 137, 145, 150, 151, 156, 158, 161, 176, 177 l, 180 b, 182, 183 b, 191, 193, 196, 199, 202, 207, 271 b, 296, 340, 341, 343

Klaas T. Noordhuis, Leens, the Netherlands: page 248, 261, 330, 332

Messrs. Onderwater, Lisse, the Netherlands: page 165, 166, 167, 168, 170

George M. Otter, IJsselstein, the Netherlands: page 23 r, 28 l+r, 35, 45 r, 61, 95, 103, 114, 120, 126, 127 l+r, 134 l+r, 149, 153 b, 159, 160, 163, 177 r, 192, 198, 200, 206, 333, 338, 342, 373

Philippe Perdereau: page 11, 15, 19, 24 rb, 112, 178, 187, 203, 205 a, 380, 381, 386, 388, 392, 394, 395

Henk Rietsema, Den Andel, the Netherlands: page 164, 166, 260, 261, 337 l+r, 339, 341

Peter Schut, Amsterdam, the Netherlands: page 7, 14 la, 16, 20, 21, 24 la, 25, 26, 34, 43, 60, 67, 74, 76, 85 la, 106, 110, 162, 180 a, 197, 199, 208 b, 268 la, 269, 344, 367

Nico Vermeulen, Groningen, the Netherlands: page 28, 65, 68 (garden of Mrs. Van Bennekom), 89, 90, 92, 94, 95, 96, 97, 99, 111, (garden of the Poley family), 113 (Priona Gardens), 123, 140, 148 , 152, 153 , 173, 200, 205, 306, 346, 347

Bibliography

Brookes, John, *Garden Design Workbook*, Dorling Kindersley
Brickell, Christopher, Ed., *The RHS Encyclopedia of Gardening*, Dorling Kindersley
Brickell, Christopher, Ed., *The RHS Gardeners' Encyclopedia of Plants and Flowers*, Dorling Kindersley
Loxton, Howard, *The Garden*, Thames & Hudson
Noordhuis, Klaas T., *Tuineren het hele jaar*, Rebo Productions
Noordhuis, Klaas T., *Encyclopaedia of Garden Plants*, Rebo Productions
Philip, C. and T. Lord, *The RHS Plant Finder* 1996/7 Edition, Moorland Publishing Co. Ltd
Stace, Clive, *New Flora of the British Isles*, Cambridge University Press

Acknowledgments

The publisher and author would like to thank the following individuals and organizations for their assistance so readily given towards the preparation of this book:

drs. Th. J.P.G. van der Heijden (Fysicon) Enkhuizen; Hermien van Wijhe-Ruys, Rhenen; Agnes Kemperman, Waarland; Tonny van der Plank, Reeuwijk; Charley Younge (Bamboo Information Centre, Netherlands) Schellinkhout: F.C.A. Verharen, Dongen; F. in 't Groen, Dongen; J. Vergeer, 's-Gravenmoer; J.P.M. Boer and family, Dongen; K. Gerris and family, Dongenvaart; M.M.L. Fleischeuer and family; G. Boon and family, Dongen; Mrs J. de Witt, Dongen; H. Merkx and family, Dongen; D. Cornelisse, Utrecht; P. van Laarhoven and family, Tilburg; S. van Gastel and family, Tilburg; Mrs C. Maas, Tilburg; W. van Tilburg and family, Oosterhout; Mrs D. Paulus van Pauwvliet, Oosterhout; Organic Gardening Foundation 'de Hovenier', Dongen; Mrs E. van Weede. Angerlo.

Addresses

Information centres

Royal Horticultural Society
80 Vincent Square
London SW1P 2PE
0171 834 4333

The Royal Botanic Gardens Kew
Richmond
Surrey TW9 3AB
0181 940 1171

The Gardens Open Scheme
The National Gardens Scheme
Hatchlands Park
East Clandon
Guildford GU4 7RT

Soil Investigation
Soil Survey and Land Research
Centre
Cranfield University
Silsoe
Beds MK45 4DT

Soil Analysis Service
RHS Advisory Service
Wisley
Woking
Surrey GU23 6QB

Nurseries

Unusual plants from seed
Chiltern Seeds
Bortree Stile
Ulverston
Cumbria LA12 7PB
Tel. 01229 581137

Thompson & Morgan
Poplar Lane
Ipswich
Suffolk IP8 3BU
Tel. 01473 688588

Box and topiary
Langley Boxwood Nursery
Rake
Liss, Hants GU33 7JL

Roses
David Austin Roses (TG)
Albrighton
Wolverhampton WV7 3HB
Tel. 01902 373931

Bamboos
The Palm Centre
563 Upper Richmond Road West
London SW14 7ED
Tel. 0181 876 3223

Unusual bulbs
Van Tubergen UK
Bressingham
Diss
Norfolk IP22 2AB
Tel. 01379 688282

Miscellaneous

Butterflies
Butterfly Conservation
Conservation Office
PO Box 444
Dorchester
Dorset DT2 7YT

Beekeeping
British Beekeepers Association
National Beekeeping Centre
National Agricultural Centre
Stoneleigh
Kenilworth
Warwickshire CV82 2LZ

Tree surgeons
Arboricultural Association
Ampfield House
Ampfield
nr Romsey
Hants SO51 9PA
Tel. 01794 68717

Organic gardening
Henry Doubleday Research
Association
Ryton Organic Gardens
Ryton on Dunsmore
Coventry CV8 3LG
Tel. 01203 303517